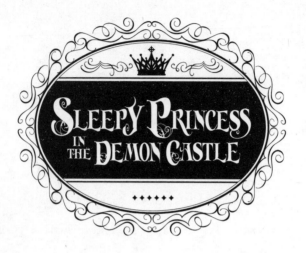

SLEEPY PRINCESS
IN THE DEMON CASTLE

17

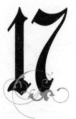

Story & Art by
KAGIJI KUMANOMATA

NIGHTS

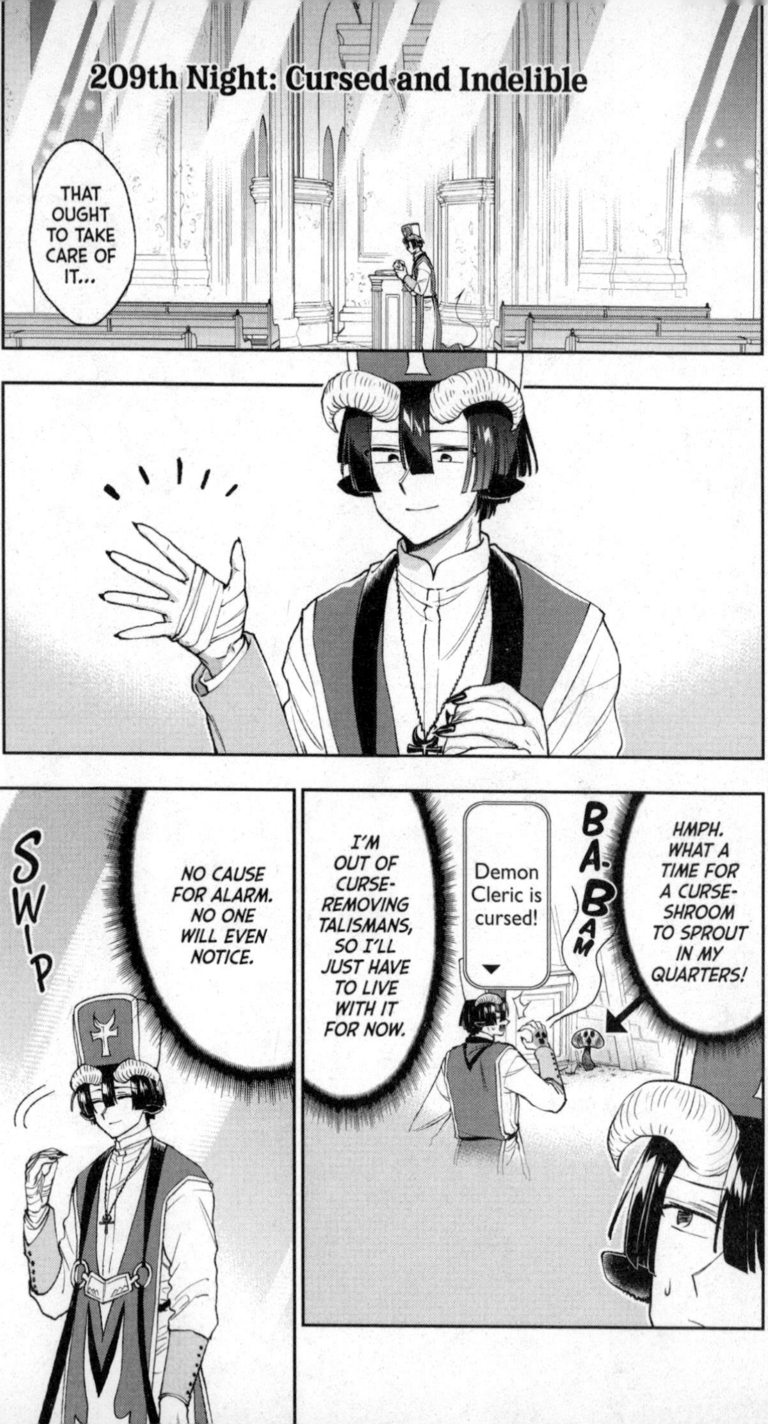
209th Night: Cursed and Indelible
THAT OUGHT TO TAKE CARE OF IT...
HMPH. WHAT A TIME FOR A CURSE-SHROOM TO SPROUT IN MY QUARTERS!
BA-BAM
Demon Cleric is cursed!
I'M OUT OF CURSE-REMOVING TALISMANS, SO I'LL JUST HAVE TO LIVE WITH IT FOR NOW.
NO CAUSE FOR ALARM. NO ONE WILL EVEN NOTICE.
SWIP

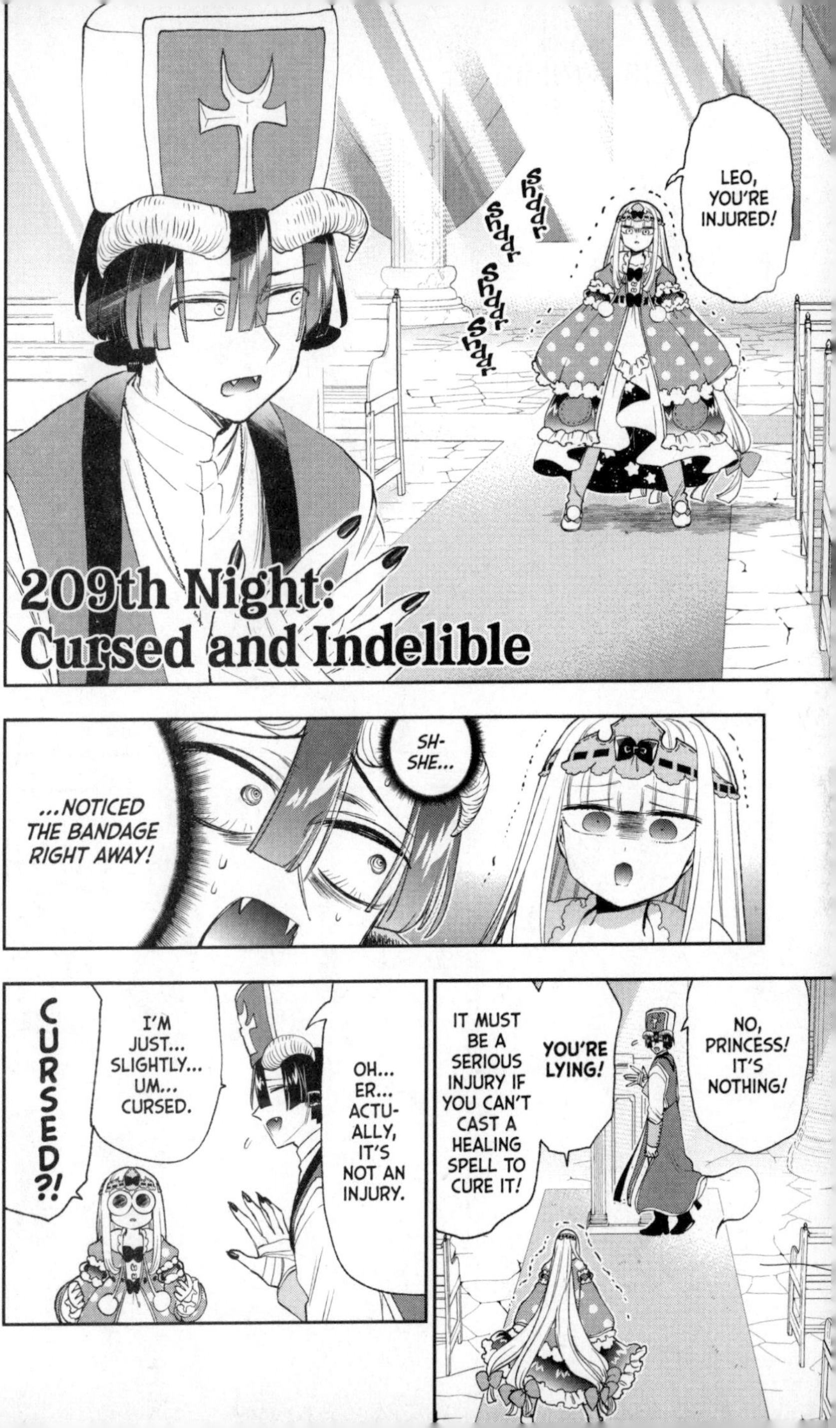
LEO, YOU'RE INJURED!
SHDDR SHDDR SHDDR SHDDR
209th Night: Cursed and Indelible
SH- SHE...
...NOTICED THE BANDAGE RIGHT AWAY!
NO, PRINCESS! IT'S NOTHING!
YOU'RE LYING!
IT MUST BE A SERIOUS INJURY IF YOU CAN'T CAST A HEALING SPELL TO CURE IT!
OH... ER... ACTU-ALLY, IT'S NOT AN INJURY.
I'M JUST... SLIGHTLY... UM... CURSED.
CURSED?!

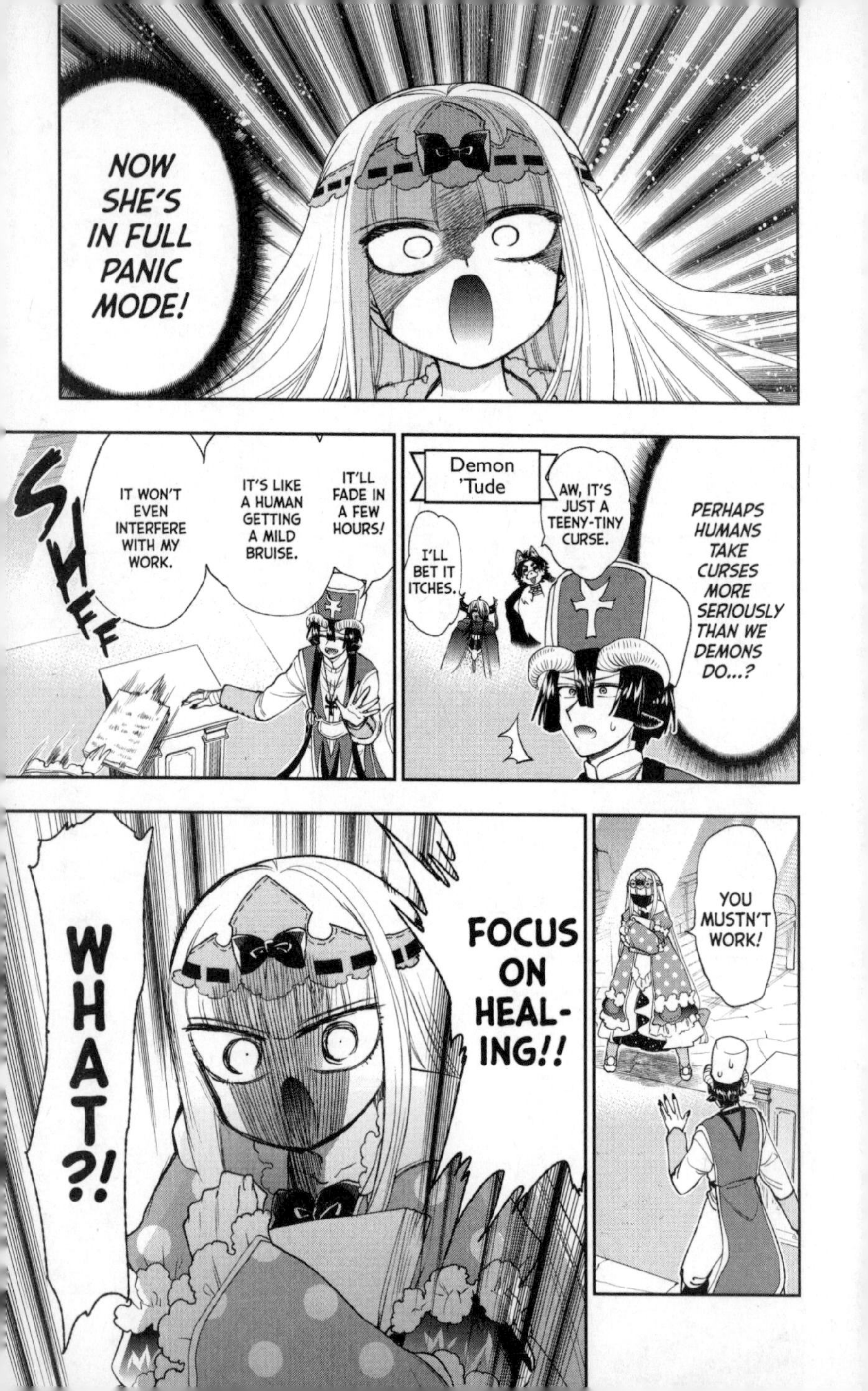
NOW SHE'S IN FULL PANIC MODE!
PERHAPS HUMANS TAKE CURSES MORE SERIOUSLY THAN WE DEMONS DO...?
AW, IT'S JUST A TEENY-TINY CURSE.
Demon 'Tude
I'LL BET IT ITCHES.
IT'LL FADE IN A FEW HOURS!
IT'S LIKE A HUMAN GETTING A MILD BRUISE.
IT WON'T EVEN INTERFERE WITH MY WORK.
SHFF
YOU MUSTN'T WORK!
FOCUS ON HEAL-ING!!
WHAT?!

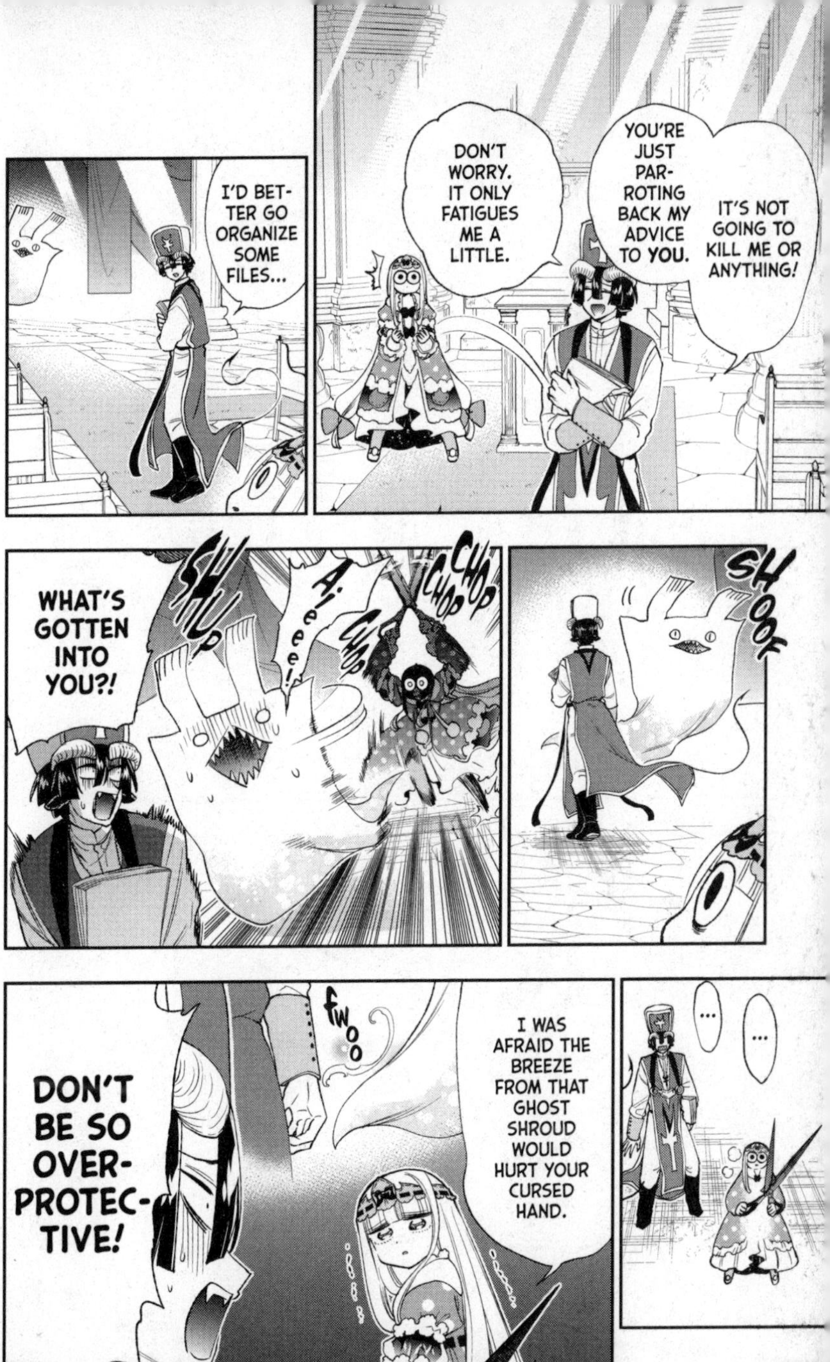
IT'S NOT GOING TO KILL ME OR ANYTHING!
YOU'RE JUST PAR-ROTING BACK MY ADVICE TO YOU.
DON'T WORRY. IT ONLY FATIGUES ME A LITTLE.
I'D BET-TER GO ORGANIZE SOME FILES...
SHOOOK
CHOP CHOP
CHOP
CHOP
Aieeee!
SHUP
WHAT'S GOTTEN INTO YOU?!
...
...
I WAS AFRAID THE BREEZE FROM THAT GHOST SHROUD WOULD HURT YOUR CURSED HAND.
fwoo
DON'T BE SO OVER-PROTEC-TIVE!

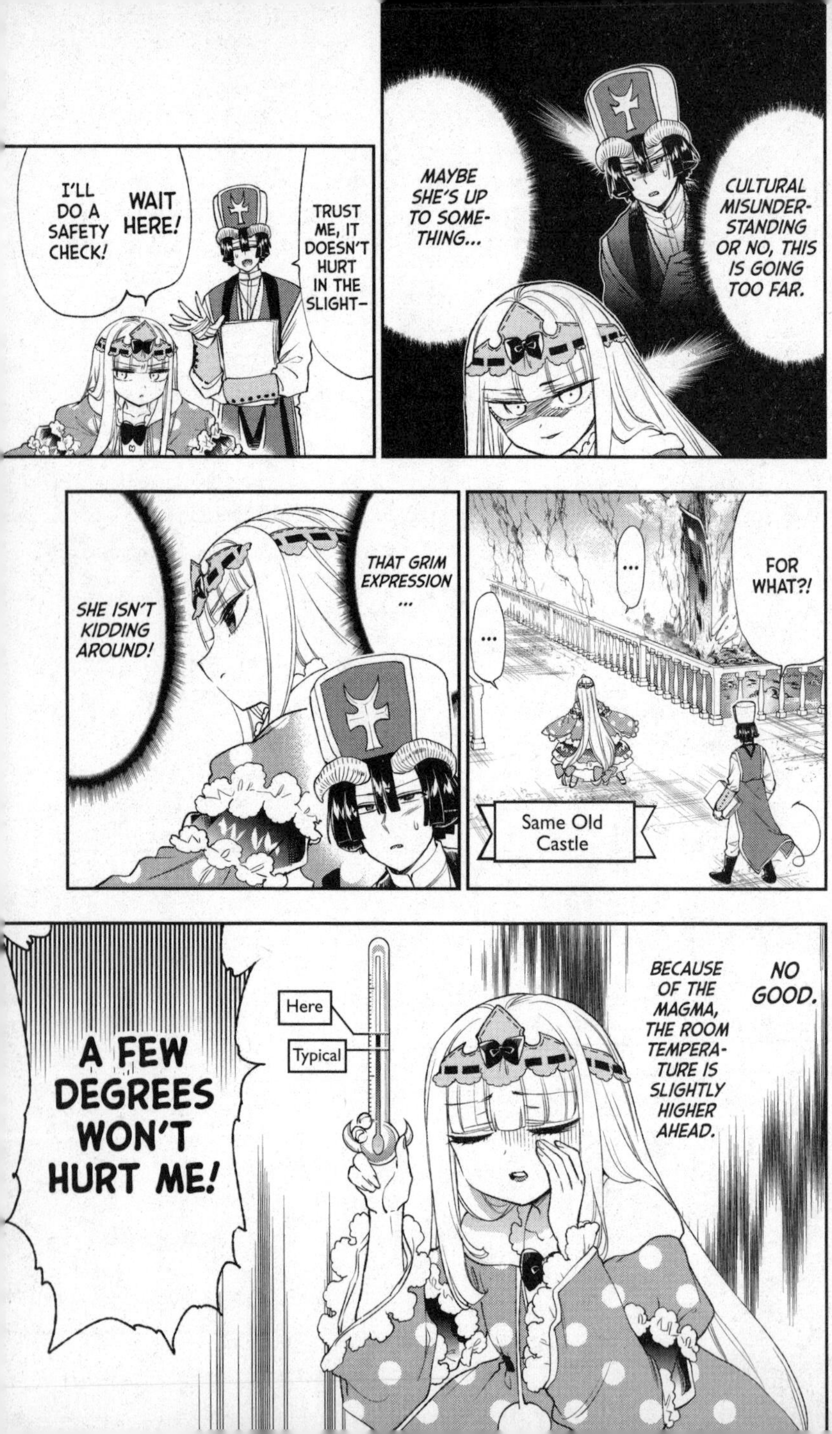
CULTURAL MISUNDERSTANDING OR NO, THIS IS GOING TOO FAR.
MAYBE SHE'S UP TO SOMETHING...
TRUST ME, IT DOESN'T HURT IN THE SLIGHT–
WAIT HERE!
I'LL DO A SAFETY CHECK!
FOR WHAT?!
...
...
Same Old Castle
THAT GRIM EXPRESSION ...
SHE ISN'T KIDDING AROUND!
NO GOOD.
BECAUSE OF THE MAGMA, THE ROOM TEMPERATURE IS SLIGHTLY HIGHER AHEAD.
Here
Typical
A FEW DEGREES WON'T HURT ME!

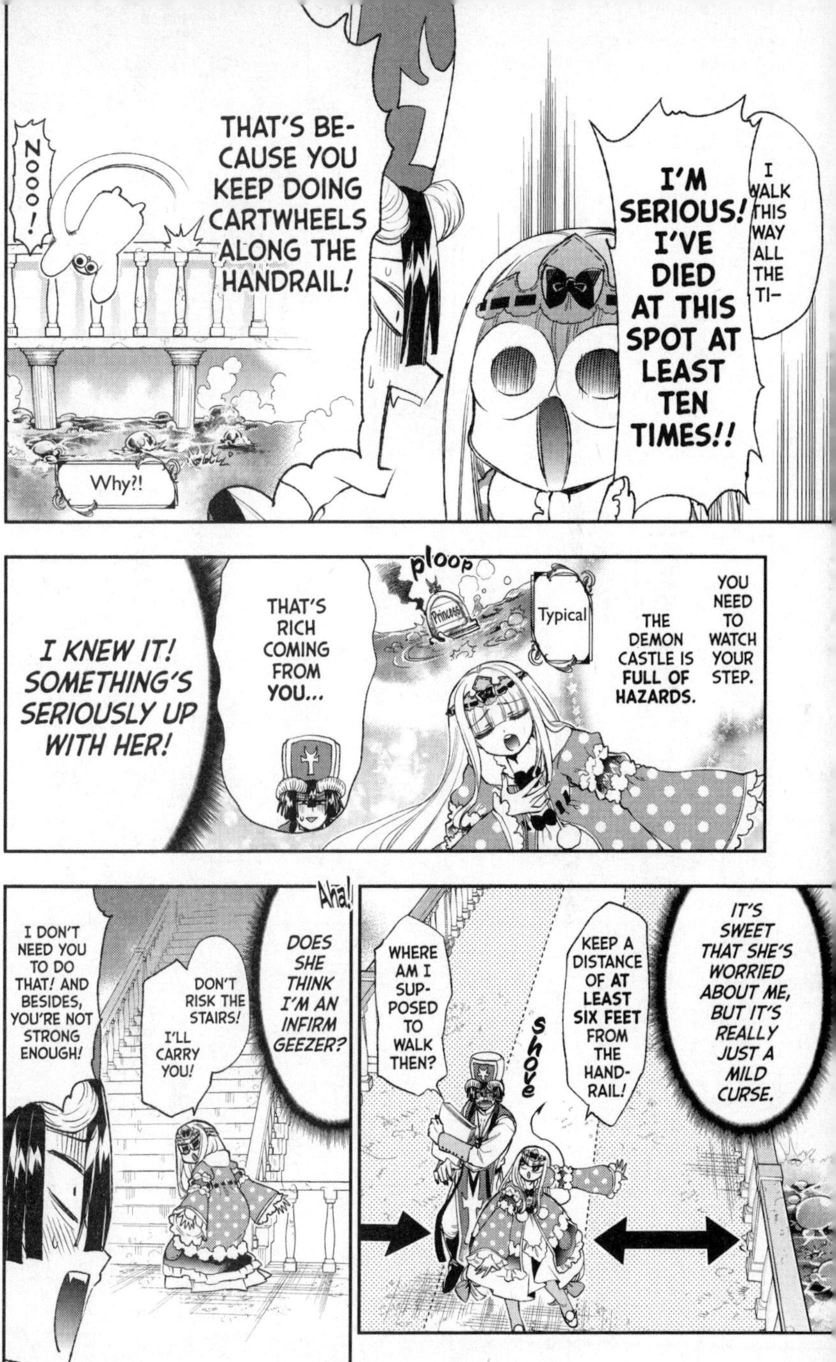
I WALK THIS WAY ALL THE TI–
I'M SERIOUS! I'VE DIED AT THIS SPOT AT LEAST TEN TIMES!!
THAT'S BE-CAUSE YOU KEEP DOING CARTWHEELS ALONG THE HANDRAIL!
NOOO!
Why?!
YOU NEED TO WATCH YOUR STEP.
THE DEMON CASTLE IS FULL OF HAZARDS.
Typical
ploop
Princess
THAT'S RICH COMING FROM YOU...
I KNEW IT! SOMETHING'S SERIOUSLY UP WITH HER!
IT'S SWEET THAT SHE'S WORRIED ABOUT ME, BUT IT'S REALLY JUST A MILD CURSE.
KEEP A DISTANCE OF AT LEAST SIX FEET FROM THE HAND-RAIL!
shove
WHERE AM I SUP-POSED TO WALK THEN?
Aha!
DOES SHE THINK I'M AN INFIRM GEEZER?
DON'T RISK THE STAIRS! I'LL CARRY YOU!
I DON'T NEED YOU TO DO THAT! AND BESIDES, YOU'RE NOT STRONG ENOUGH!

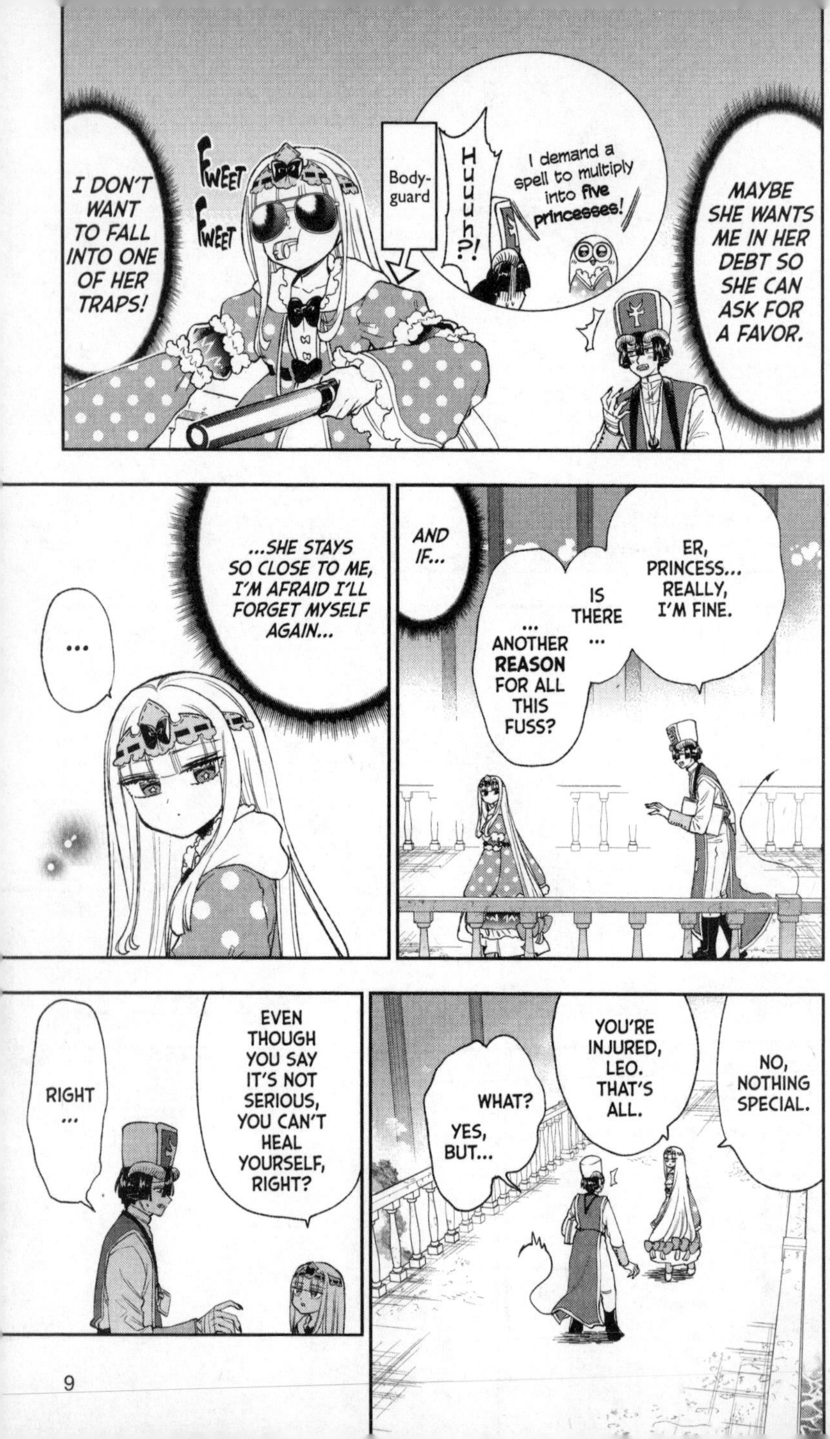
MAYBE SHE WANTS ME IN HER DEBT SO SHE CAN ASK FOR A FAVOR.
I demand a spell to multiply into five princesses!
Huuuh?!
Body-guard
FWEET
FWEET
I DON'T WANT TO FALL INTO ONE OF HER TRAPS!
ER, PRINCESS... REALLY, I'M FINE.
IS THERE ...
... ANOTHER REASON FOR ALL THIS FUSS?
AND IF...
...SHE STAYS SO CLOSE TO ME, I'M AFRAID I'LL FORGET MYSELF AGAIN...
...
NO, NOTHING SPECIAL.
YOU'RE INJURED, LEO. THAT'S ALL.
WHAT?
YES, BUT...
EVEN THOUGH YOU SAY IT'S NOT SERIOUS, YOU CAN'T HEAL YOURSELF, RIGHT?
RIGHT ...

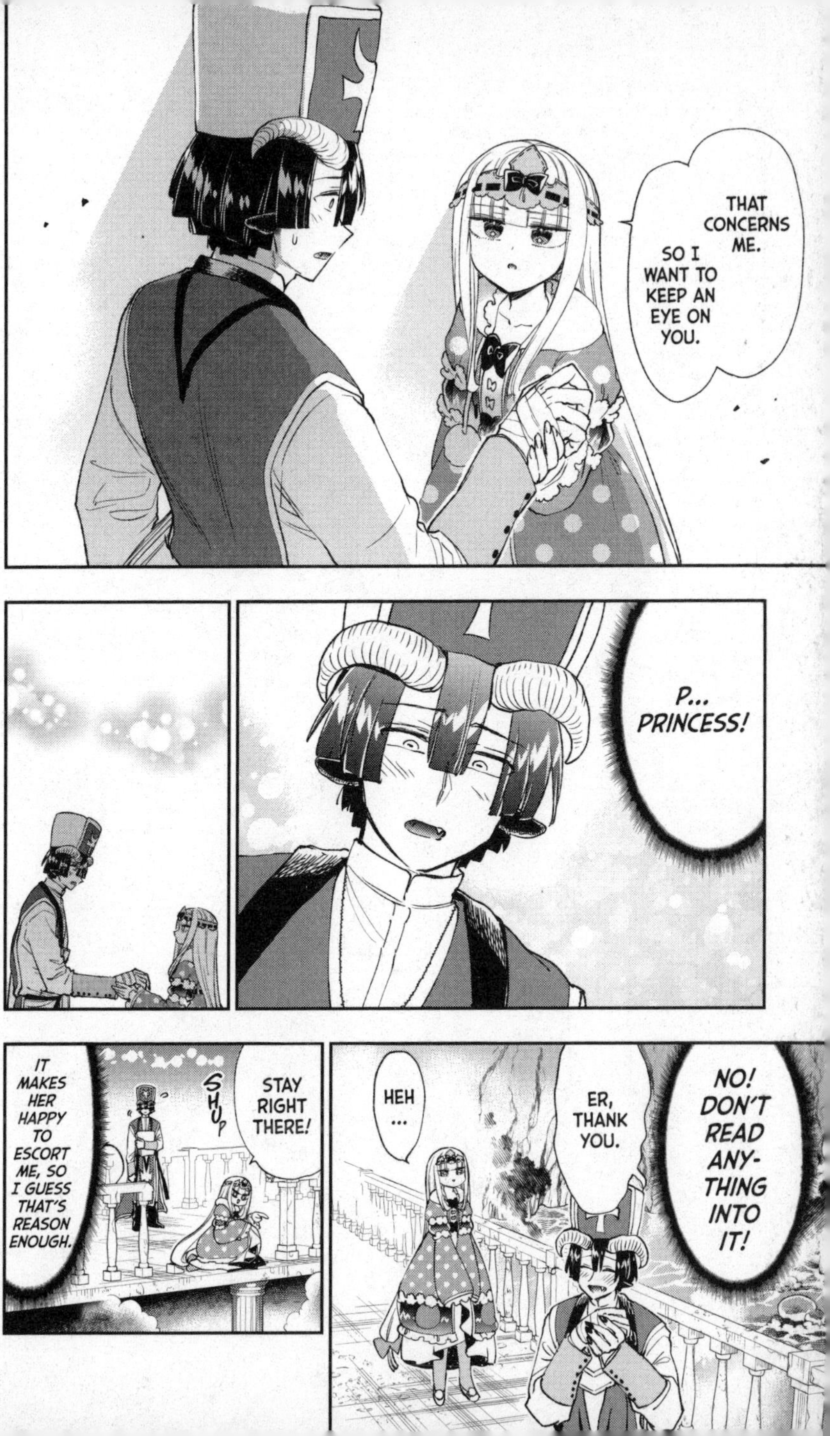
THAT CONCERNS ME.
SO I WANT TO KEEP AN EYE ON YOU.
P... PRINCESS!
NO! DON'T READ ANY-THING INTO IT!
ER, THANK YOU.
HEH ...
STAY RIGHT THERE!
SHUP
IT MAKES HER HAPPY TO ESCORT ME, SO I GUESS THAT'S REASON ENOUGH.

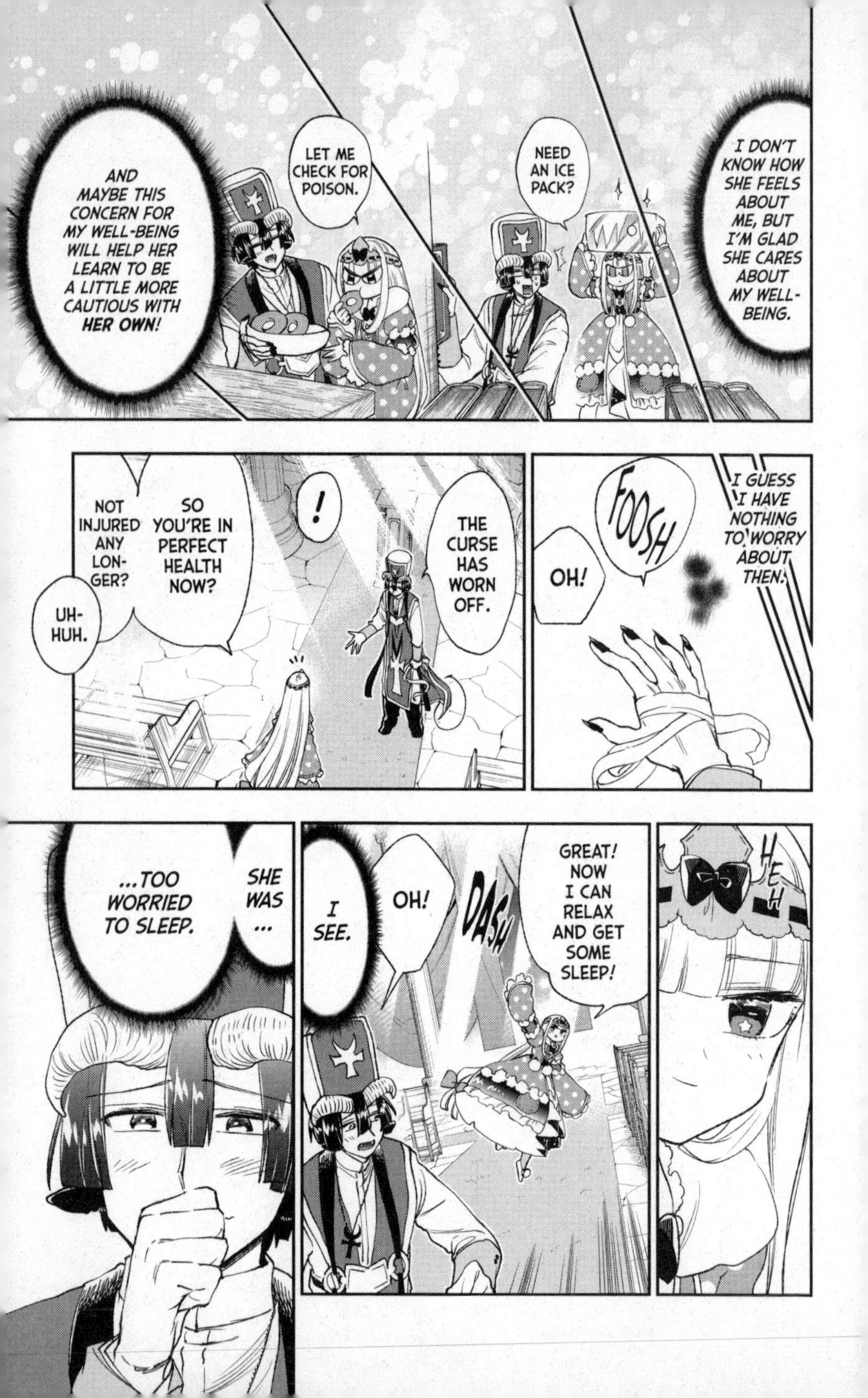
I DON'T KNOW HOW SHE FEELS ABOUT ME, BUT I'M GLAD SHE CARES ABOUT MY WELL-BEING.
NEED AN ICE PACK?
LET ME CHECK FOR POISON.
AND MAYBE THIS CONCERN FOR MY WELL-BEING WILL HELP HER LEARN TO BE A LITTLE MORE CAUTIOUS WITH **HER OWN**!
FOOSH
OH!
I GUESS I HAVE NOTHING TO WORRY ABOUT THEN.
THE CURSE HAS WORN OFF.
!
SO YOU'RE IN PERFECT HEALTH NOW?
NOT INJURED ANY LON-GER?
UH-HUH.
HEH
GREAT! NOW I CAN RELAX AND GET SOME SLEEP!
DASH
OH!
I SEE.
SHE WAS...
...TOO WORRIED TO SLEEP.

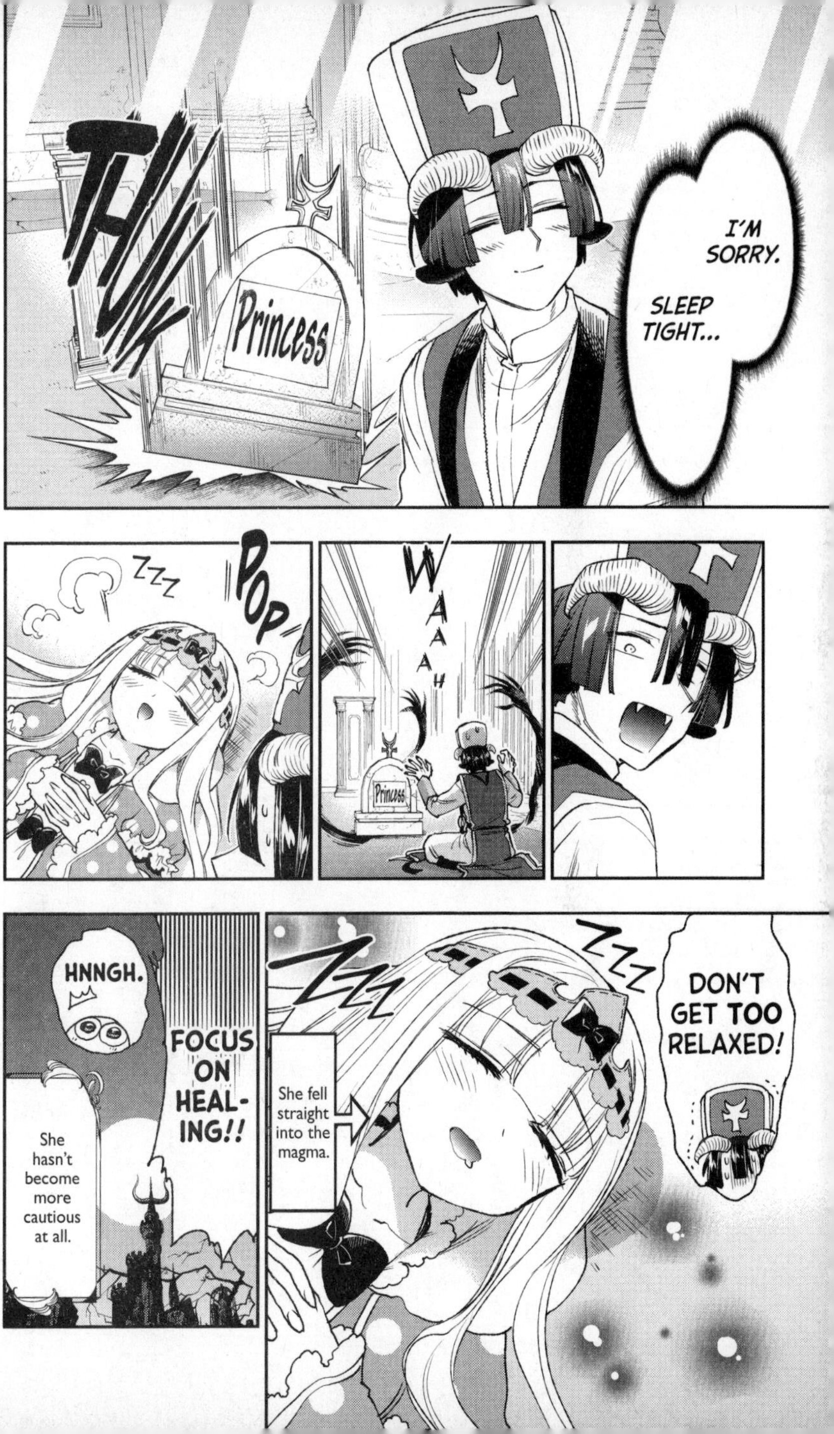
I'M SORRY.
SLEEP TIGHT...
THUNK
Princess
WAAAH
Princess
POP
ZZZ
ZZZ
DON'T GET TOO RELAXED!
ZZZ
She fell straight into the magma.
HNNGH.
FOCUS ON HEAL-ING!!
She hasn't become more cautious at all.

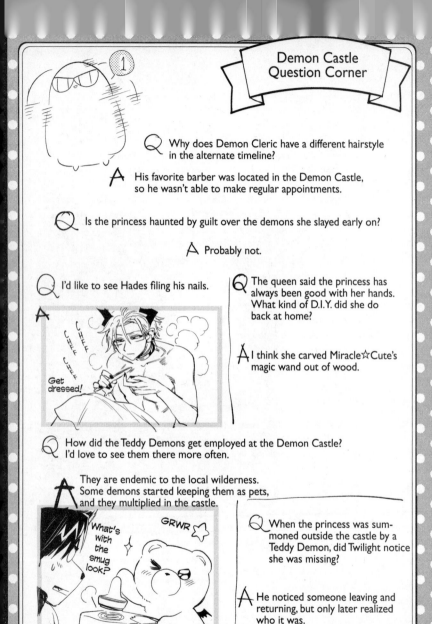

Demon Castle Question Corner

①

Q Why does Demon Cleric have a different hairstyle in the alternate timeline?

A His favorite barber was located in the Demon Castle, so he wasn't able to make regular appointments.

Q Is the princess haunted by guilt over the demons she slayed early on?

A Probably not.

Q I'd like to see Hades filing his nails.

A

CHEF
CHEF
CHEF

Get dressed!

Q The queen said the princess has always been good with her hands. What kind of D.I.Y. did she do back at home?

A I think she carved Miracle☆Cute's magic wand out of wood.

Q How did the Teddy Demons get employed at the Demon Castle? I'd love to see them there more often.

A They are endemic to the local wilderness. Some demons started keeping them as pets, and they multiplied in the castle.

What's with the smug look?

GRWR

Q When the princess was summoned outside the castle by a Teddy Demon, did Twilight notice she was missing?

A He noticed someone leaving and returning, but only later realized who it was.

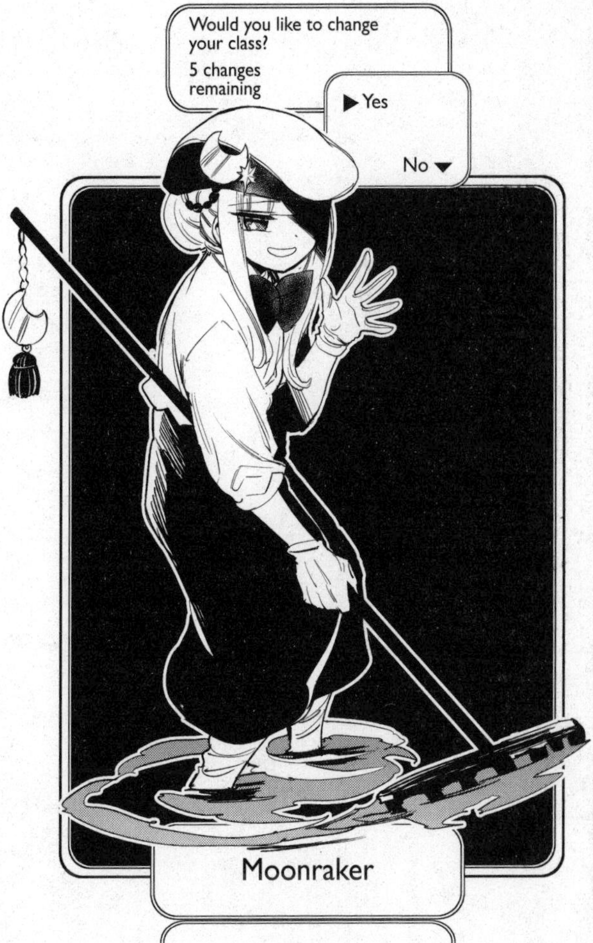
Would you like to change your class?
5 changes remaining
▶Yes
No ▼
Moonraker
"I'm not that bright, you see."

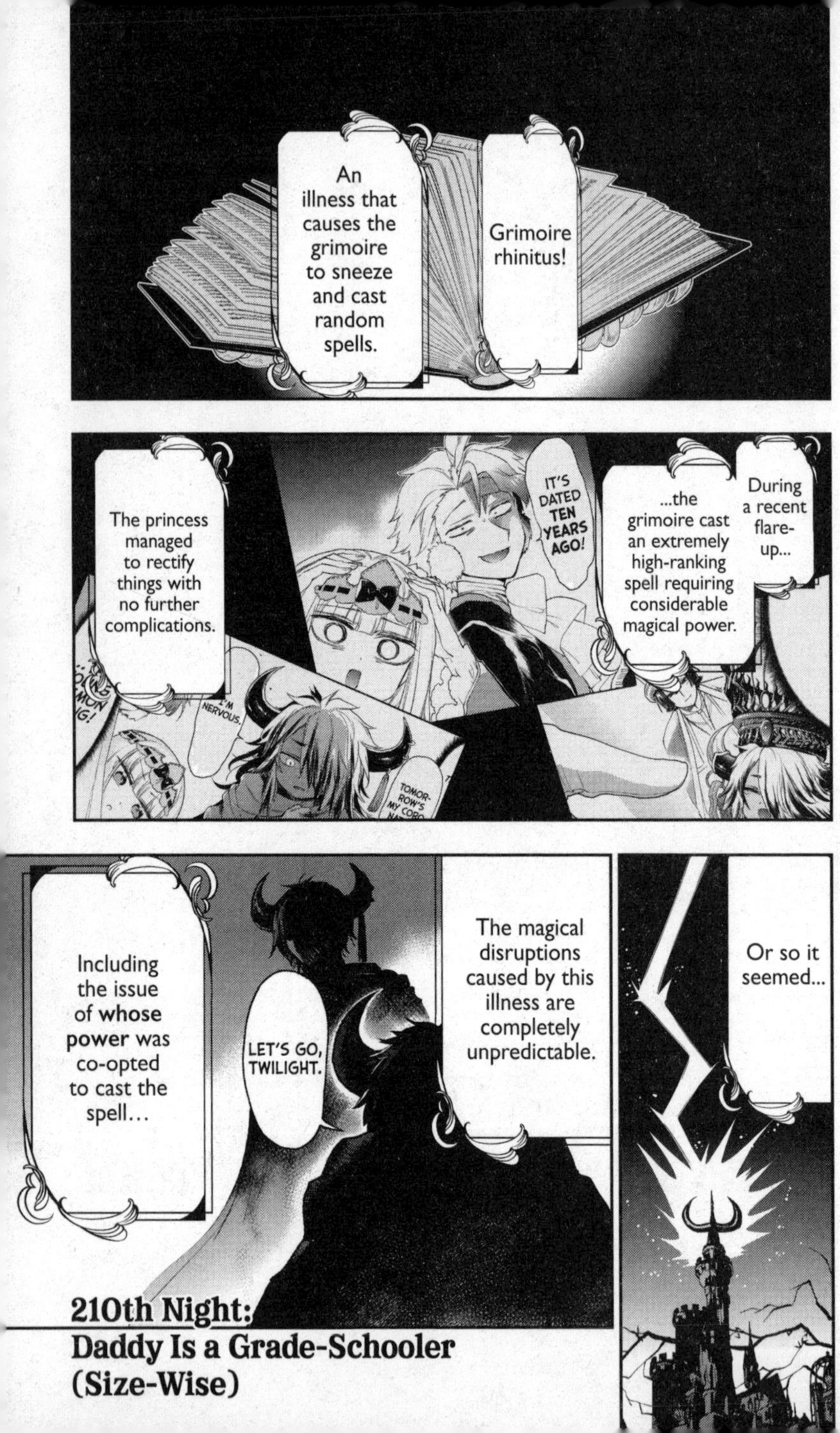
Grimoire rhinitus!
An illness that causes the grimoire to sneeze and cast random spells.
During a recent flare-up...
...the grimoire cast an extremely high-ranking spell requiring considerable magical power.
IT'S DATED TEN YEARS AGO!
The princess managed to rectify things with no further complications.
I'M NERVOUS.
Or so it seemed...
The magical disruptions caused by this illness are completely unpredictable.
LET'S GO, TWILIGHT.
Including the issue of whose power was co-opted to cast the spell...

210th Night: Daddy Is a Grade-Schooler (Size-Wise)

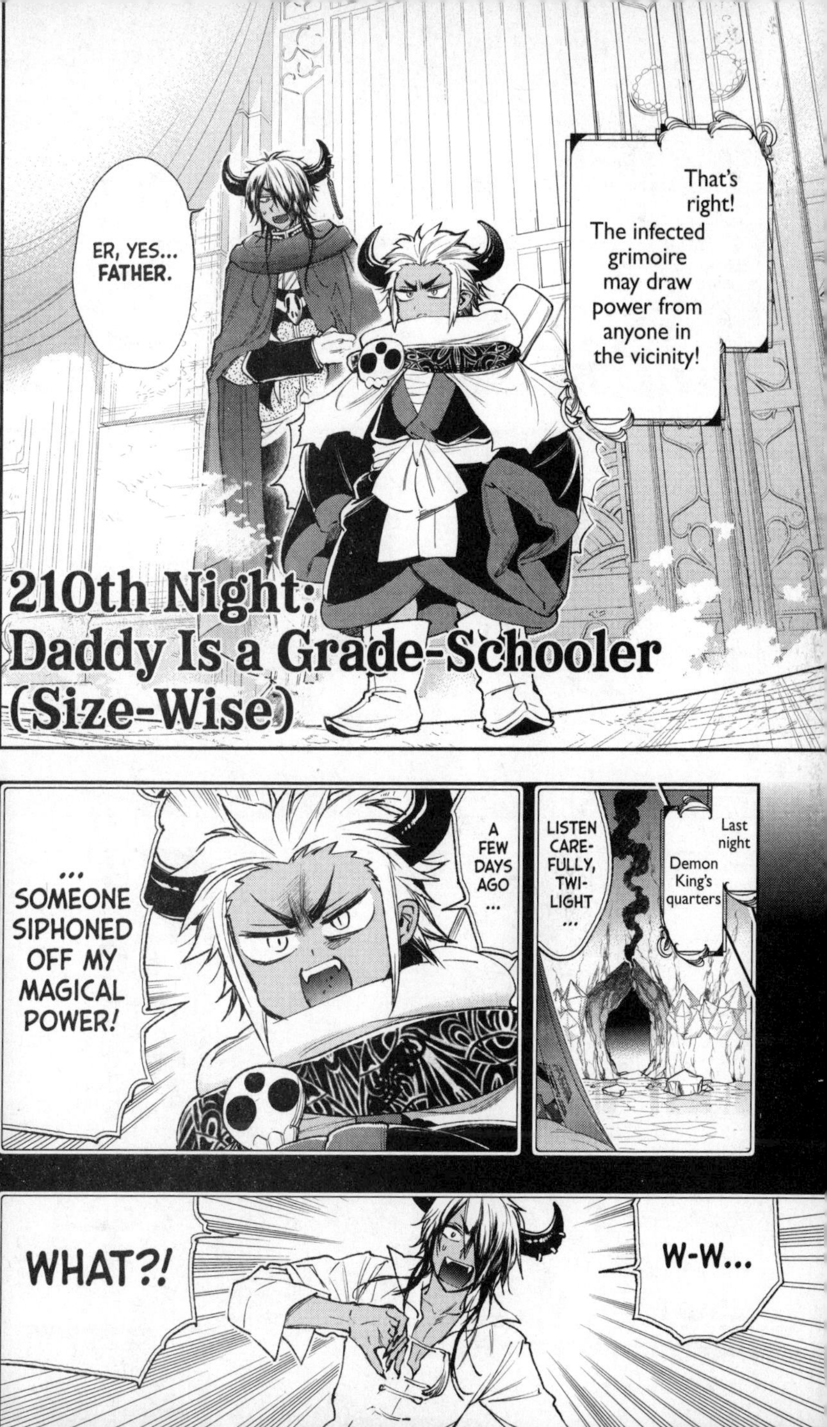
That's right! The infected grimoire may draw power from anyone in the vicinity!
ER, YES... FATHER.
210th Night: Daddy Is a Grade-Schooler (Size-Wise)
Last night Demon King's quarters
LISTEN CAREFULLY, TWILIGHT...
A FEW DAYS AGO...
...SOMEONE SIPHONED OFF MY MAGICAL POWER!
W-W...
WHAT?!

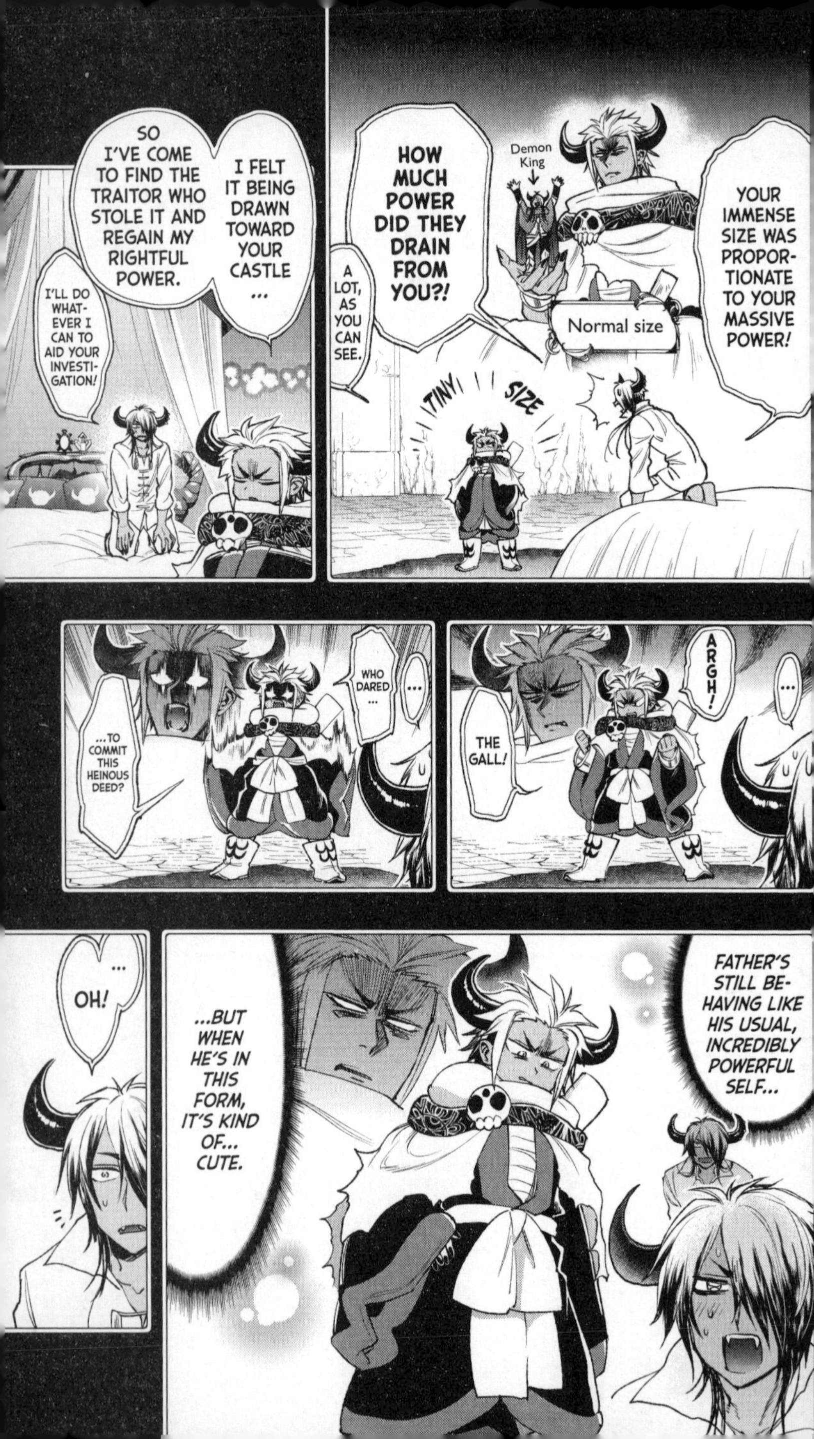

YOUR IMMENSE SIZE WAS PROPORTIONATE TO YOUR MASSIVE POWER!
Demon King
Normal size
HOW MUCH POWER DID THEY DRAIN FROM YOU?!
A LOT, AS YOU CAN SEE.
TINY SIZE
I FELT IT BEING DRAWN TOWARD YOUR CASTLE ...
SO I'VE COME TO FIND THE TRAITOR WHO STOLE IT AND REGAIN MY RIGHTFUL POWER.
I'LL DO WHATEVER I CAN TO AID YOUR INVESTIGATION!
...
ARGH!
THE GALL!
...
WHO DARED ...
...TO COMMIT THIS HEINOUS DEED?
FATHER'S STILL BEHAVING LIKE HIS USUAL, INCREDIBLY POWERFUL SELF...
...BUT WHEN HE'S IN THIS FORM, IT'S KIND OF... CUTE.
... OH!

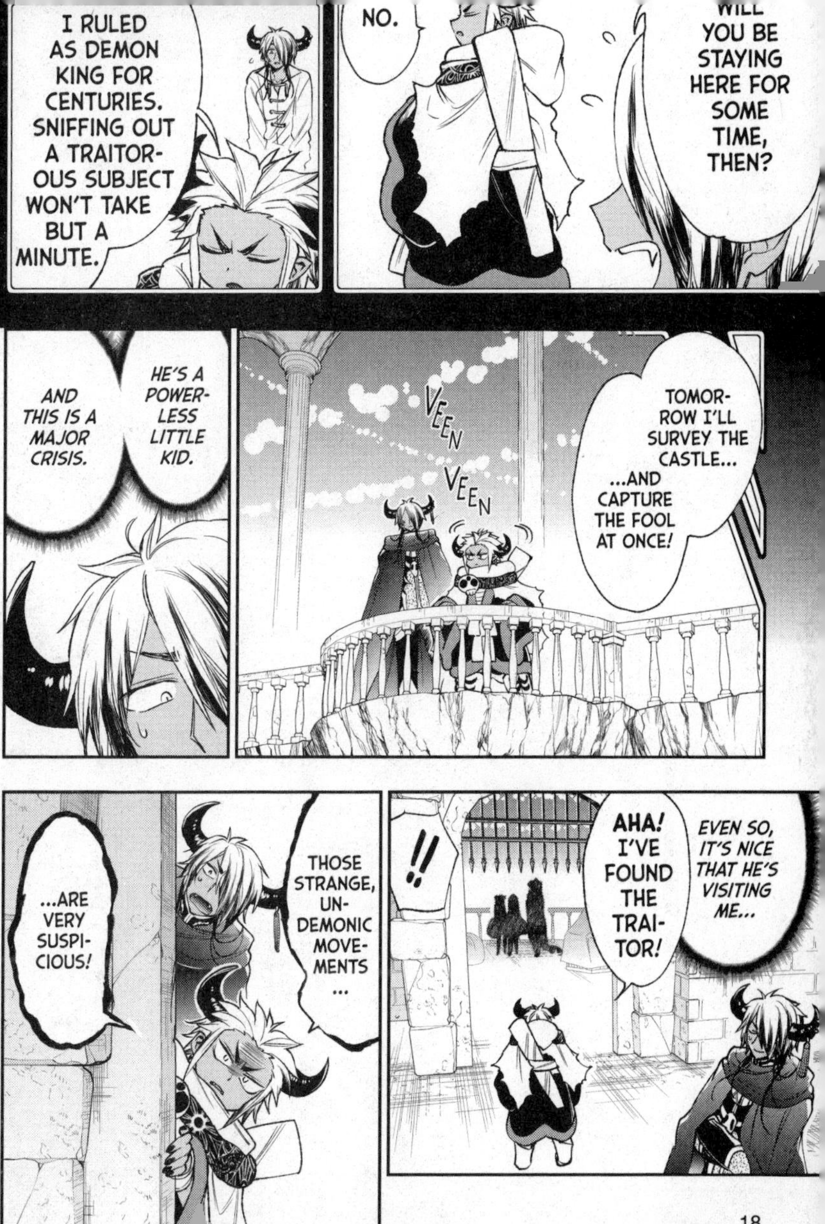
WILL YOU BE STAYING HERE FOR SOME TIME, THEN?
NO.
I RULED AS DEMON KING FOR CENTURIES. SNIFFING OUT A TRAITOROUS SUBJECT WON'T TAKE BUT A MINUTE.
TOMORROW I'LL SURVEY THE CASTLE...
...AND CAPTURE THE FOOL AT ONCE!
VEEN
VEEN
HE'S A POWERLESS LITTLE KID.
AND THIS IS A MAJOR CRISIS.
EVEN SO, IT'S NICE THAT HE'S VISITING ME...
AHA! I'VE FOUND THE TRAITOR!
!!
THOSE STRANGE, UNDEMONIC MOVEMENTS...
...ARE VERY SUSPICIOUS!

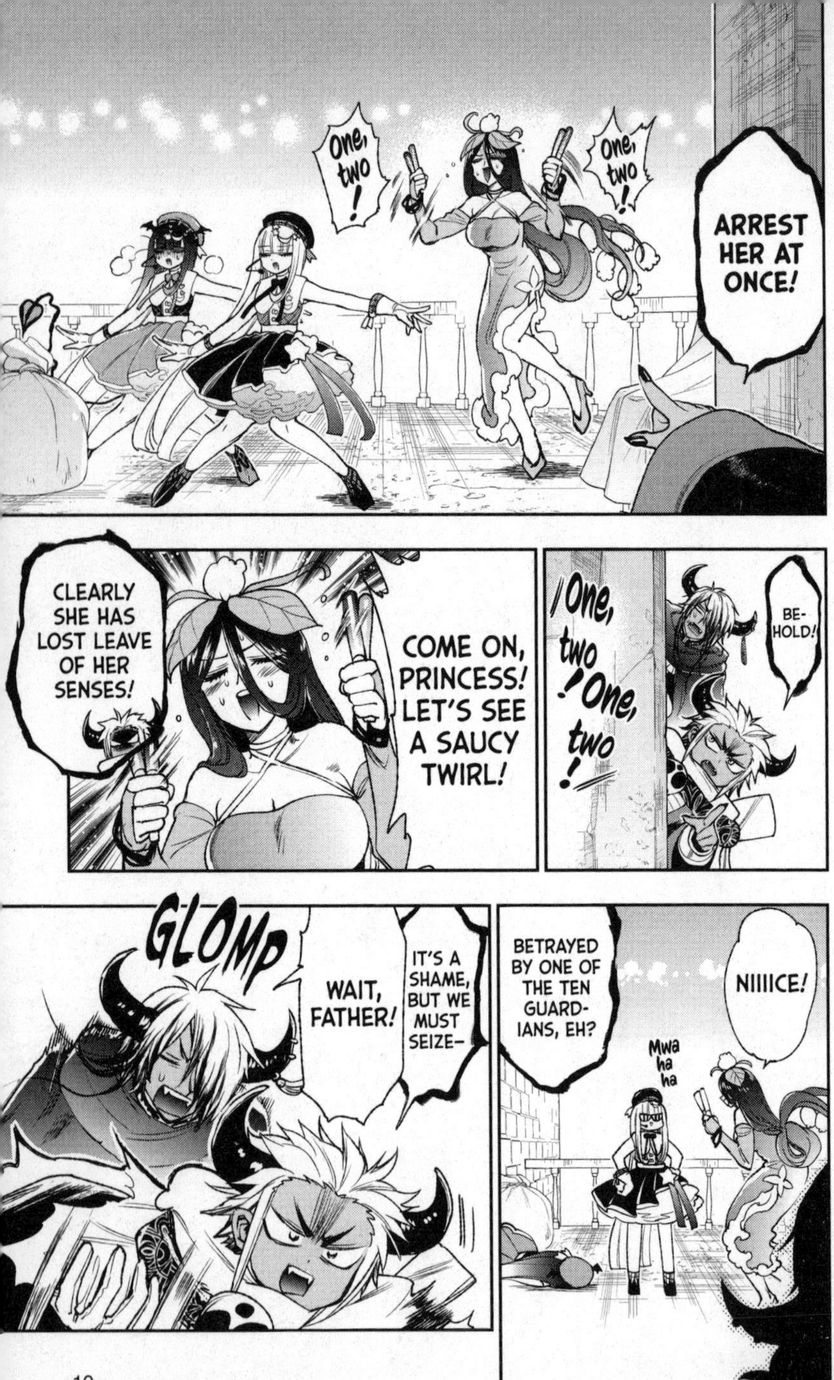
ARREST HER AT ONCE!
One, two!
One, two!
BE-HOLD!
One, two! One, two!
COME ON, PRINCESS! LET'S SEE A SAUCY TWIRL!
CLEARLY SHE HAS LOST LEAVE OF HER SENSES!
NIIIICE!
BETRAYED BY ONE OF THE TEN GUARD-IANS, EH?
Mwa ha ha
IT'S A SHAME, BUT WE MUST SEIZE—
WAIT, FATHER!
GLOMP

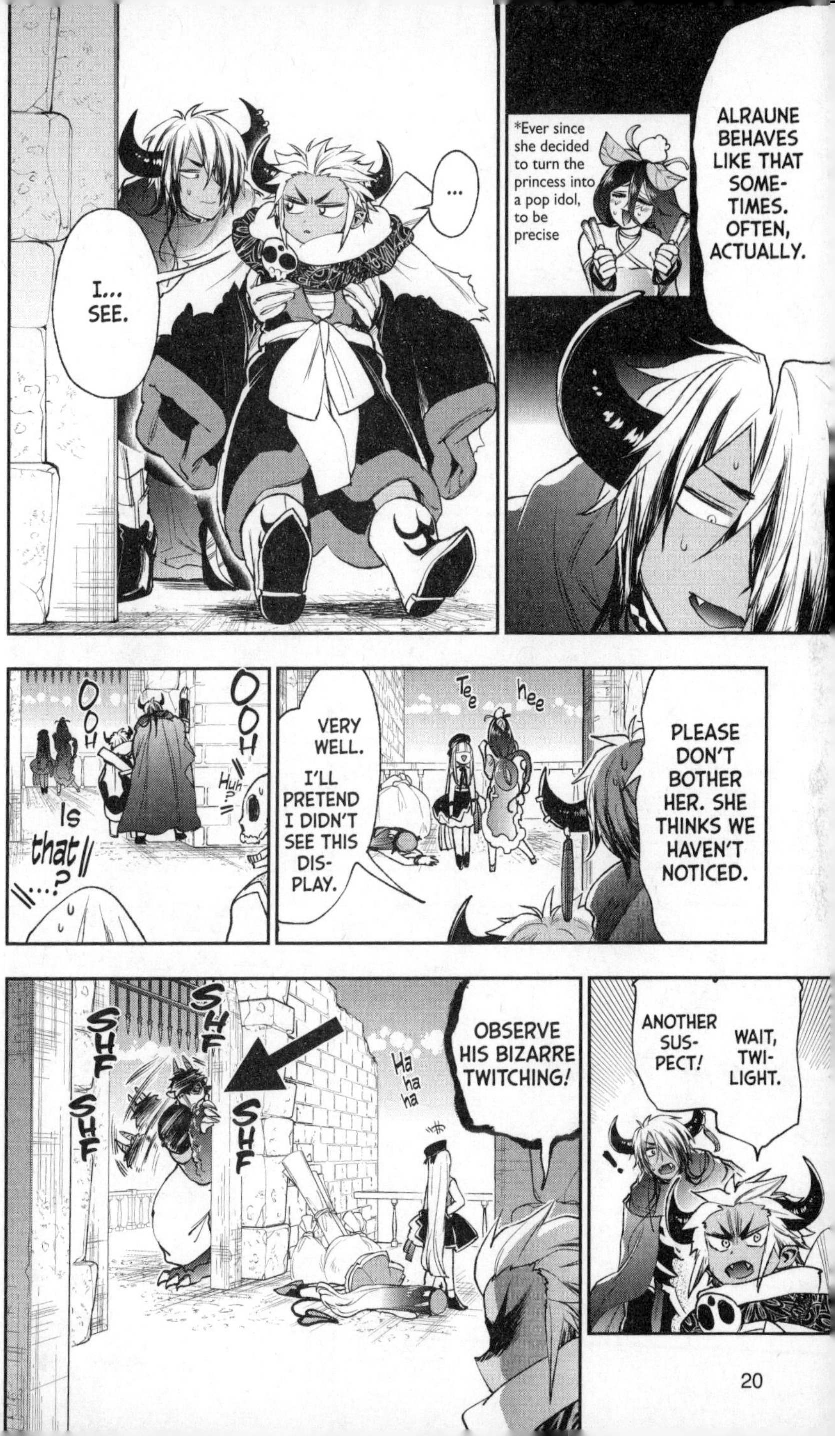
ALRAUNE BEHAVES LIKE THAT SOMETIMES. OFTEN, ACTUALLY.
*Ever since she decided to turn the princess into a pop idol, to be precise
...
I... SEE.
PLEASE DON'T BOTHER HER. SHE THINKS WE HAVEN'T NOTICED.
Tee hee
VERY WELL.
I'LL PRETEND I DIDN'T SEE THIS DIS-PLAY.
OOH
OOH
Huh?
Is that...?
WAIT, TWI-LIGHT.
ANOTHER SUS-PECT!
!
OBSERVE HIS BIZARRE TWITCHING!
Ha ha ha
SHF
SHF
SHF
SHF
SHF

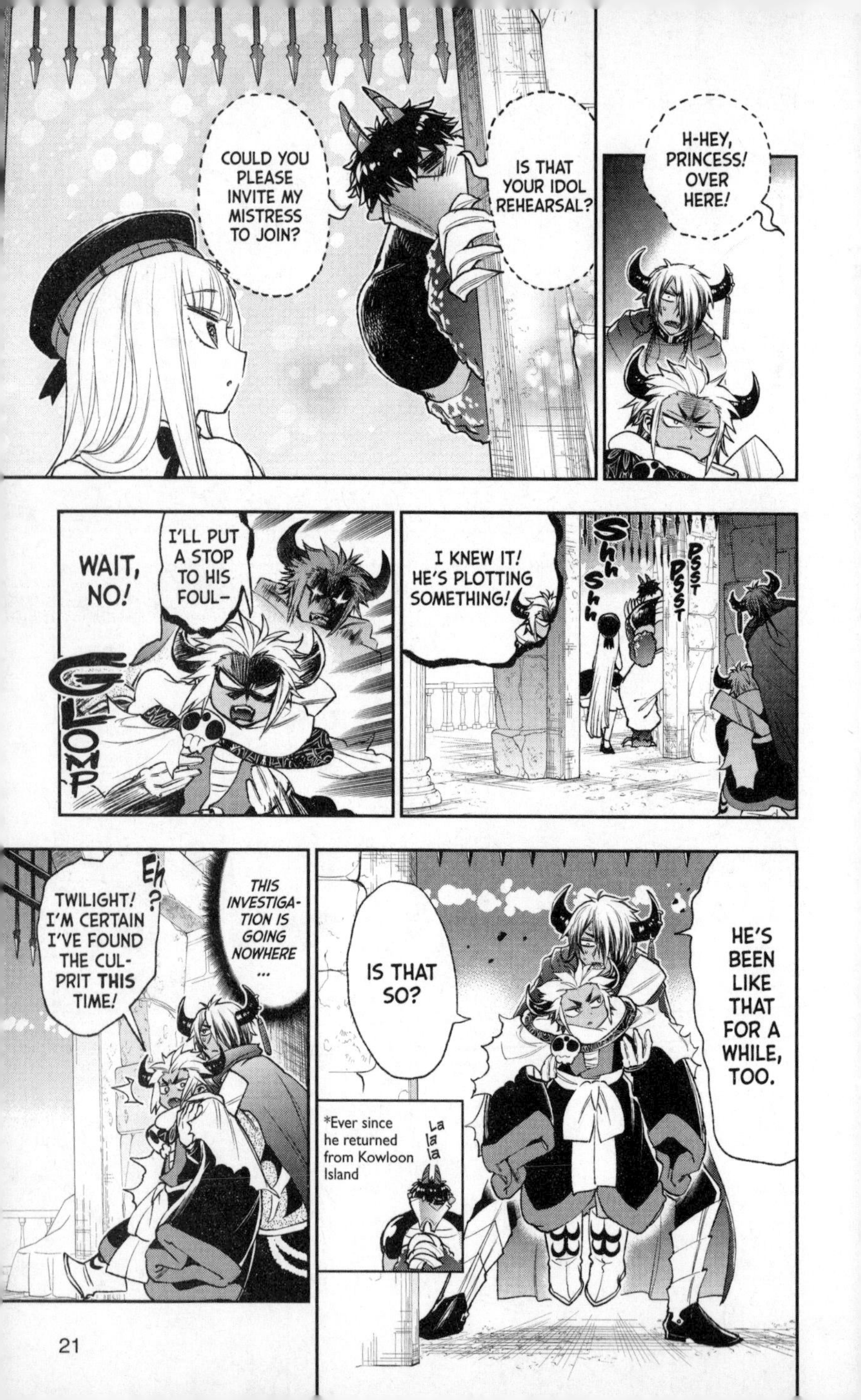
H-HEY, PRINCESS! OVER HERE!
IS THAT YOUR IDOL REHEARSAL?
COULD YOU PLEASE INVITE MY MISTRESS TO JOIN?
Shh Shh
Pssst Pssst
I KNEW IT! HE'S PLOTTING SOMETHING!
I'LL PUT A STOP TO HIS FOUL–
WAIT, NO!
GLOMP
HE'S BEEN LIKE THAT FOR A WHILE, TOO.
IS THAT SO?
*Ever since he returned from Kowloon Island
La la la
THIS INVESTIGATION IS GOING NOWHERE...
Eh?
TWILIGHT! I'M CERTAIN I'VE FOUND THE CULPRIT THIS TIME!

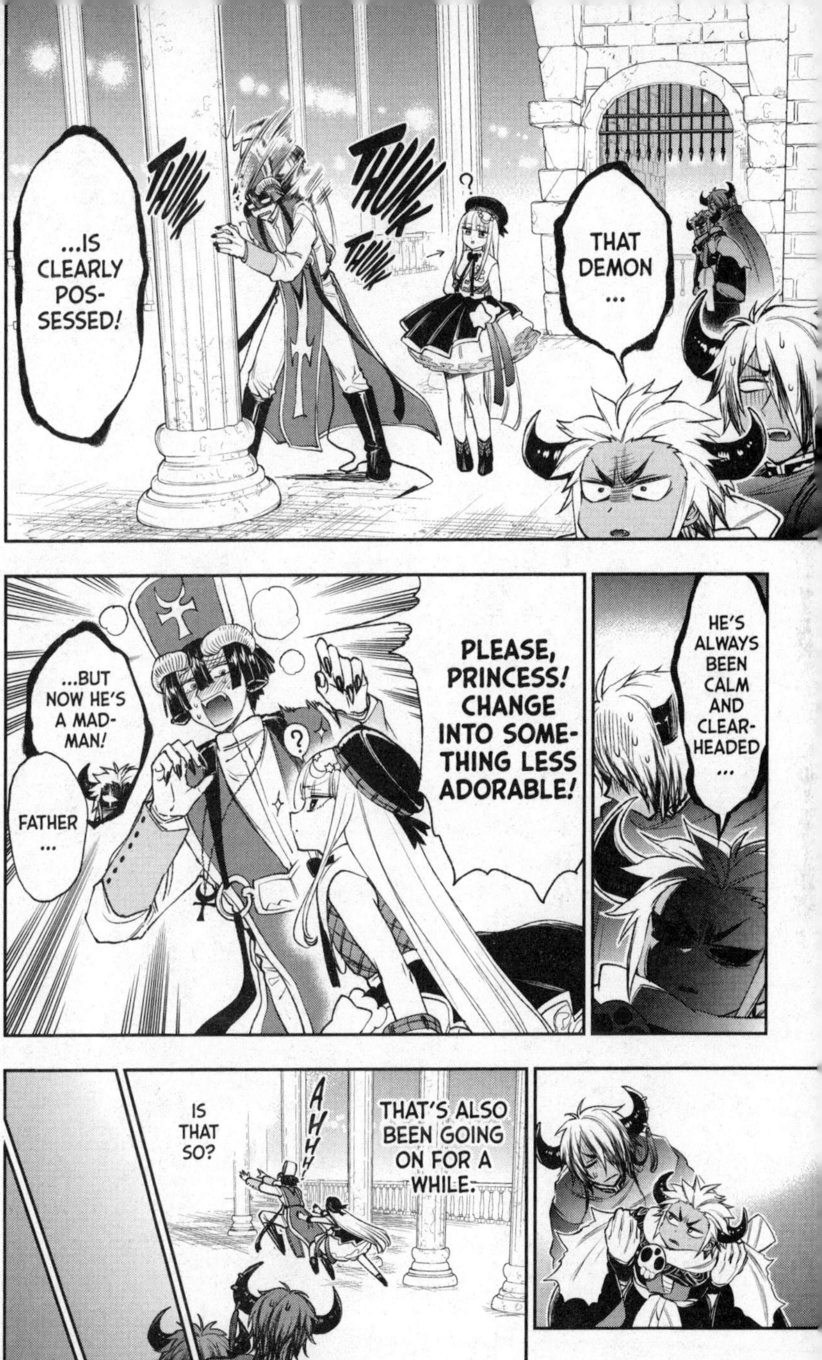
THAT DEMON ...
THUNK
THUNK
THUNK
...IS CLEARLY POS-SESSED!
HE'S ALWAYS BEEN CALM AND CLEAR-HEADED ...
PLEASE, PRINCESS! CHANGE INTO SOME-THING LESS ADORABLE!
...BUT NOW HE'S A MAD-MAN!
FATHER ...
THAT'S ALSO BEEN GOING ON FOR A WHILE.
AHHH
IS THAT SO?

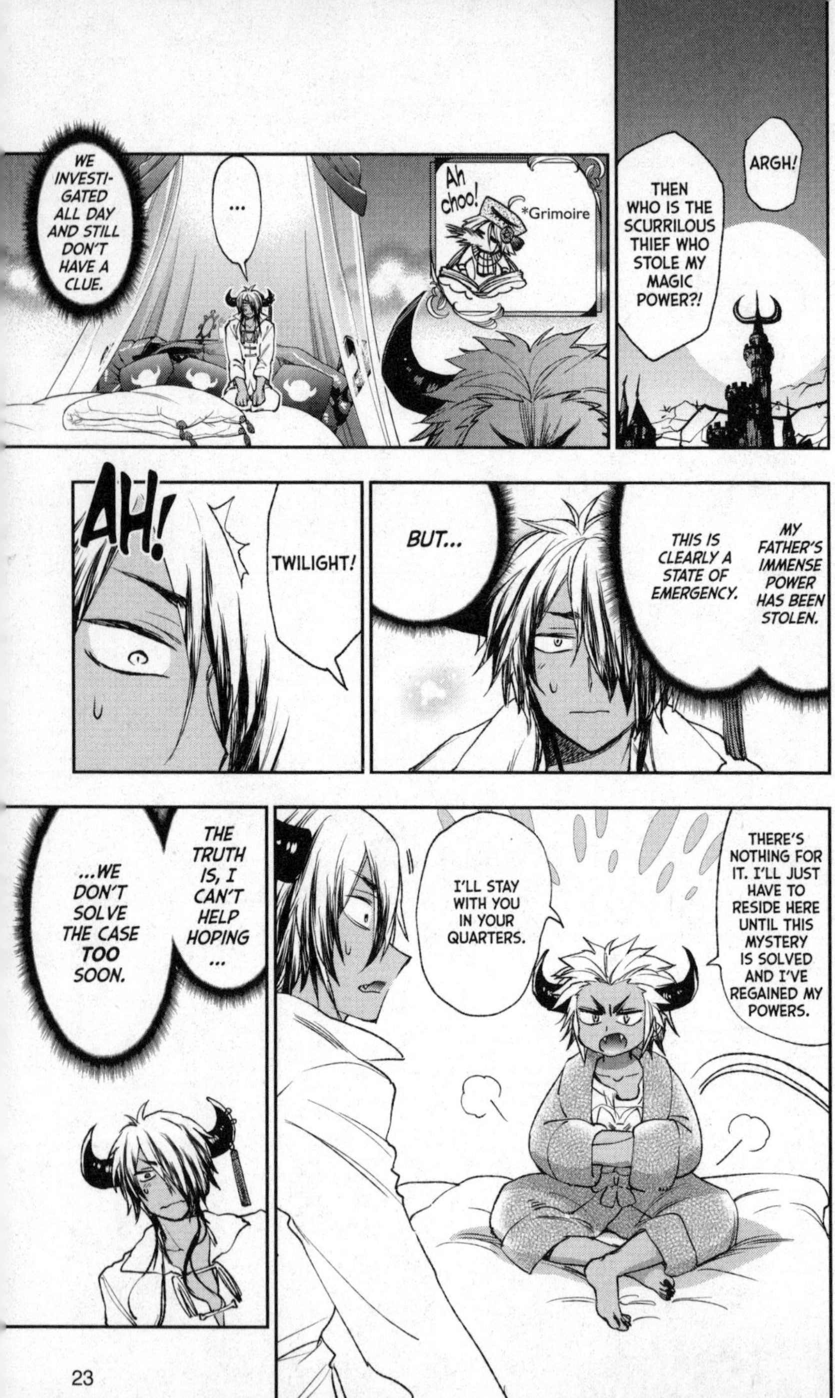
ARGH!
THEN WHO IS THE SCURRILOUS THIEF WHO STOLE MY MAGIC POWER?!
Ah choo!
*Grimoire
...
WE INVESTI-GATED ALL DAY AND STILL DON'T HAVE A CLUE.
MY FATHER'S IMMENSE POWER HAS BEEN STOLEN.
THIS IS CLEARLY A STATE OF EMERGENCY.
BUT...
TWILIGHT!
AH!
THERE'S NOTHING FOR IT. I'LL JUST HAVE TO RESIDE HERE UNTIL THIS MYSTERY IS SOLVED AND I'VE REGAINED MY POWERS.
I'LL STAY WITH YOU IN YOUR QUARTERS.
THE TRUTH IS, I CAN'T HELP HOPING...
...WE DON'T SOLVE THE CASE TOO SOON.

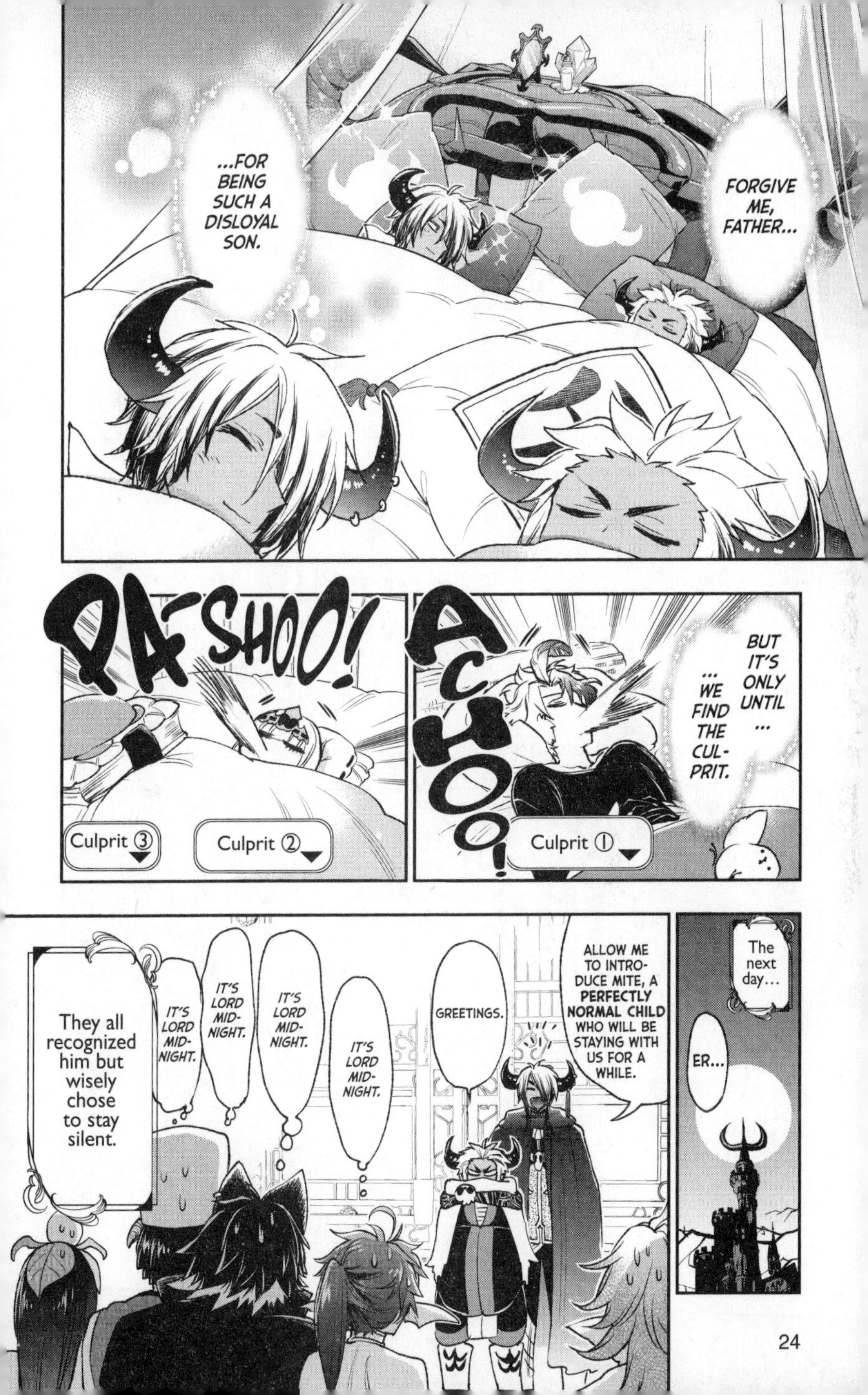
FORGIVE ME, FATHER...
...FOR BEING SUCH A DISLOYAL SON.
BUT IT'S ONLY UNTIL...
...WE FIND THE CUL-PRIT.
ACHOO!
Culprit ①
PA-SHOO!
Culprit ②
Culprit ③
The next day...
ER...
ALLOW ME TO INTRO-DUCE MITE, A **PERFECTLY NORMAL CHILD** WHO WILL BE STAYING WITH US FOR A WHILE.
GREETINGS.
IT'S LORD MID-NIGHT.
IT'S LORD MID-NIGHT.
IT'S LORD MID-NIGHT.
IT'S LORD MID-NIGHT.
They all recognized him but wisely chose to stay silent.

211th Night: Damn Bird, Figuring It Out So Quickly

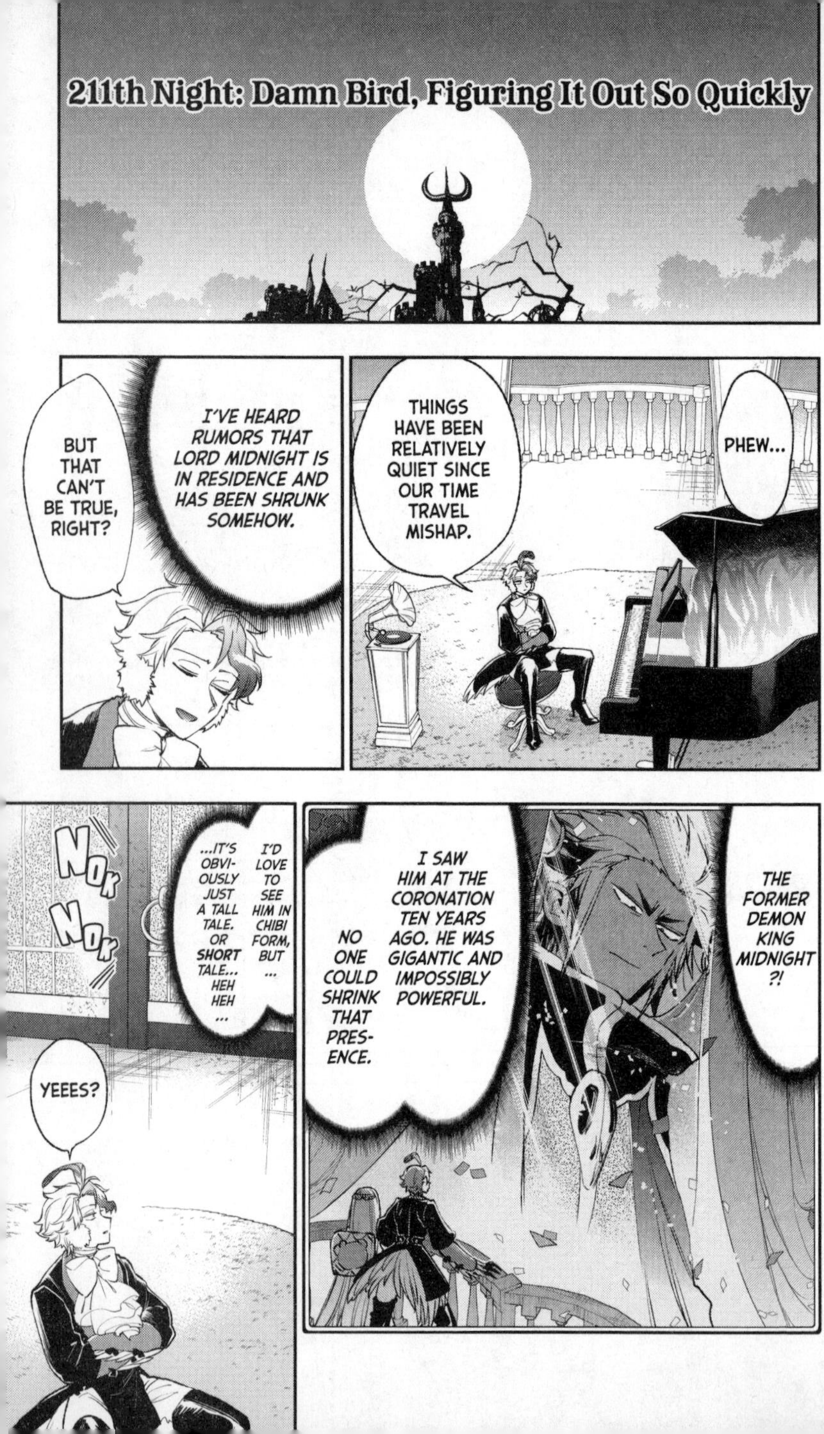
PHEW...
THINGS HAVE BEEN RELATIVELY QUIET SINCE OUR TIME TRAVEL MISHAP.
I'VE HEARD RUMORS THAT LORD MIDNIGHT IS IN RESIDENCE AND HAS BEEN SHRUNK SOMEHOW.
BUT THAT CAN'T BE TRUE, RIGHT?
THE FORMER DEMON KING MIDNIGHT?!
I SAW HIM AT THE CORONATION TEN YEARS AGO. HE WAS GIGANTIC AND IMPOSSIBLY POWERFUL.
NO ONE COULD SHRINK THAT PRESENCE.
I'D LOVE TO SEE HIM IN CHIBI FORM, BUT...
...IT'S OBVIOUSLY JUST A TALL TALE. OR **SHORT** TALE... HEH HEH...
NOK NOK
YEEES?

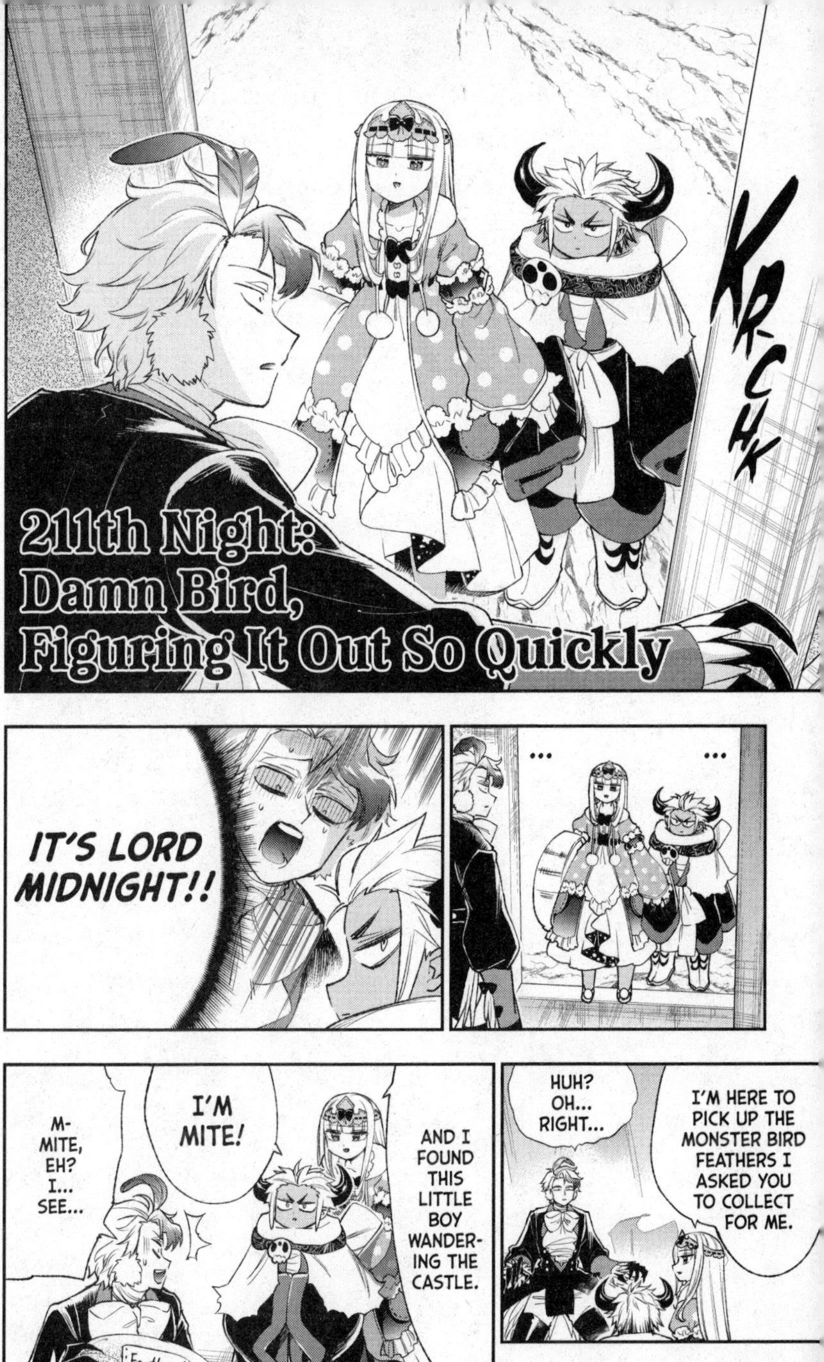
KR-CHK
211th Night: Damn Bird, Figuring It Out So Quickly
...
...
IT'S LORD MIDNIGHT!!
I'M HERE TO PICK UP THE MONSTER BIRD FEATHERS I ASKED YOU TO COLLECT FOR ME.
HUH? OH... RIGHT...
AND I FOUND THIS LITTLE BOY WANDERING THE CASTLE.
I'M MITE!
M-MITE, EH? I... SEE...
Feathers

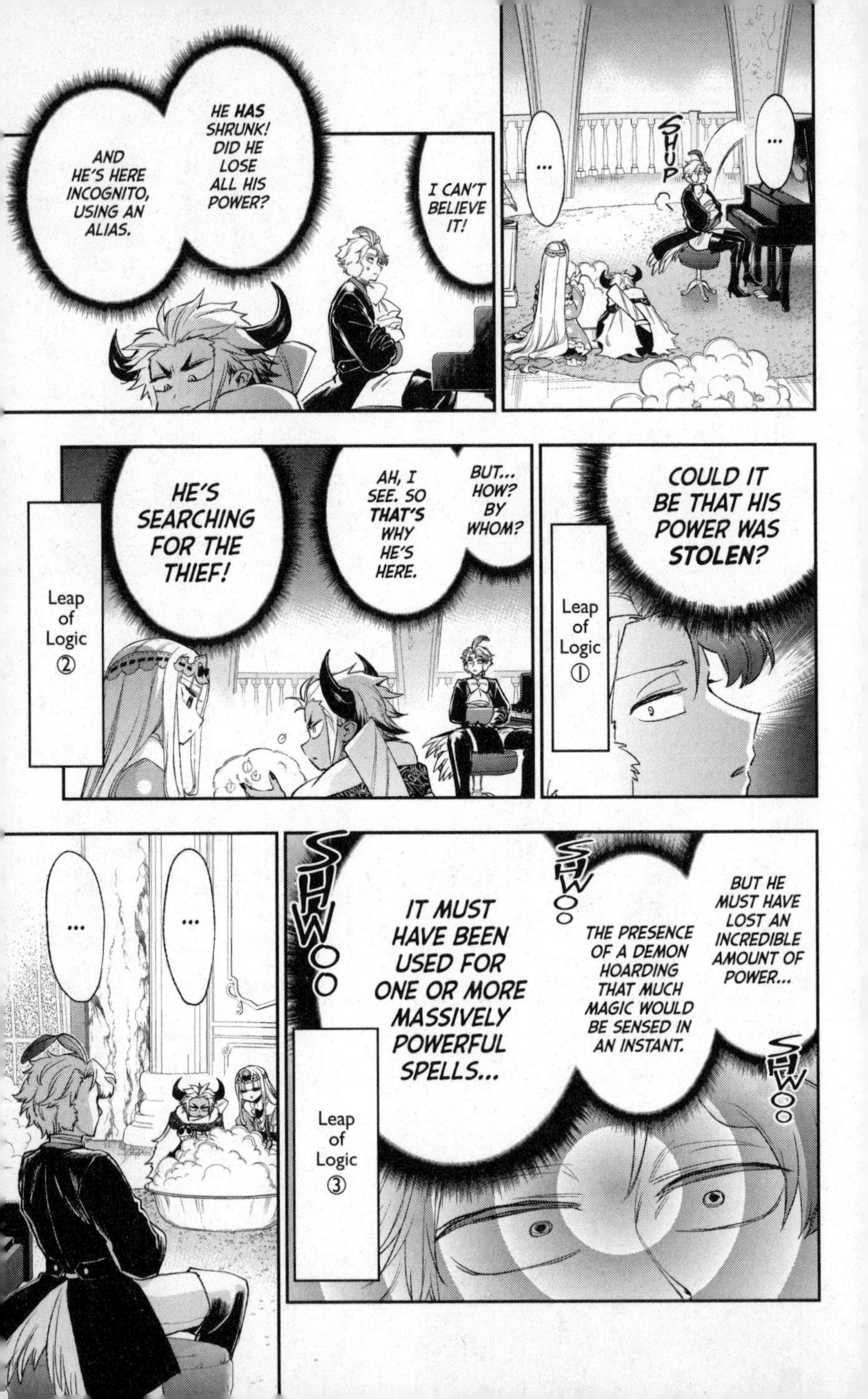
...
SHUP
...
I CAN'T BELIEVE IT!
HE HAS SHRUNK! DID HE LOSE ALL HIS POWER?
AND HE'S HERE INCOGNITO, USING AN ALIAS.
COULD IT BE THAT HIS POWER WAS STOLEN?
Leap of Logic ①
BUT... HOW? BY WHOM?
AH, I SEE. SO THAT'S WHY HE'S HERE.
HE'S SEARCHING FOR THE THIEF!
Leap of Logic ②
SHWOO
BUT HE MUST HAVE LOST AN INCREDIBLE AMOUNT OF POWER...
SHWOO
THE PRESENCE OF A DEMON HOARDING THAT MUCH MAGIC WOULD BE SENSED IN AN INSTANT.
SHWOO
IT MUST HAVE BEEN USED FOR ONE OR MORE MASSIVELY POWERFUL SPELLS...
Leap of Logic ③
...
...

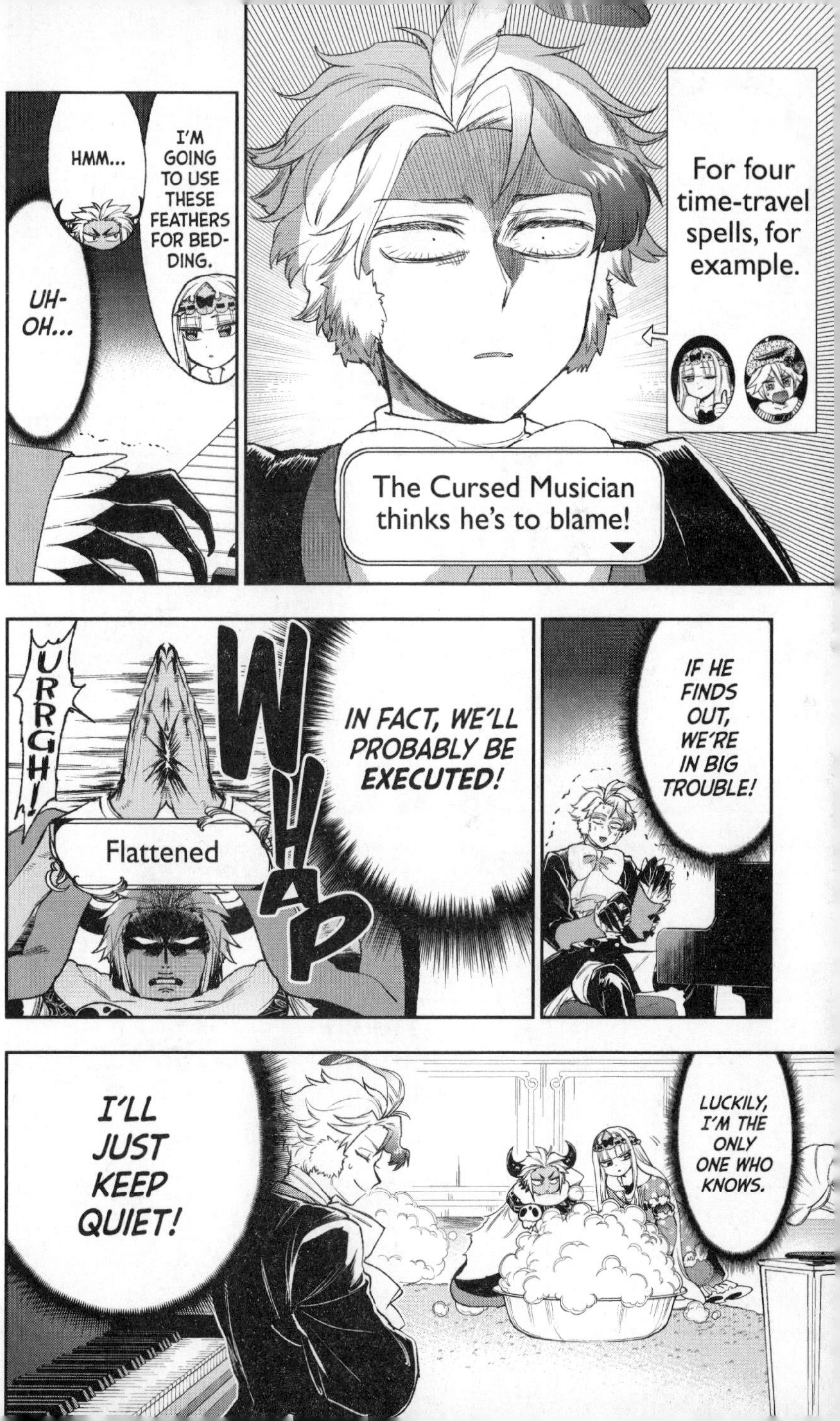
For four time-travel spells, for example.
The Cursed Musician thinks he's to blame!
I'M GOING TO USE THESE FEATHERS FOR BEDDING.
HMM...
UH-OH...
IF HE FINDS OUT, WE'RE IN BIG TROUBLE!
IN FACT, WE'LL PROBABLY BE EXECUTED!
WHAP
URRGH!
Flattened
LUCKILY, I'M THE ONLY ONE WHO KNOWS.
I'LL JUST KEEP QUIET!

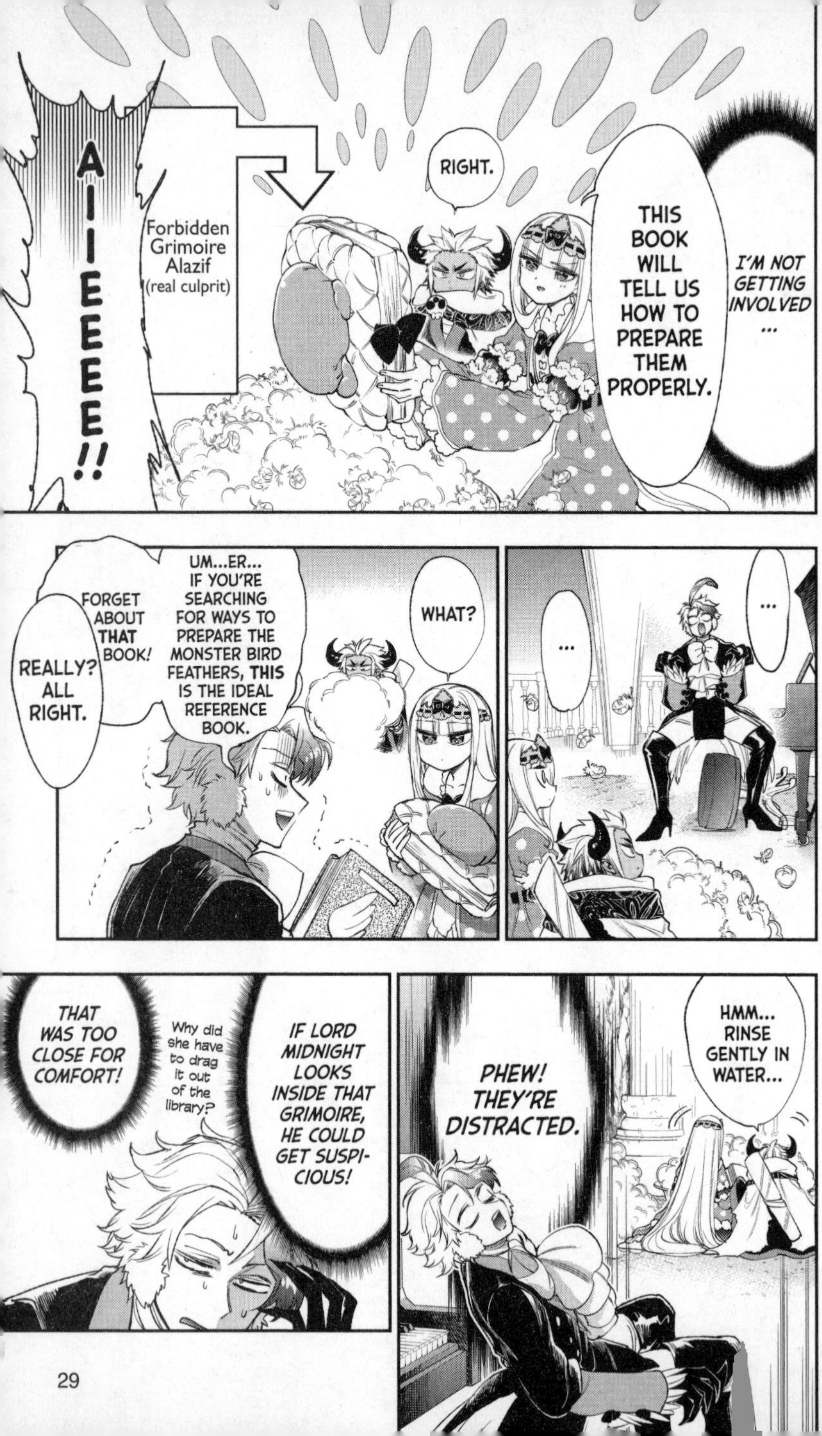
I'M NOT GETTING INVOLVED...
THIS BOOK WILL TELL US HOW TO PREPARE THEM PROPERLY.
RIGHT.
Forbidden Grimoire Alazif (real culprit)
AIIEEEE!!
...
...
WHAT?
UM...ER... IF YOU'RE SEARCHING FOR WAYS TO PREPARE THE MONSTER BIRD FEATHERS, **THIS** IS THE IDEAL REFERENCE BOOK.
FORGET ABOUT **THAT** BOOK!
REALLY? ALL RIGHT.
HMM... RINSE GENTLY IN WATER...
PHEW! THEY'RE DISTRACTED.
IF LORD MIDNIGHT LOOKS INSIDE THAT GRIMOIRE, HE COULD GET SUSPICIOUS!
Why did she have to drag it out of the library?
THAT WAS TOO CLOSE FOR COMFORT!

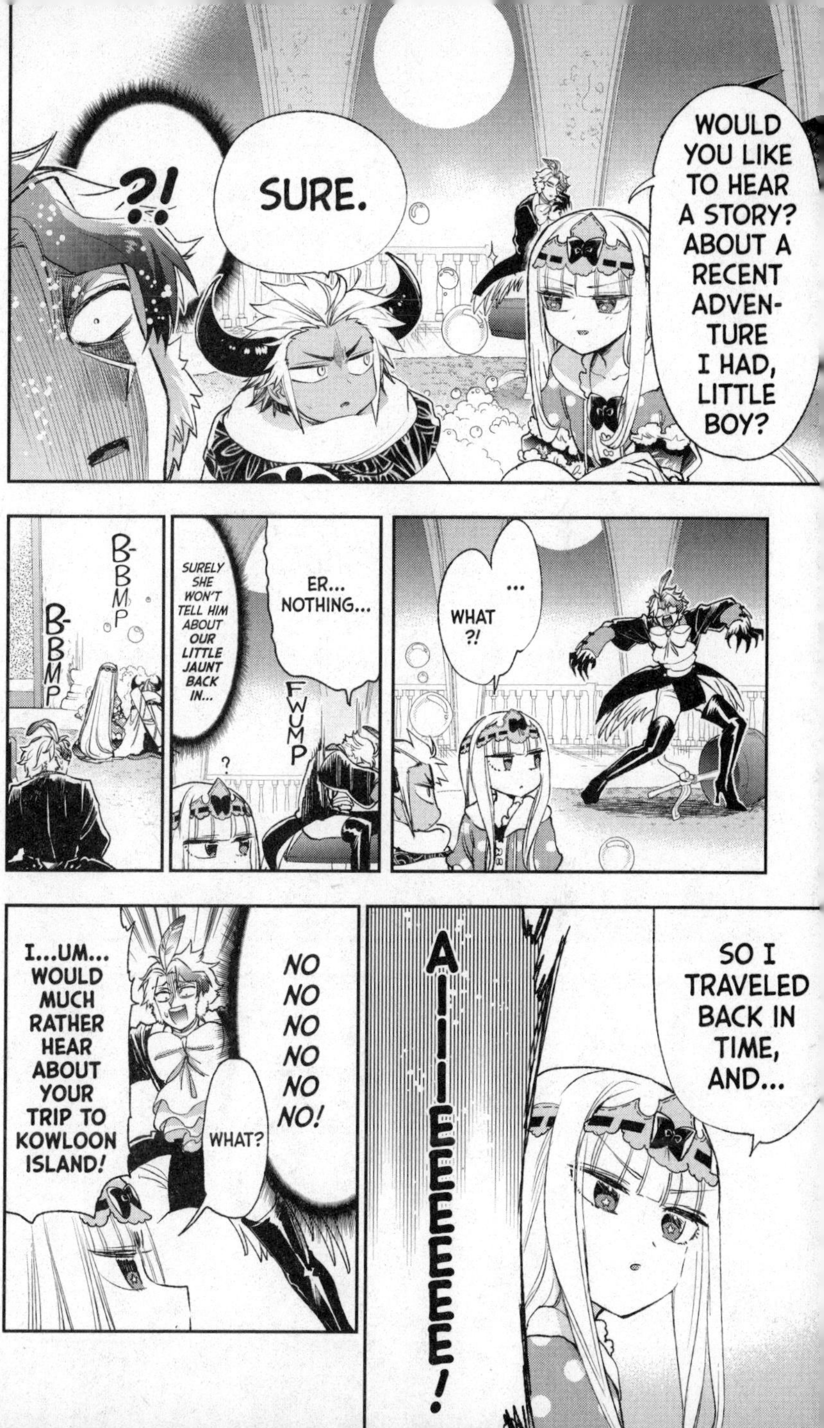
WOULD YOU LIKE TO HEAR A STORY? ABOUT A RECENT ADVEN-TURE I HAD, LITTLE BOY?
SURE.
?!
...
WHAT ?!
ER... NOTHING...
SURELY SHE WON'T TELL HIM ABOUT OUR LITTLE JAUNT BACK IN...
FWUMP
?
B-BBMP
B-BBMP
SO I TRAVELED BACK IN TIME, AND...
AIIIEEEEEEEE!
NO NO NO NO NO NO!
WHAT?
I...UM... WOULD MUCH RATHER HEAR ABOUT YOUR TRIP TO KOWLOON ISLAND!

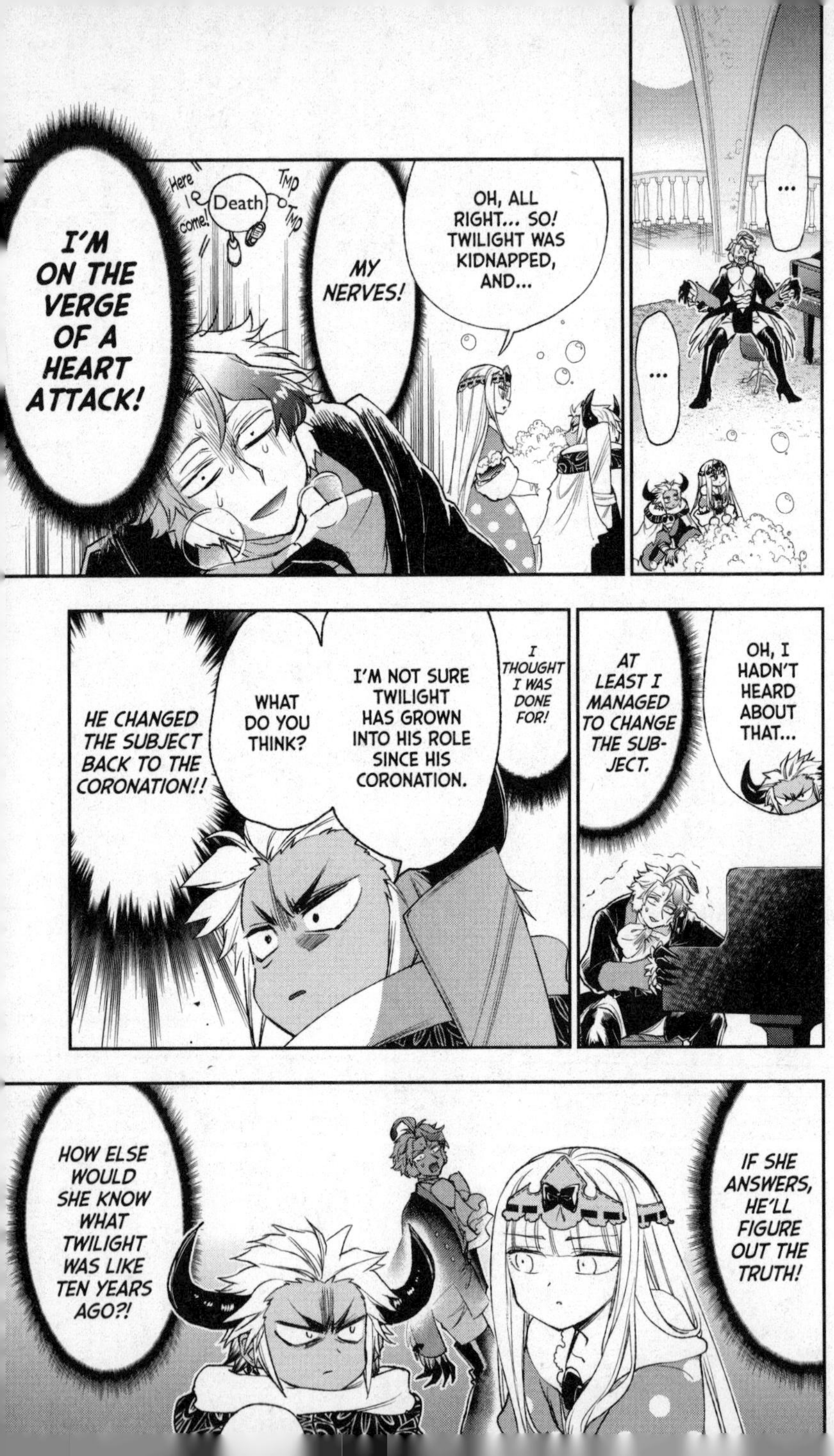
...
...
OH, ALL RIGHT... SO! TWILIGHT WAS KIDNAPPED, AND...
MY NERVES!
Tmp
Tmp
Death
Here I come!
I'M ON THE VERGE OF A HEART ATTACK!
OH, I HADN'T HEARD ABOUT THAT...
AT LEAST I MANAGED TO CHANGE THE SUB-JECT.
I THOUGHT I WAS DONE FOR!
I'M NOT SURE TWILIGHT HAS GROWN INTO HIS ROLE SINCE HIS CORONATION.
WHAT DO YOU THINK?
HE CHANGED THE SUBJECT BACK TO THE CORONATION!!
IF SHE ANSWERS, HE'LL FIGURE OUT THE TRUTH!
HOW ELSE WOULD SHE KNOW WHAT TWILIGHT WAS LIKE TEN YEARS AGO?!

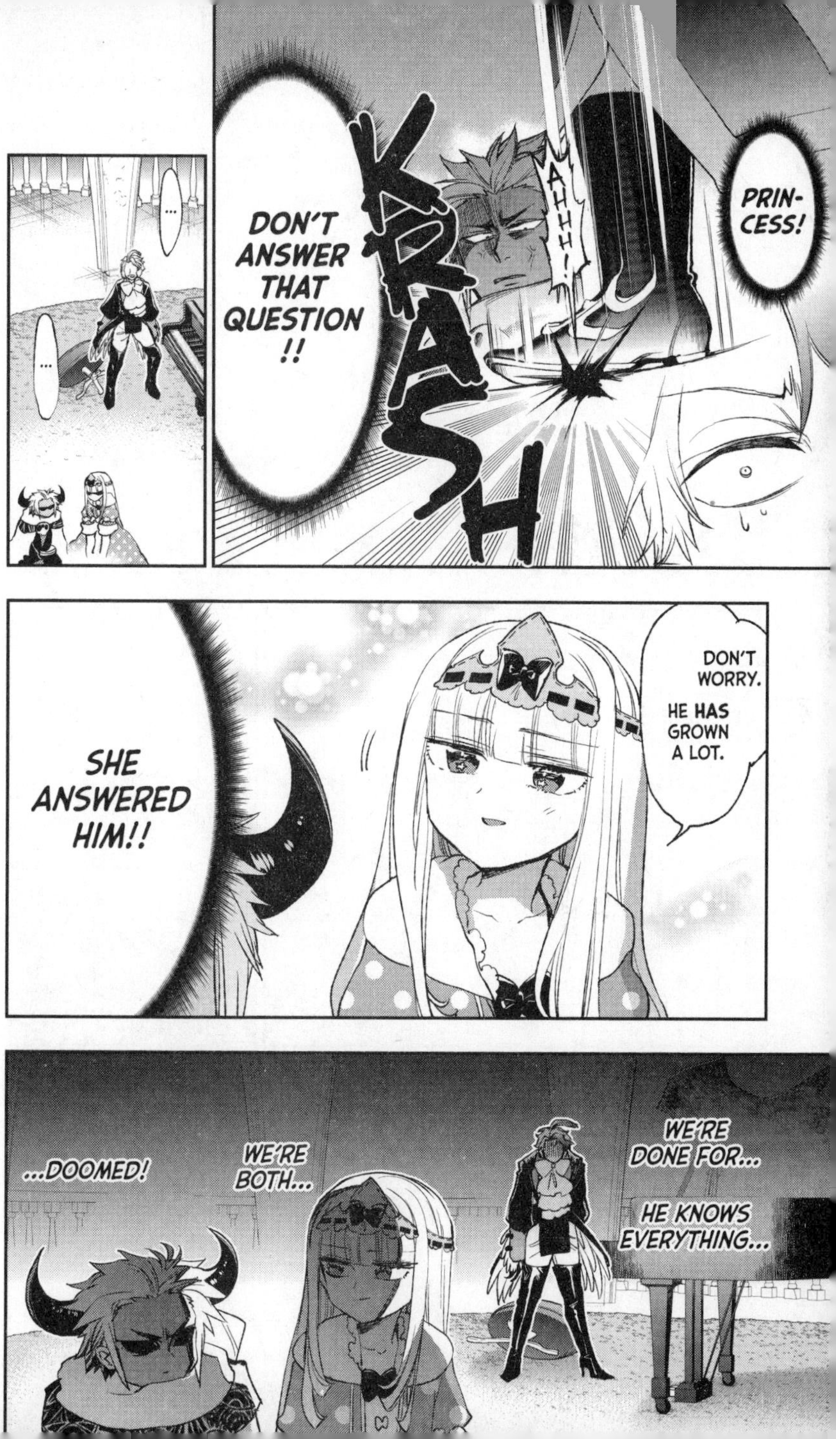
PRIN-CESS!
AHHH!
DON'T ANSWER THAT QUESTION!!
KRASH
...
...
DON'T WORRY.
HE HAS GROWN A LOT.
SHE ANSWERED HIM!!
WE'RE DONE FOR...
HE KNOWS EVERYTHING...
WE'RE BOTH...
...DOOMED!

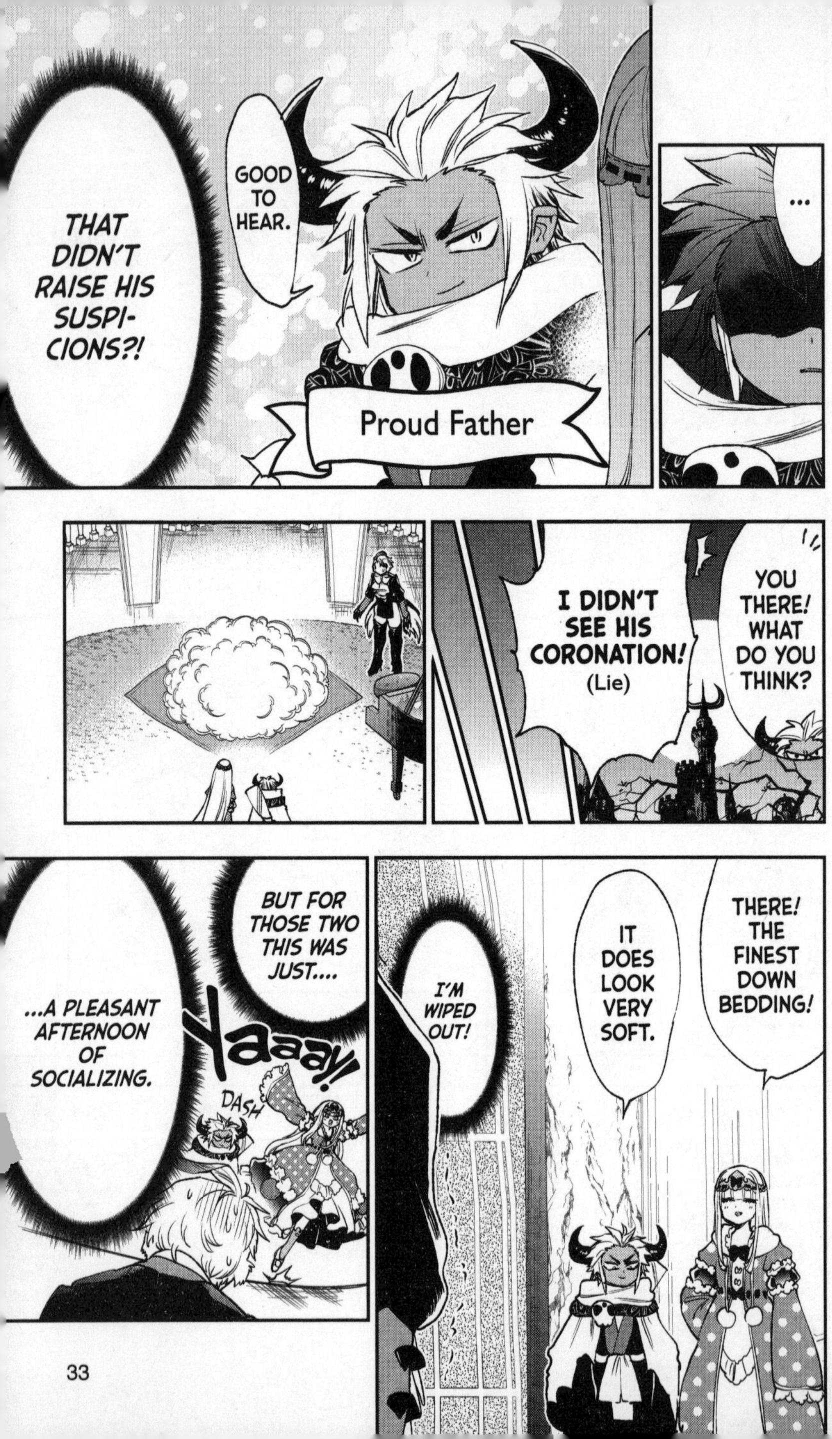
...
GOOD TO HEAR.
THAT DIDN'T RAISE HIS SUSPI-CIONS?!
Proud Father
YOU THERE! WHAT DO YOU THINK?
I DIDN'T SEE HIS CORONATION!
(Lie)
THERE! THE FINEST DOWN BEDDING!
IT DOES LOOK VERY SOFT.
I'M WIPED OUT!
BUT FOR THOSE TWO THIS WAS JUST....
Yaaay!!
DASH
...A PLEASANT AFTERNOON OF SOCIALIZING.

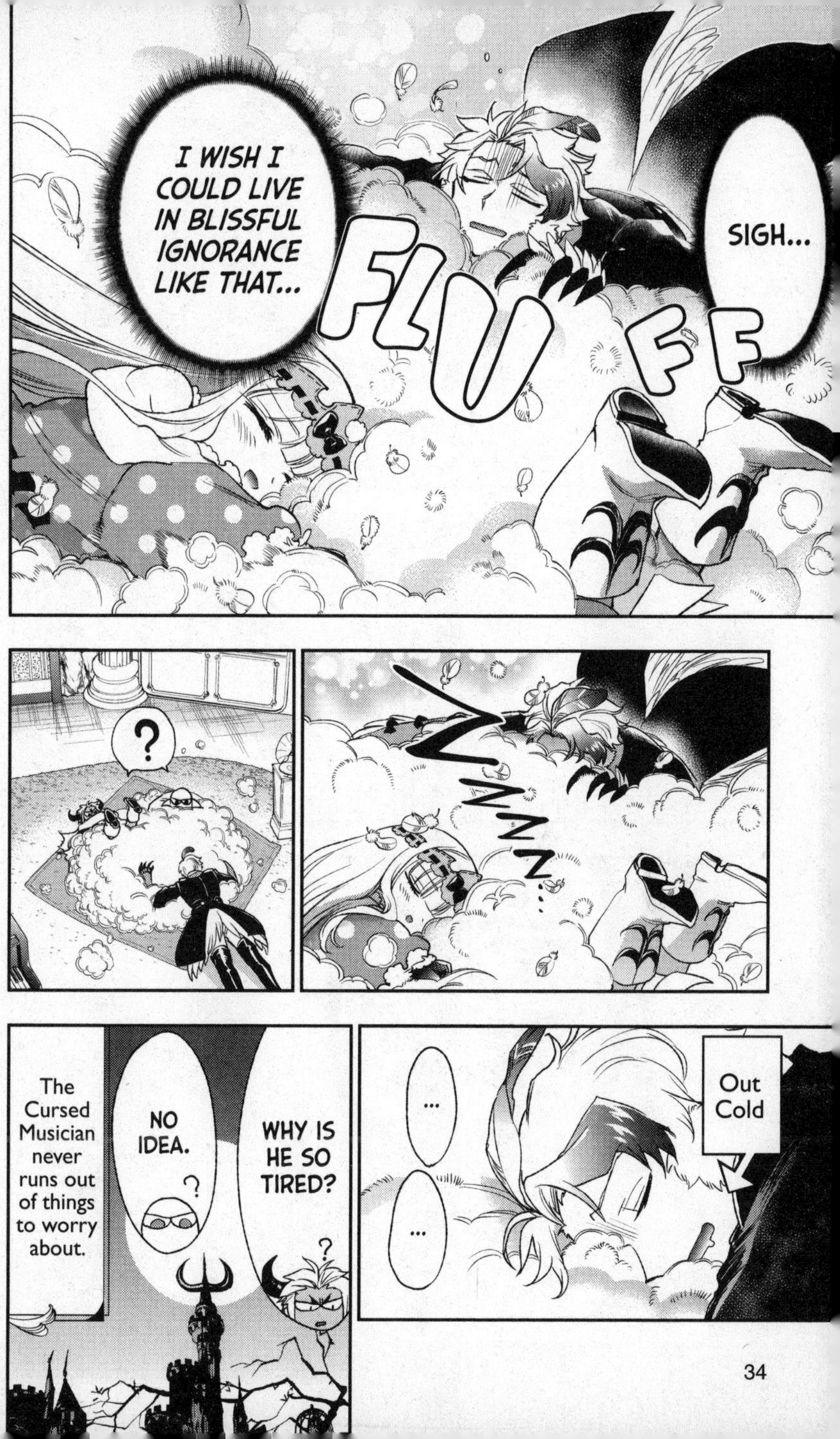
SIGH...
FLUFF
I WISH I COULD LIVE IN BLISSFUL IGNORANCE LIKE THAT...
ZZZZ...
?
Out Cold
...
...
WHY IS HE SO TIRED?
?
NO IDEA.
?
The Cursed Musician never runs out of things to worry about.

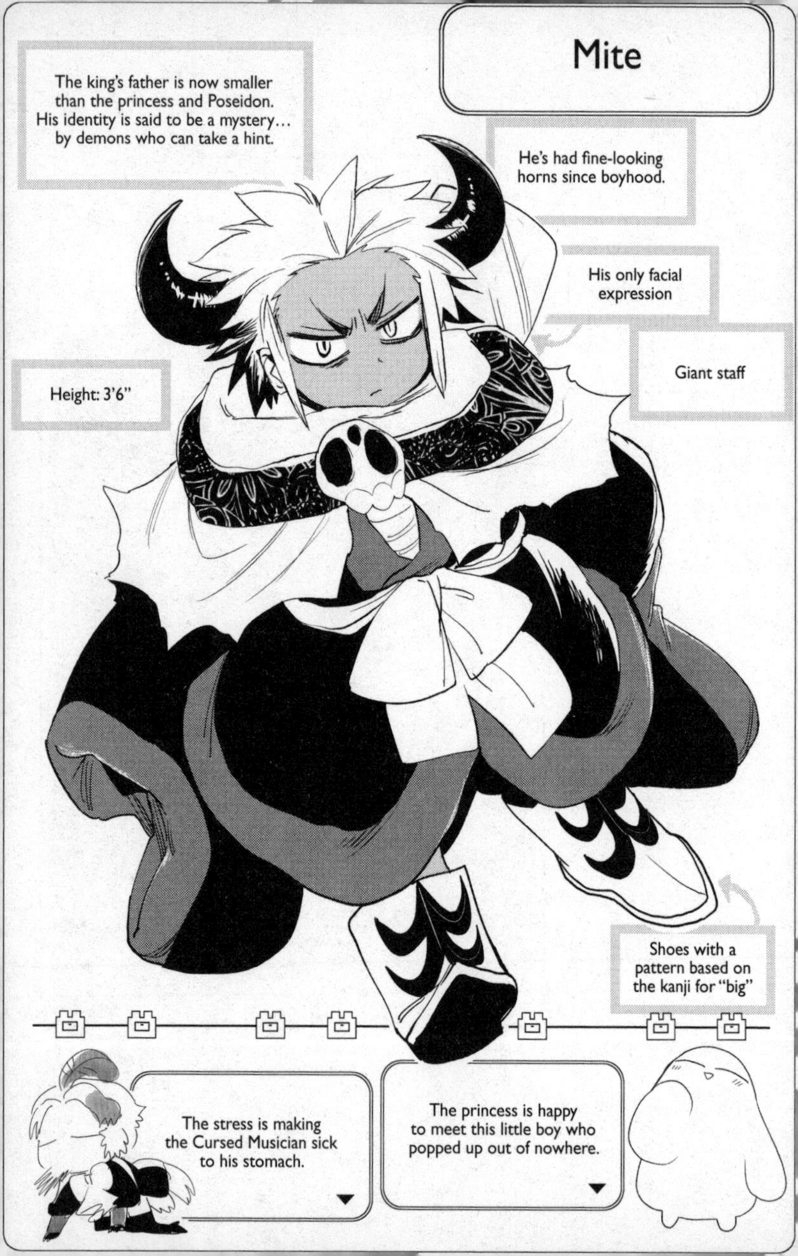
Mite
The king's father is now smaller than the princess and Poseidon. His identity is said to be a mystery… by demons who can take a hint.
He's had fine-looking horns since boyhood.
His only facial expression
Giant staff
Height: 3'6"
Shoes with a pattern based on the kanji for "big"
The princess is happy to meet this little boy who popped up out of nowhere.
The stress is making the Cursed Musician sick to his stomach.

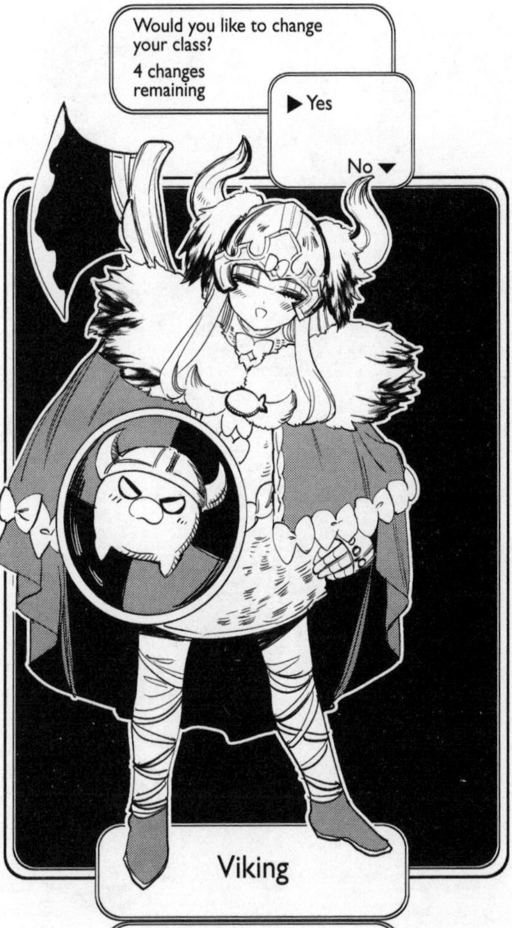
Would you like to change your class?
4 changes remaining
▶ Yes
No ▼
Viking
"This shield is sooo cool. ♡"

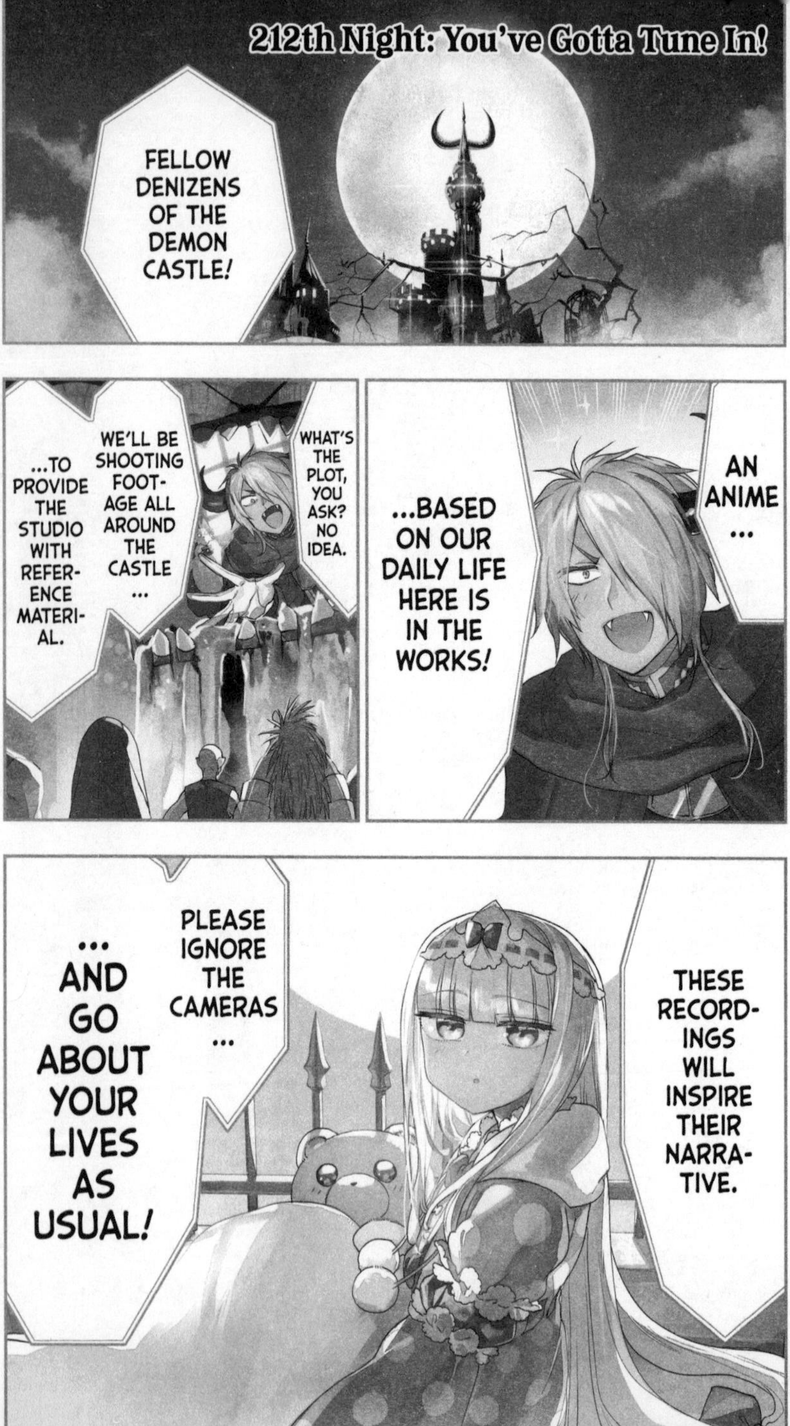
212th Night: You've Gotta Tune In!
FELLOW DENIZENS OF THE DEMON CASTLE!
AN ANIME...
...BASED ON OUR DAILY LIFE HERE IS IN THE WORKS!
WHAT'S THE PLOT, YOU ASK? NO IDEA.
WE'LL BE SHOOTING FOOTAGE ALL AROUND THE CASTLE...
...TO PROVIDE THE STUDIO WITH REFERENCE MATERIAL.
THESE RECORDINGS WILL INSPIRE THEIR NARRATIVE.
PLEASE IGNORE THE CAMERAS...
...AND GO ABOUT YOUR LIVES AS USUAL!

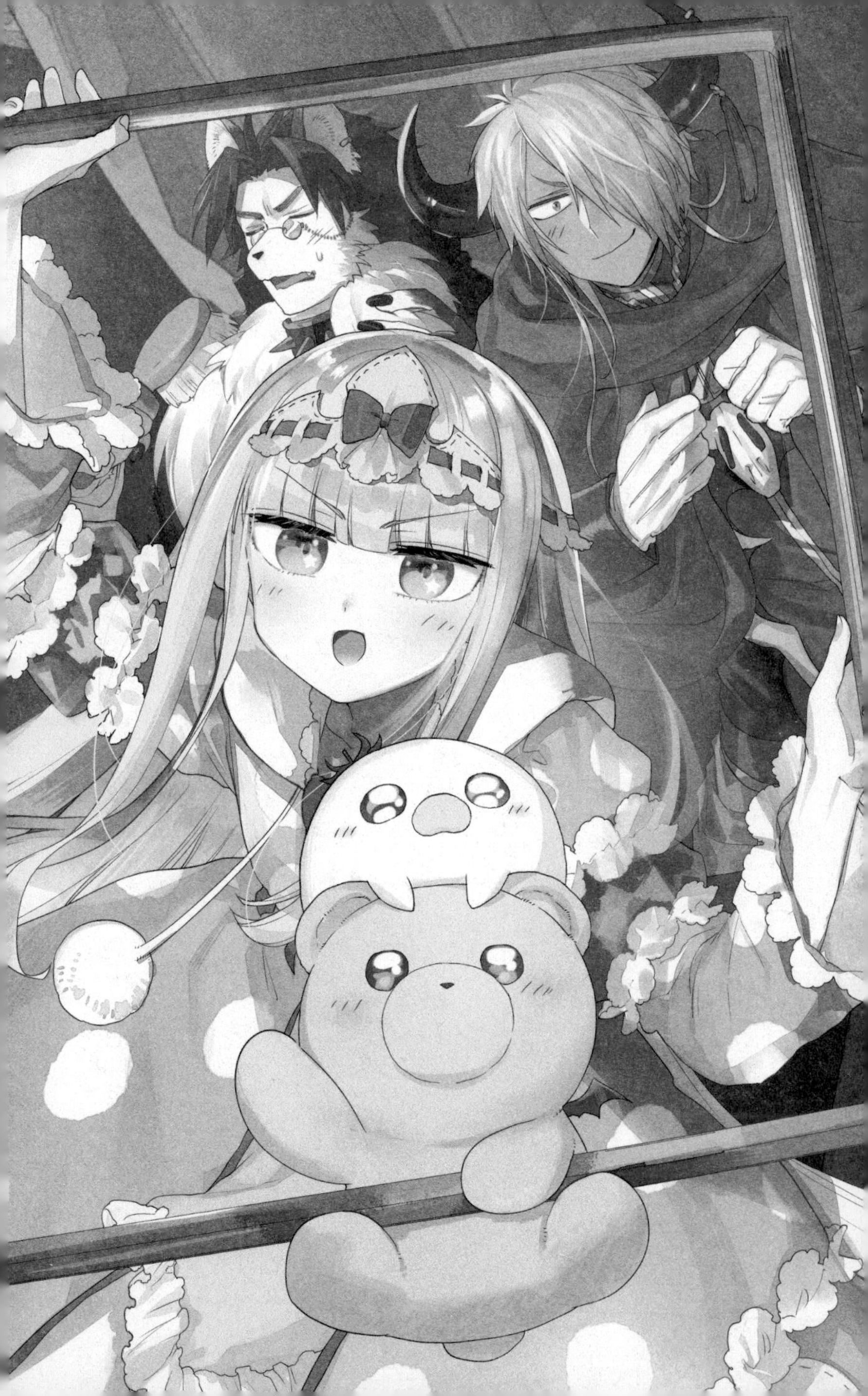

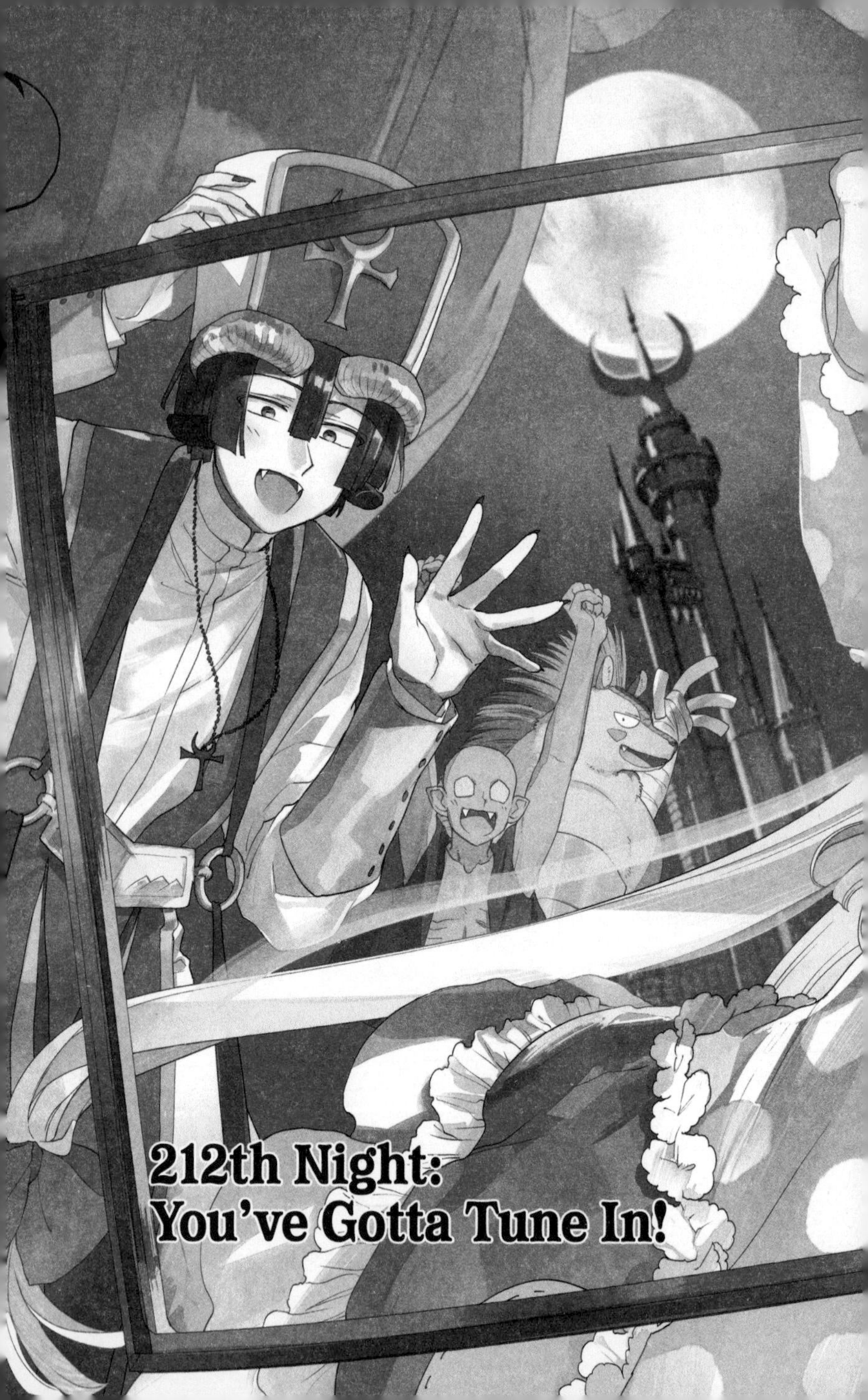
212th Night:
You've Gotta Tune In!

SLEEPY PRINCESS
IN THE
DEMON CASTLE

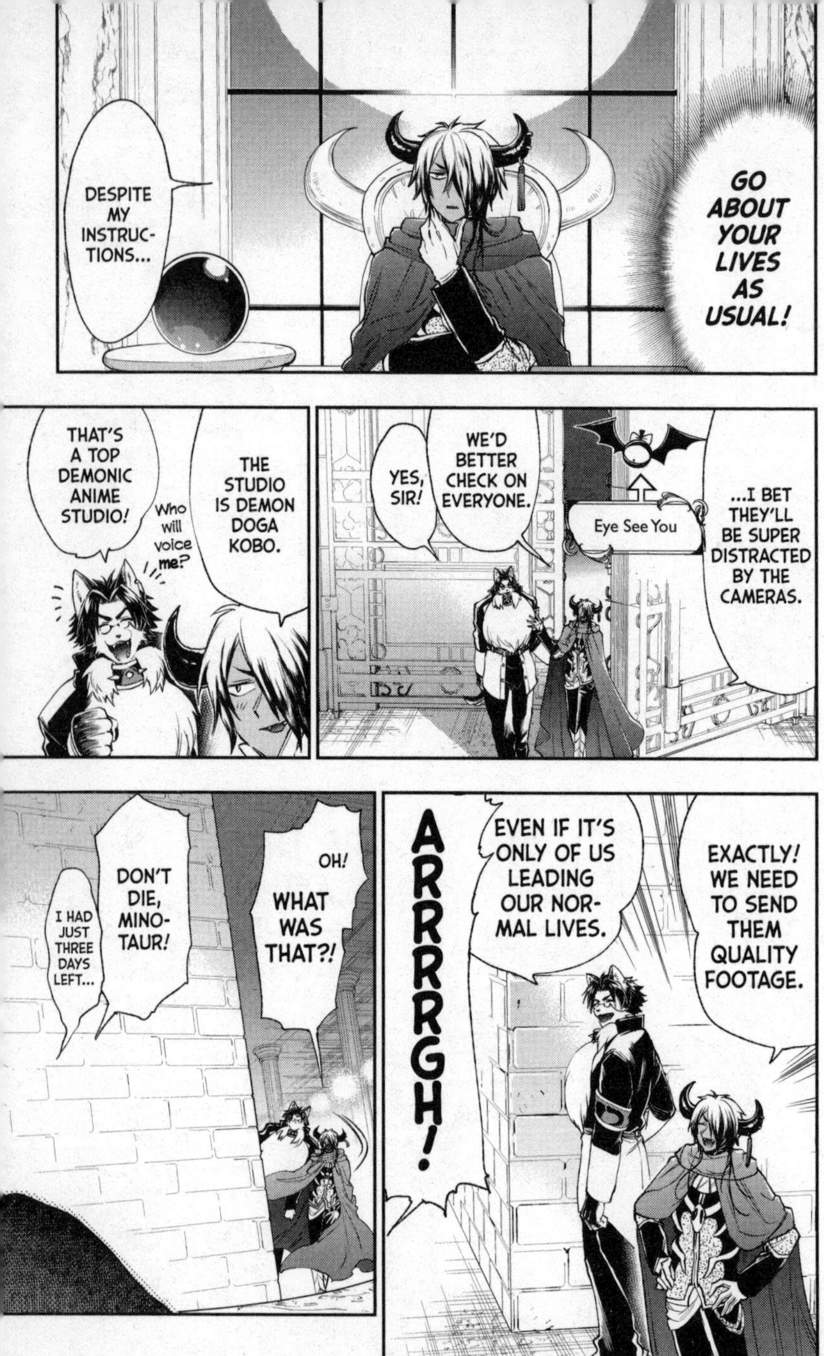
GO ABOUT YOUR LIVES AS USUAL!
DESPITE MY INSTRUCTIONS...
...I BET THEY'LL BE SUPER DISTRACTED BY THE CAMERAS.
Eye See You
WE'D BETTER CHECK ON EVERYONE.
YES, SIR!
THE STUDIO IS DEMON DOGA KOBO.
THAT'S A TOP DEMONIC ANIME STUDIO!
Who will voice me?
EXACTLY! WE NEED TO SEND THEM QUALITY FOOTAGE.
EVEN IF IT'S ONLY OF US LEADING OUR NORMAL LIVES.
ARRRRGH!
OH!
WHAT WAS THAT?!
DON'T DIE, MINOTAUR!
I HAD JUST THREE DAYS LEFT...

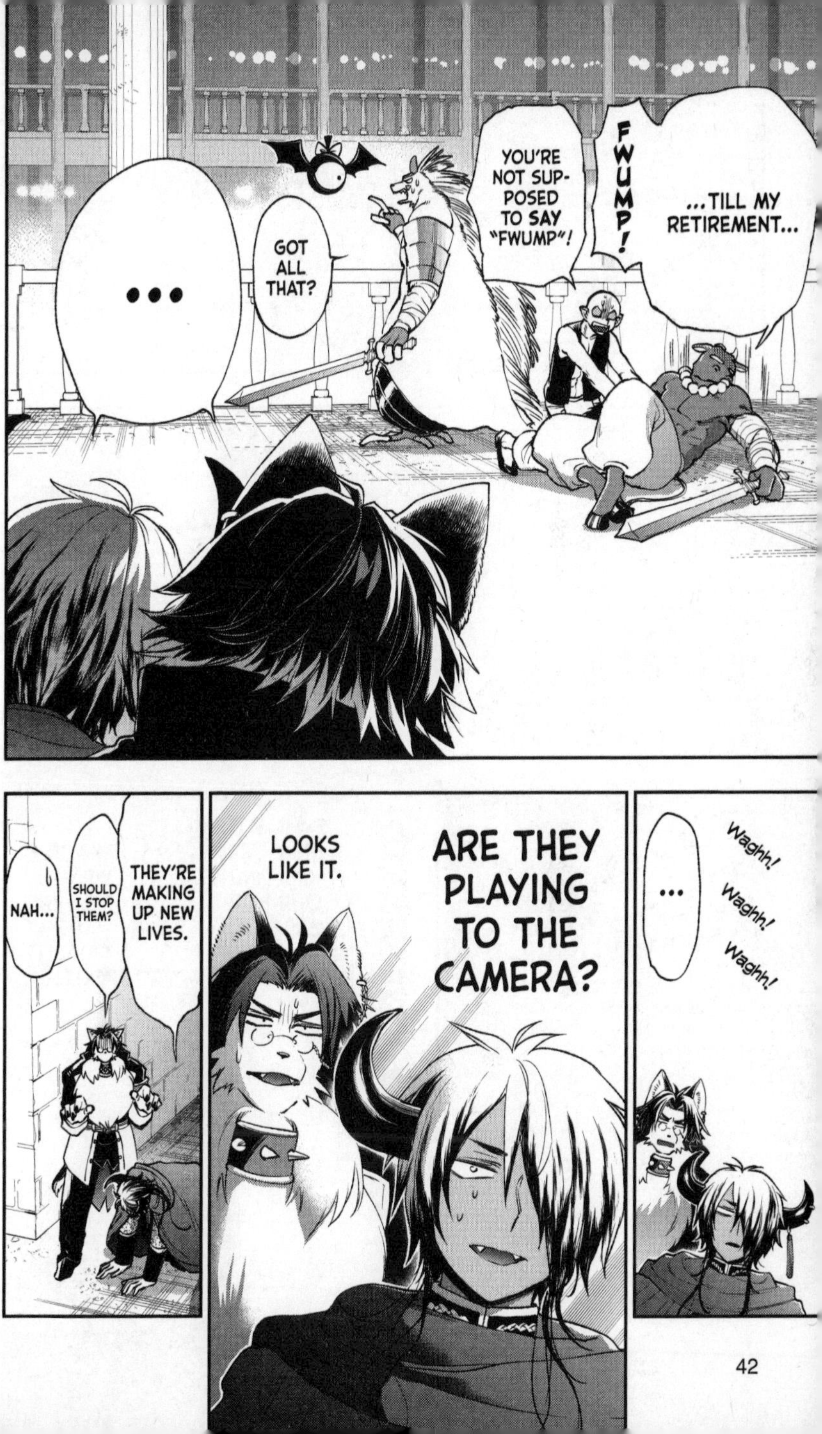
...TILL MY RETIREMENT...
FWUMP!
YOU'RE NOT SUP-POSED TO SAY "FWUMP"!
GOT ALL THAT?
...
...
Waghh! Waghh! Waghh!
ARE THEY PLAYING TO THE CAMERA?
LOOKS LIKE IT.
THEY'RE MAKING UP NEW LIVES.
SHOULD I STOP THEM?
NAH...

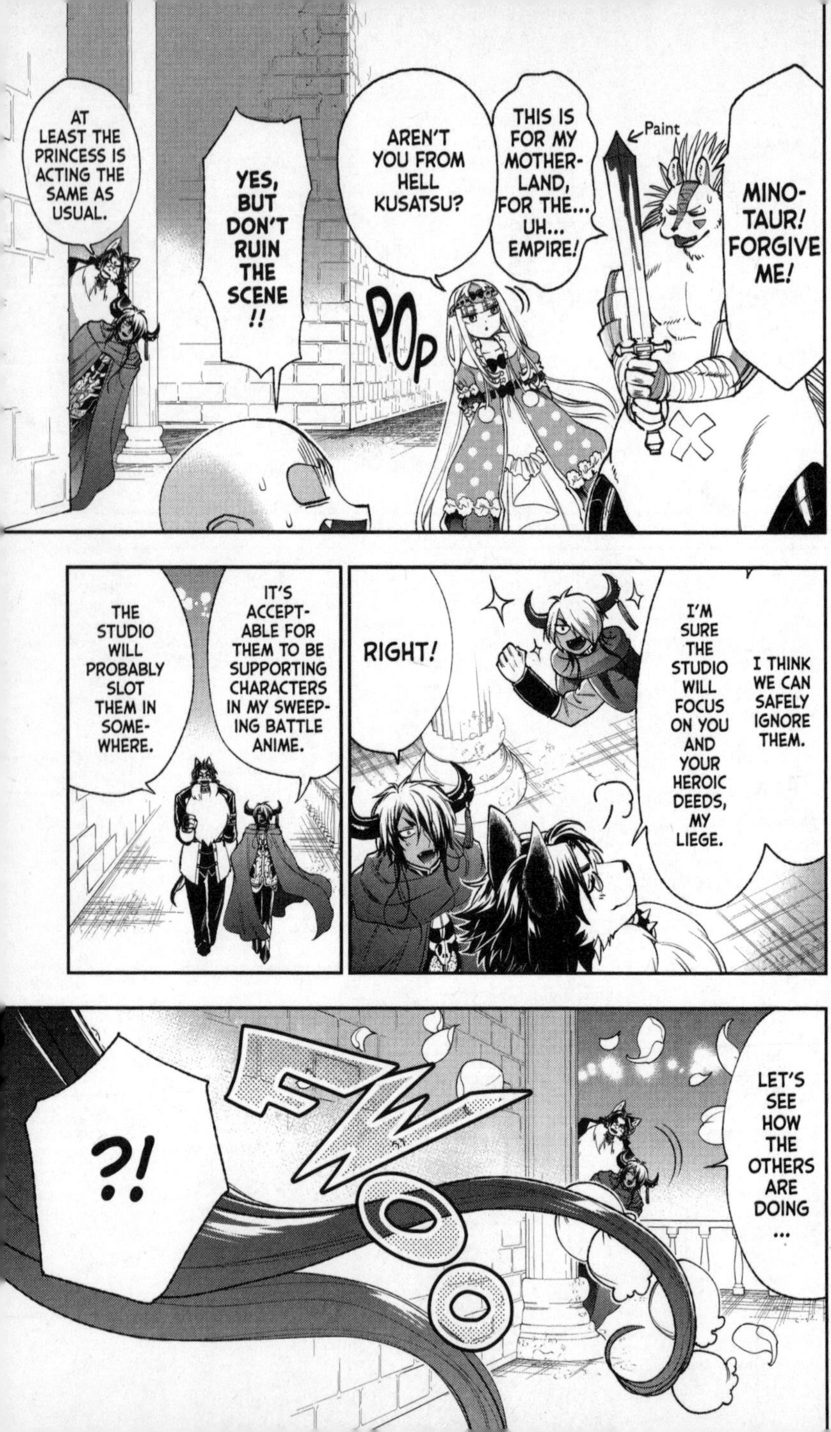
MINOTAUR! FORGIVE ME!
Paint
THIS IS FOR MY MOTHERLAND, FOR THE... UH... EMPIRE!
AREN'T YOU FROM HELL KUSATSU?
POP
YES, BUT DON'T RUIN THE SCENE!!
AT LEAST THE PRINCESS IS ACTING THE SAME AS USUAL.
I THINK WE CAN SAFELY IGNORE THEM.
I'M SURE THE STUDIO WILL FOCUS ON YOU AND YOUR HEROIC DEEDS, MY LIEGE.
RIGHT!
IT'S ACCEPTABLE FOR THEM TO BE SUPPORTING CHARACTERS IN MY SWEEPING BATTLE ANIME.
THE STUDIO WILL PROBABLY SLOT THEM IN SOMEWHERE.
LET'S SEE HOW THE OTHERS ARE DOING...
FWOO
?!

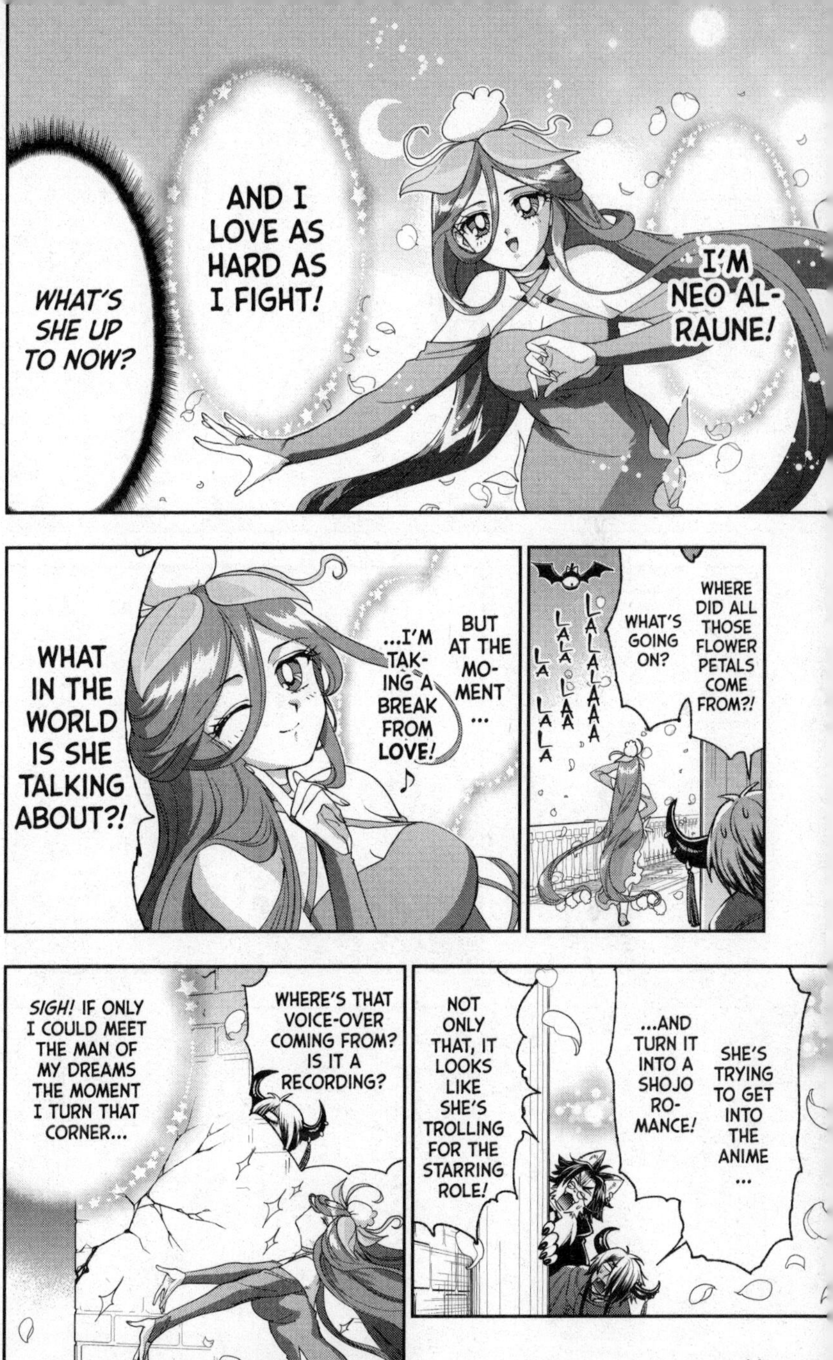
I'M NEO AL-RAUNE!
AND I LOVE AS HARD AS I FIGHT!
WHAT'S SHE UP TO NOW?
WHERE DID ALL THOSE FLOWER PETALS COME FROM?!
WHAT'S GOING ON?
LALALAAAA LALALAA LA LALA
BUT AT THE MOMENT...
...I'M TAKING A BREAK FROM LOVE! ♪
WHAT IN THE WORLD IS SHE TALKING ABOUT?!
SHE'S TRYING TO GET INTO THE ANIME...
...AND TURN IT INTO A SHOJO ROMANCE!
NOT ONLY THAT, IT LOOKS LIKE SHE'S TROLLING FOR THE STARRING ROLE!
WHERE'S THAT VOICE-OVER COMING FROM? IS IT A RECORDING?
SIGH! IF ONLY I COULD MEET THE MAN OF MY DREAMS THE MOMENT I TURN THAT CORNER...

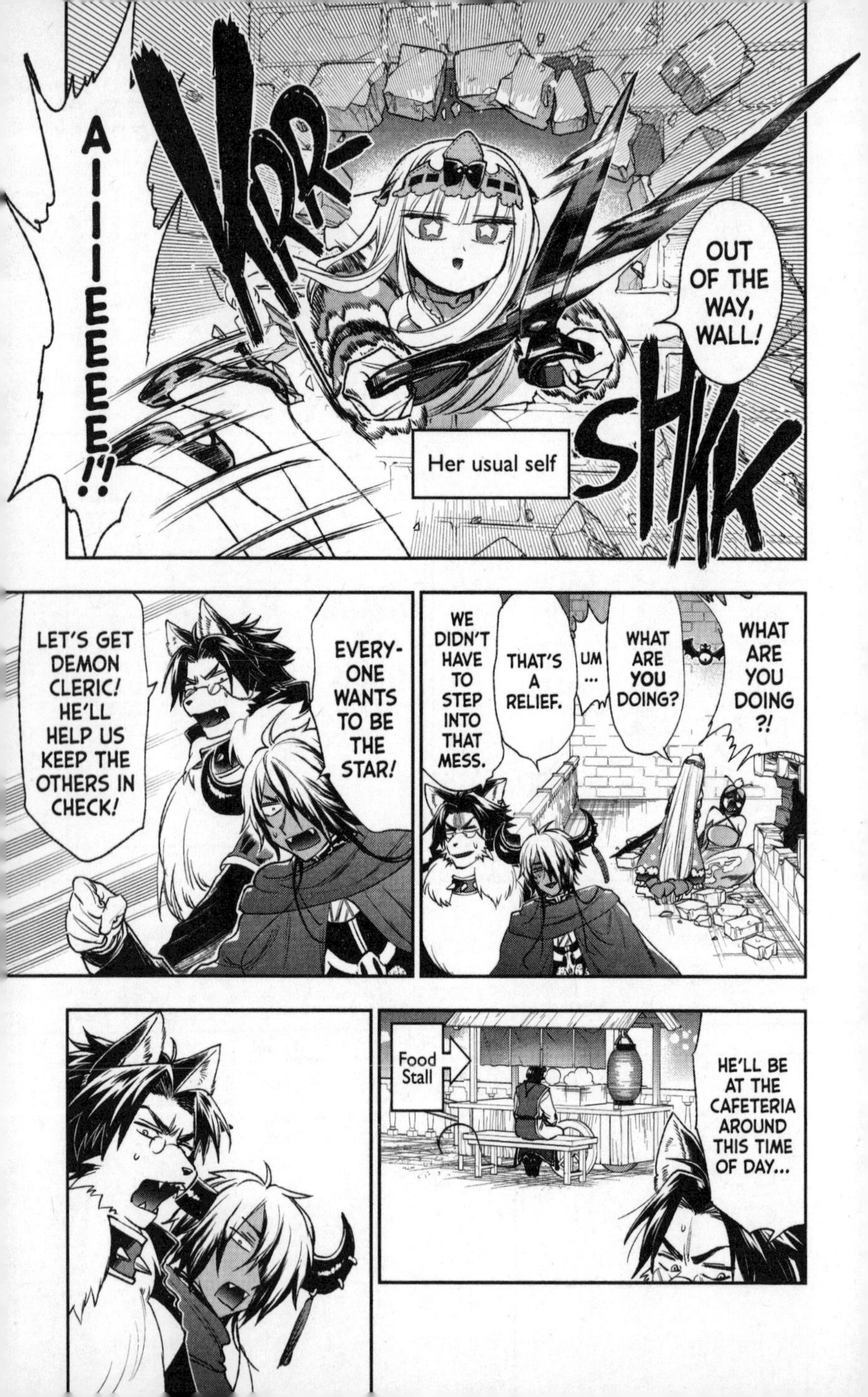
OUT OF THE WAY, WALL!
KRR-
AIIIEEEEE!!
SHKK
Her usual self
WHAT ARE YOU DOING?!
WHAT ARE YOU DOING?
UM...
THAT'S A RELIEF.
WE DIDN'T HAVE TO STEP INTO THAT MESS.
EVERY-ONE WANTS TO BE THE STAR!
LET'S GET DEMON CLERIC! HE'LL HELP US KEEP THE OTHERS IN CHECK!
HE'LL BE AT THE CAFETERIA AROUND THIS TIME OF DAY...
Food Stall

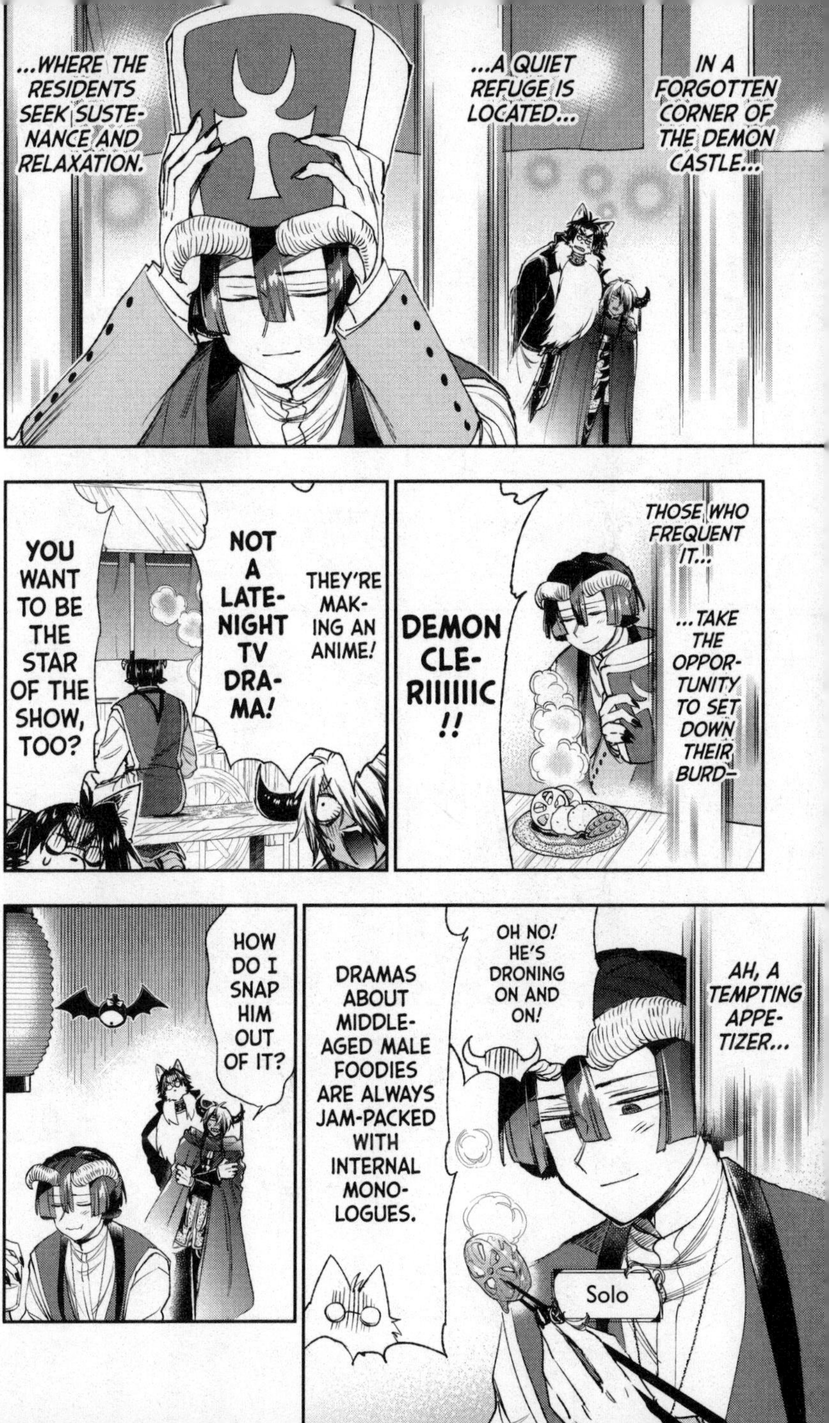
IN A FORGOTTEN CORNER OF THE DEMON CASTLE...
...A QUIET REFUGE IS LOCATED...
...WHERE THE RESIDENTS SEEK SUSTENANCE AND RELAXATION.
THOSE WHO FREQUENT IT...
...TAKE THE OPPORTUNITY TO SET DOWN THEIR BURD—
DEMON CLERIIIIIIC!!
THEY'RE MAKING AN ANIME!
NOT A LATE-NIGHT TV DRAMA!
YOU WANT TO BE THE STAR OF THE SHOW, TOO?
AH, A TEMPTING APPETIZER...
Solo
OH NO! HE'S DRONING ON AND ON!
DRAMAS ABOUT MIDDLE-AGED MALE FOODIES ARE ALWAYS JAM-PACKED WITH INTERNAL MONOLOGUES.
HOW DO I SNAP HIM OUT OF IT?

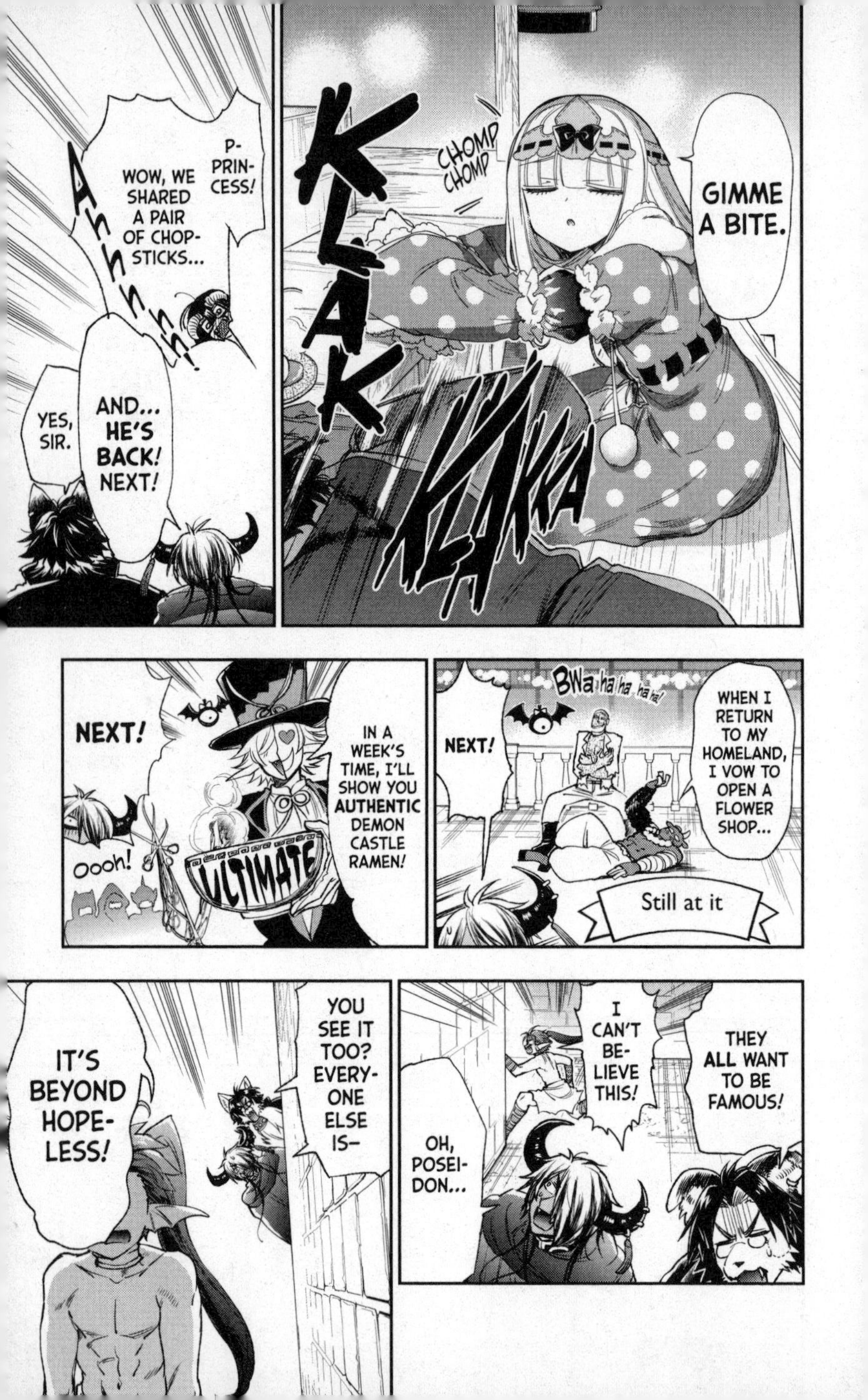
GIMME A BITE.
CHOMP CHOMP
KLAK
KLAKKA
P-PRINCESS!
WOW, WE SHARED A PAIR OF CHOPSTICKS...
Ahhhhh!
AND... HE'S BACK! NEXT!
YES, SIR.
BWa ha ha ha ha!
WHEN I RETURN TO MY HOMELAND, I VOW TO OPEN A FLOWER SHOP...
NEXT!
Still at it
IN A WEEK'S TIME, I'LL SHOW YOU AUTHENTIC DEMON CASTLE RAMEN!
NEXT!
ULTIMATE
Oooh!
THEY ALL WANT TO BE FAMOUS!
I CAN'T BELIEVE THIS!
OH, POSEIDON...
YOU SEE IT TOO? EVERYONE ELSE IS–
IT'S BEYOND HOPELESS!

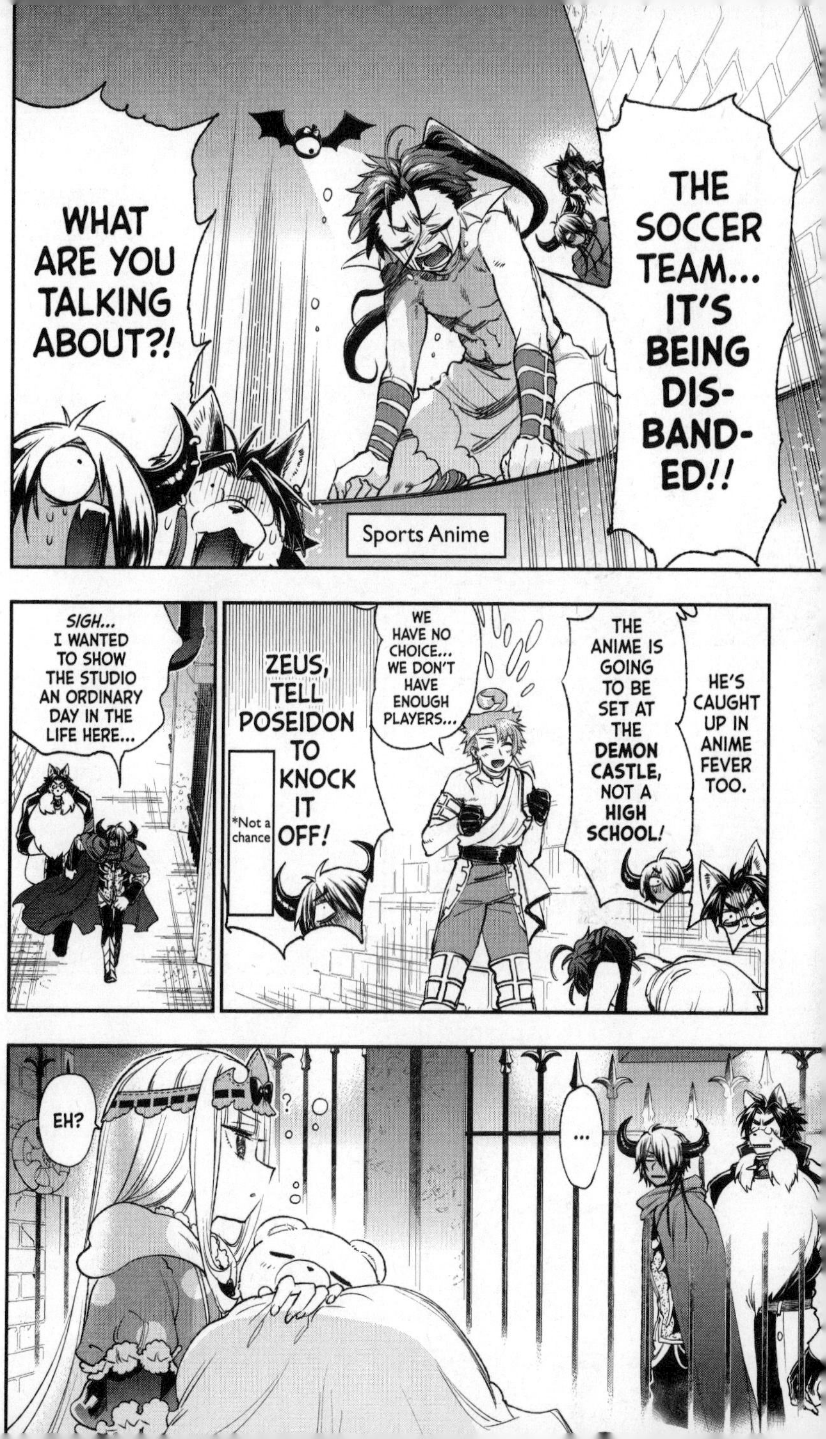
THE SOCCER TEAM... IT'S BEING DIS-BAND-ED!!
WHAT ARE YOU TALKING ABOUT?!
Sports Anime
HE'S CAUGHT UP IN ANIME FEVER TOO.
THE ANIME IS GOING TO BE SET AT THE DEMON CASTLE, NOT A HIGH SCHOOL!
WE HAVE NO CHOICE... WE DON'T HAVE ENOUGH PLAYERS...
ZEUS, TELL POSEIDON TO KNOCK IT OFF!
*Not a chance
SIGH... I WANTED TO SHOW THE STUDIO AN ORDINARY DAY IN THE LIFE HERE...
...
EH?

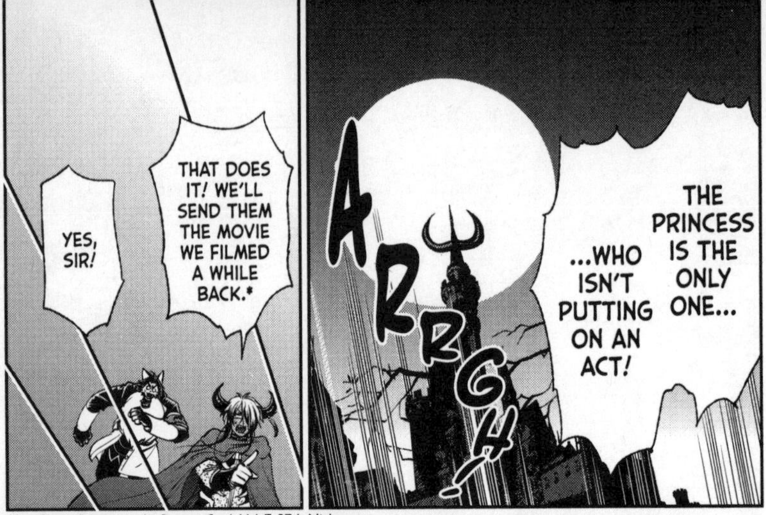
THE PRINCESS IS THE ONLY ONE...
...WHO ISN'T PUTTING ON AN ACT!
ARRGH!
THAT DOES IT! WE'LL SEND THEM THE MOVIE WE FILMED A WHILE BACK.*
YES, SIR!

*See *Sleepy Princess in the Demon Castle* Vol. 7, 87th Night

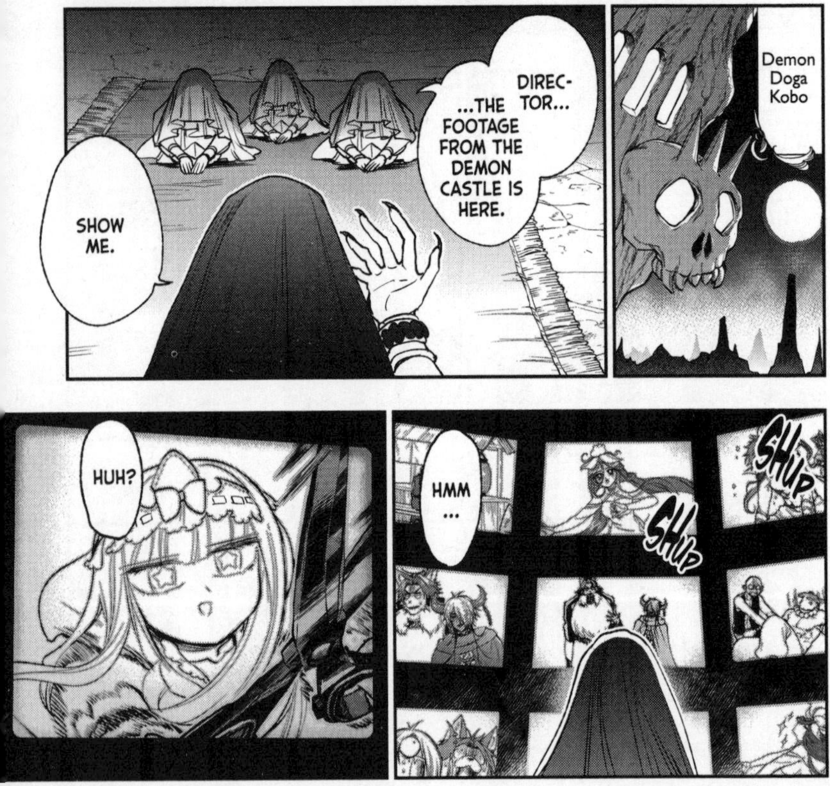
Demon Doga Kobo
DIRECTOR... ...THE FOOTAGE FROM THE DEMON CASTLE IS HERE.
SHOW ME.
SHUP
SHUP
HMM...
HUH?

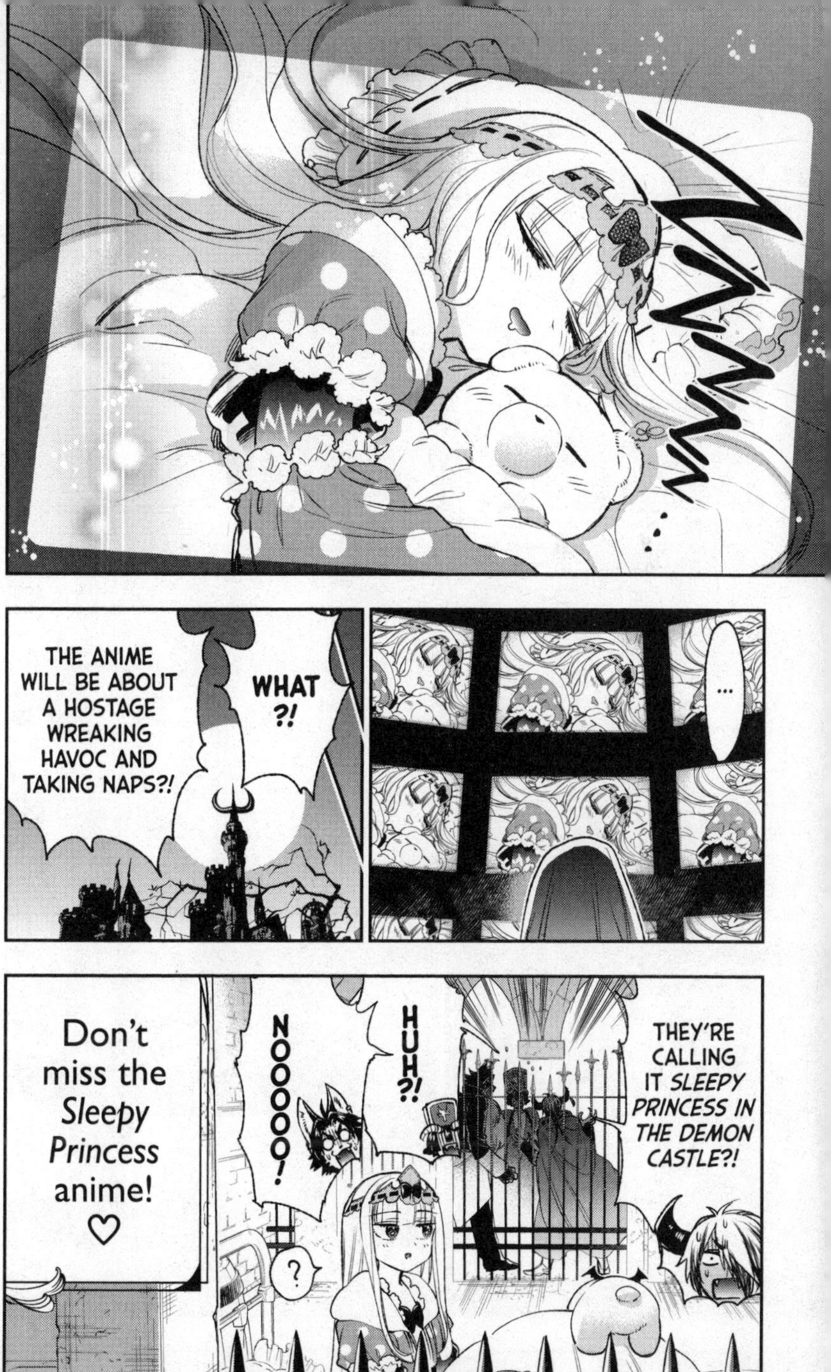
...
WHAT?!
THE ANIME WILL BE ABOUT A HOSTAGE WREAKING HAVOC AND TAKING NAPS?!
THEY'RE CALLING IT *SLEEPY PRINCESS IN THE DEMON CASTLE*?!
HUH?!
NOOOOOO!
?
Don't miss the *Sleepy Princess* anime! ♡

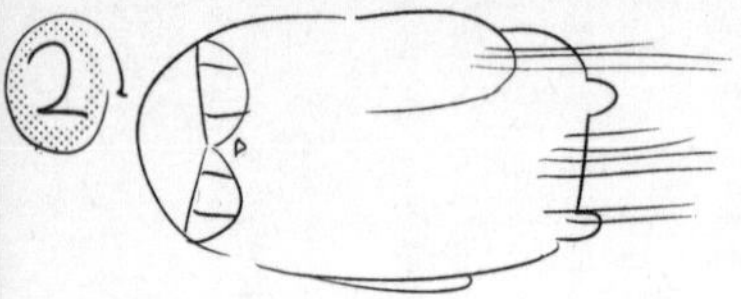

2

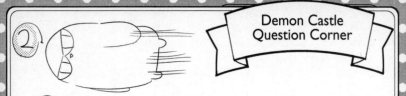

Demon Castle Question Corner

Q Mr. Oh My wears a mask all the time because M.O.T.H.E.R. is worried about data leaks. Does he ever remove it?

A He wears a sleeping mask to bed, so there must be a brief time when he switches masks and washes his face.

Q I'd like to know Stray Sickle Weasel's real name.

I'm interested in this demon's ↓ name too.

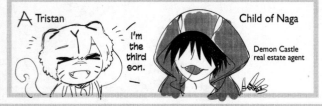

A Tristan

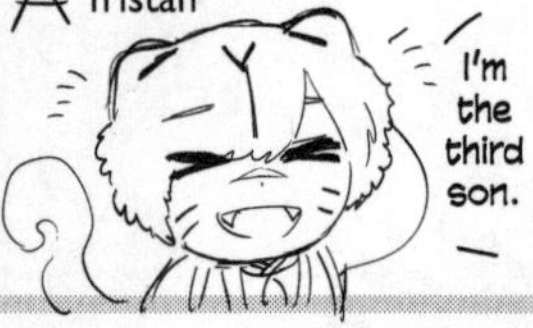

I'm the third son.

Child of Naga

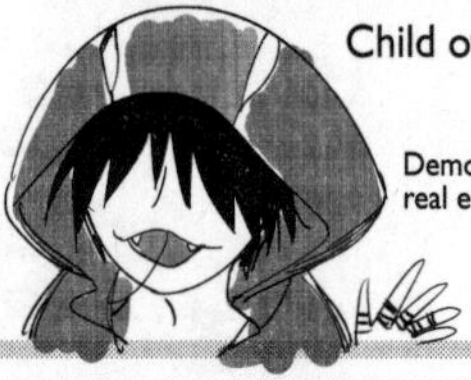

Demon Castle real estate agent

Q What would the Demon Castle crew do on social media?

A Guess who's who!

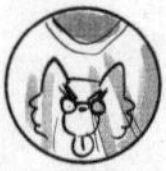
Horny

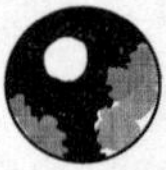
Goat
Tweets about back problems

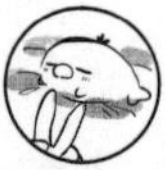
I'm Seal
Collects cute animal pics

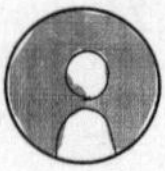
New Account
Only tweets to Horny

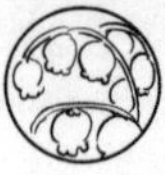
Lily Girl
Freaks out over depressing news

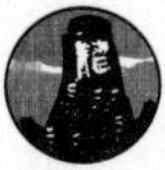
Mack
Last tweet was several years ago

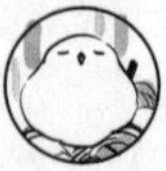
Fried Chicken☆
Posts pics of every meal

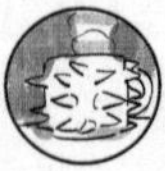
@Studying
An account created just to read the Goat's tweets

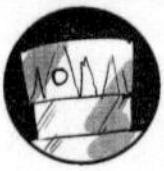
Ice Golem
Latest updates on the Ice Zone and Eggplant Seal photos

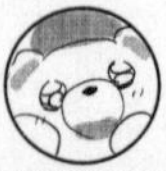
Aurora Sya Lis Goodereste
Mostly tweets about sleeping

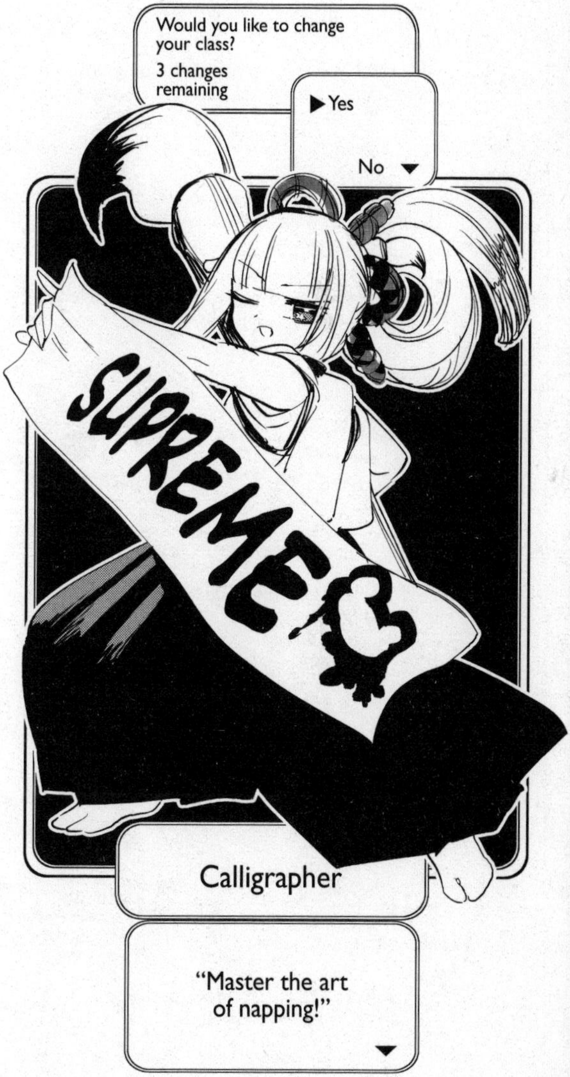
Would you like to change your class?
3 changes remaining
▶Yes
No
SUPREME
Calligrapher
"Master the art of napping!"

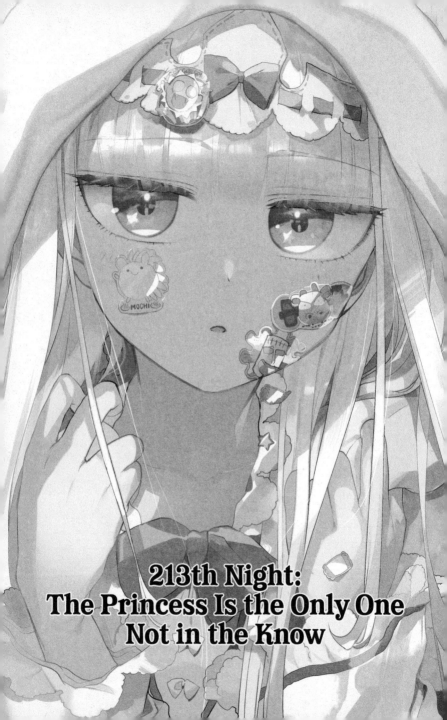

213th Night:
The Princess Is the Only One Not in the Know

SLEEPY PRINCESS IN THE DEMON CASTLE

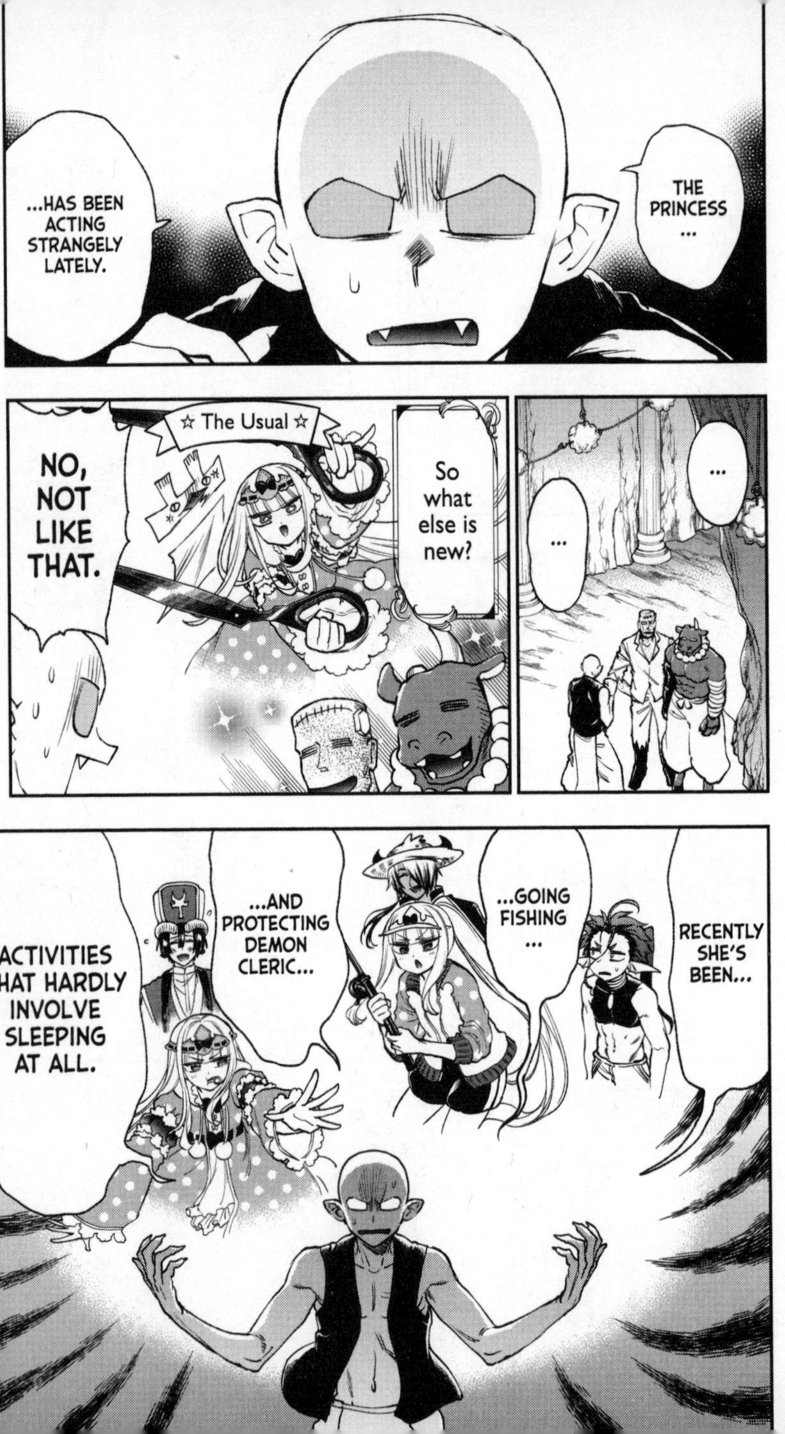
THE PRINCESS ...
...HAS BEEN ACTING STRANGELY LATELY.
...
...
So what else is new?
☆ The Usual ☆
NO, NOT LIKE THAT.
RECENTLY SHE'S BEEN...
...GOING FISHING ...
...AND PROTECTING DEMON CLERIC...
ACTIVITIES THAT HARDLY INVOLVE SLEEPING AT ALL.

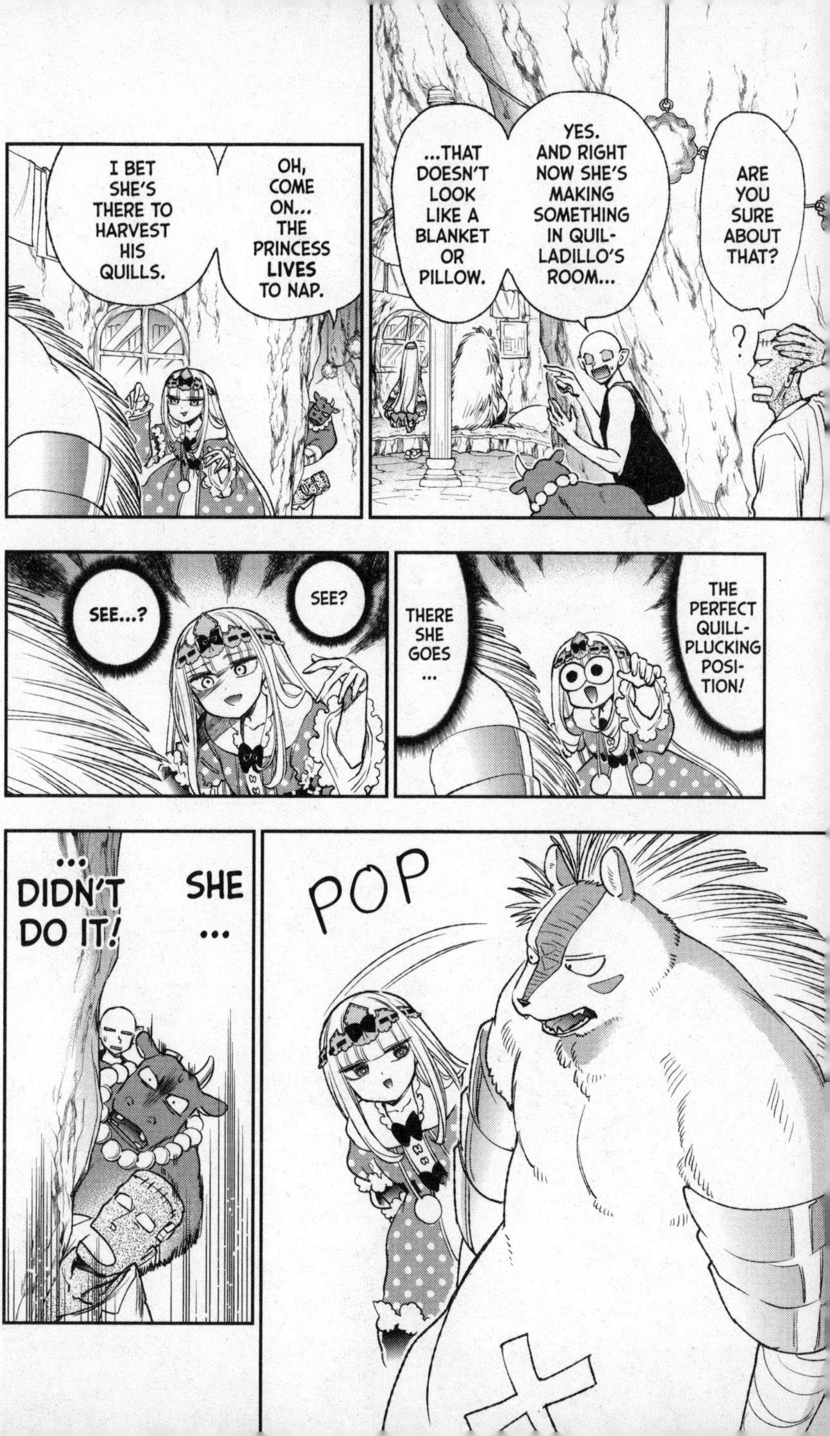
ARE YOU SURE ABOUT THAT?
YES. AND RIGHT NOW SHE'S MAKING SOMETHING IN QUIL-LADILLO'S ROOM...
...THAT DOESN'T LOOK LIKE A BLANKET OR PILLOW.
OH, COME ON... THE PRINCESS **LIVES** TO NAP.
I BET SHE'S THERE TO HARVEST HIS QUILLS.
THE PERFECT QUILL-PLUCKING POSI-TION!
THERE SHE GOES ...
SEE?
SEE...?
POP
SHE ...
... DIDN'T DO IT!

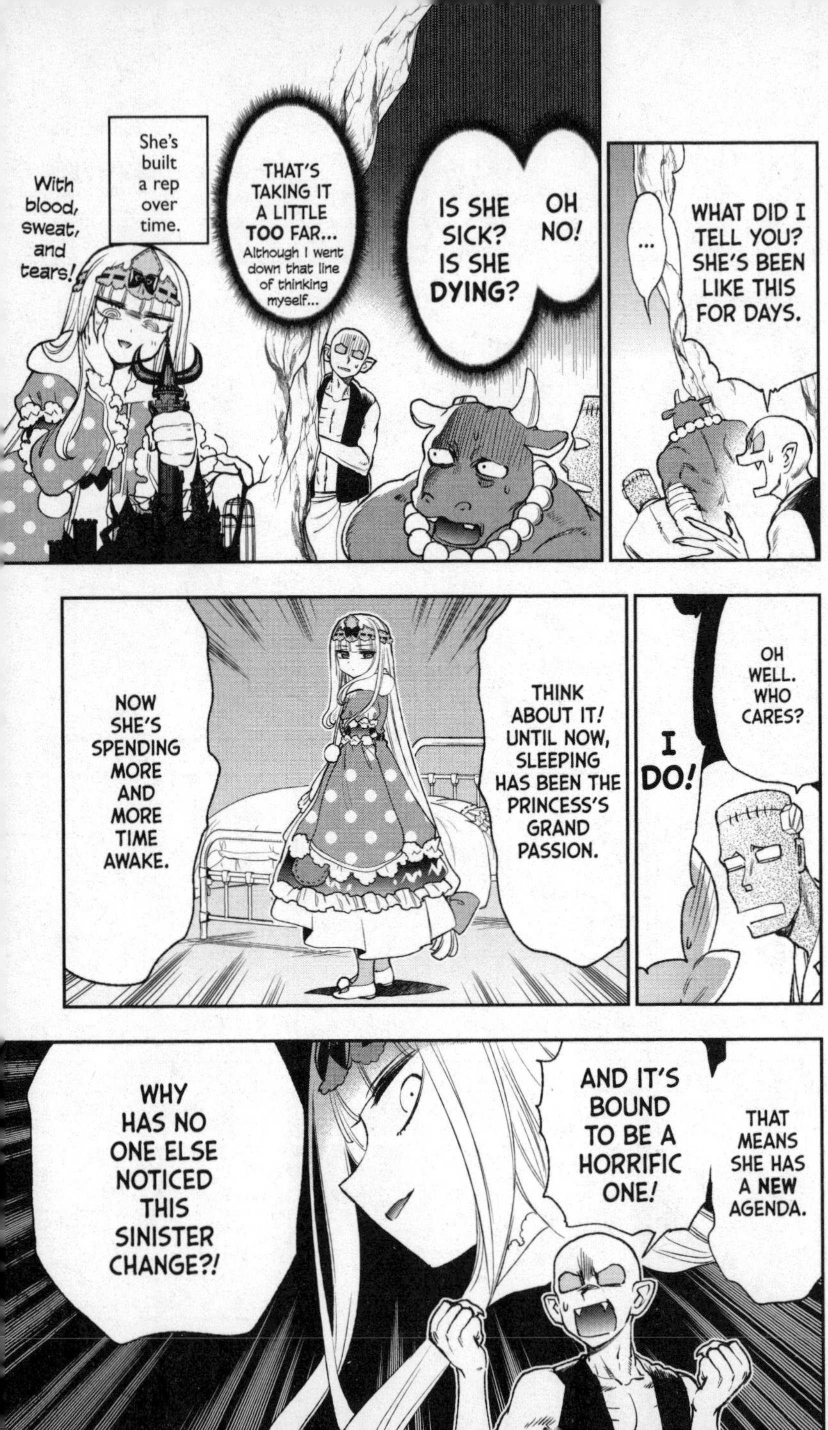
WHAT DID I TELL YOU? SHE'S BEEN LIKE THIS FOR DAYS.
...
OH NO!
IS SHE SICK? IS SHE DYING?
THAT'S TAKING IT A LITTLE TOO FAR... Although I went down that line of thinking myself...
She's built a rep over time.
With blood, sweat, and tears!
OH WELL. WHO CARES?
I DO!
THINK ABOUT IT! UNTIL NOW, SLEEPING HAS BEEN THE PRINCESS'S GRAND PASSION.
NOW SHE'S SPENDING MORE AND MORE TIME AWAKE.
THAT MEANS SHE HAS A NEW AGENDA.
AND IT'S BOUND TO BE A HORRIFIC ONE!
WHY HAS NO ONE ELSE NOTICED THIS SINISTER CHANGE?!

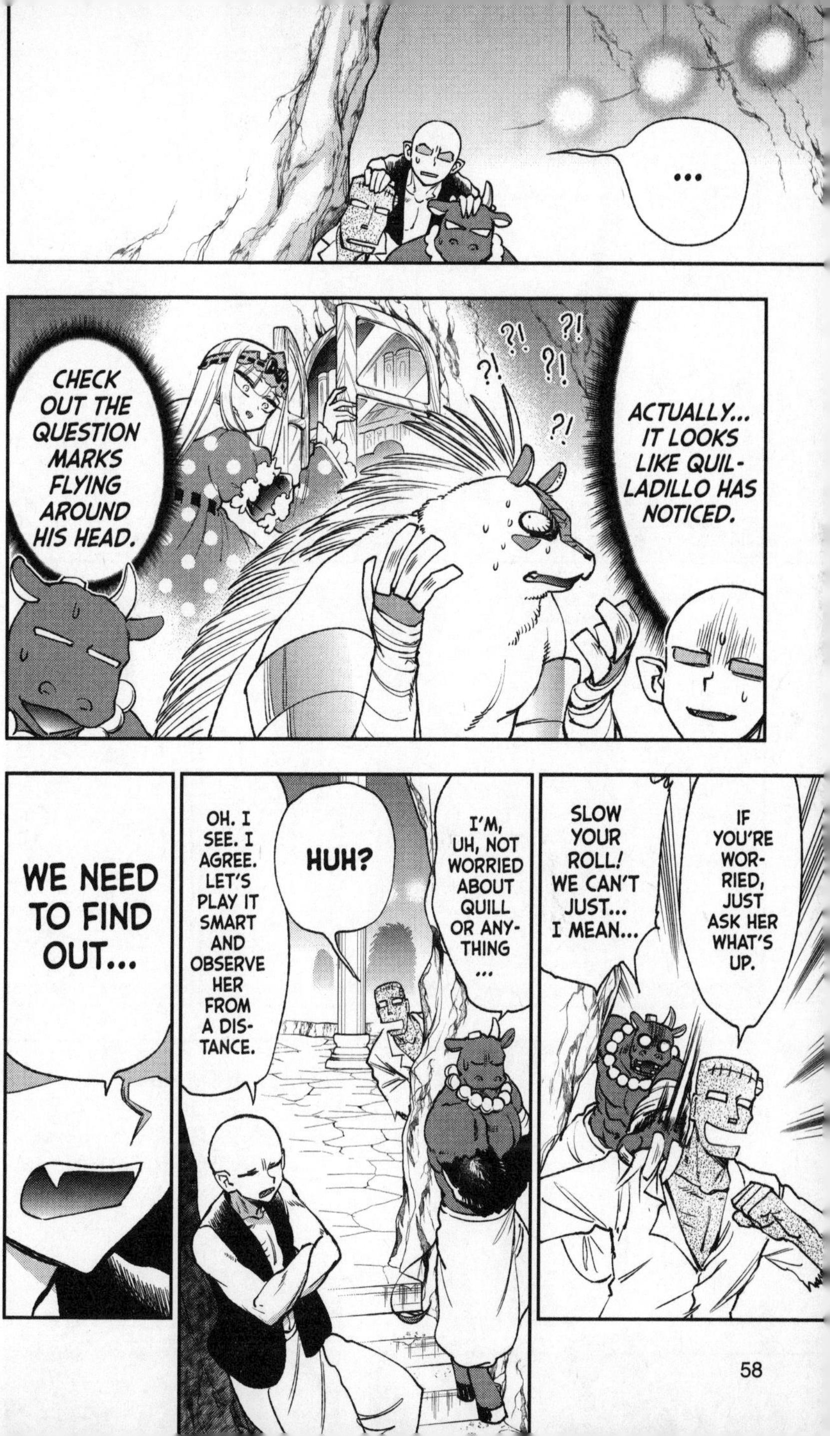
...
ACTUALLY... IT LOOKS LIKE QUIL-LADILLO HAS NOTICED.
?! ?! ?! ?! ?!
CHECK OUT THE QUESTION MARKS FLYING AROUND HIS HEAD.
IF YOU'RE WOR-RIED, JUST ASK HER WHAT'S UP.
SLOW YOUR ROLL! WE CAN'T JUST... I MEAN...
I'M, UH, NOT WORRIED ABOUT QUILL OR ANY-THING...
HUH?
OH. I SEE. I AGREE. LET'S PLAY IT SMART AND OBSERVE HER FROM A DIS-TANCE.
WE NEED TO FIND OUT...

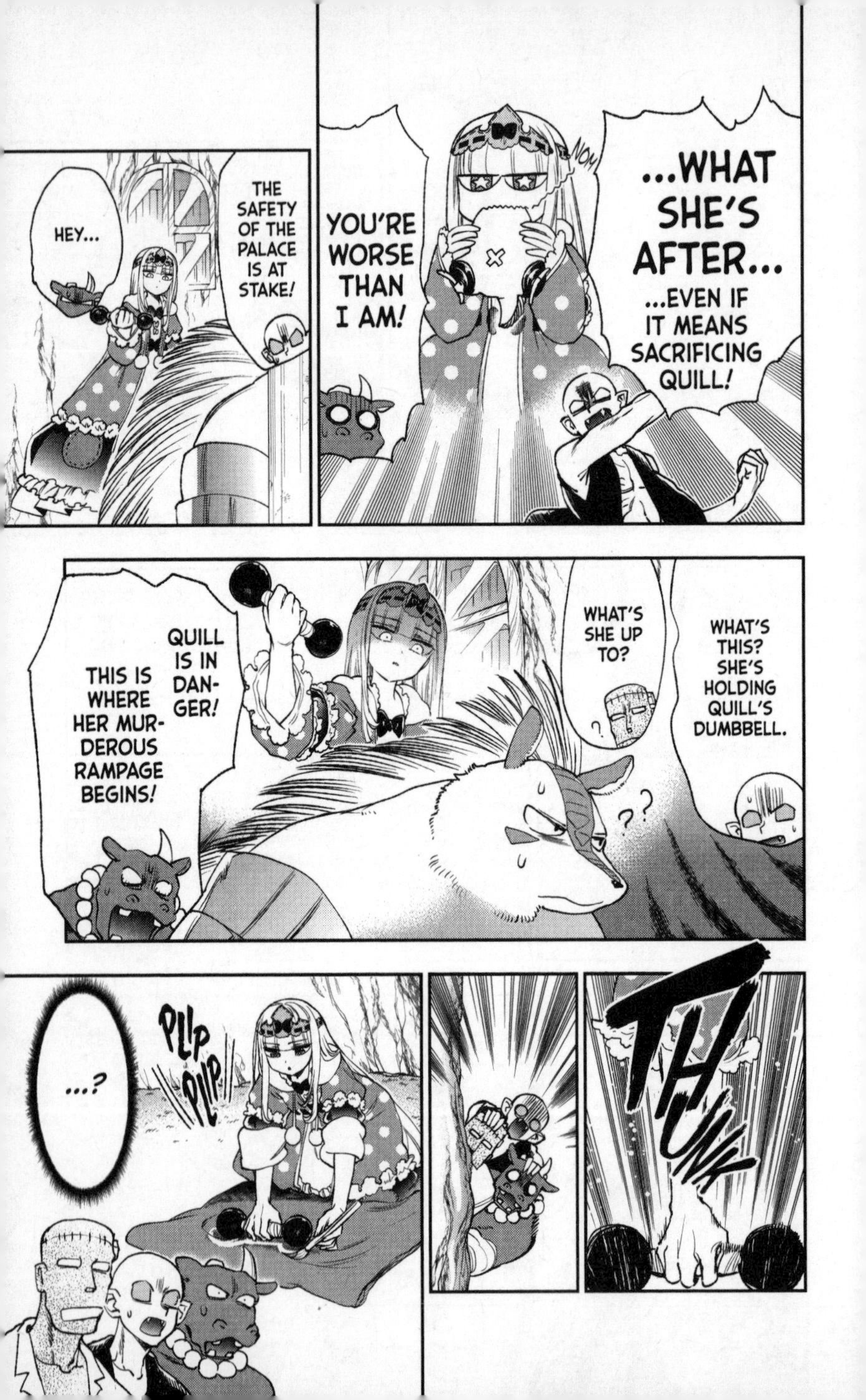
...WHAT SHE'S AFTER...
...EVEN IF IT MEANS SACRIFICING QUILL!
NOM
YOU'RE WORSE THAN I AM!
THE SAFETY OF THE PALACE IS AT STAKE!
HEY...
WHAT'S THIS? SHE'S HOLDING QUILL'S DUMBBELL.
WHAT'S SHE UP TO?
QUILL IS IN DAN-GER!
THIS IS WHERE HER MUR-DEROUS RAMPAGE BEGINS!
THUNK
PLIP PLIP
...?

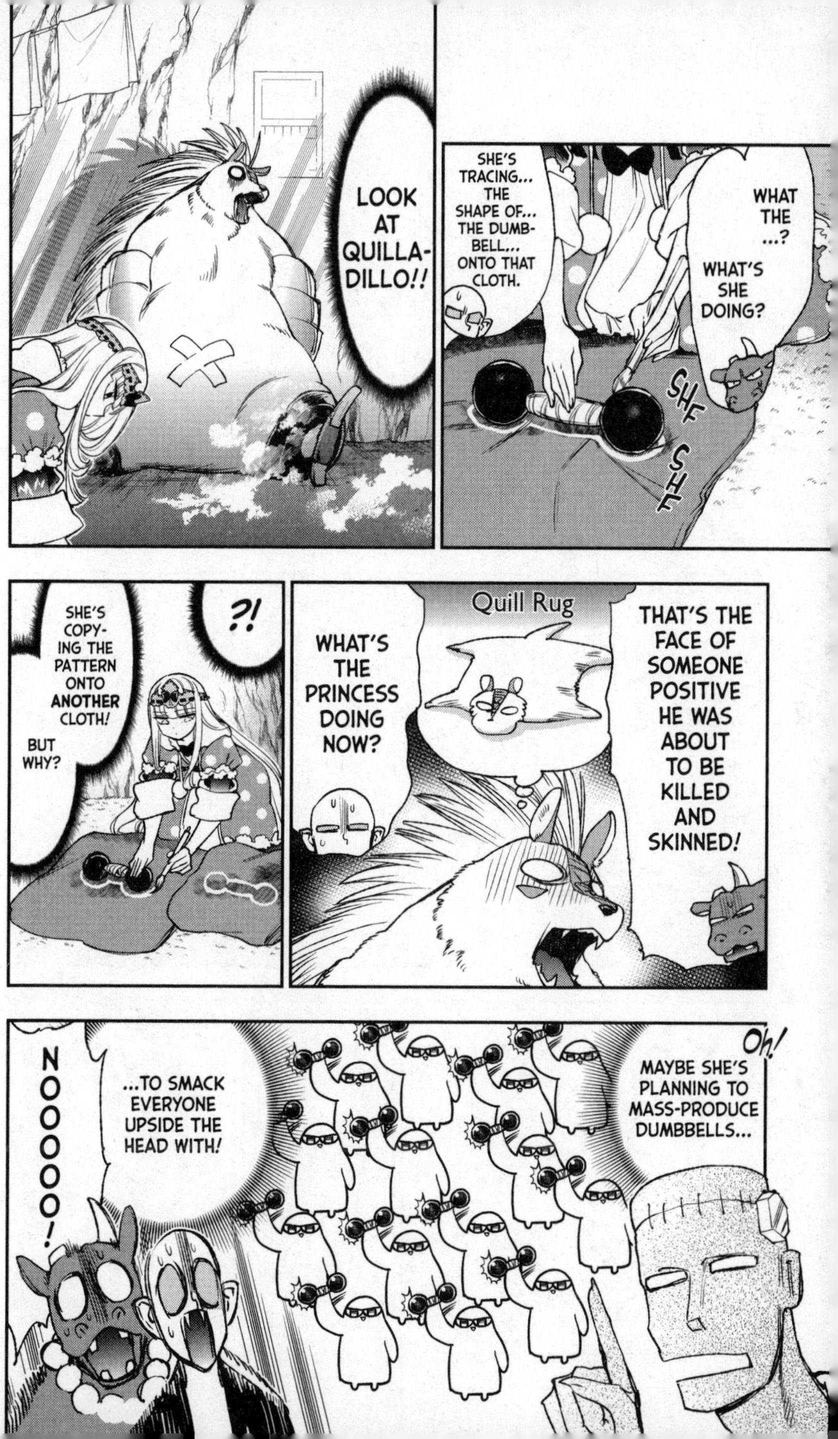
WHAT THE ...?
WHAT'S SHE DOING?
SHE'S TRACING... THE SHAPE OF... THE DUMB-BELL... ONTO THAT CLOTH.
SHF SHF
LOOK AT QUILLA-DILLO!!
THAT'S THE FACE OF SOMEONE POSITIVE HE WAS ABOUT TO BE KILLED AND SKINNED!
Quill Rug
WHAT'S THE PRINCESS DOING NOW?
?!
SHE'S COPYING THE PATTERN ONTO ANOTHER CLOTH!
BUT WHY?
Oh!
MAYBE SHE'S PLANNING TO MASS-PRODUCE DUMBBELLS...
...TO SMACK EVERYONE UPSIDE THE HEAD WITH!
NOOOOOO!

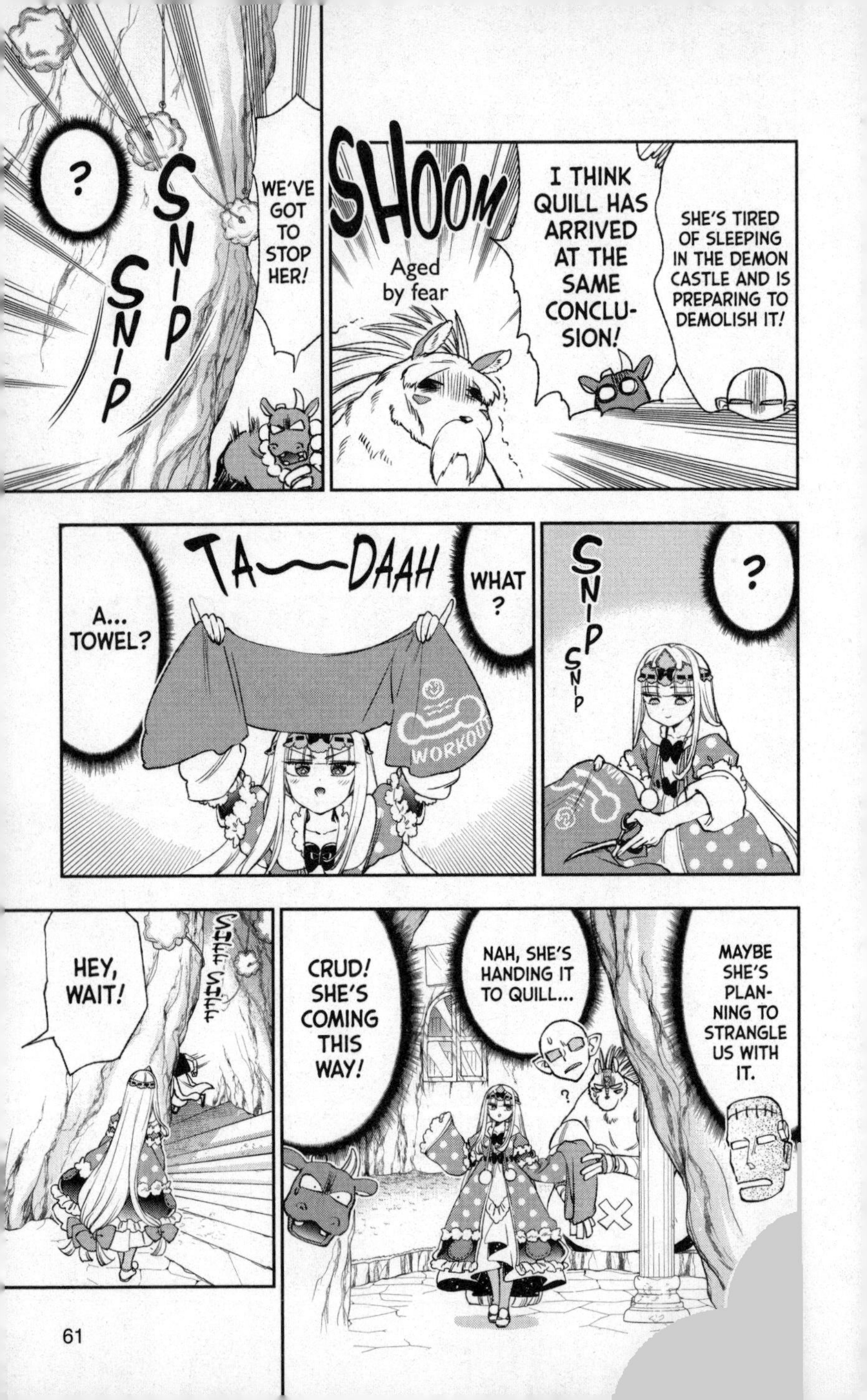

SHE'S TIRED OF SLEEPING IN THE DEMON CASTLE AND IS PREPARING TO DEMOLISH IT!
I THINK QUILL HAS ARRIVED AT THE SAME CONCLUSION!
SHOOM
Aged by fear
WE'VE GOT TO STOP HER!
SNIP
SNIP
?
?
SNIP
SNIP
WHAT?
TA—DAAH
A... TOWEL?
WORKOUT
MAYBE SHE'S PLANNING TO STRANGLE US WITH IT.
NAH, SHE'S HANDING IT TO QUILL...
CRUD! SHE'S COMING THIS WAY!
?
SHFF SHFF
HEY, WAIT!

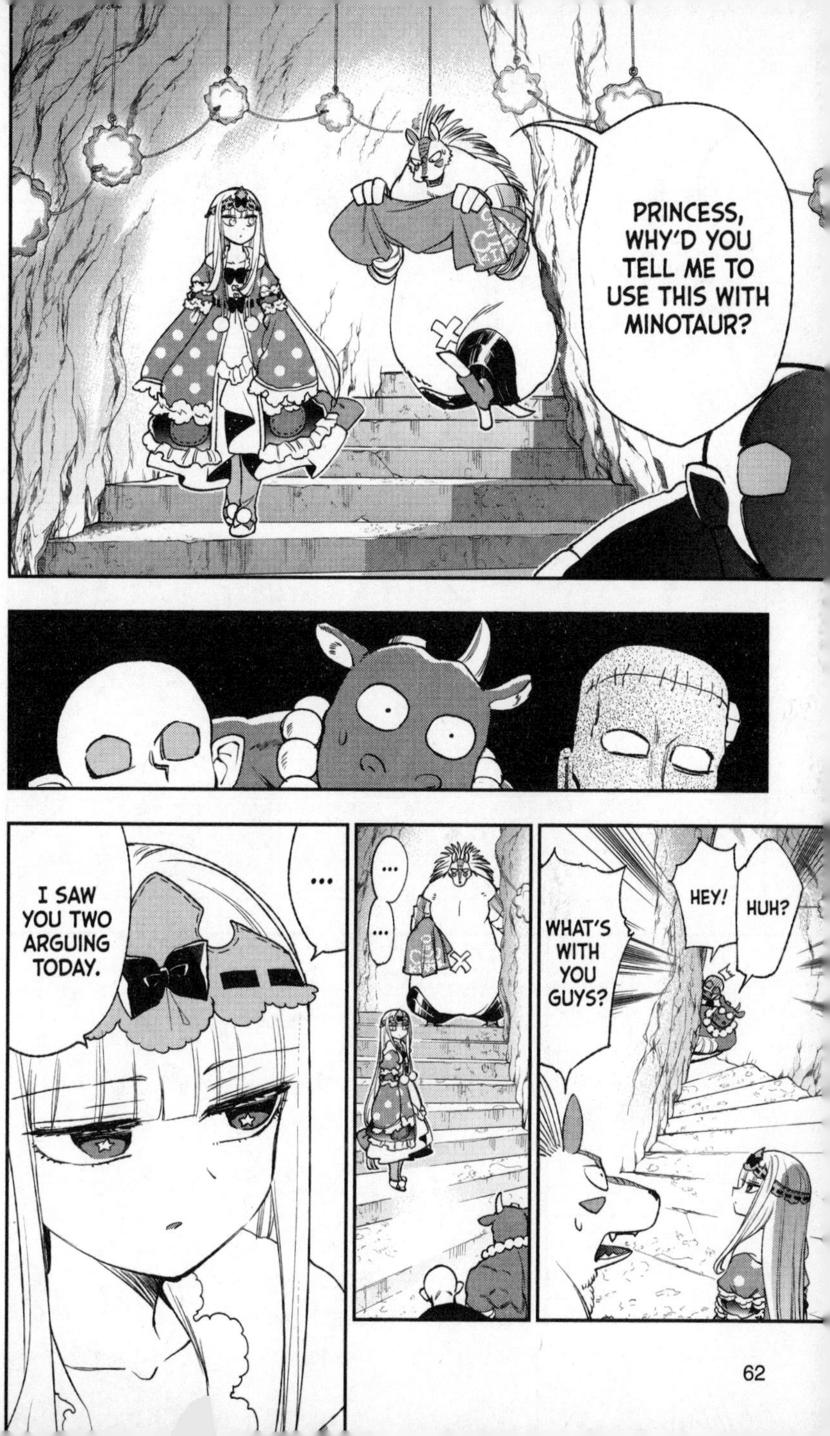
PRINCESS, WHY'D YOU TELL ME TO USE THIS WITH MINOTAUR?
HUH?
HEY!
WHAT'S WITH YOU GUYS?
...
...
...
I SAW YOU TWO ARGUING TODAY.

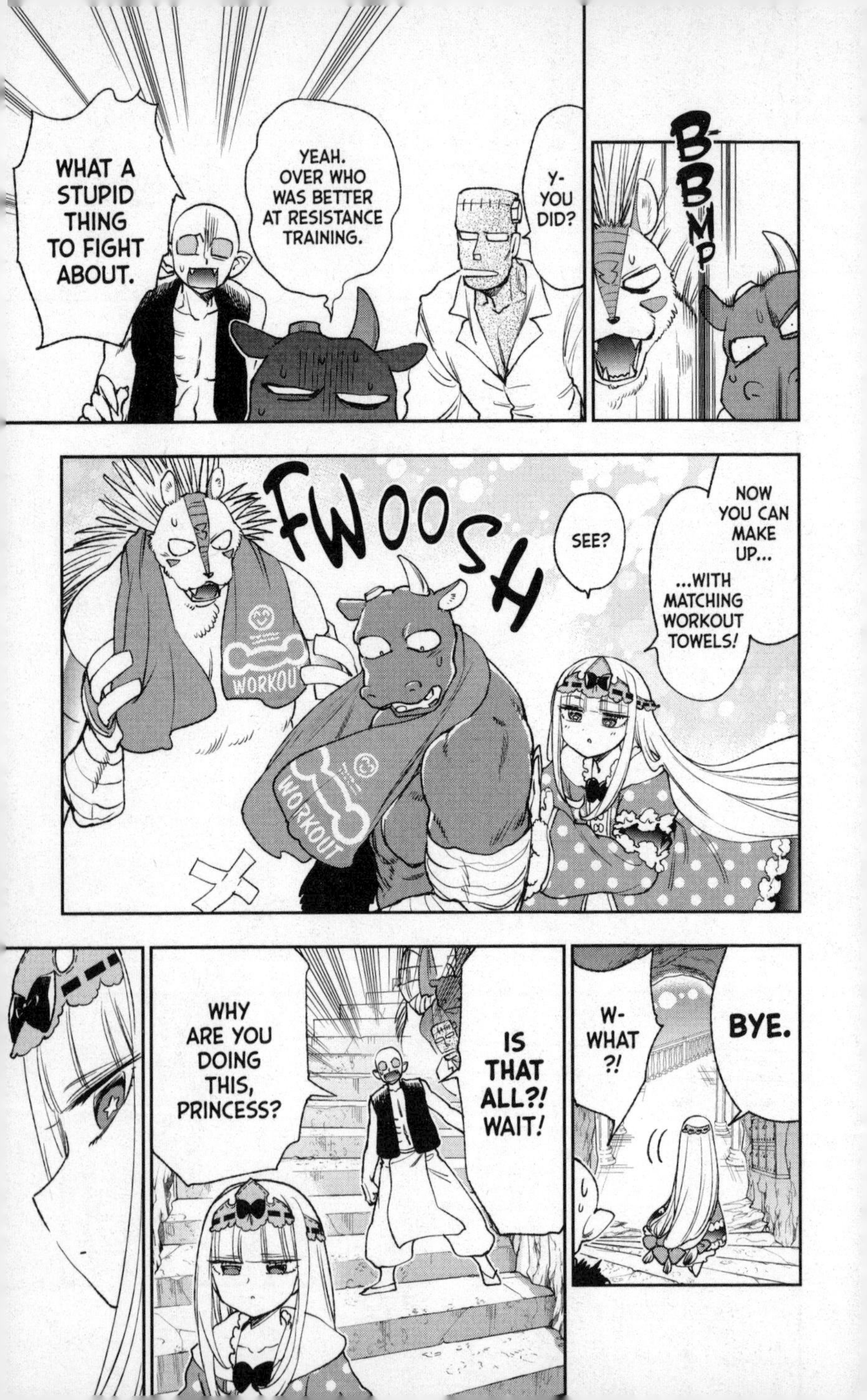
B-BMP
Y- YOU DID?
YEAH. OVER WHO WAS BETTER AT RESISTANCE TRAINING.
WHAT A STUPID THING TO FIGHT ABOUT.
NOW YOU CAN MAKE UP...
...WITH MATCHING WORKOUT TOWELS!
SEE?
FWOOSH
WORKOU
WORKOUT
BYE.
W- WHAT ?!
IS THAT ALL?! WAIT!
WHY ARE YOU DOING THIS, PRINCESS?

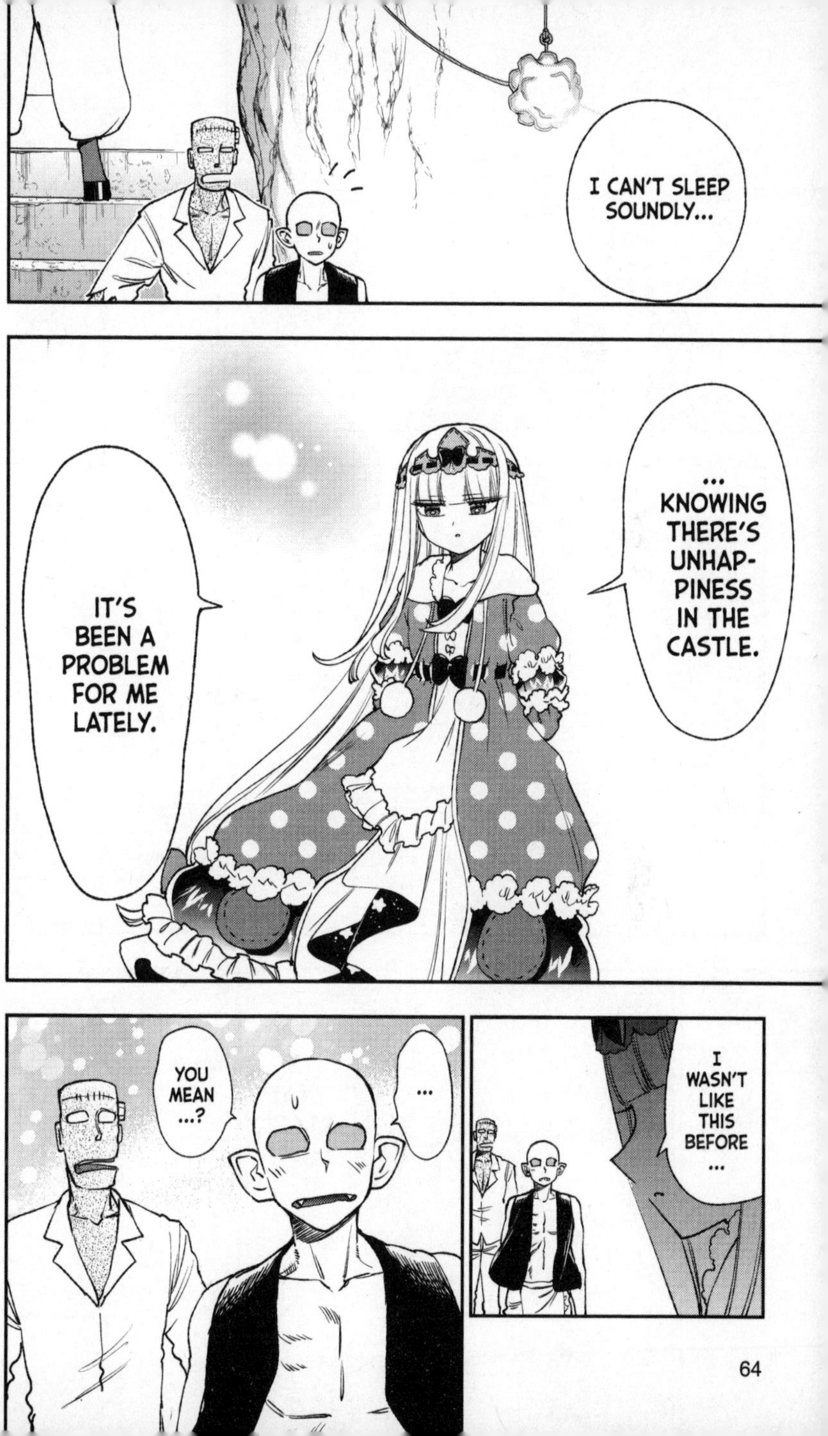
I CAN'T SLEEP SOUNDLY...
...KNOWING THERE'S UNHAP-PINESS IN THE CASTLE.
IT'S BEEN A PROBLEM FOR ME LATELY.
I WASN'T LIKE THIS BEFORE...
...
YOU MEAN...?

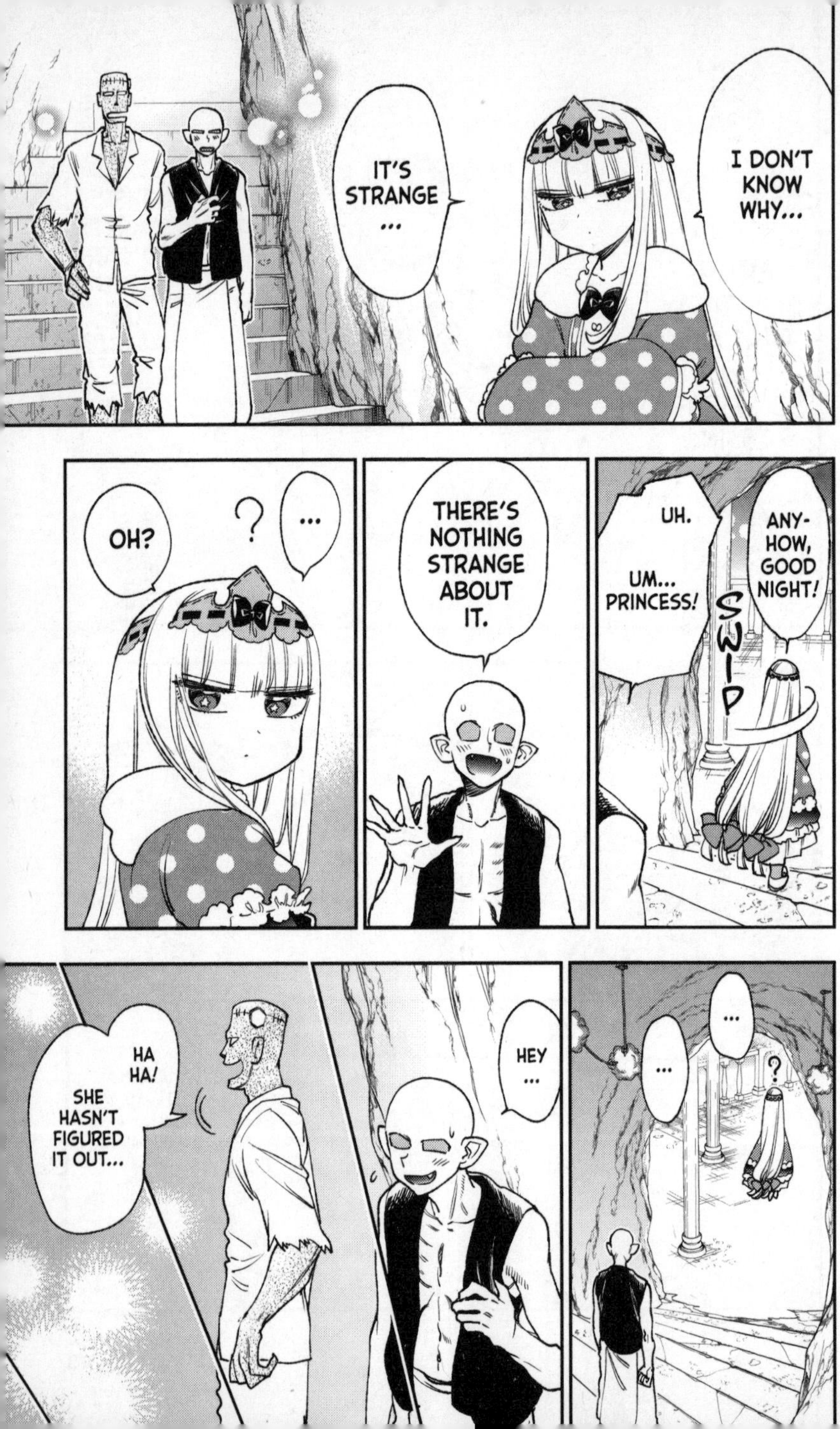
I DON'T KNOW WHY...
IT'S STRANGE ...
ANY-HOW, GOOD NIGHT!
SWIP
UH.
UM... PRINCESS!
THERE'S NOTHING STRANGE ABOUT IT.
...
?
OH?
...
?
...
HEY ...
HA HA!
SHE HASN'T FIGURED IT OUT...

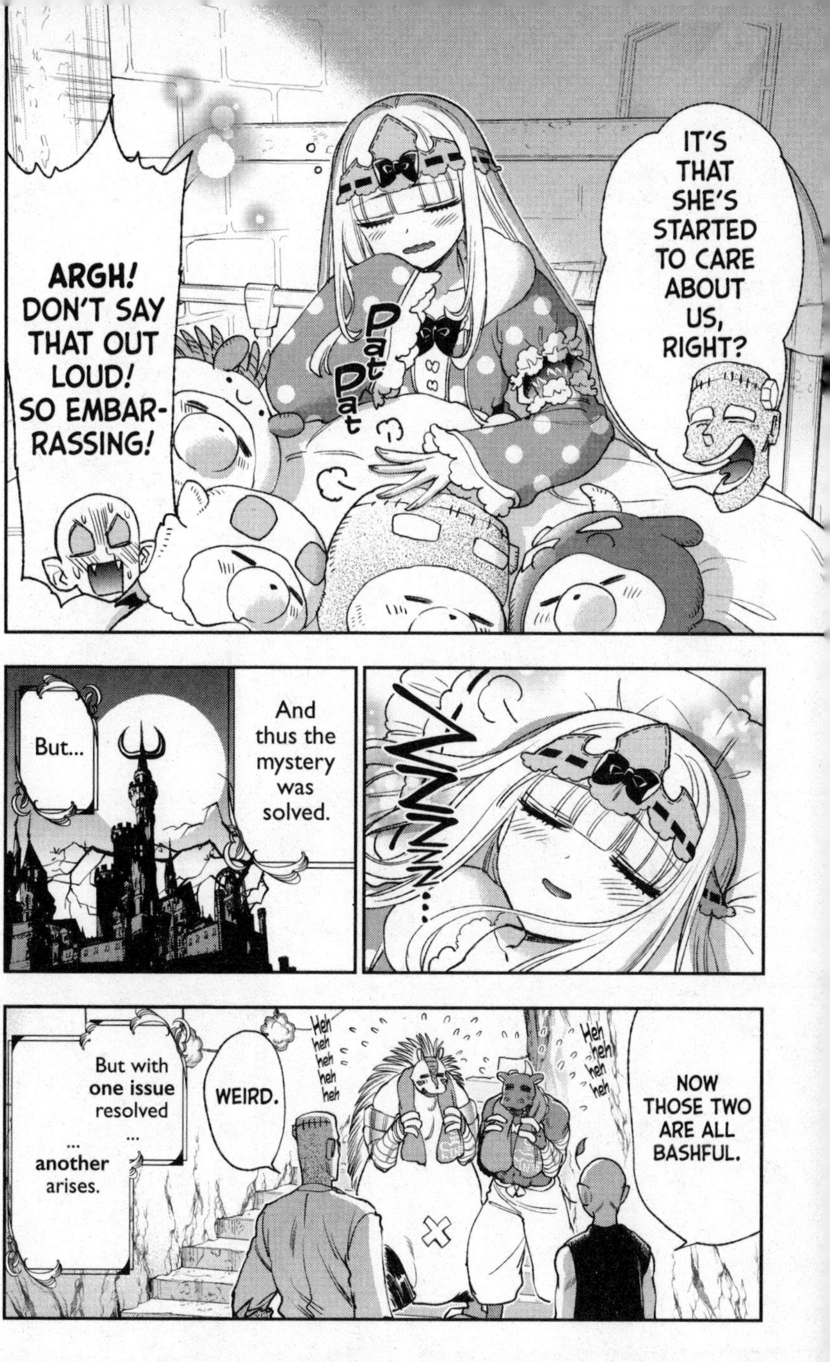
IT'S THAT SHE'S STARTED TO CARE ABOUT US, RIGHT?
Pat Pat
ARGH! DON'T SAY THAT OUT LOUD! SO EMBARRASSING!
And thus the mystery was solved.
But...
NOW THOSE TWO ARE ALL BASHFUL.
Heh heh heh heh
Heh heh heh heh heh
WEIRD.
But with one issue resolved ...
... another arises.

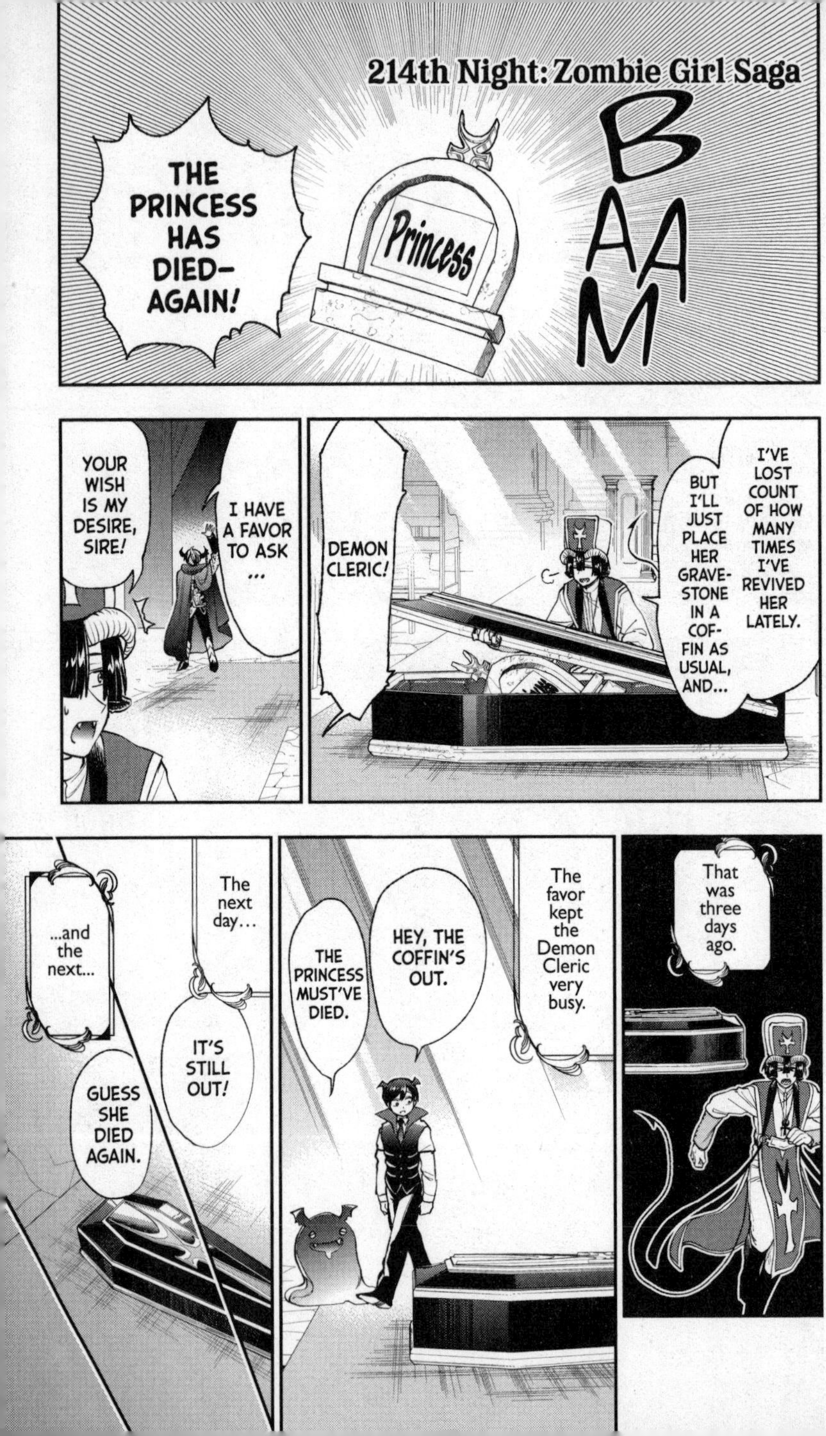
214th Night: Zombie Girl Saga
BAAAM
Princess
THE PRINCESS HAS DIED—AGAIN!
I'VE LOST COUNT OF HOW MANY TIMES I'VE REVIVED HER LATELY.
BUT I'LL JUST PLACE HER GRAVE-STONE IN A COF-FIN AS USUAL, AND...
DEMON CLERIC!
I HAVE A FAVOR TO ASK ...
YOUR WISH IS MY DESIRE, SIRE!
That was three days ago.
The favor kept the Demon Cleric very busy.
HEY, THE COFFIN'S OUT.
THE PRINCESS MUST'VE DIED.
The next day...
IT'S STILL OUT!
...and the next...
GUESS SHE DIED AGAIN.

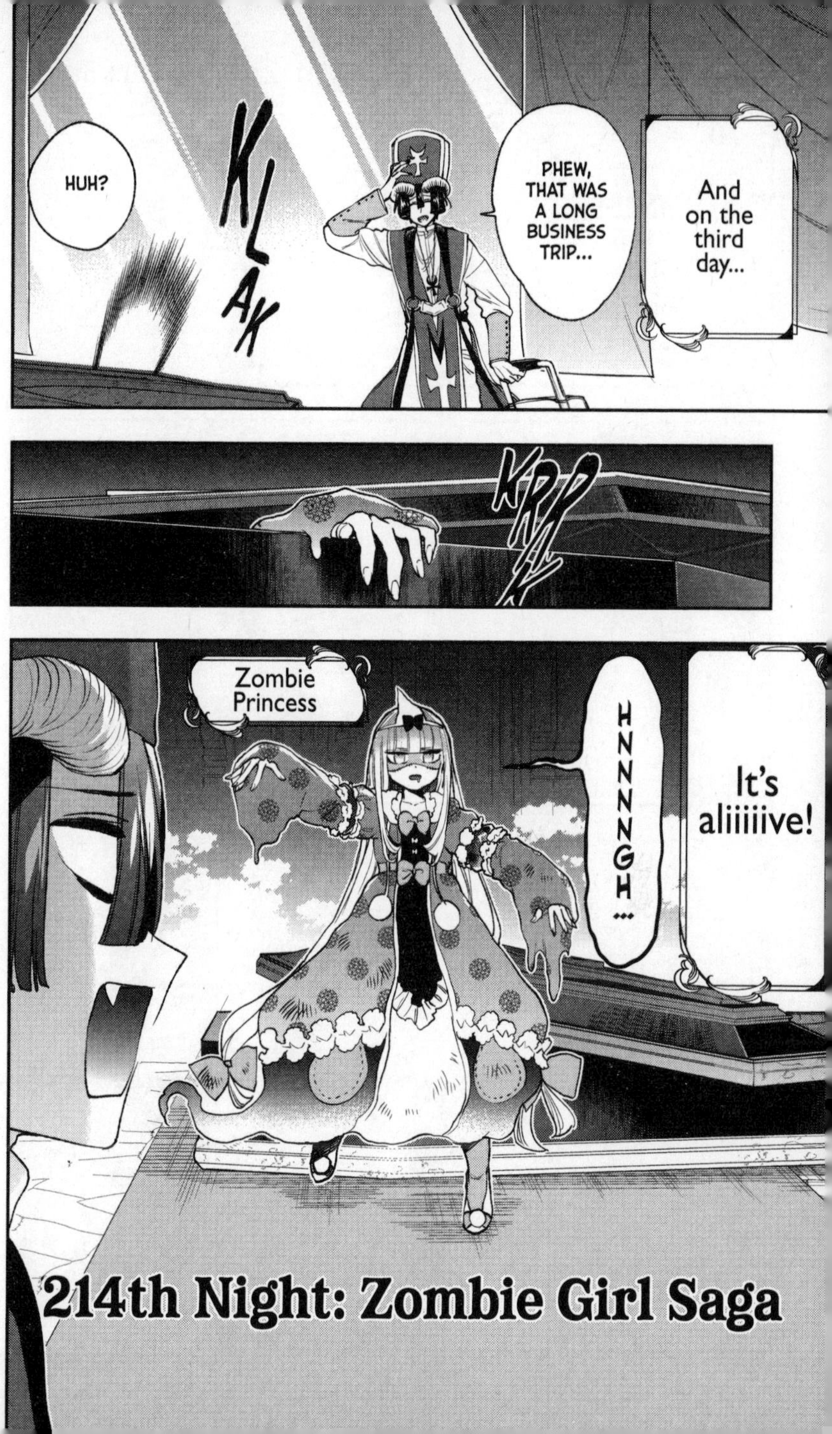
And on the third day...
PHEW, THAT WAS A LONG BUSINESS TRIP...
KLAK
HUH?
It's aliiiiiive!
HNNNNGH...
Zombie Princess

214th Night: Zombie Girl Saga

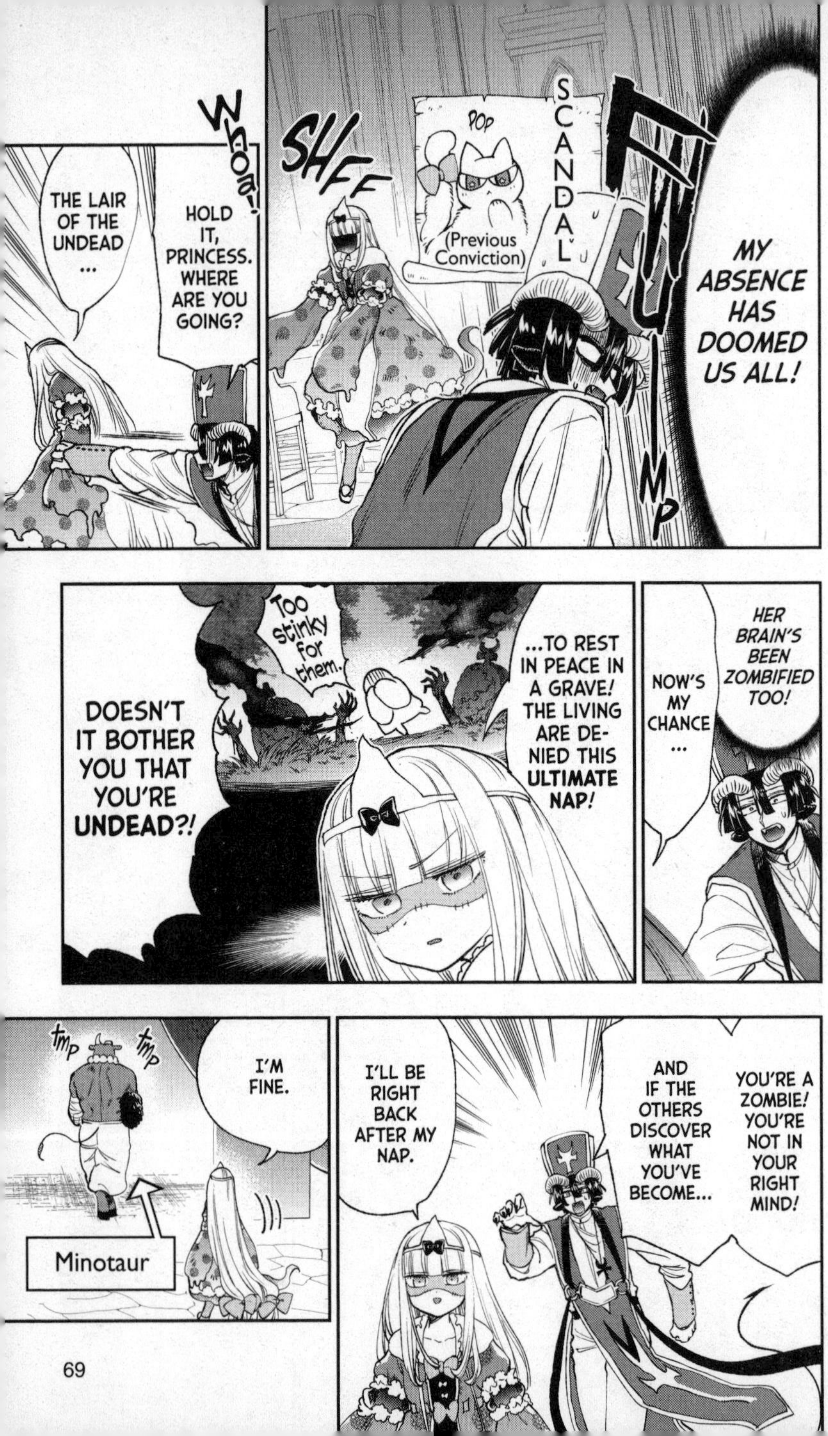
MY ABSENCE HAS DOOMED US ALL!
FWUMP
SCANDAL
(Previous Conviction)
POP
SHFF
Whoa!
HOLD IT, PRINCESS. WHERE ARE YOU GOING?
THE LAIR OF THE UNDEAD ...
HER BRAIN'S BEEN ZOMBIFIED TOO!
NOW'S MY CHANCE ...
...TO REST IN PEACE IN A GRAVE! THE LIVING ARE DENIED THIS ULTIMATE NAP!
Too stinky for them.
DOESN'T IT BOTHER YOU THAT YOU'RE UNDEAD?!
YOU'RE A ZOMBIE! YOU'RE NOT IN YOUR RIGHT MIND!
AND IF THE OTHERS DISCOVER WHAT YOU'VE BECOME...
I'LL BE RIGHT BACK AFTER MY NAP.
I'M FINE.
tmp
tmp
Minotaur

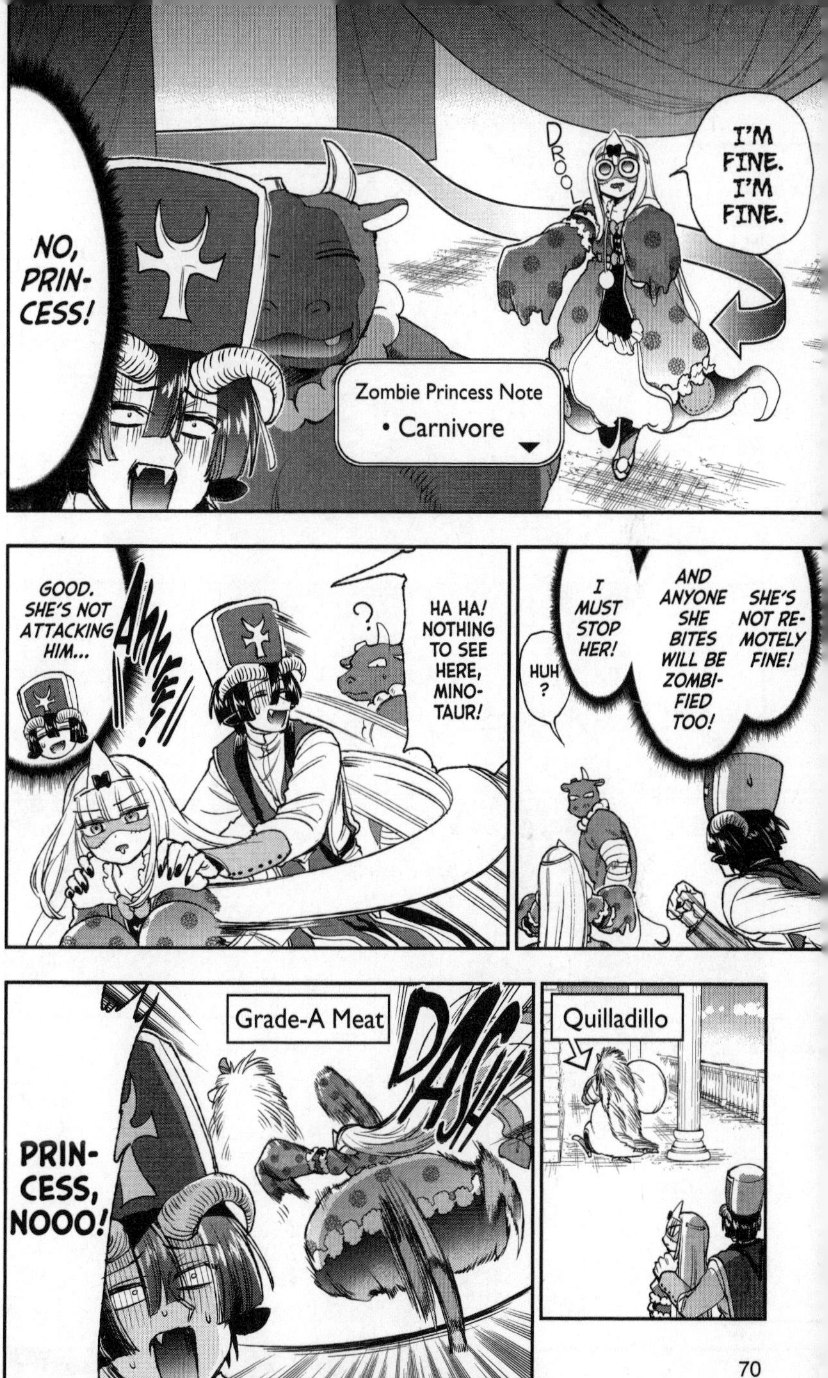
I'M FINE. I'M FINE.
DROOL
NO, PRIN-CESS!
Zombie Princess Note
• Carnivore
SHE'S NOT RE-MOTELY FINE!
AND ANYONE SHE BITES WILL BE ZOMBI-FIED TOO!
I MUST STOP HER!
HUH?
HA HA! NOTHING TO SEE HERE, MINO-TAUR!
?
GOOD. SHE'S NOT ATTACKING HIM...
Quilladillo
Grade-A Meat
DASH
PRIN-CESS, NOOO!

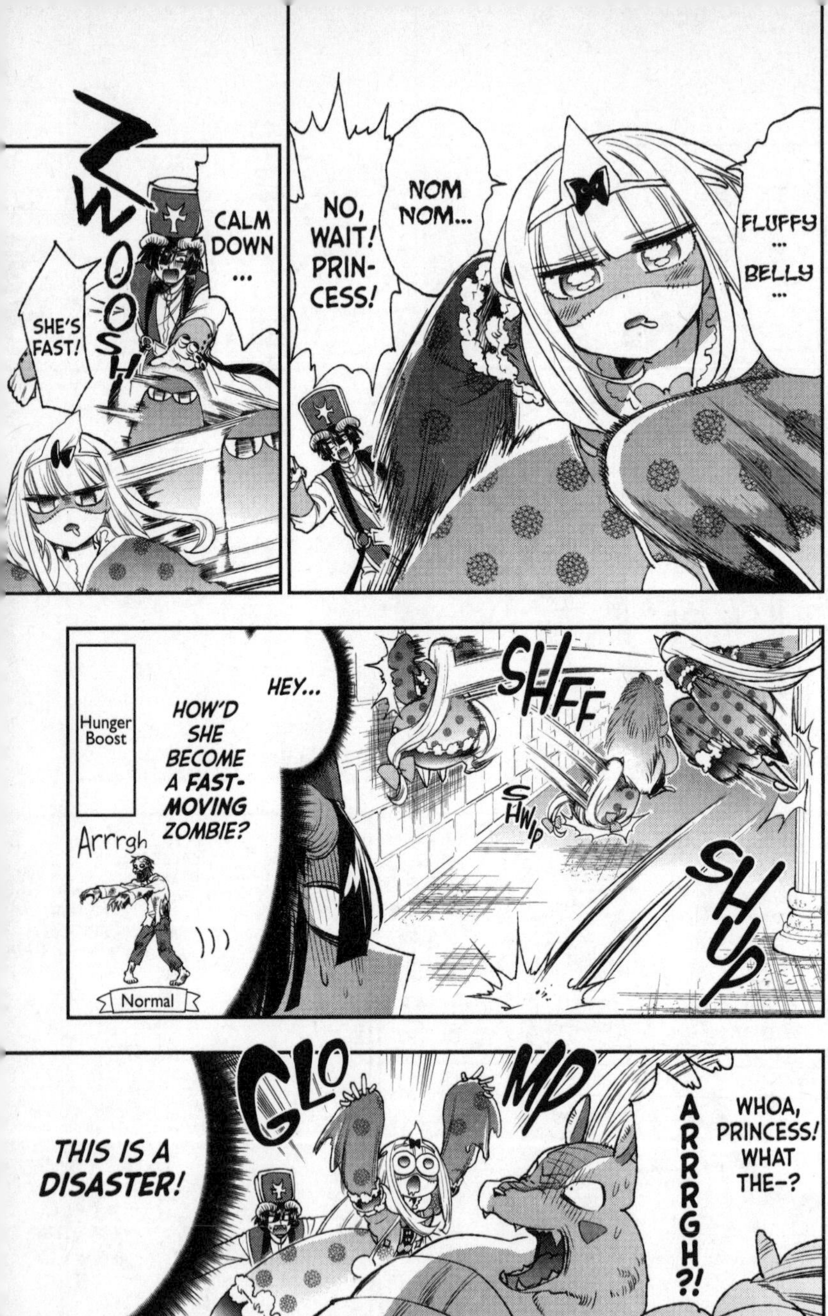

FLUFFY ... BELLY ...
NOM NOM...
NO, WAIT! PRIN-CESS!
CALM DOWN ...
ZWOOOSH
SHE'S FAST!
SHUP
SHFF
SHWIP
HEY...
HOW'D SHE BECOME A FAST-MOVING ZOMBIE?
Hunger Boost
Arrrgh
Normal
WHOA, PRINCESS! WHAT THE-?
ARRRGH?!
GLOMP
THIS IS A DISASTER!

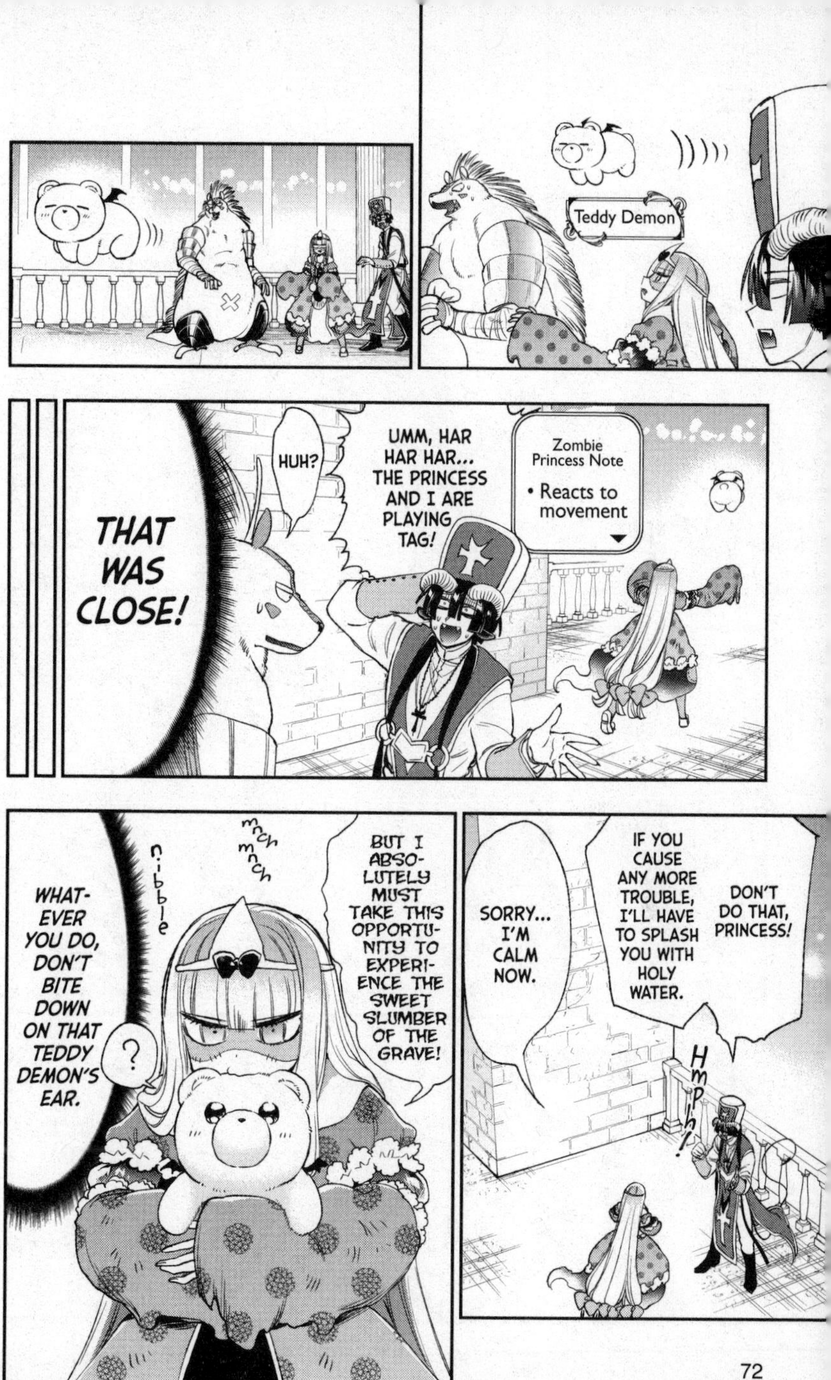

Teddy Demon
Zombie Princess Note
• Reacts to movement
UMM, HAR HAR HAR... THE PRINCESS AND I ARE PLAYING TAG!
HUH?
THAT WAS CLOSE!
DON'T DO THAT, PRINCESS!
IF YOU CAUSE ANY MORE TROUBLE, I'LL HAVE TO SPLASH YOU WITH HOLY WATER.
SORRY... I'M CALM NOW.
Hmph!
BUT I ABSO-LUTELY MUST TAKE THIS OPPORTU-NITY TO EXPERI-ENCE THE SWEET SLUMBER OF THE GRAVE!
mnch mnch
nibble
?
WHAT-EVER YOU DO, DON'T BITE DOWN ON THAT TEDDY DEMON'S EAR.

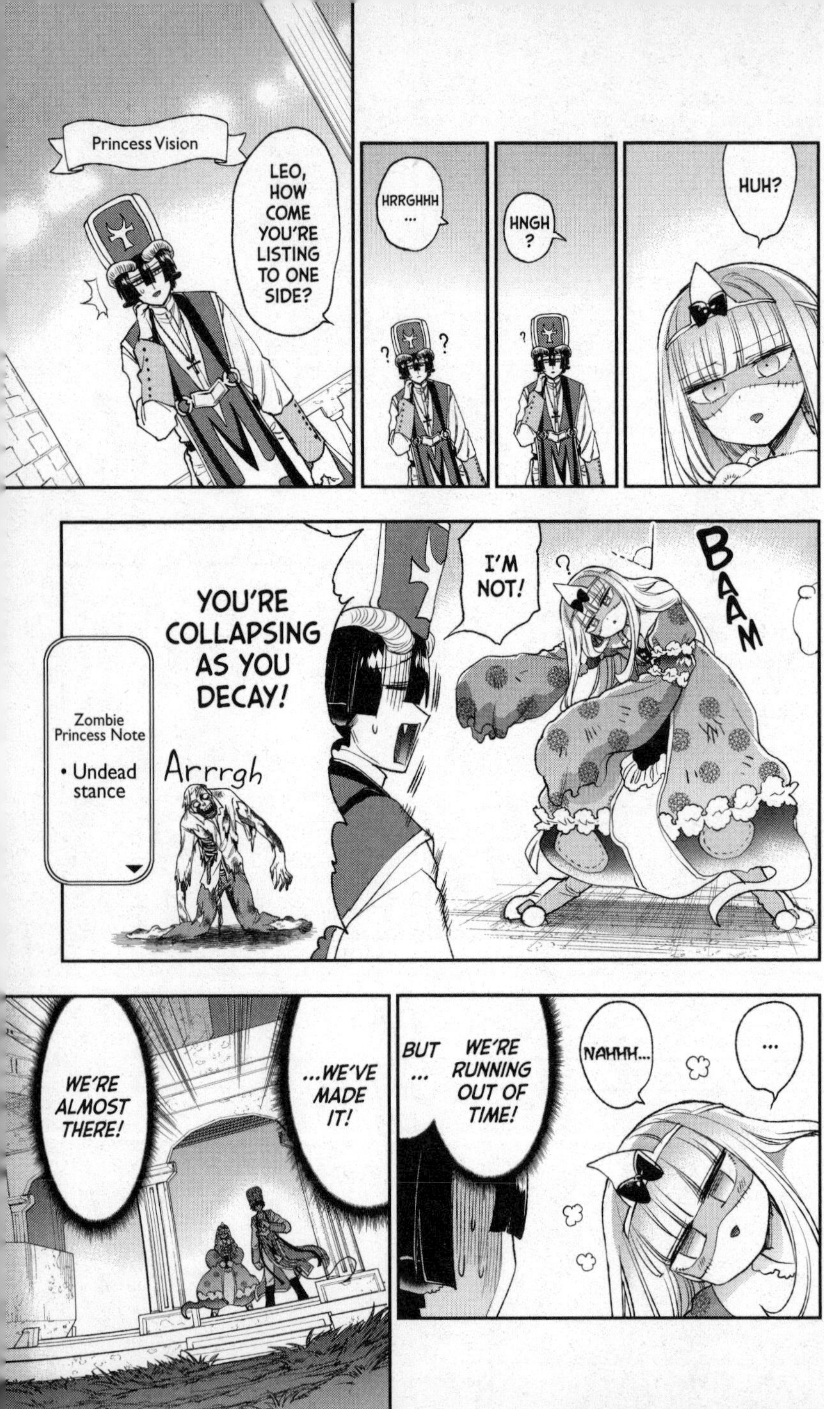
HUH?
HNGH ?
HRRGHHH ...
Princess Vision
LEO, HOW COME YOU'RE LISTING TO ONE SIDE?
BAAAM
I'M NOT!
YOU'RE COLLAPSING AS YOU DECAY!
Zombie Princess Note
• Undead stance
Arrrgh
...
NAHHH...
WE'RE RUNNING OUT OF TIME!
BUT ...
...WE'VE MADE IT!
WE'RE ALMOST THERE!

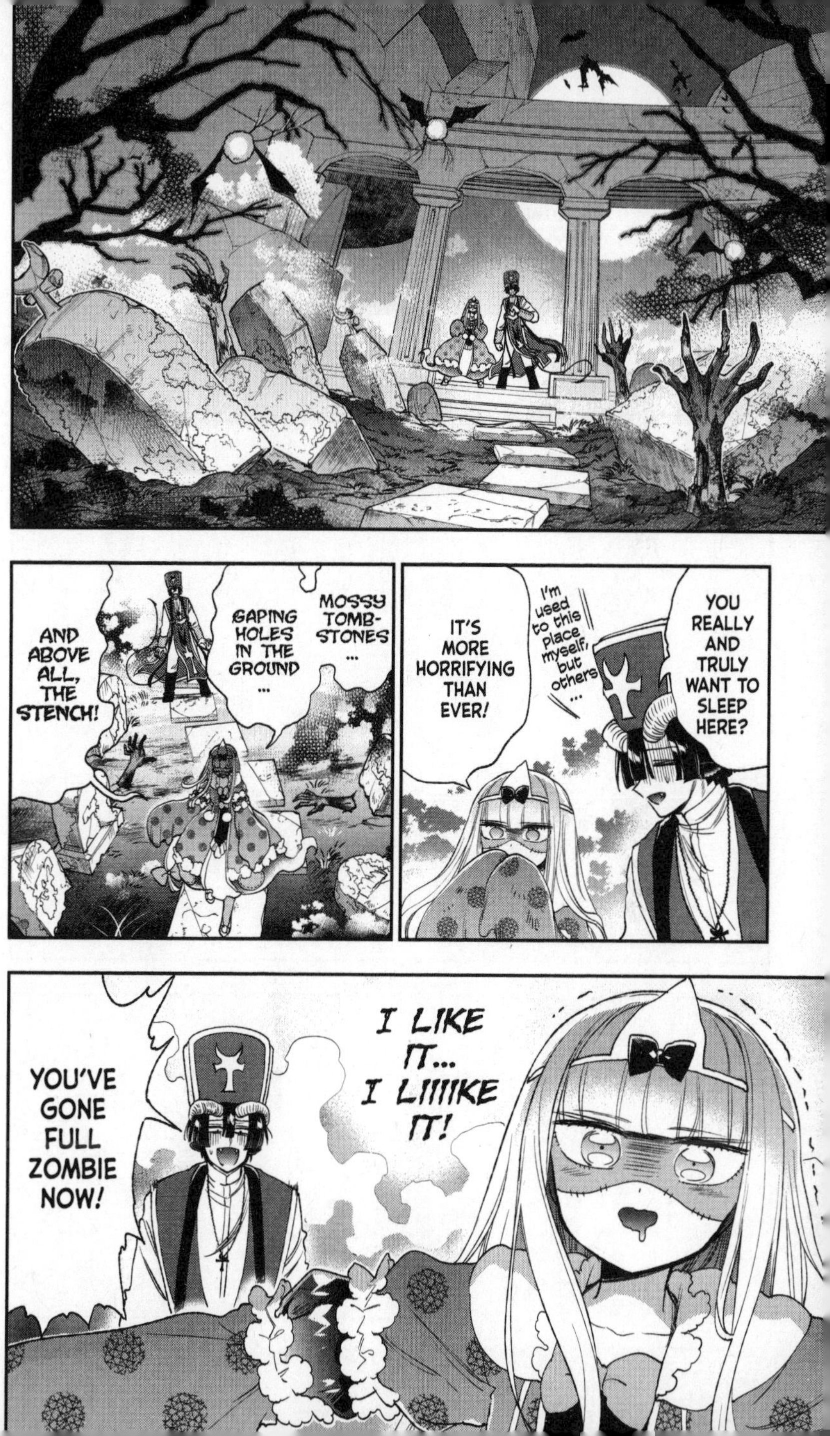
YOU REALLY AND TRULY WANT TO SLEEP HERE?
I'm used to this place myself, but others...
IT'S MORE HORRIFYING THAN EVER!
MOSSY TOMB-STONES...
GAPING HOLES IN THE GROUND...
AND ABOVE ALL, THE STENCH!
I LIKE IT... I LIIIIKE IT!
YOU'VE GONE FULL ZOMBIE NOW!

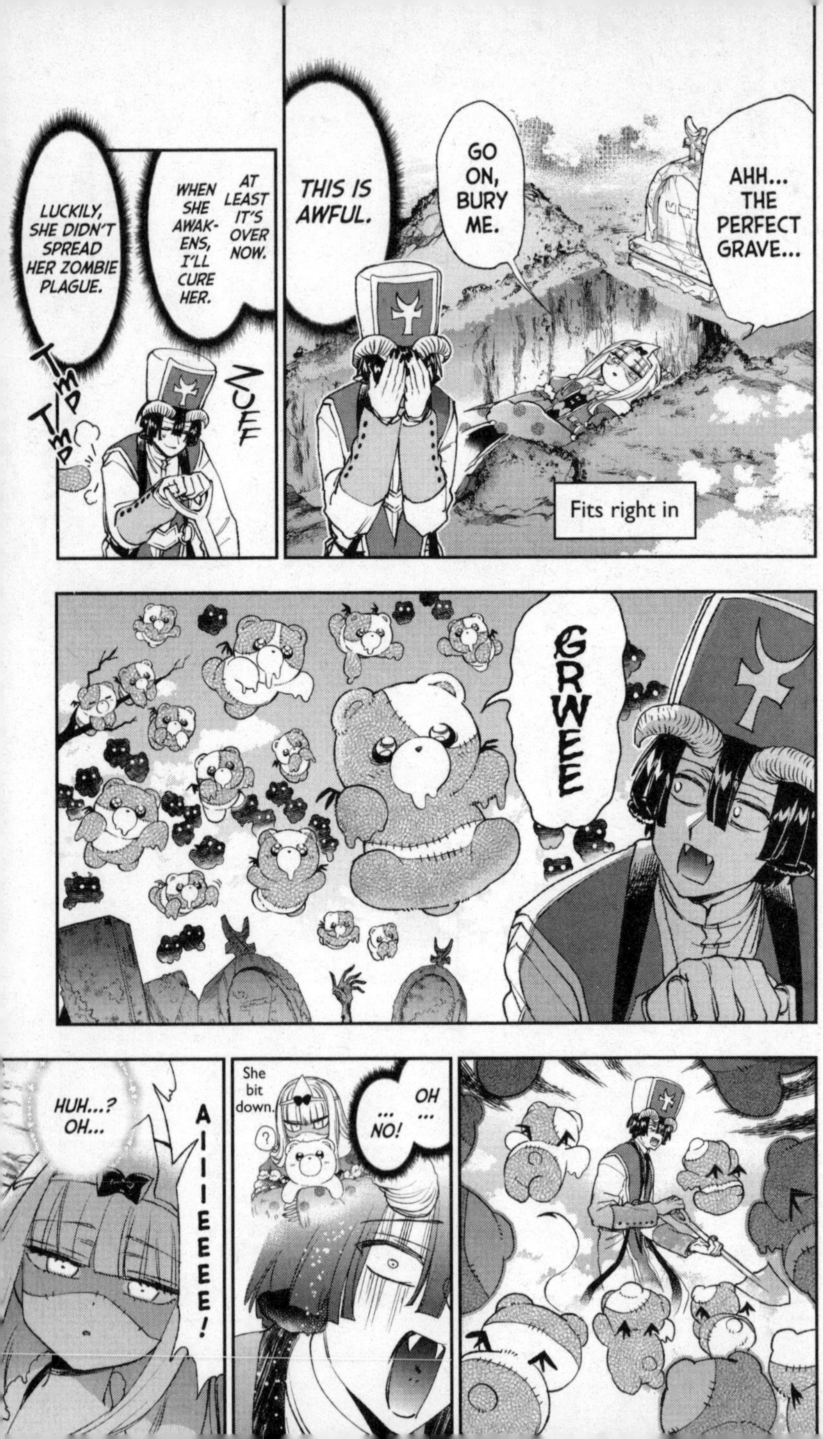
AHH... THE PERFECT GRAVE...
GO ON, BURY ME.
THIS IS AWFUL.
Fits right in
AT LEAST IT'S OVER NOW.
WHEN SHE AWAKENS, I'LL CURE HER.
LUCKILY, SHE DIDN'T SPREAD HER ZOMBIE PLAGUE.
ZUFF
TMP TMP
GRWEE
OH ... NO!
She bit down.
?
AIIIEEEEE!
HUH...? OH...

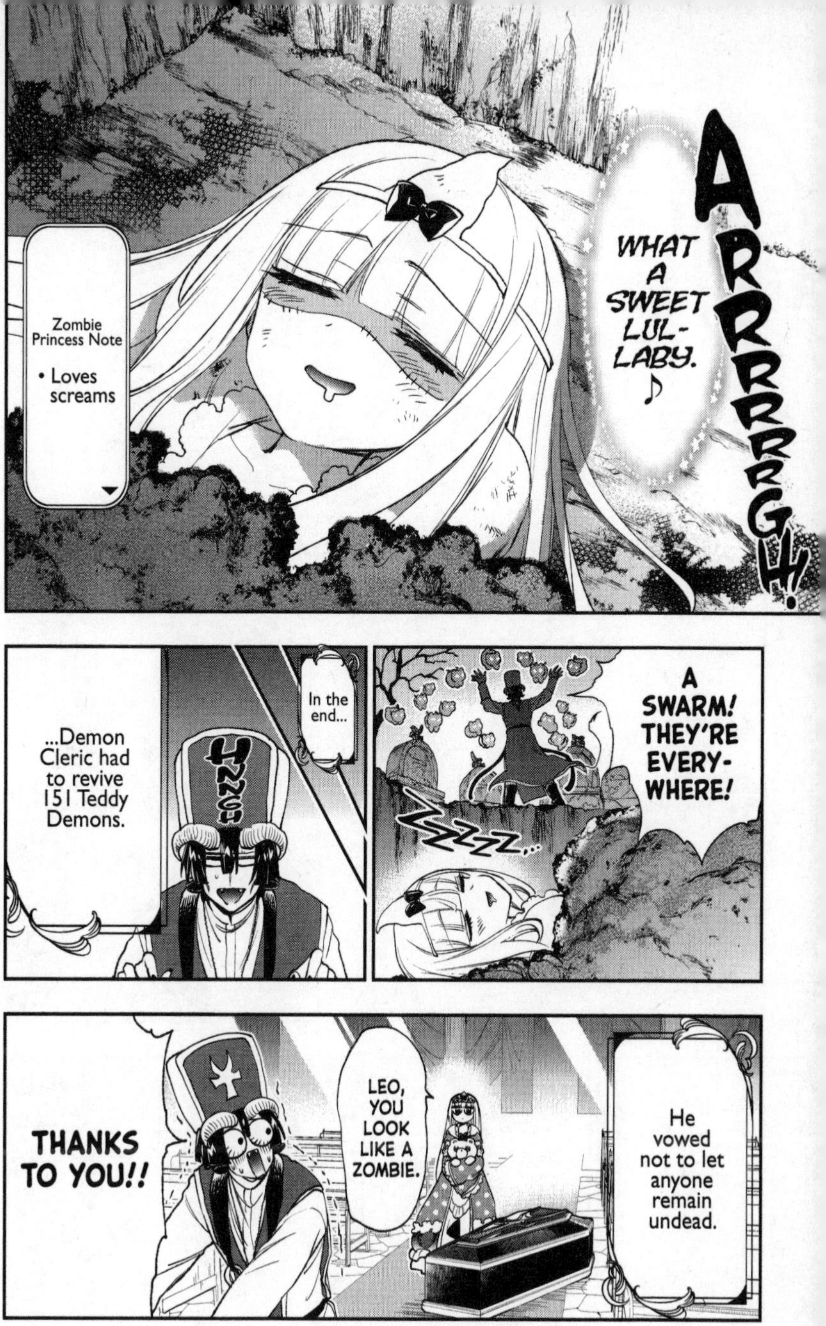
ARRRRRGH!
WHAT A SWEET LULLABY. ♪
Zombie Princess Note
• Loves screams
A SWARM! THEY'RE EVERYWHERE!
ZZZZZ...
In the end...
...Demon Cleric had to revive 151 Teddy Demons.
HNNGH
He vowed not to let anyone remain undead.
LEO, YOU LOOK LIKE A ZOMBIE.
THANKS TO YOU!!

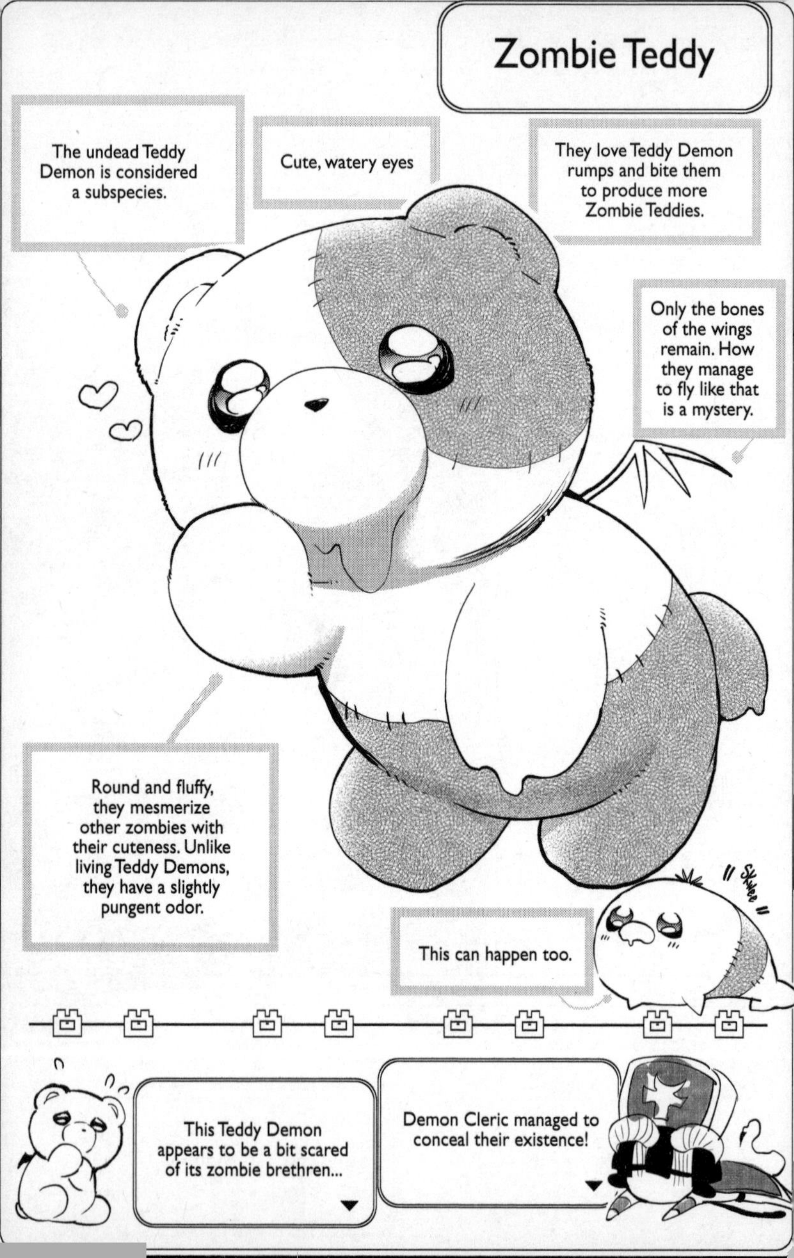
Zombie Teddy
The undead Teddy Demon is considered a subspecies.
Cute, watery eyes
They love Teddy Demon rumps and bite them to produce more Zombie Teddies.
Only the bones of the wings remain. How they manage to fly like that is a mystery.
Round and fluffy, they mesmerize other zombies with their cuteness. Unlike living Teddy Demons, they have a slightly pungent odor.
Skwee
This can happen too.
This Teddy Demon appears to be a bit scared of its zombie brethren...
Demon Cleric managed to conceal their existence!

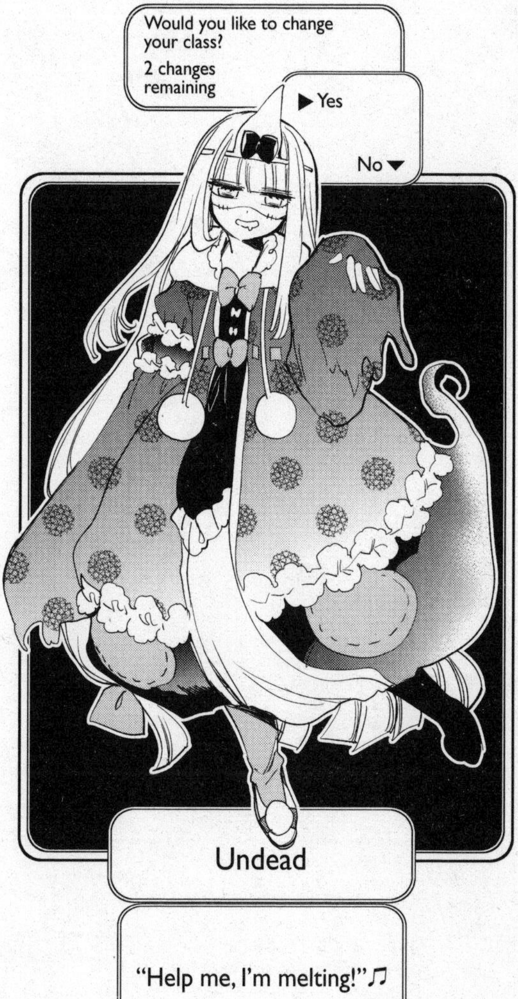
Would you like to change your class?
2 changes remaining
▶ Yes
No ▼
Undead
"Help me, I'm melting!" ♫
▼

215th Night: Endless Changes

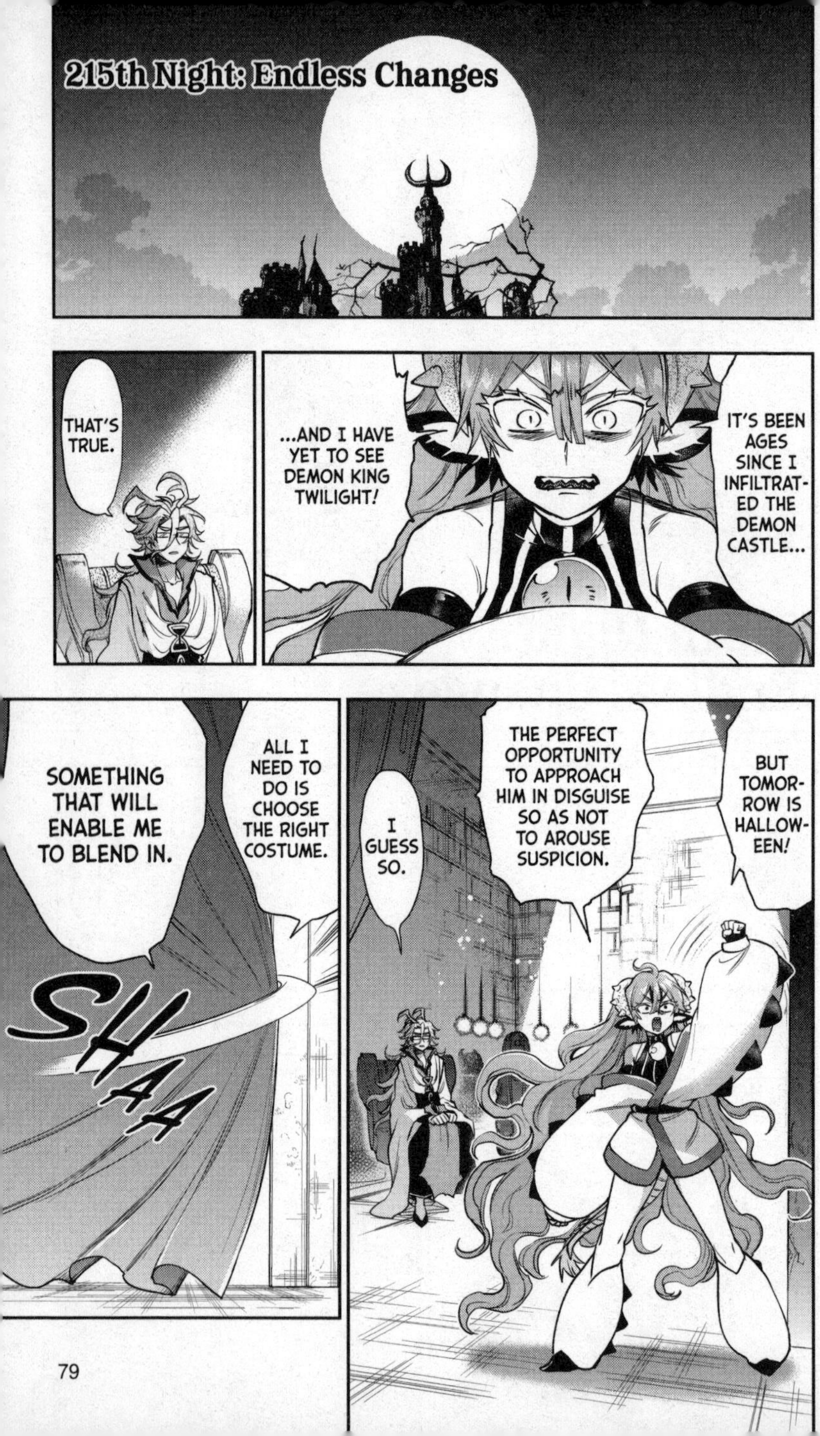
IT'S BEEN AGES SINCE I INFILTRAT-ED THE DEMON CASTLE...
...AND I HAVE YET TO SEE DEMON KING TWILIGHT!
THAT'S TRUE.
BUT TOMOR-ROW IS HALLOW-EEN!
THE PERFECT OPPORTUNITY TO APPROACH HIM IN DISGUISE SO AS NOT TO AROUSE SUSPICION.
I GUESS SO.
ALL I NEED TO DO IS CHOOSE THE RIGHT COSTUME.
SOMETHING THAT WILL ENABLE ME TO BLEND IN.
SHAA

215th Night: Endless Changes

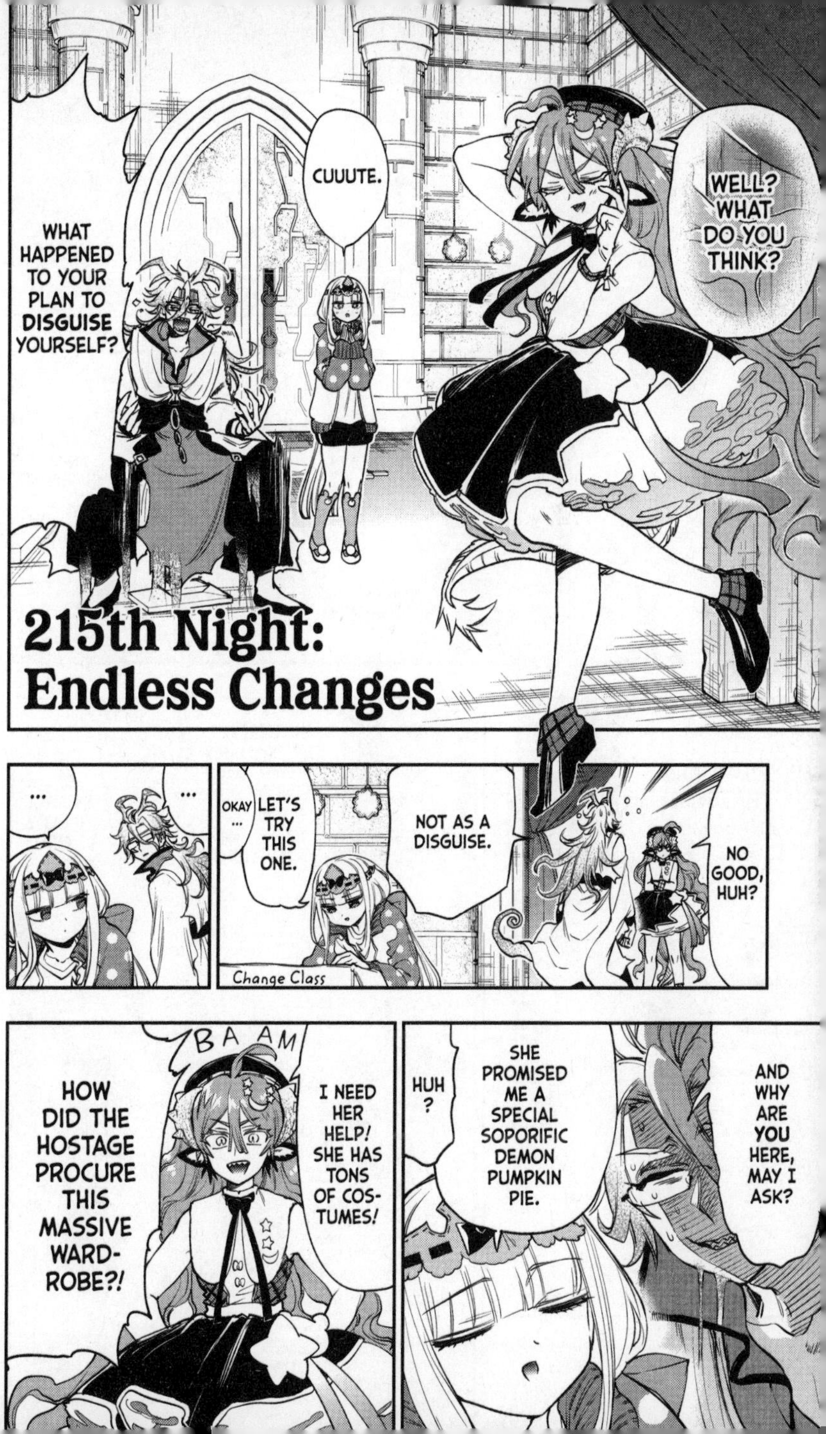
WELL? WHAT DO YOU THINK?
CUUUTE.
WHAT HAPPENED TO YOUR PLAN TO DISGUISE YOURSELF?
NO GOOD, HUH?
NOT AS A DISGUISE.
LET'S TRY THIS ONE.
OKAY...
Change Class
...
...
AND WHY ARE YOU HERE, MAY I ASK?
SHE PROMISED ME A SPECIAL SOPORIFIC DEMON PUMPKIN PIE.
HUH?
BAAM
I NEED HER HELP! SHE HAS TONS OF COS-TUMES!
HOW DID THE HOSTAGE PROCURE THIS MASSIVE WARD-ROBE?!

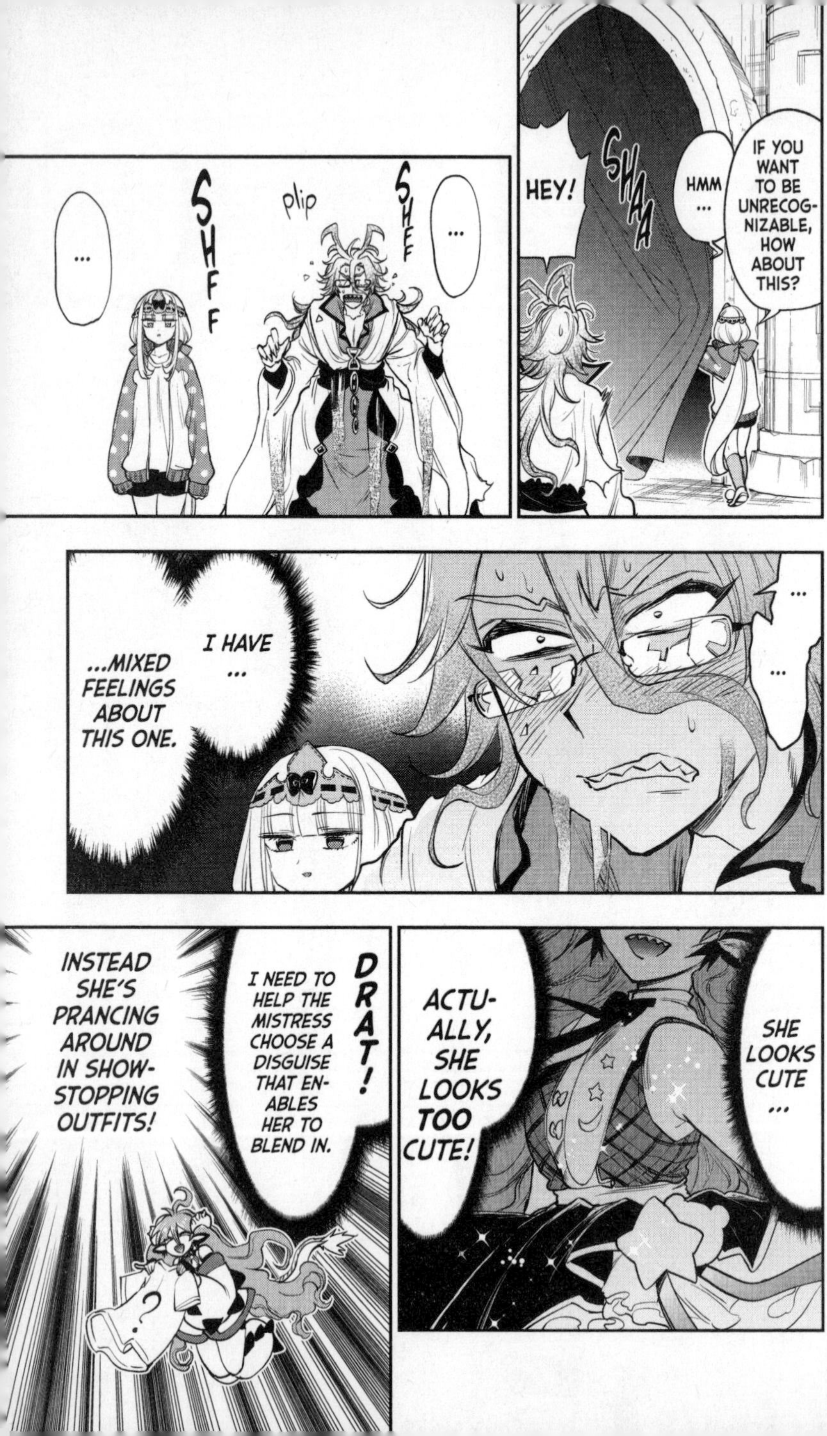
IF YOU WANT TO BE UNRECOG-NIZABLE, HOW ABOUT THIS?
HMM ...
SHAA
HEY!
...
SHFF
plip
SHFF
...
...
...
I HAVE ...
...MIXED FEELINGS ABOUT THIS ONE.
SHE LOOKS CUTE ...
ACTU-ALLY, SHE LOOKS TOO CUTE!
DRAT!
I NEED TO HELP THE MISTRESS CHOOSE A DISGUISE THAT EN-ABLES HER TO BLEND IN.
INSTEAD SHE'S PRANCING AROUND IN SHOW-STOPPING OUTFITS!

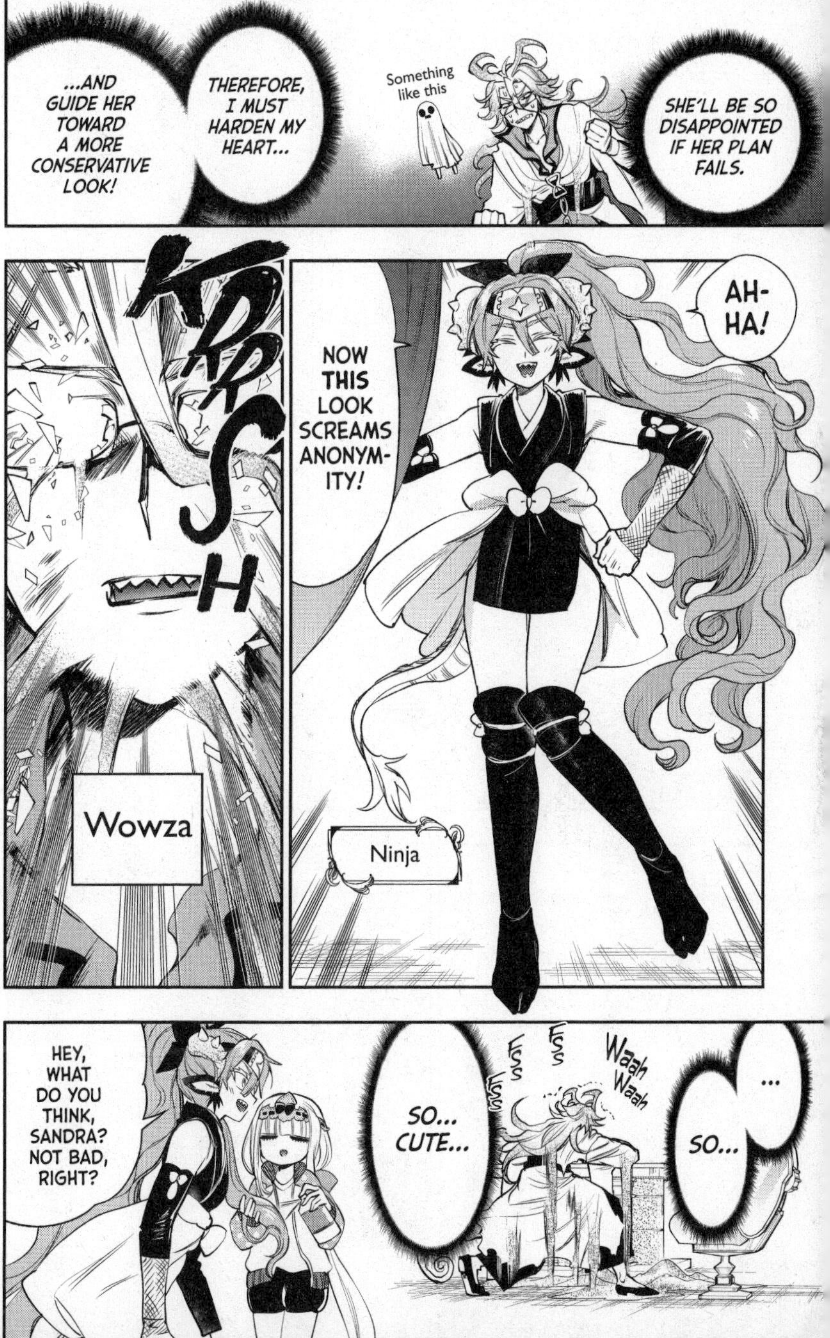
SHE'LL BE SO DISAPPOINTED IF HER PLAN FAILS.
Something like this
THEREFORE, I MUST HARDEN MY HEART...
...AND GUIDE HER TOWARD A MORE CONSERVATIVE LOOK!
AH-HA!
NOW THIS LOOK SCREAMS ANONYM-ITY!
Ninja
KRRSSH
Wowza
...SO...
Waah Waah
Fss Fss Fss Fss
SO... CUTE...
HEY, WHAT DO YOU THINK, SANDRA? NOT BAD, RIGHT?

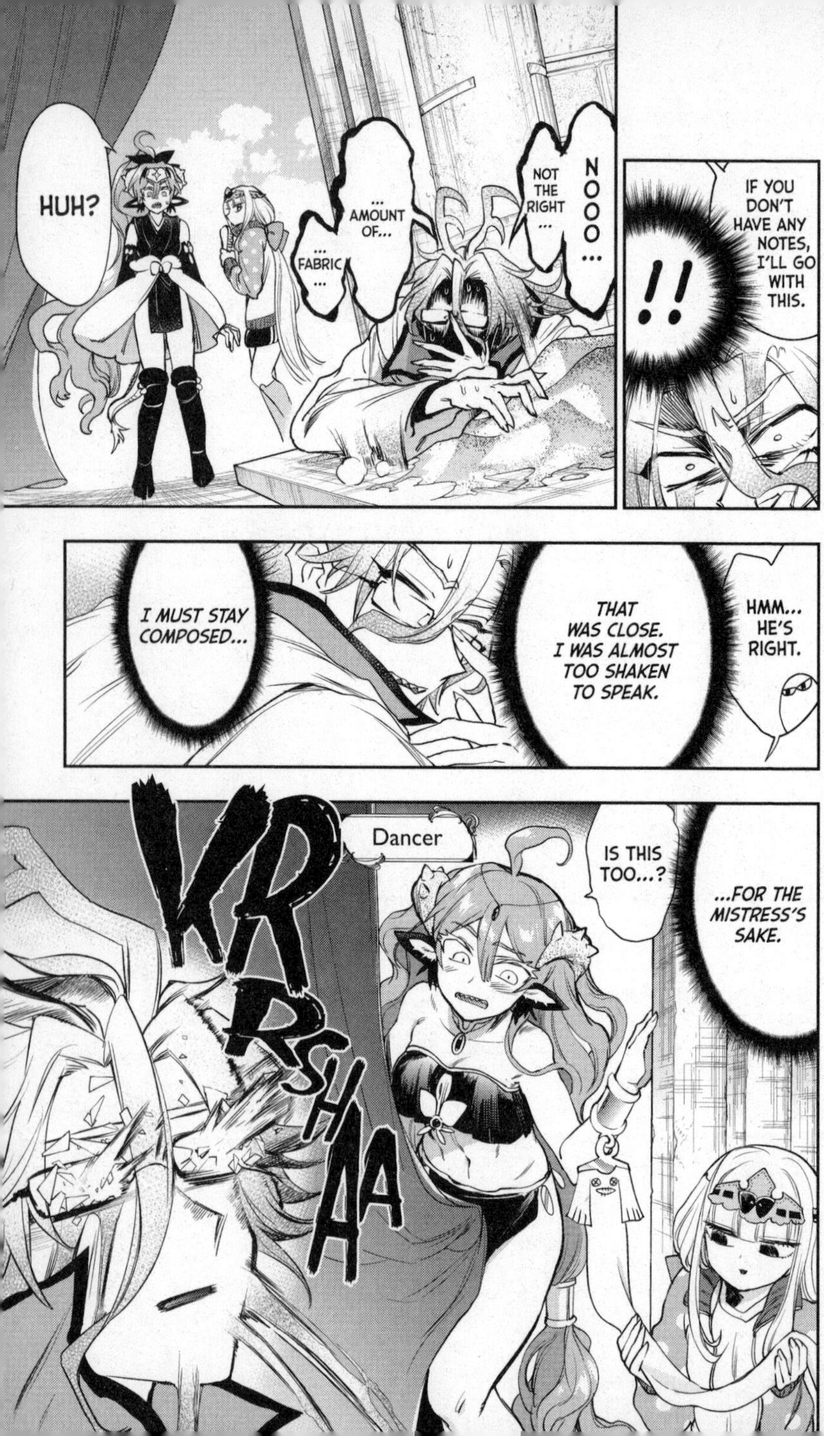
IF YOU DON'T HAVE ANY NOTES, I'LL GO WITH THIS.
!!
NOOO...
NOT THE RIGHT...
...AMOUNT OF...
...FABRIC...
HUH?
HMM... HE'S RIGHT.
THAT WAS CLOSE. I WAS ALMOST TOO SHAKEN TO SPEAK.
I MUST STAY COMPOSED...
...FOR THE MISTRESS'S SAKE.
IS THIS TOO...?
Dancer
KRRSHAA

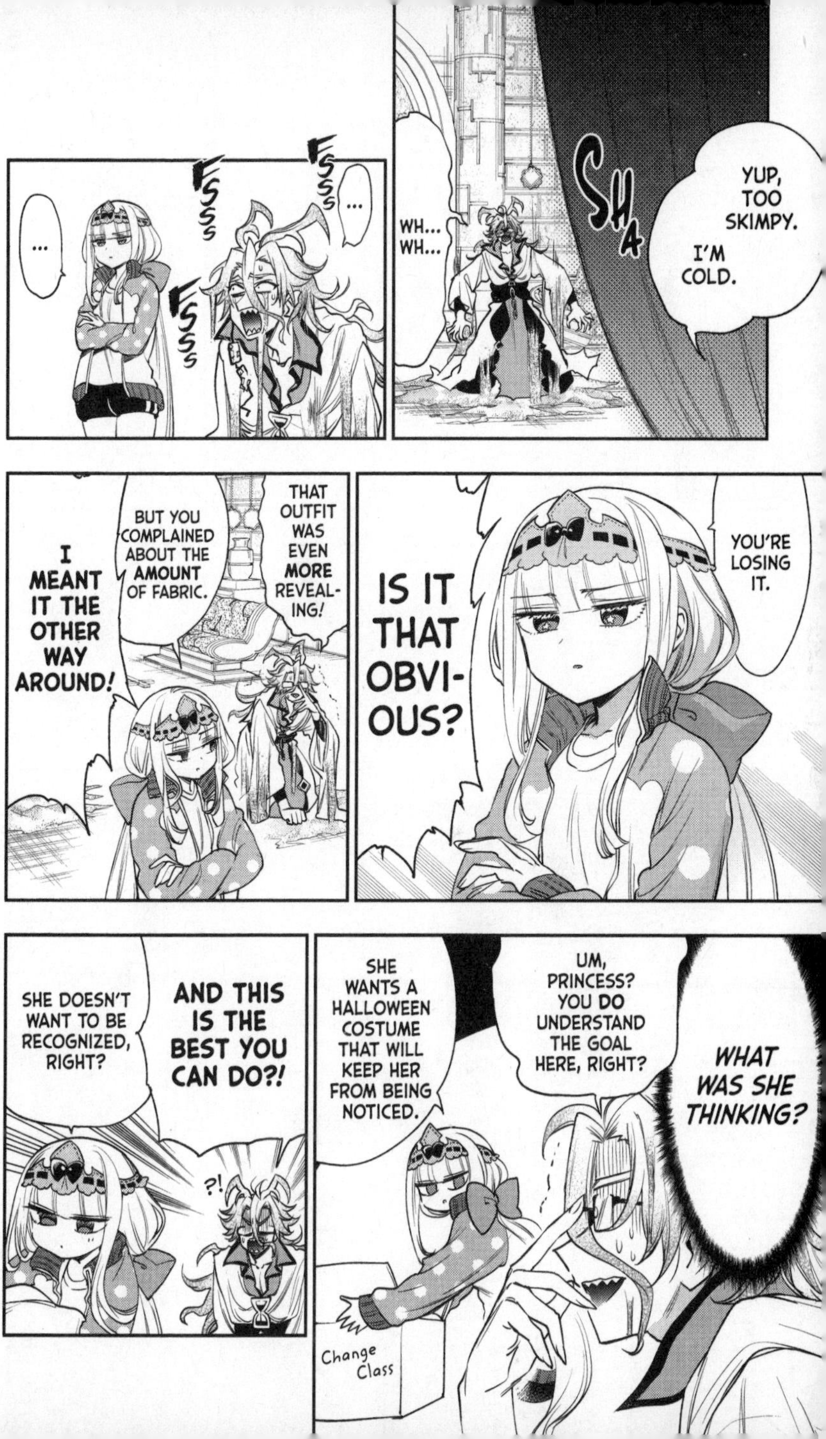
YUP, TOO SKIMPY.
I'M COLD.
SHA
WH... WH...
...
FSSS
FSSS
FSSS
...
YOU'RE LOSING IT.
IS IT THAT OBVIOUS?
THAT OUTFIT WAS EVEN MORE REVEALING!
BUT YOU COMPLAINED ABOUT THE AMOUNT OF FABRIC.
I MEANT IT THE OTHER WAY AROUND!
WHAT WAS SHE THINKING?
UM, PRINCESS? YOU DO UNDERSTAND THE GOAL HERE, RIGHT?
SHE WANTS A HALLOWEEN COSTUME THAT WILL KEEP HER FROM BEING NOTICED.
Change Class
AND THIS IS THE BEST YOU CAN DO?!
SHE DOESN'T WANT TO BE RECOGNIZED, RIGHT?
?!

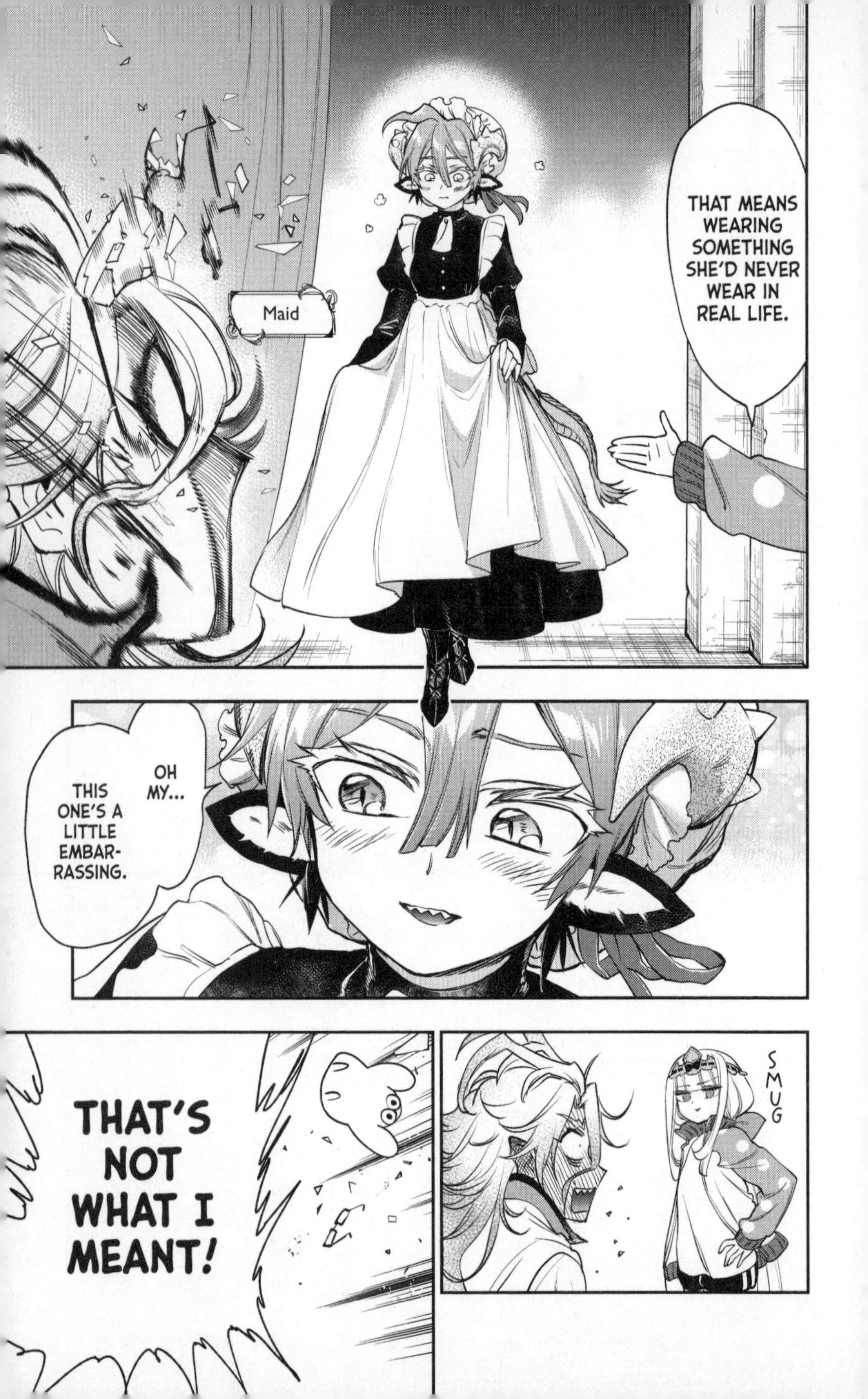
THAT MEANS WEARING SOMETHING SHE'D NEVER WEAR IN REAL LIFE.
Maid
OH MY...
THIS ONE'S A LITTLE EMBAR-RASSING.
SMUG
THAT'S NOT WHAT I MEANT!

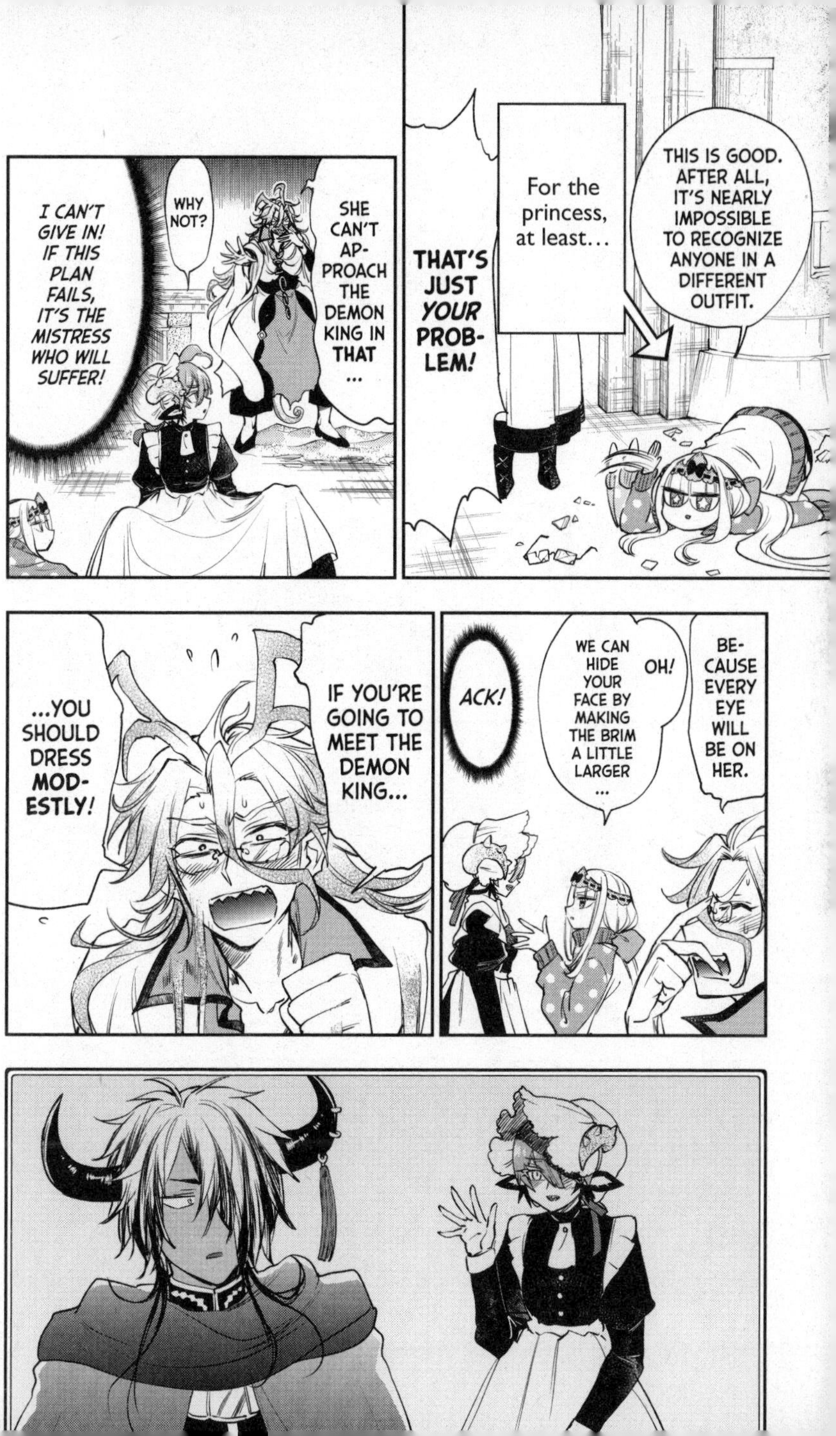
THIS IS GOOD. AFTER ALL, IT'S NEARLY IMPOSSIBLE TO RECOGNIZE ANYONE IN A DIFFERENT OUTFIT.
For the princess, at least…
THAT'S JUST *YOUR* PROBLEM!
SHE CAN'T APPROACH THE DEMON KING IN THAT ...
WHY NOT?
I CAN'T GIVE IN! IF THIS PLAN FAILS, IT'S THE MISTRESS WHO WILL SUFFER!
BECAUSE EVERY EYE WILL BE ON HER.
OH!
WE CAN HIDE YOUR FACE BY MAKING THE BRIM A LITTLE LARGER ...
ACK!
IF YOU'RE GOING TO MEET THE DEMON KING...
...YOU SHOULD DRESS **MODESTLY**!

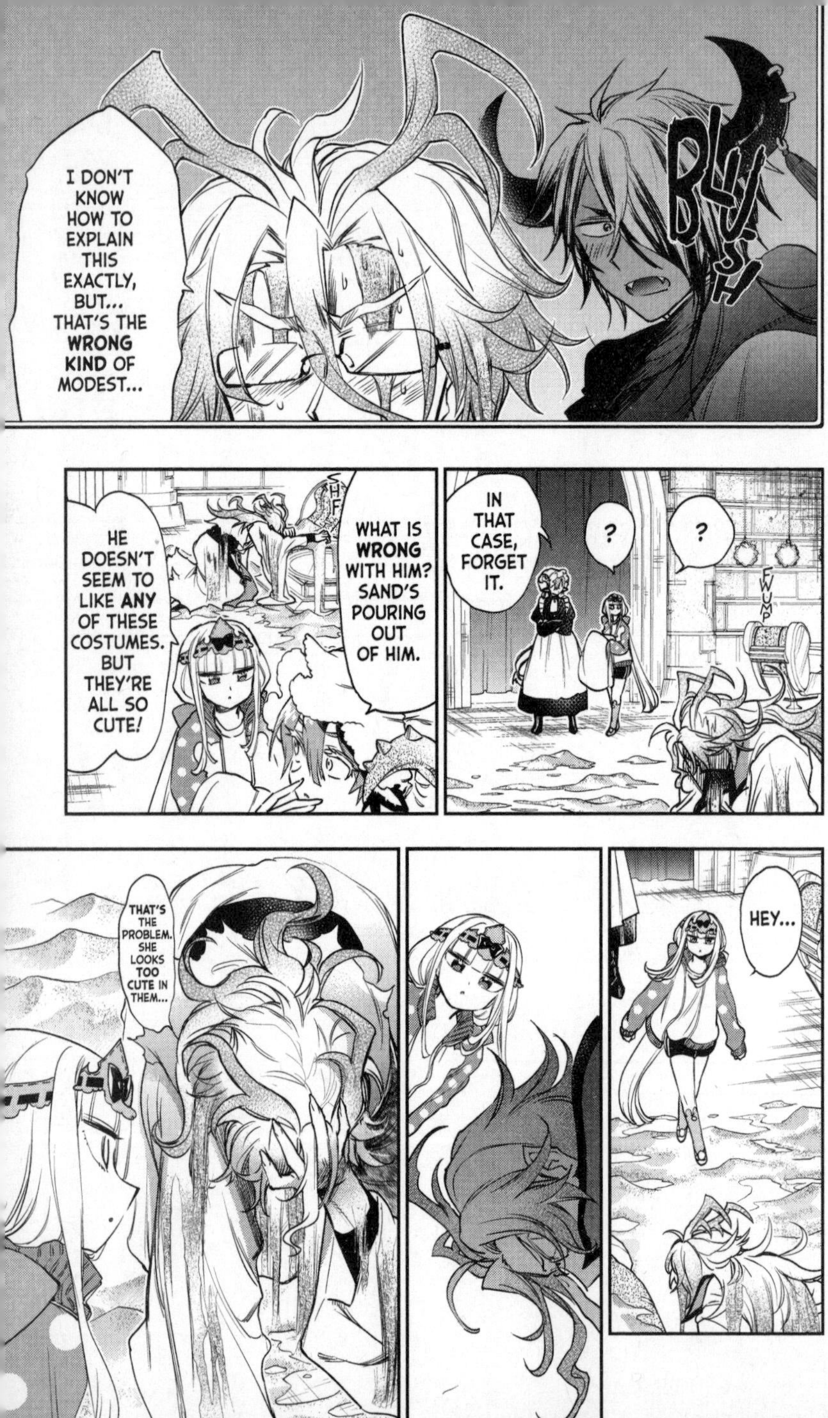
BLUSH
I DON'T KNOW HOW TO EXPLAIN THIS EXACTLY, BUT... THAT'S THE WRONG KIND OF MODEST...
?
?
IN THAT CASE, FORGET IT.
FWUMP
SHF
WHAT IS WRONG WITH HIM? SAND'S POURING OUT OF HIM.
HE DOESN'T SEEM TO LIKE ANY OF THESE COSTUMES. BUT THEY'RE ALL SO CUTE!
HEY...
THAT'S THE PROBLEM. SHE LOOKS TOO CUTE IN THEM...

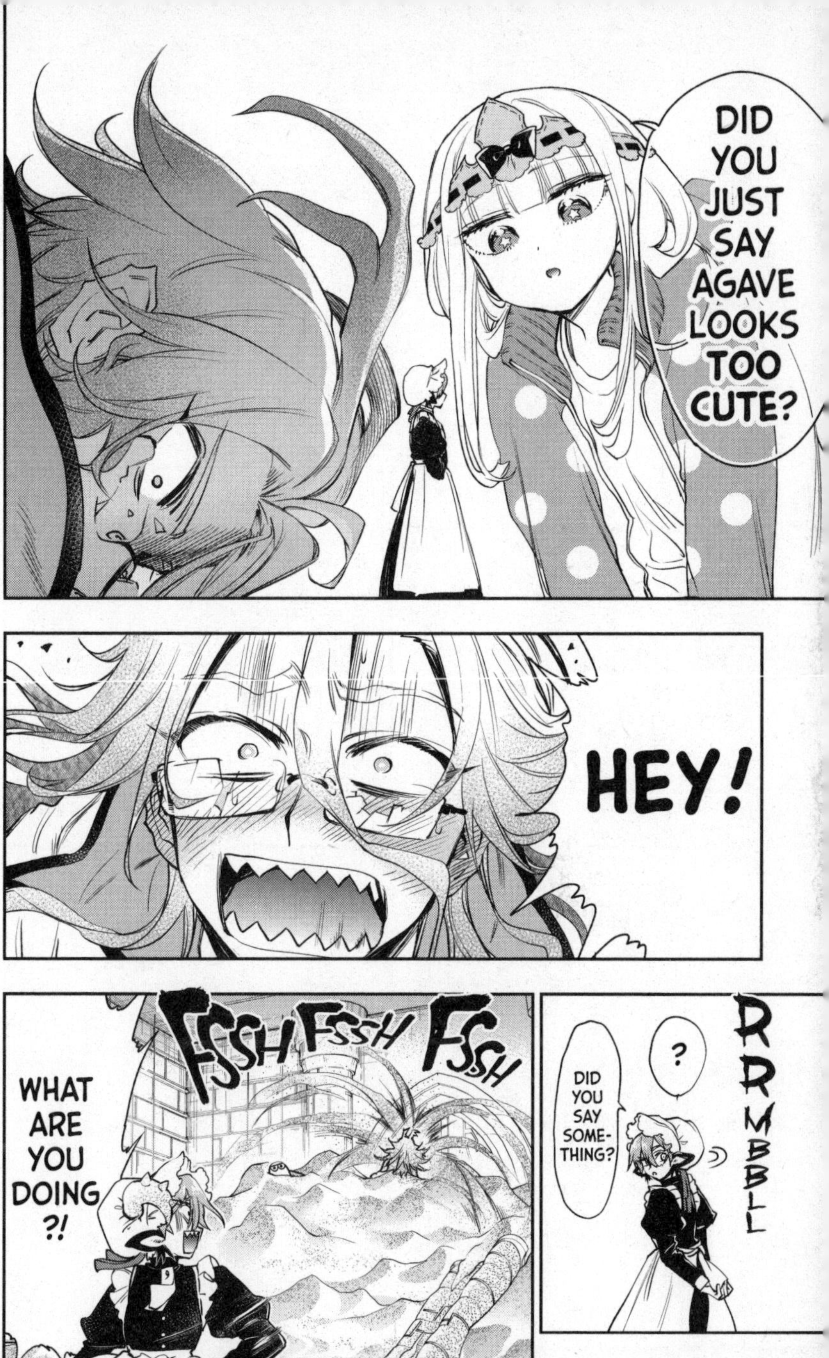
DID YOU JUST SAY AGAVE LOOKS TOO CUTE?
HEY!
DRRMBBLL
?
DID YOU SAY SOME-THING?
FSSH FSSH FSSH
WHAT ARE YOU DOING ?!

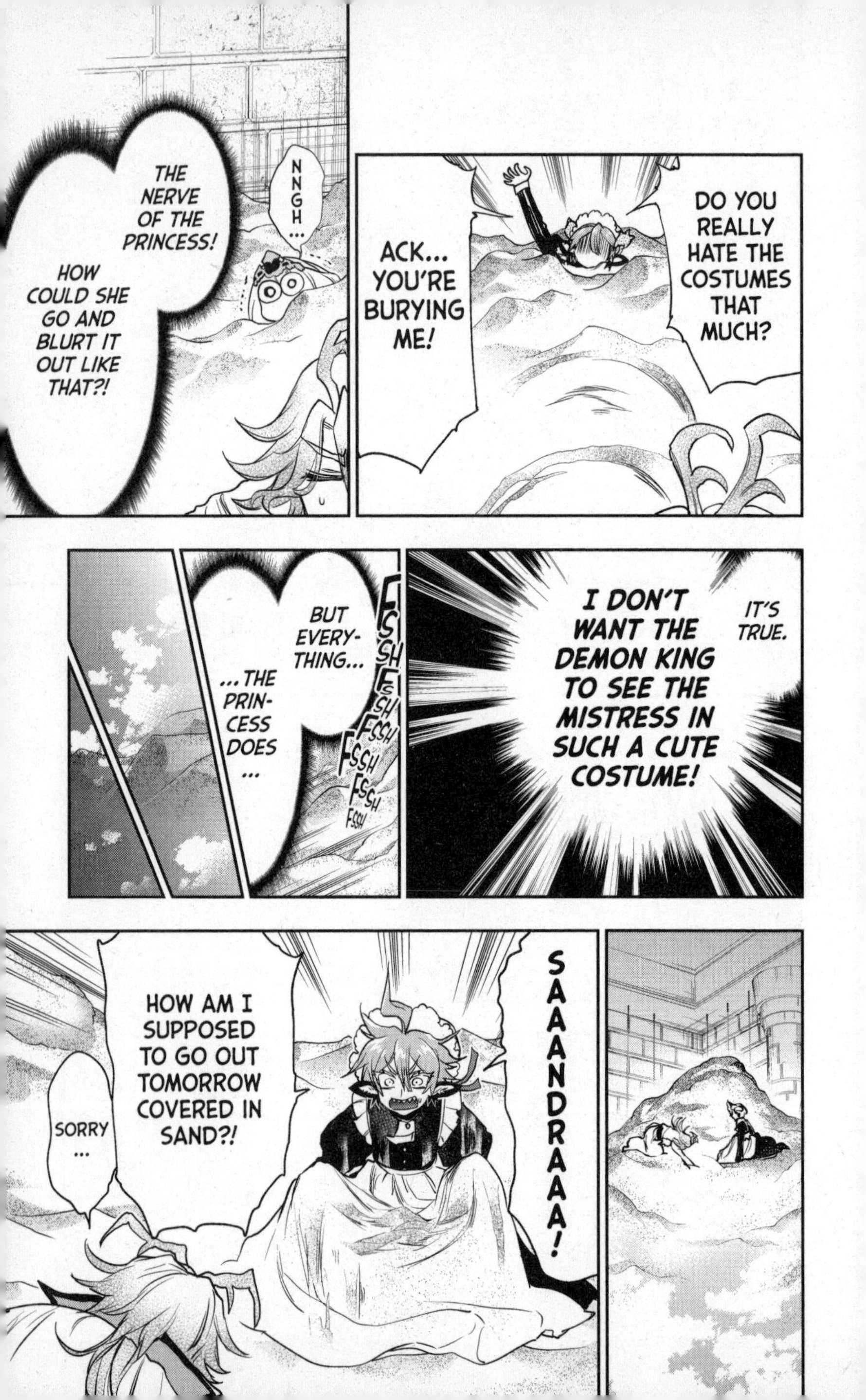
DO YOU REALLY HATE THE COSTUMES THAT MUCH?
ACK... YOU'RE BURYING ME!
NNGH...
THE NERVE OF THE PRINCESS!
HOW COULD SHE GO AND BLURT IT OUT LIKE THAT?!
IT'S TRUE.
I DON'T WANT THE DEMON KING TO SEE THE MISTRESS IN SUCH A CUTE COSTUME!
FSSH FSSH FSSH FSSH FSSH FSSH
BUT EVERY-THING...
...THE PRIN-CESS DOES ...
SAAAANDRAAAA!
HOW AM I SUPPOSED TO GO OUT TOMORROW COVERED IN SAND?!
SORRY ...

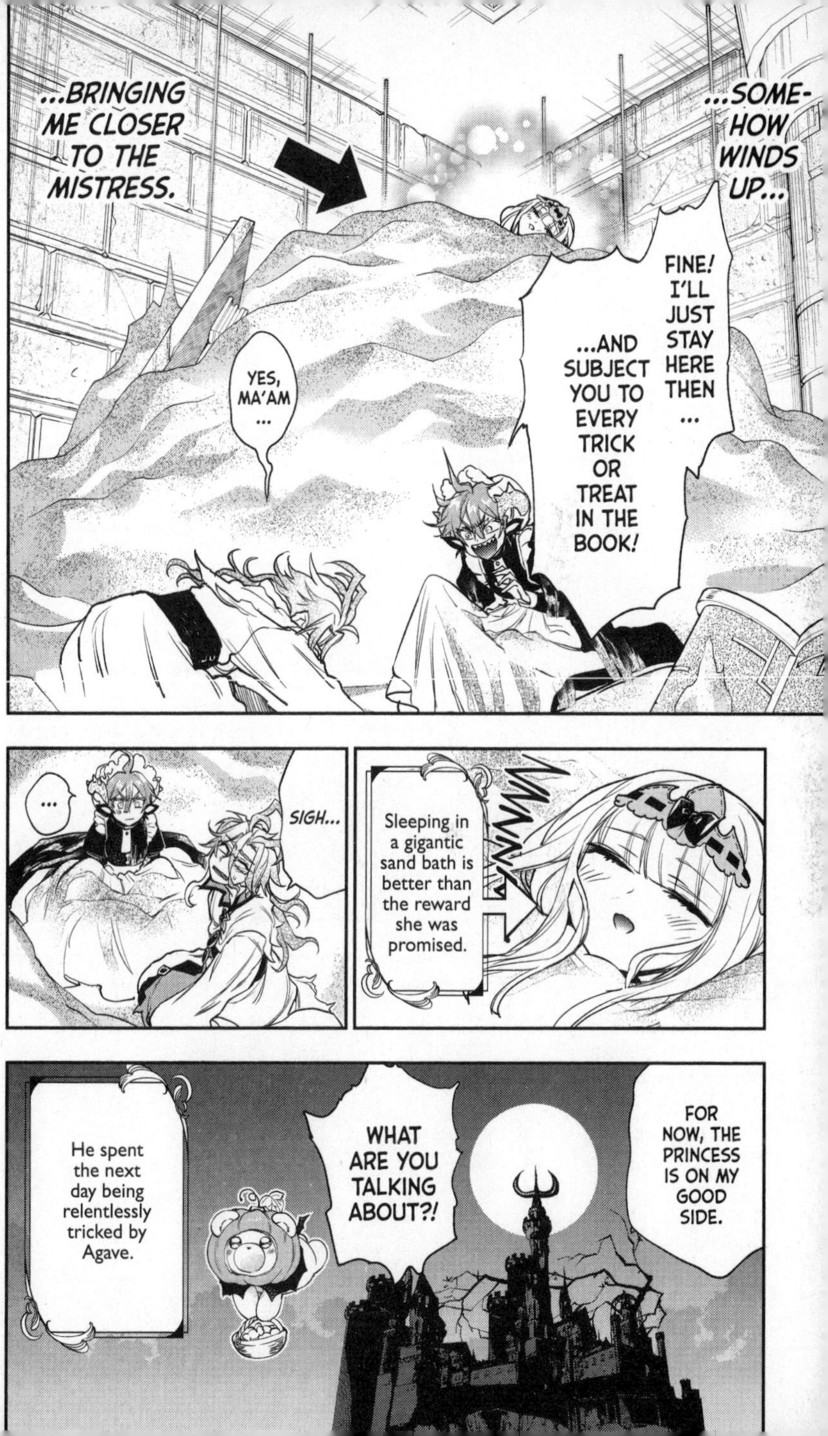
...SOME-HOW WINDS UP...
...BRINGING ME CLOSER TO THE MISTRESS.
FINE! I'LL JUST STAY HERE THEN ...
...AND SUBJECT YOU TO EVERY TRICK OR TREAT IN THE BOOK!
YES, MA'AM ...
Sleeping in a gigantic sand bath is better than the reward she was promised.
SIGH...
...
FOR NOW, THE PRINCESS IS ON MY GOOD SIDE.
WHAT ARE YOU TALKING ABOUT?!
He spent the next day being relentlessly tricked by Agave.

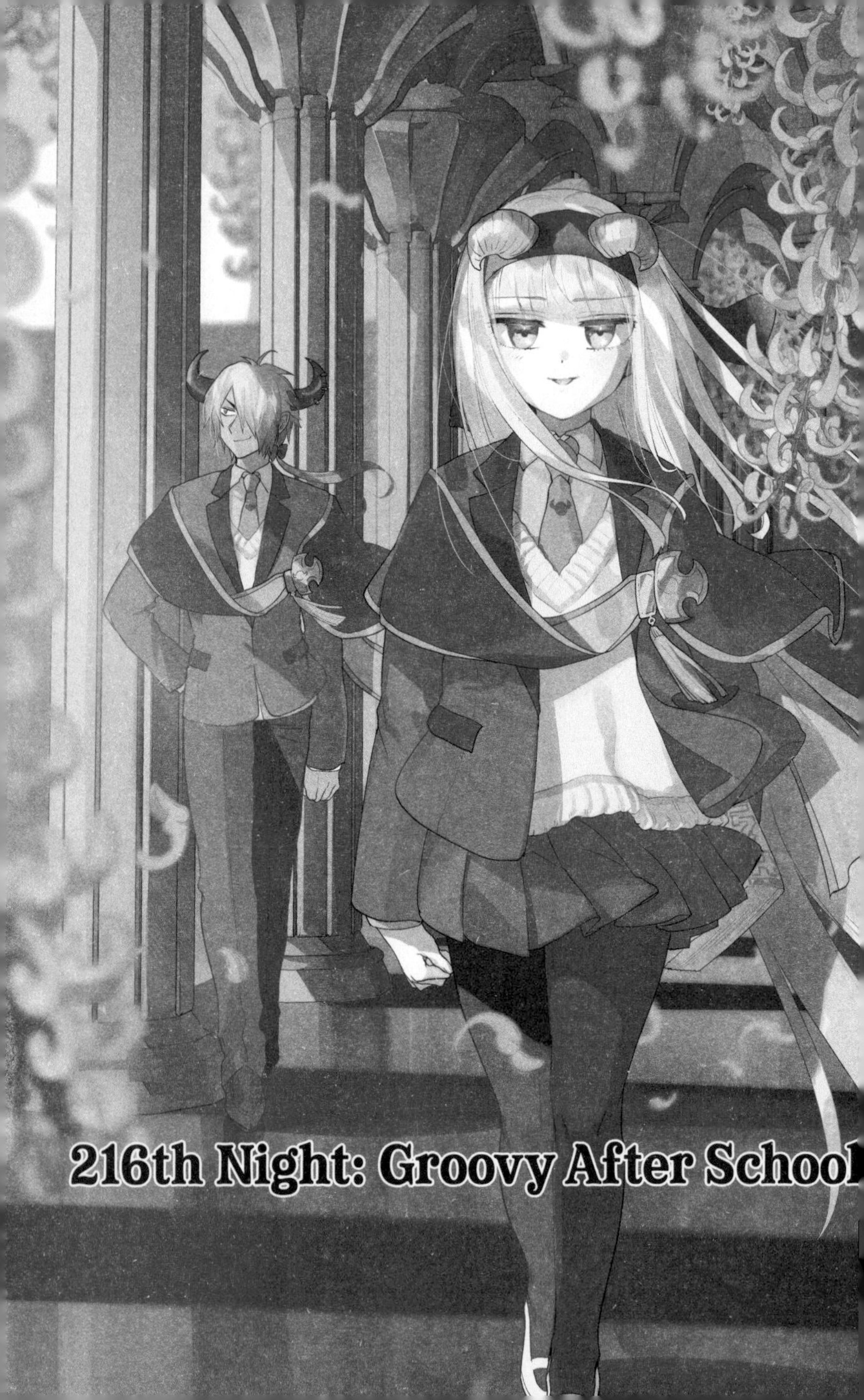
216th Night: Groovy After School

SLEEPY PRINCESS
IN THE
DEMON CASTLE

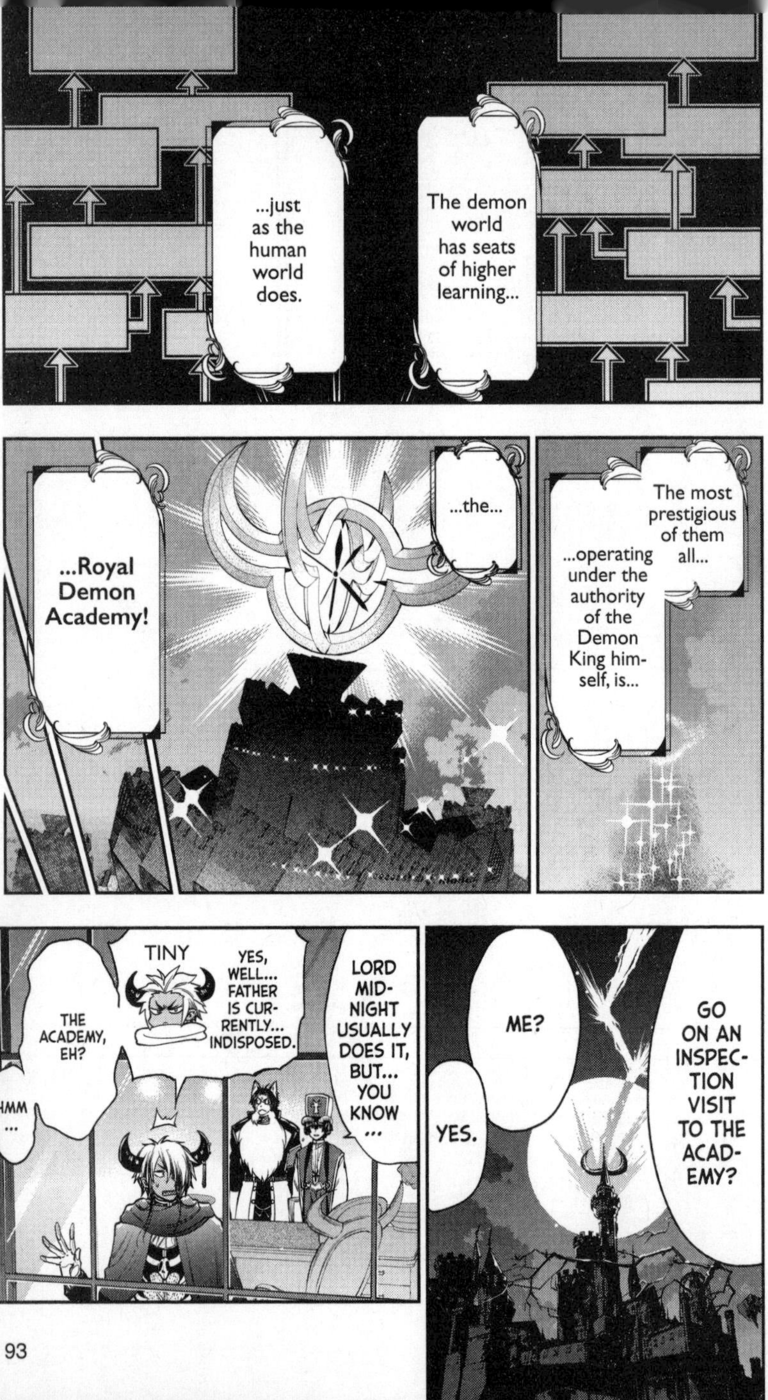
The demon world has seats of higher learning...
...just as the human world does.
The most prestigious of them all...
...operating under the authority of the Demon King himself, is...
...the...
...Royal Demon Academy!
GO ON AN INSPECTION VISIT TO THE ACADEMY?
ME?
YES.
LORD MIDNIGHT USUALLY DOES IT, BUT... YOU KNOW...
YES, WELL... FATHER IS CURRENTLY... INDISPOSED.
TINY
THE ACADEMY, EH?
HMM...

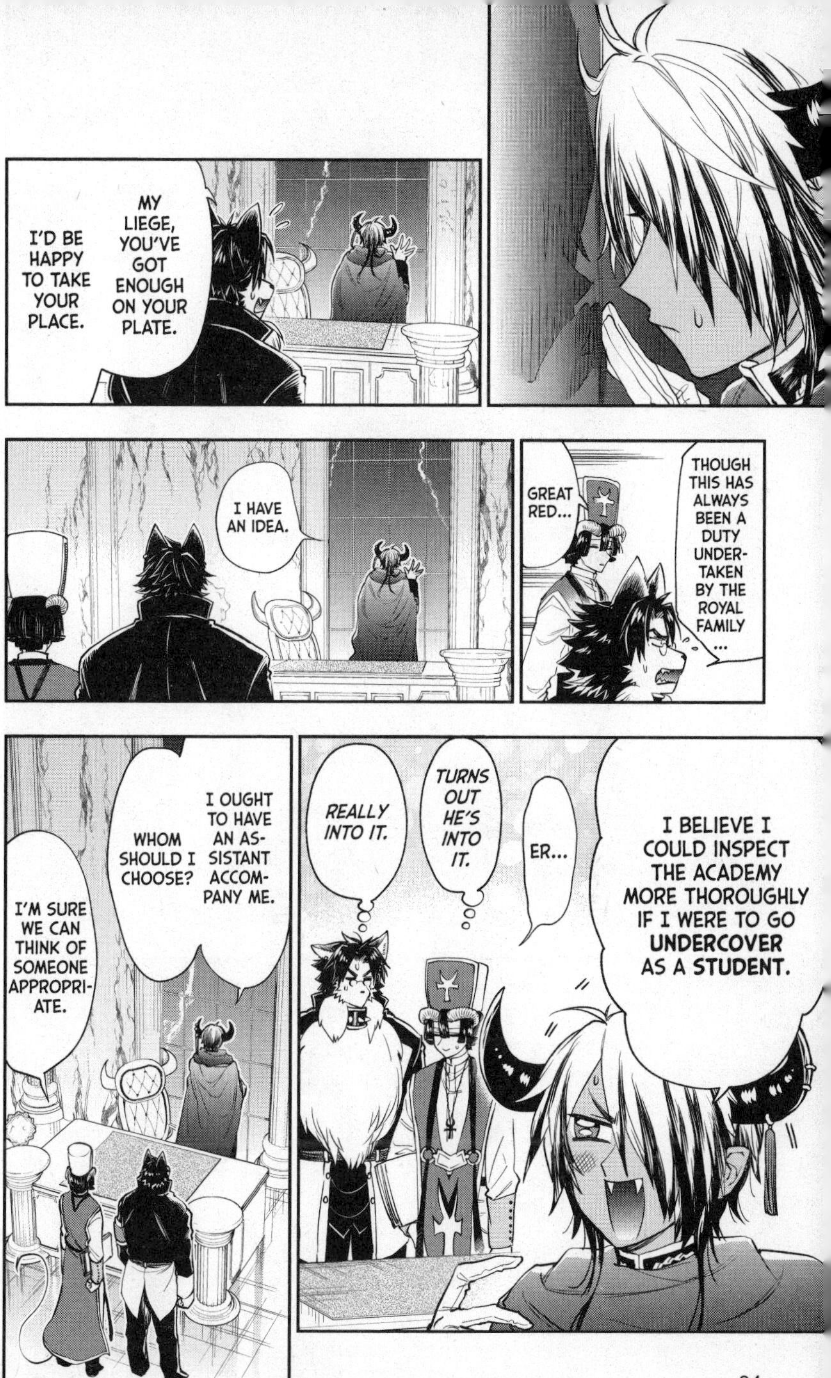
MY LIEGE, YOU'VE GOT ENOUGH ON YOUR PLATE.
I'D BE HAPPY TO TAKE YOUR PLACE.
THOUGH THIS HAS ALWAYS BEEN A DUTY UNDER-TAKEN BY THE ROYAL FAMILY...
GREAT RED...
I HAVE AN IDEA.
I BELIEVE I COULD INSPECT THE ACADEMY MORE THOROUGHLY IF I WERE TO GO **UNDERCOVER** AS A **STUDENT**.
ER...
TURNS OUT HE'S INTO IT.
REALLY INTO IT.
I OUGHT TO HAVE AN AS-SISTANT ACCOM-PANY ME.
WHOM SHOULD I CHOOSE?
I'M SURE WE CAN THINK OF SOMEONE APPROPRI-ATE.

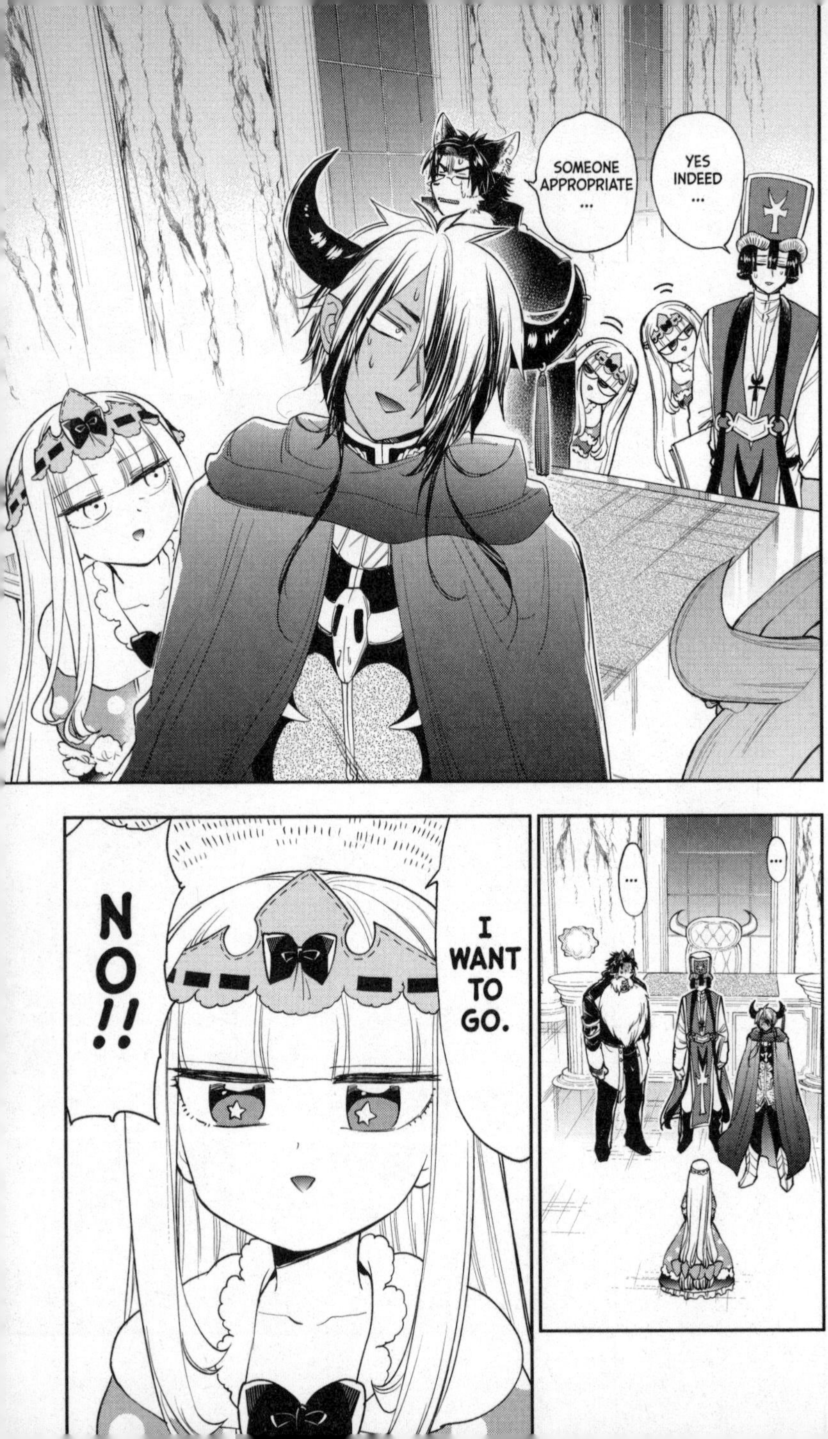
YES INDEED ...
SOMEONE APPROPRIATE ...
...
...
I WANT TO GO.
NO!!

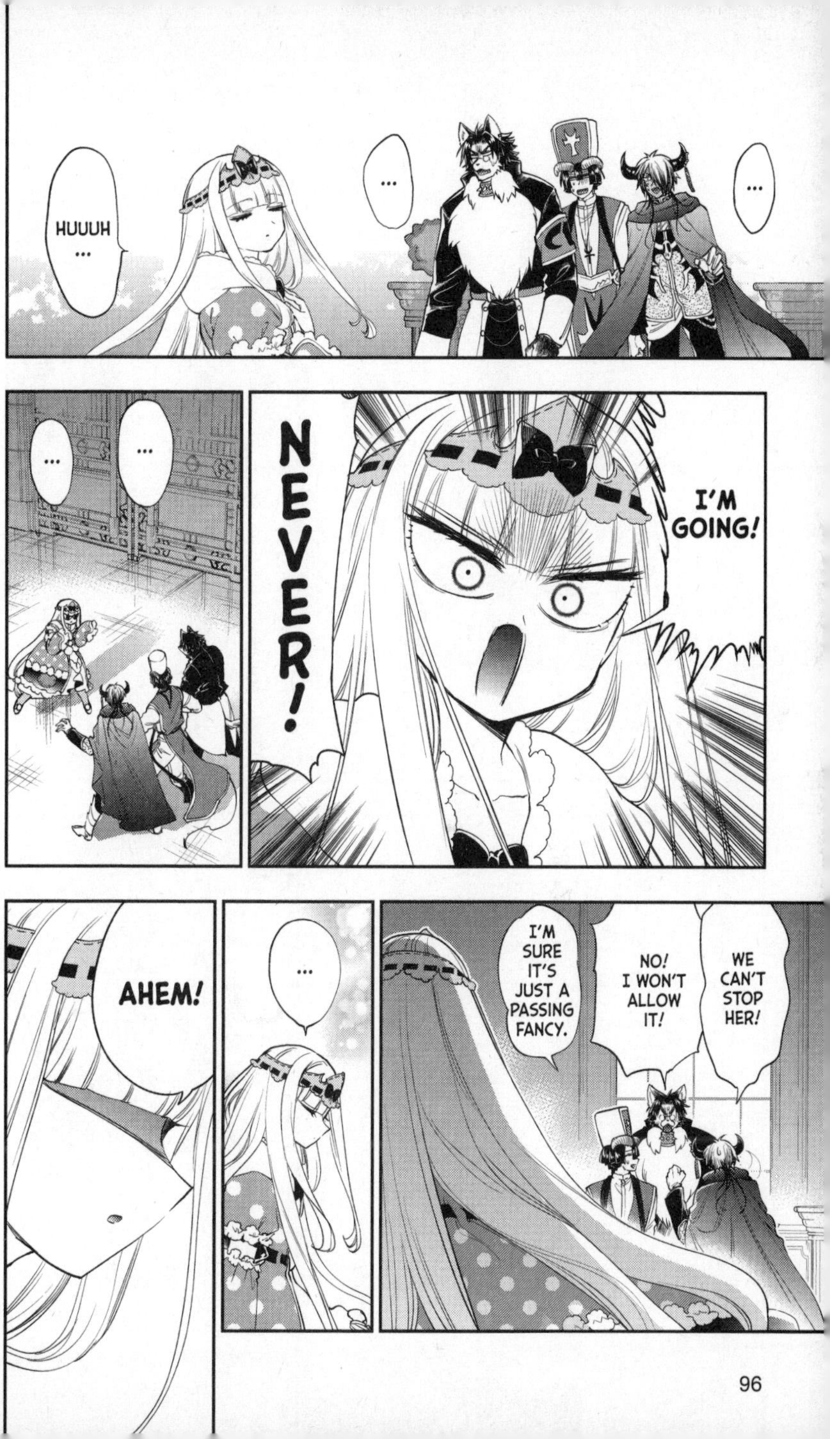
...
...
HUUUH ...
I'M GOING!
NEVER!
...
...
WE CAN'T STOP HER!
NO! I WON'T ALLOW IT!
I'M SURE IT'S JUST A PASSING FANCY.
...
AHEM!

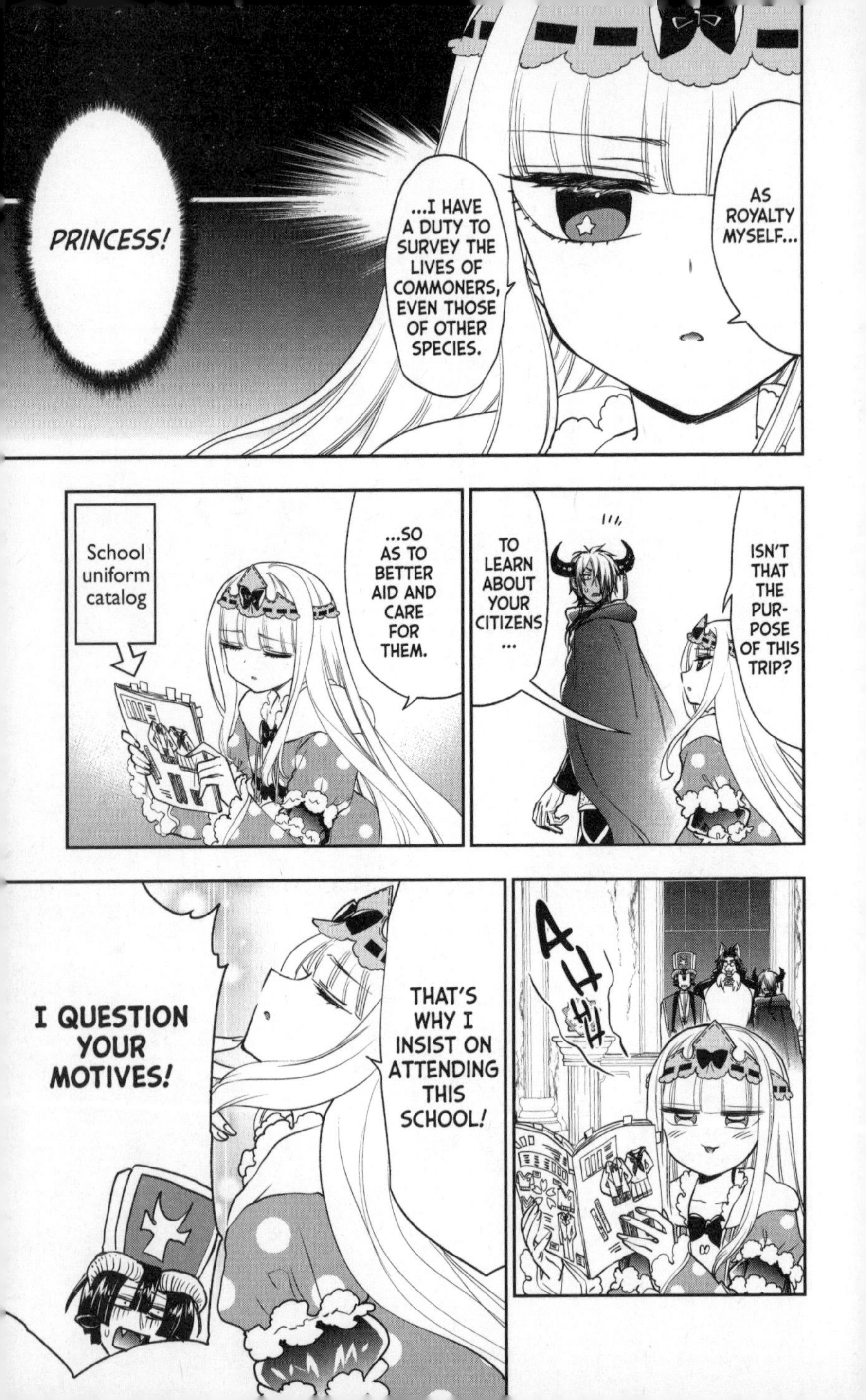
AS ROYALTY MYSELF...
...I HAVE A DUTY TO SURVEY THE LIVES OF COMMONERS, EVEN THOSE OF OTHER SPECIES.
PRINCESS!
ISN'T THAT THE PURPOSE OF THIS TRIP?
TO LEARN ABOUT YOUR CITIZENS...
...SO AS TO BETTER AID AND CARE FOR THEM.
School uniform catalog
AHHH
THAT'S WHY I INSIST ON ATTENDING THIS SCHOOL!
I QUESTION YOUR MOTIVES!

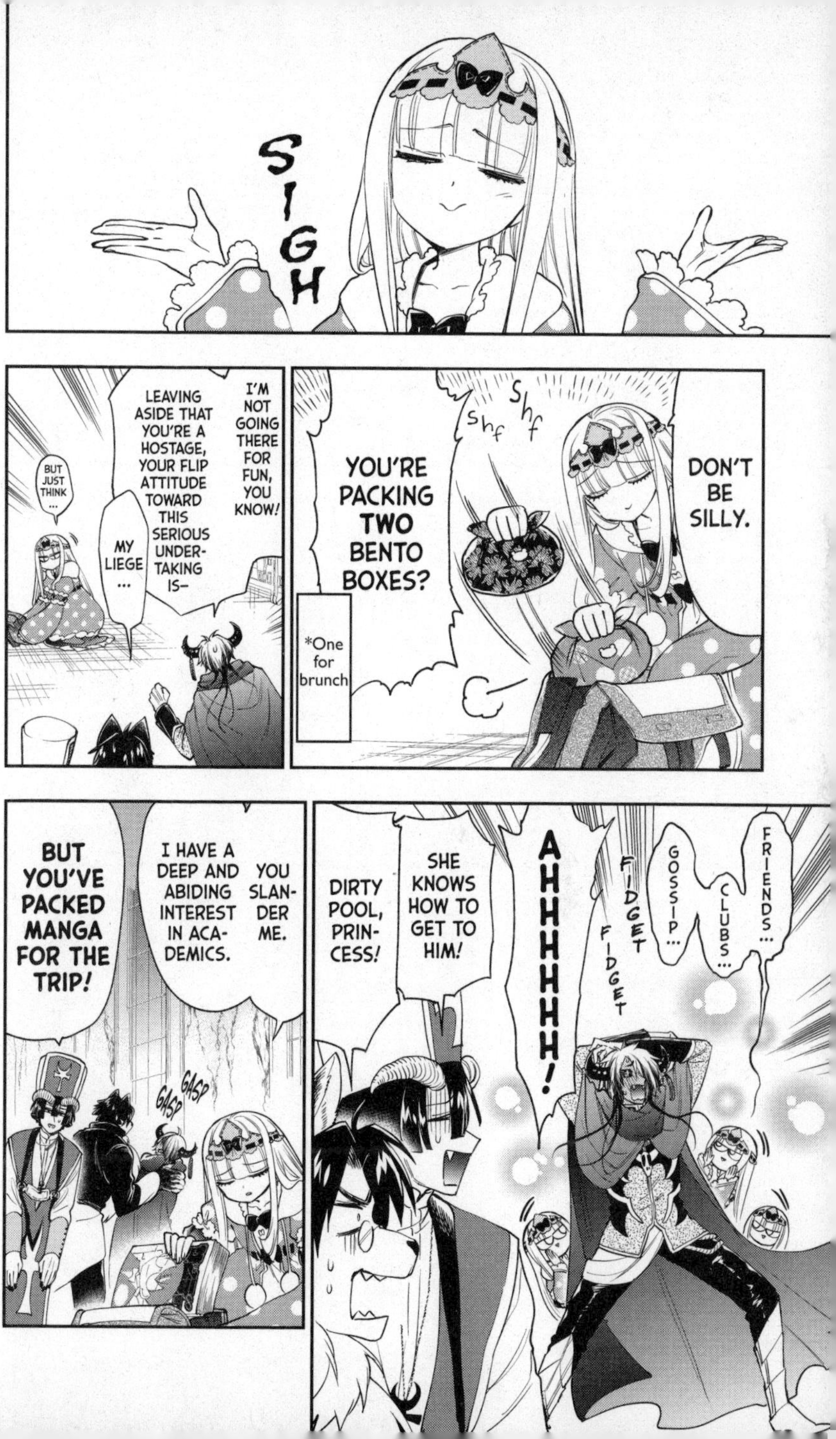
SIGH
DON'T BE SILLY.
shf shf
YOU'RE PACKING TWO BENTO BOXES?
*One for brunch
I'M NOT GOING THERE FOR FUN, YOU KNOW!
LEAVING ASIDE THAT YOU'RE A HOSTAGE, YOUR FLIP ATTITUDE TOWARD THIS SERIOUS UNDER-TAKING IS—
MY LIEGE...
BUT JUST THINK...
FRIENDS...
CLUBS...
GOSSIP...
FIDGET
FIDGET
AHHHHHHH!
SHE KNOWS HOW TO GET TO HIM!
DIRTY POOL, PRIN-CESS!
YOU SLAN-DER ME.
I HAVE A DEEP AND ABIDING INTEREST IN ACA-DEMICS.
BUT YOU'VE PACKED MANGA FOR THE TRIP!
GASP
GASP

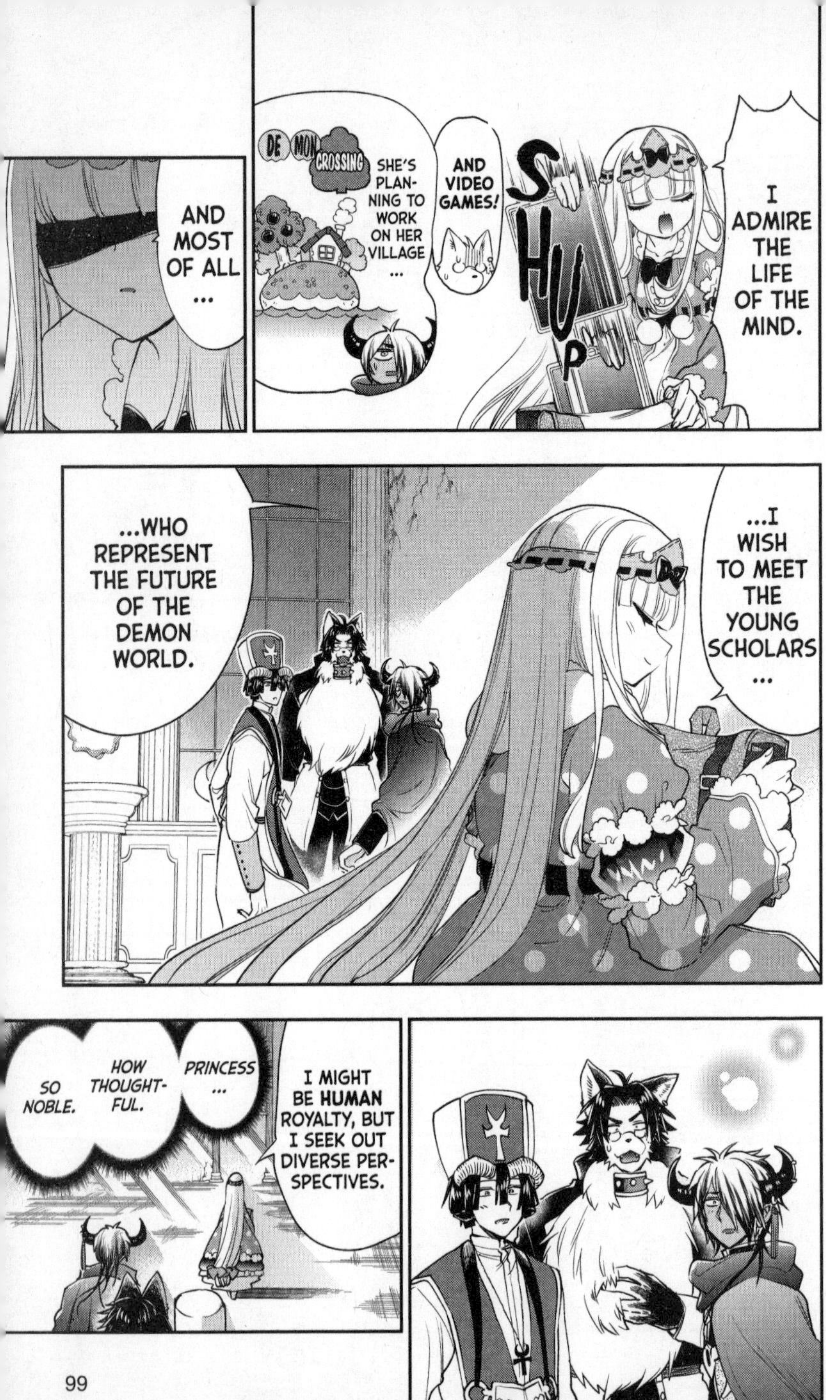
I ADMIRE THE LIFE OF THE MIND.
SHUP
AND VIDEO GAMES!
SHE'S PLAN-NING TO WORK ON HER VILLAGE ...
DE MON CROSSING
AND MOST OF ALL ...
...I WISH TO MEET THE YOUNG SCHOLARS ...
...WHO REPRESENT THE FUTURE OF THE DEMON WORLD.
I MIGHT BE **HUMAN** ROYALTY, BUT I SEEK OUT DIVERSE PER-SPECTIVES.
PRINCESS ...
HOW THOUGHT-FUL.
SO NOBLE.

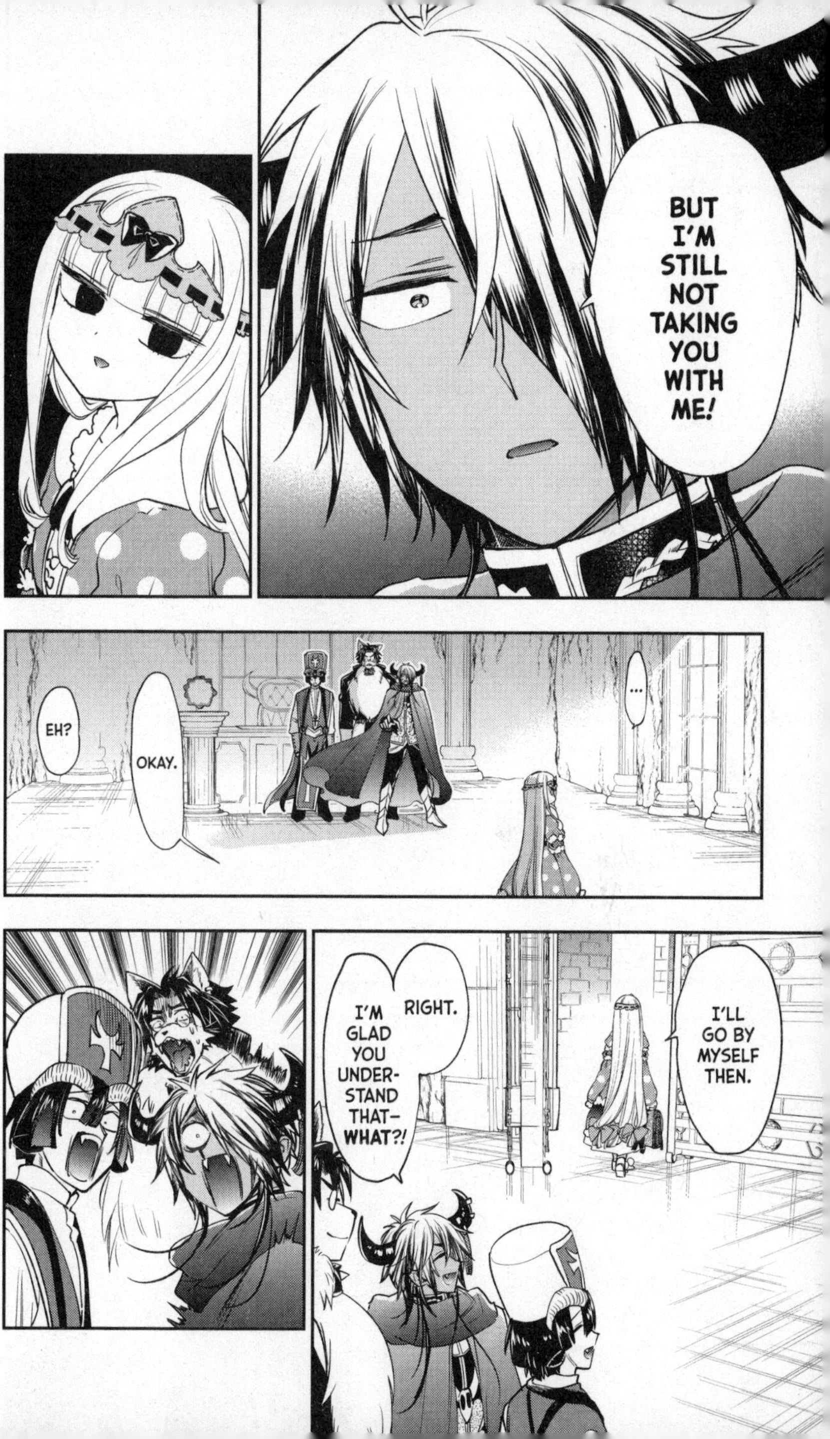
BUT I'M STILL NOT TAKING YOU WITH ME!
...
OKAY.
EH?
I'LL GO BY MYSELF THEN.
RIGHT.
I'M GLAD YOU UNDER-STAND THAT— WHAT?!

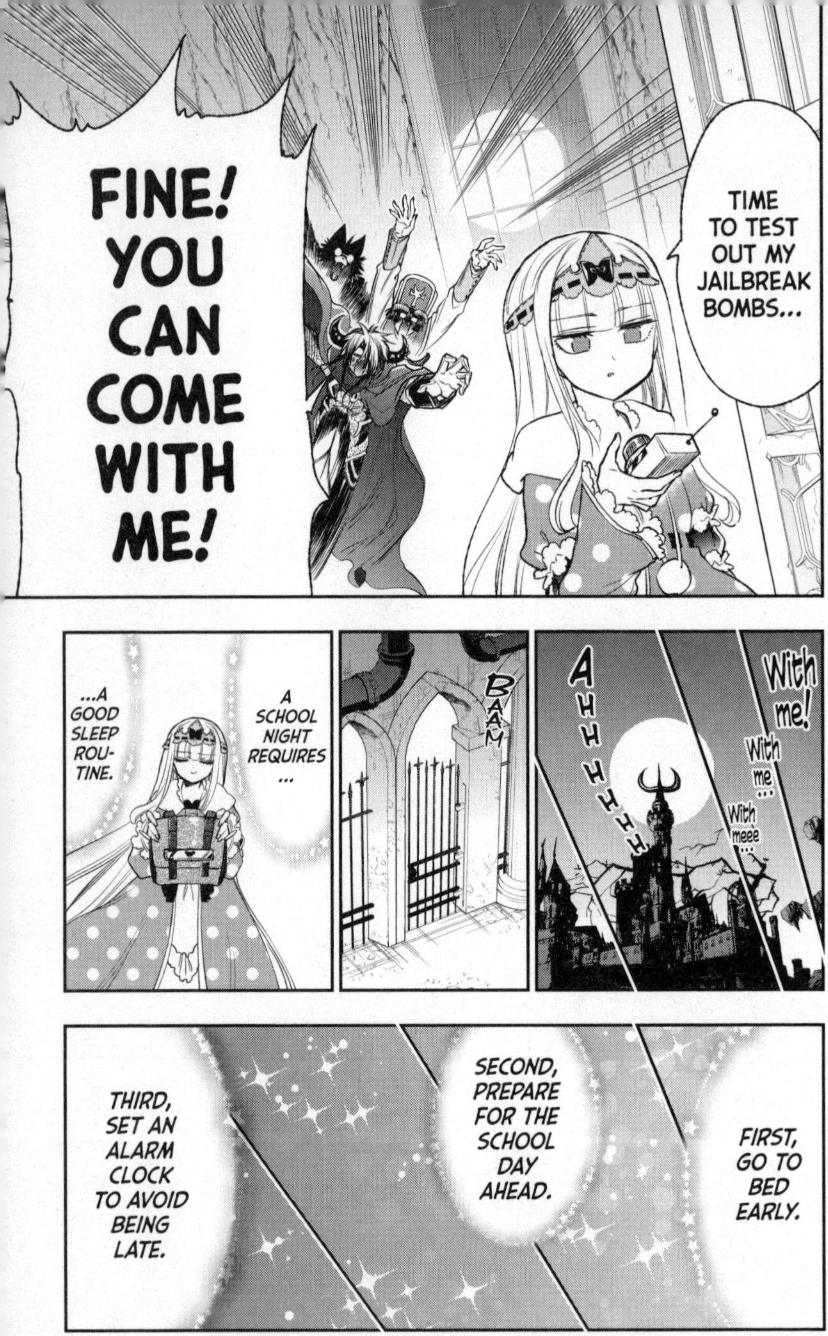
TIME TO TEST OUT MY JAILBREAK BOMBS...
FINE! YOU CAN COME WITH ME!
With me!
With me...
With meee...
AHHHHHH
BAAM
A SCHOOL NIGHT REQUIRES...
...A GOOD SLEEP ROUTINE.
FIRST, GO TO BED EARLY.
SECOND, PREPARE FOR THE SCHOOL DAY AHEAD.
THIRD, SET AN ALARM CLOCK TO AVOID BEING LATE.

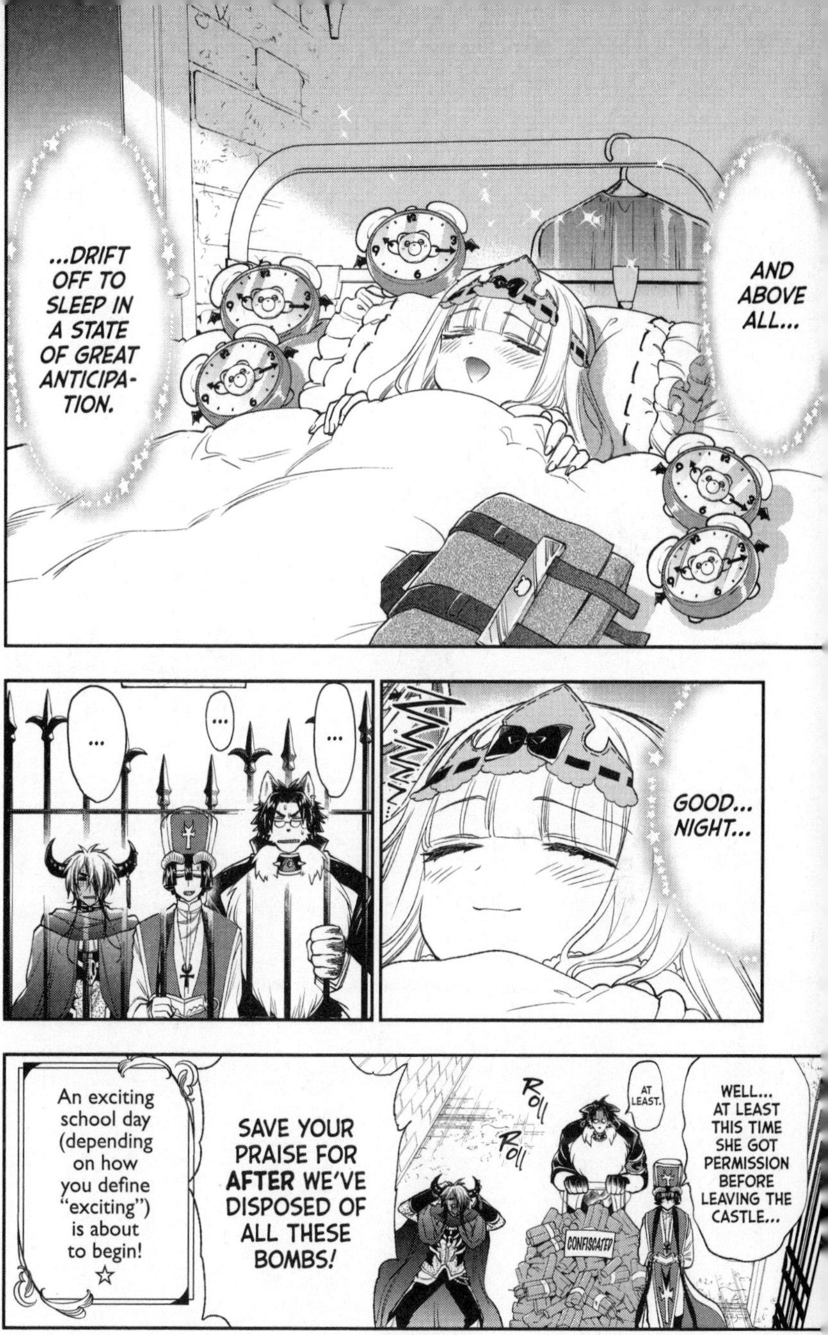
AND ABOVE ALL...
...DRIFT OFF TO SLEEP IN A STATE OF GREAT ANTICIPATION.
GOOD... NIGHT...
...
...
...
WELL... AT LEAST THIS TIME SHE GOT PERMISSION BEFORE LEAVING THE CASTLE...
AT LEAST.
ROLL
ROLL
CONFISCATED
SAVE YOUR PRAISE FOR AFTER WE'VE DISPOSED OF ALL THESE BOMBS!
An exciting school day (depending on how you define "exciting") is about to begin! ☆

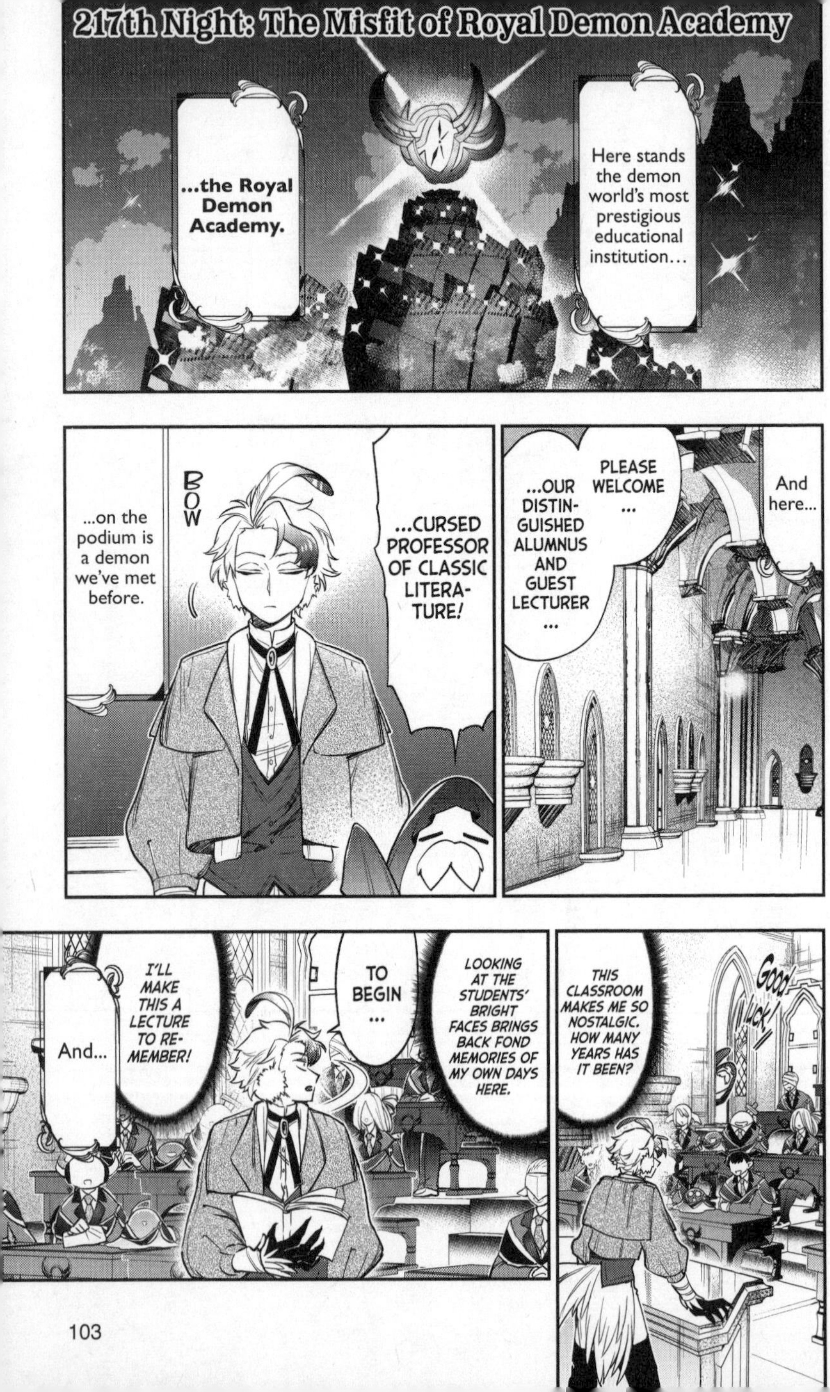
217th Night: The Misfit of Royal Demon Academy
Here stands the demon world's most prestigious educational institution…
...the Royal Demon Academy.
And here...
PLEASE WELCOME ...
...OUR DISTIN-GUISHED ALUMNUS AND GUEST LECTURER ...
...CURSED PROFESSOR OF CLASSIC LITERA-TURE!
BOW
...on the podium is a demon we've met before.
Good luck!
THIS CLASSROOM MAKES ME SO NOSTALGIC. HOW MANY YEARS HAS IT BEEN?
LOOKING AT THE STUDENTS' BRIGHT FACES BRINGS BACK FOND MEMORIES OF MY OWN DAYS HERE.
TO BEGIN ...
I'LL MAKE THIS A LECTURE TO RE-MEMBER!
And...

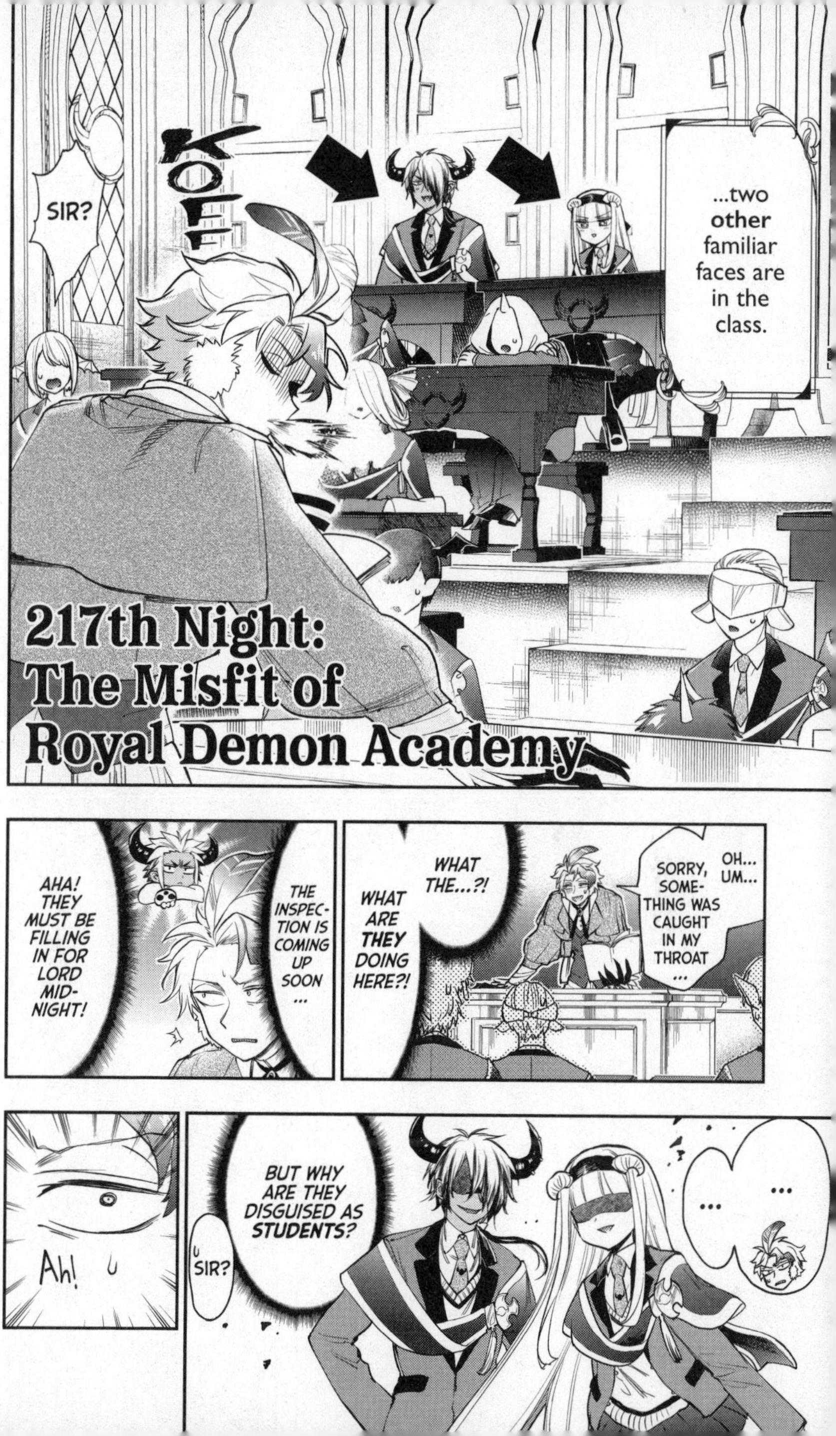
...two other familiar faces are in the class.
KOFF
SIR?
217th Night: The Misfit of Royal Demon Academy
OH... UM...
SORRY, SOMETHING WAS CAUGHT IN MY THROAT...
WHAT THE...?!
WHAT ARE THEY DOING HERE?!
THE INSPECTION IS COMING UP SOON...
AHA! THEY MUST BE FILLING IN FOR LORD MIDNIGHT!
...
...
BUT WHY ARE THEY DISGUISED AS STUDENTS?
SIR?
Ah!

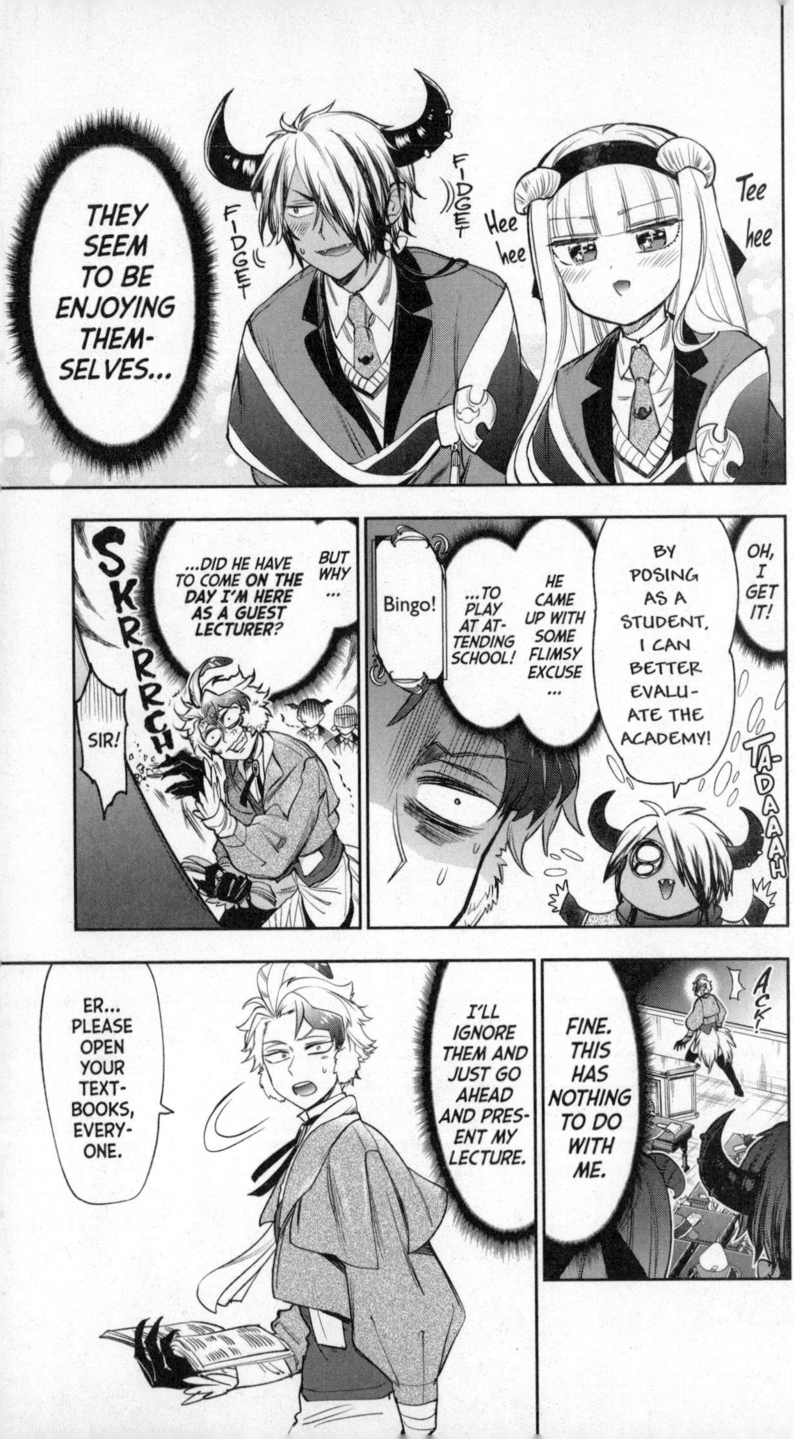
Tee hee
Hee hee
FIDGET
FIDGET
THEY SEEM TO BE ENJOYING THEM-SELVES...
OH, I GET IT!
BY POSING AS A STUDENT, I CAN BETTER EVALU-ATE THE ACADEMY!
TA-DAAAAAH
HE CAME UP WITH SOME FLIMSY EXCUSE...
...TO PLAY AT AT-TENDING SCHOOL!
Bingo!
BUT WHY...
...DID HE HAVE TO COME ON THE DAY I'M HERE AS A GUEST LECTURER?
SKRRRCH
SIR!
ACK!
FINE. THIS HAS NOTHING TO DO WITH ME.
I'LL IGNORE THEM AND JUST GO AHEAD AND PRES-ENT MY LECTURE.
ER... PLEASE OPEN YOUR TEXT-BOOKS, EVERY-ONE.

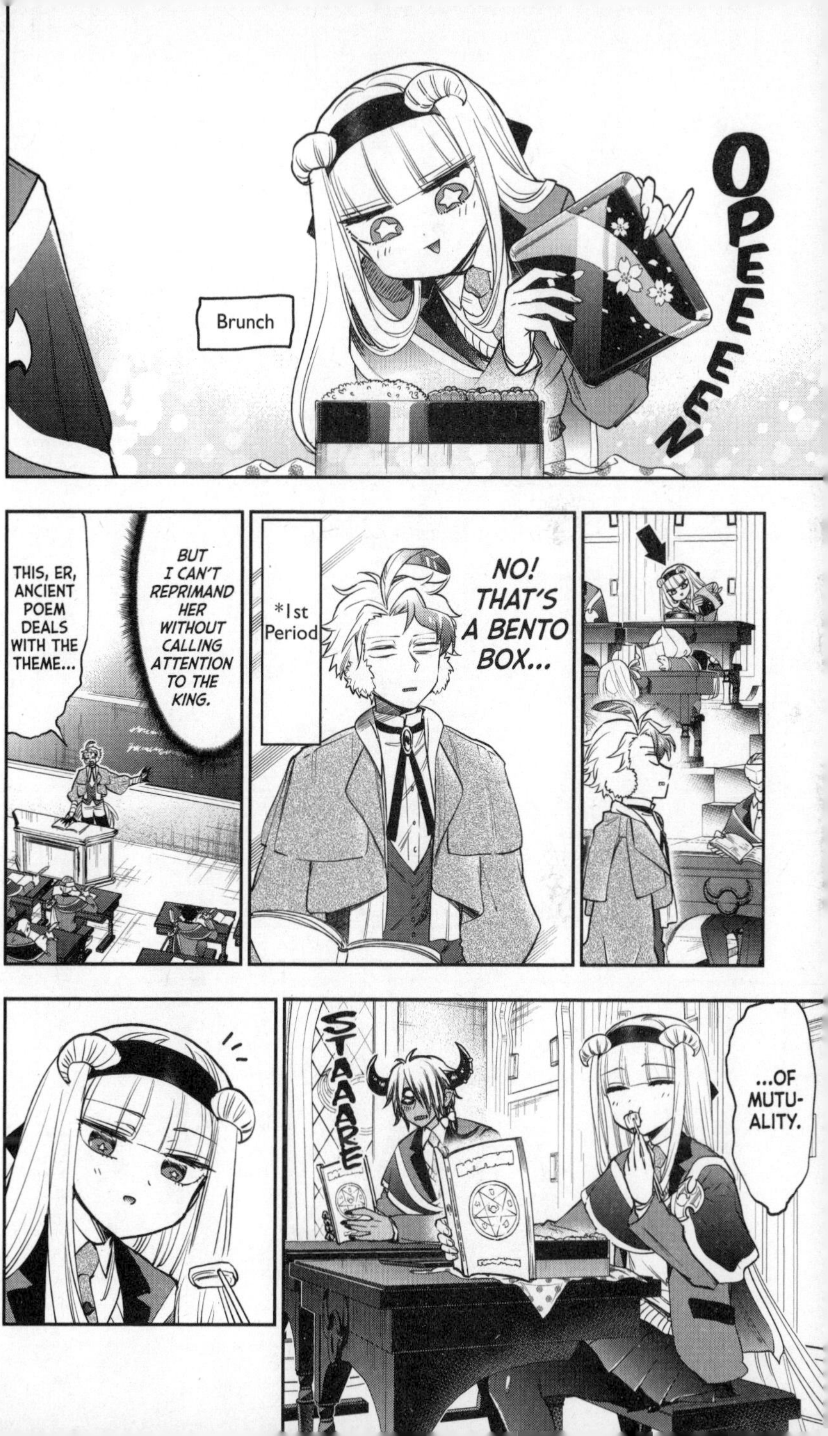
OPEEEEEN
Brunch
NO! THAT'S A BENTO BOX...
*1st Period
BUT I CAN'T REPRIMAND HER WITHOUT CALLING ATTENTION TO THE KING.
THIS, ER, ANCIENT POEM DEALS WITH THE THEME...
...OF MUTUALITY.
STAAARE

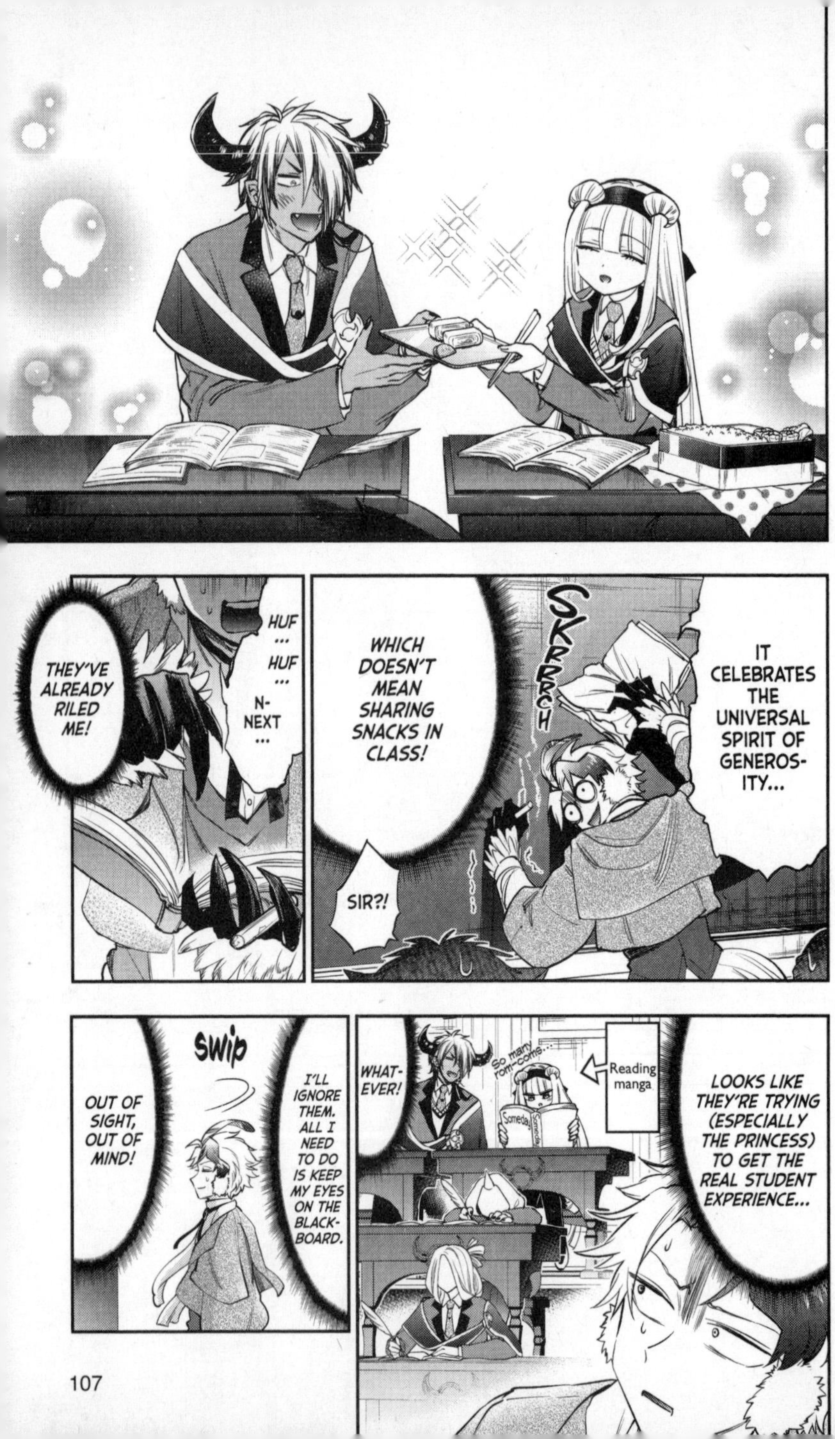
IT CELEBRATES THE UNIVERSAL SPIRIT OF GENEROS-ITY...
SKRRRCH
WHICH DOESN'T MEAN SHARING SNACKS IN CLASS!
SIR?!
HUF... HUF... N-NEXT...
THEY'VE ALREADY RILED ME!
LOOKS LIKE THEY'RE TRYING (ESPECIALLY THE PRINCESS) TO GET THE REAL STUDENT EXPERIENCE...
Reading manga
So many rom-coms...
WHAT-EVER!
I'LL IGNORE THEM. ALL I NEED TO DO IS KEEP MY EYES ON THE BLACK-BOARD.
SWIP
OUT OF SIGHT, OUT OF MIND!

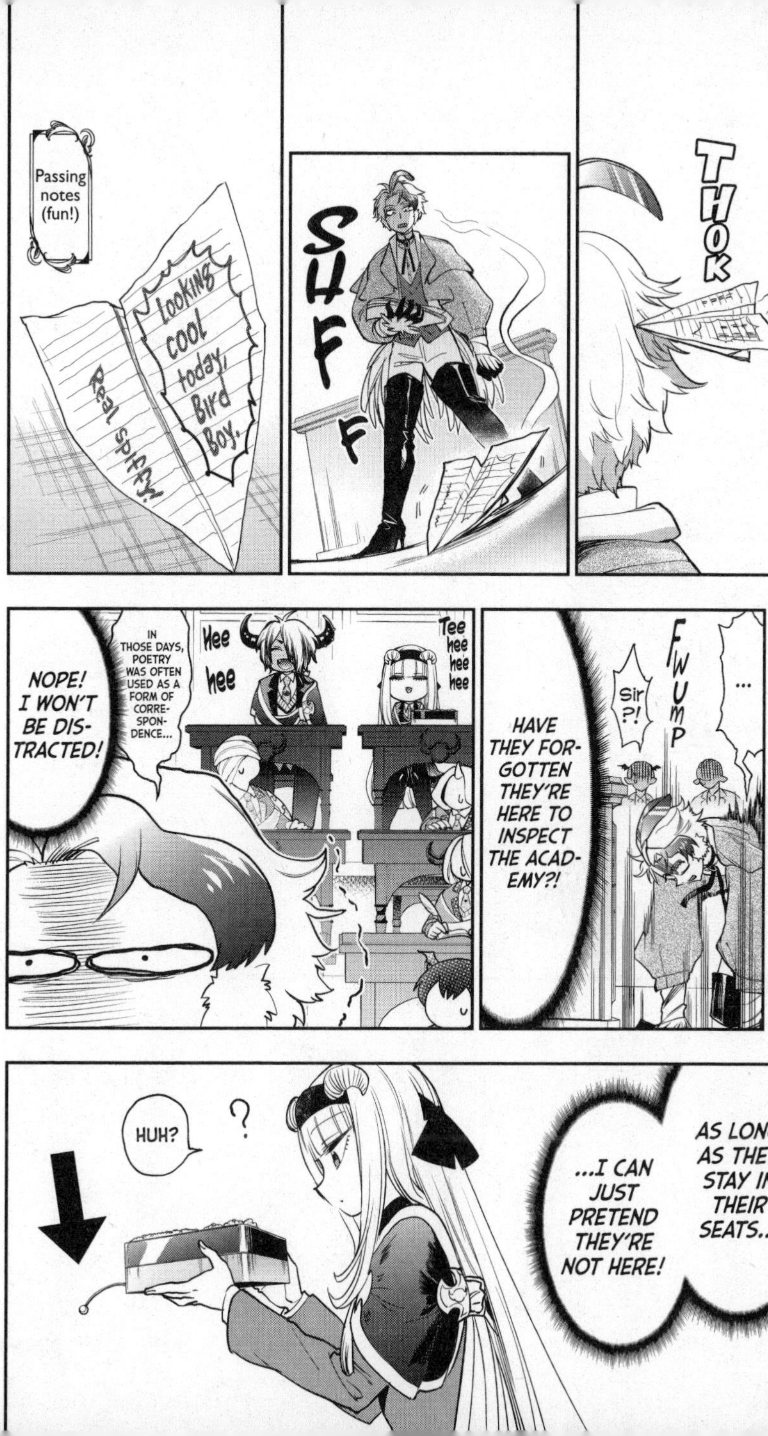
THOK
SHUFF
Passing notes (fun!)
Looking cool today, Bird Boy.
Real spiffy!
...
FWUMP
Sir?!
HAVE THEY FORGOTTEN THEY'RE HERE TO INSPECT THE ACADEMY?!
Tee hee hee hee
Hee hee
IN THOSE DAYS, POETRY WAS OFTEN USED AS A FORM OF CORRESPONDENCE...
NOPE! I WON'T BE DISTRACTED!
AS LONG AS THEY STAY IN THEIR SEATS...
...I CAN JUST PRETEND THEY'RE NOT HERE!
?
HUH?

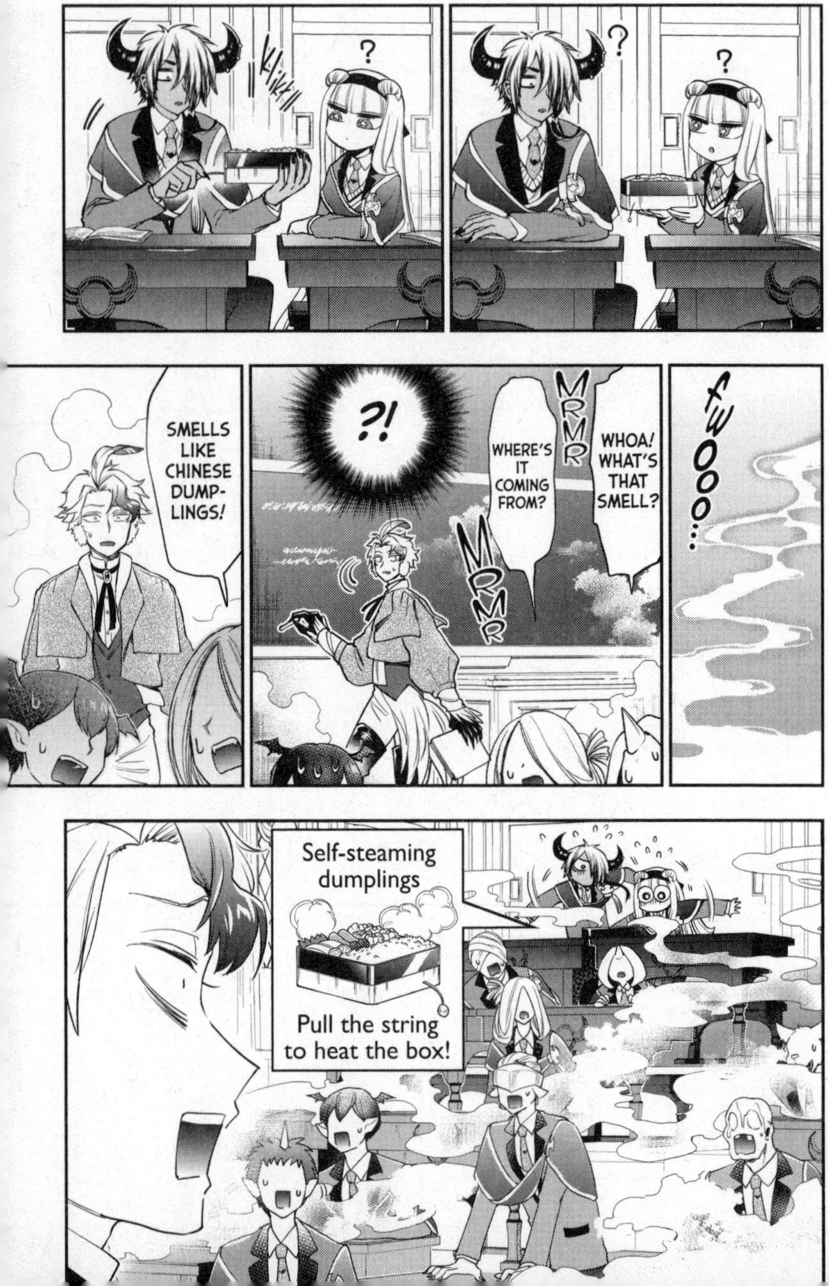
?
?
?
KLIKK
FWOOOO...
WHOA! WHAT'S THAT SMELL?
MRMR
WHERE'S IT COMING FROM?
MRMR
?!
SMELLS LIKE CHINESE DUMP-LINGS!
Self-steaming dumplings
Pull the string to heat the box!

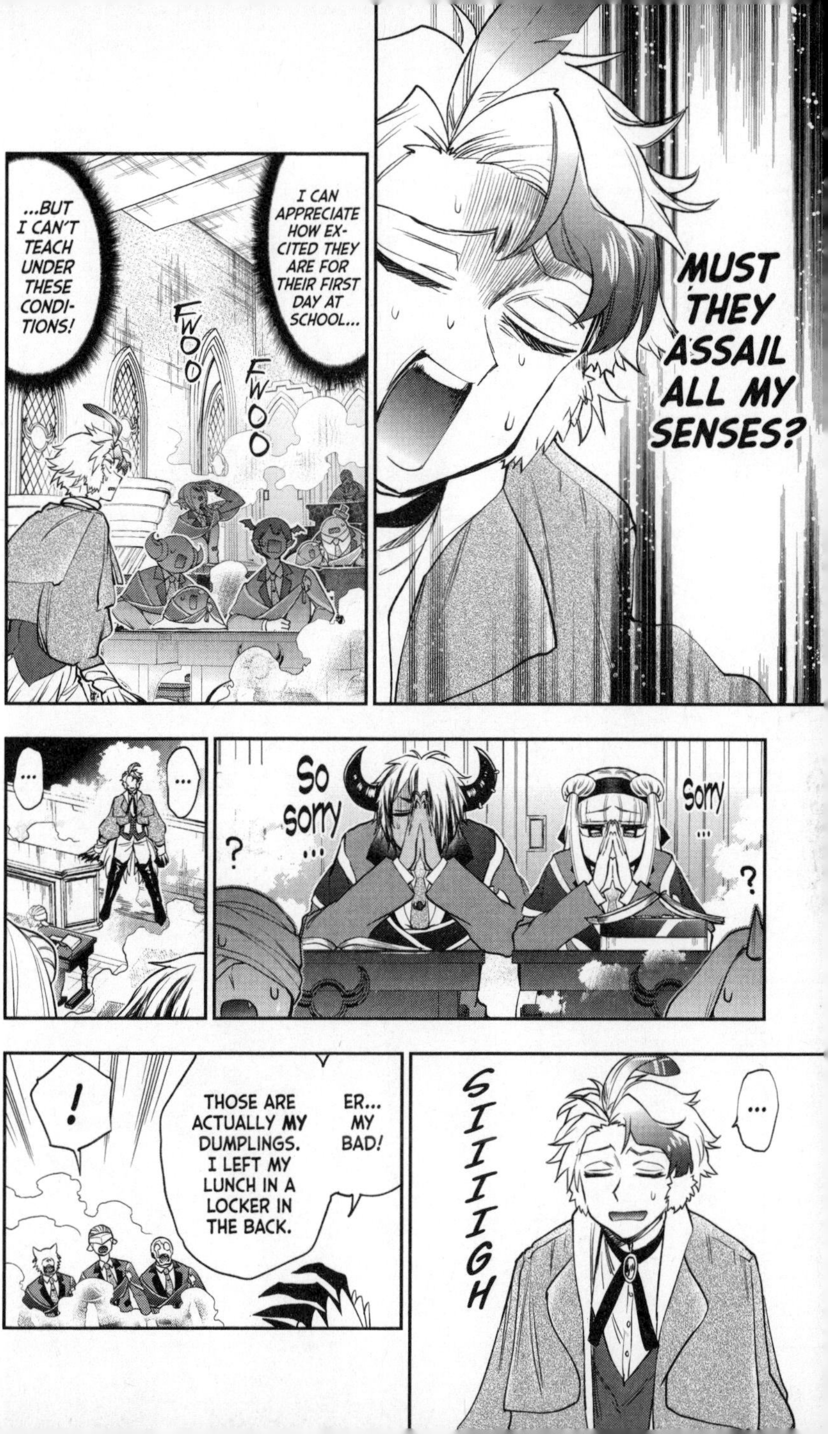
MUST THEY ASSAIL ALL MY SENSES?
I CAN APPRECIATE HOW EXCITED THEY ARE FOR THEIR FIRST DAY AT SCHOOL...
...BUT I CAN'T TEACH UNDER THESE CONDITIONS!
FWOO
FWOO
Sorry...
?
So sorry...
?
...
...
SIIIIGH
...
ER... MY BAD!
THOSE ARE ACTUALLY MY DUMPLINGS. I LEFT MY LUNCH IN A LOCKER IN THE BACK.
!

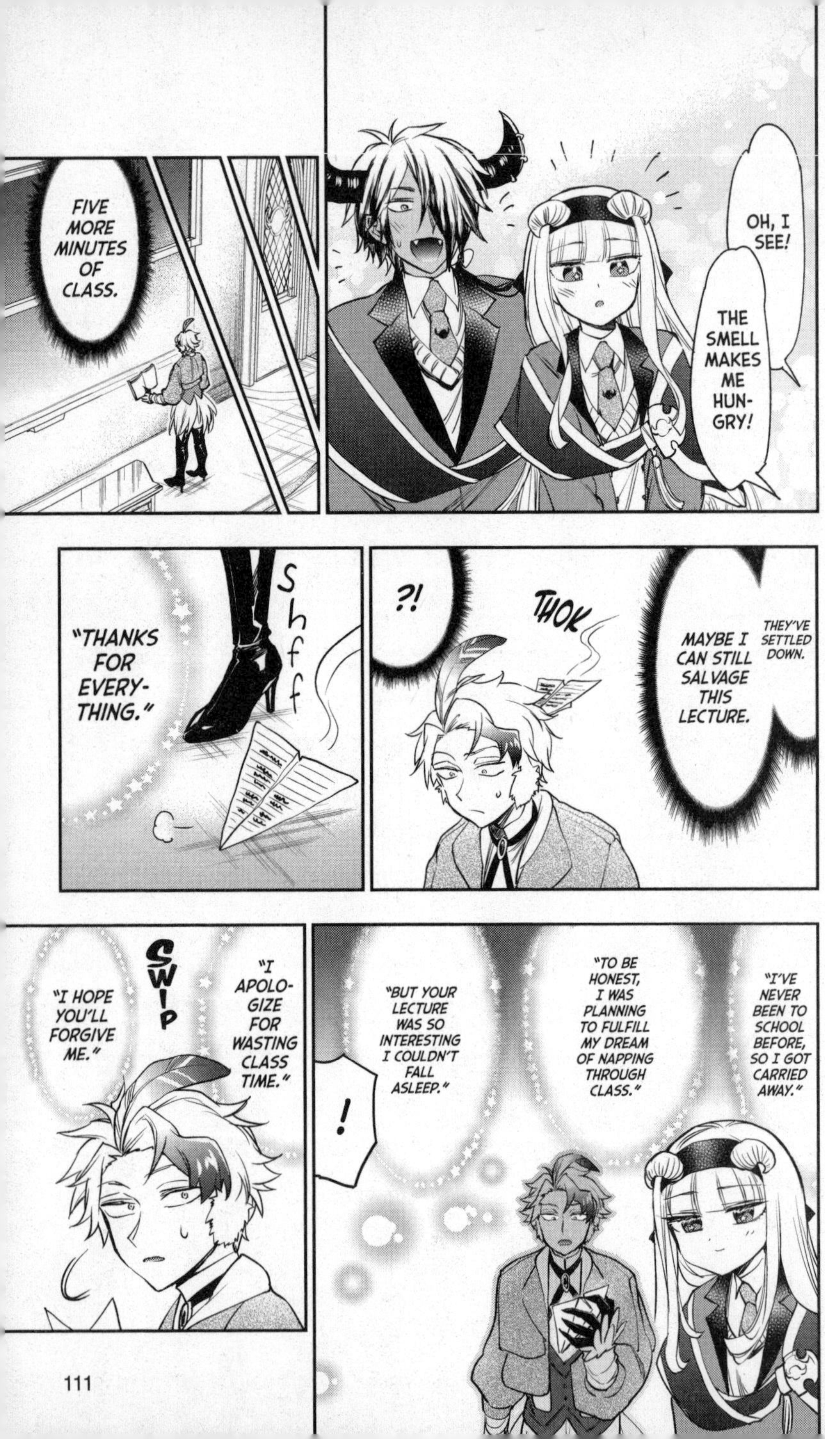
OH, I SEE!
THE SMELL MAKES ME HUNGRY!
FIVE MORE MINUTES OF CLASS.
THEY'VE SETTLED DOWN.
MAYBE I CAN STILL SALVAGE THIS LECTURE.
THOK
?!
Shff
"THANKS FOR EVERY-THING."
"I'VE NEVER BEEN TO SCHOOL BEFORE, SO I GOT CARRIED AWAY."
"TO BE HONEST, I WAS PLANNING TO FULFILL MY DREAM OF NAPPING THROUGH CLASS."
"BUT YOUR LECTURE WAS SO INTERESTING I COULDN'T FALL ASLEEP."
!
"I APOLO-GIZE FOR WASTING CLASS TIME."
SWIP
"I HOPE YOU'LL FORGIVE ME."

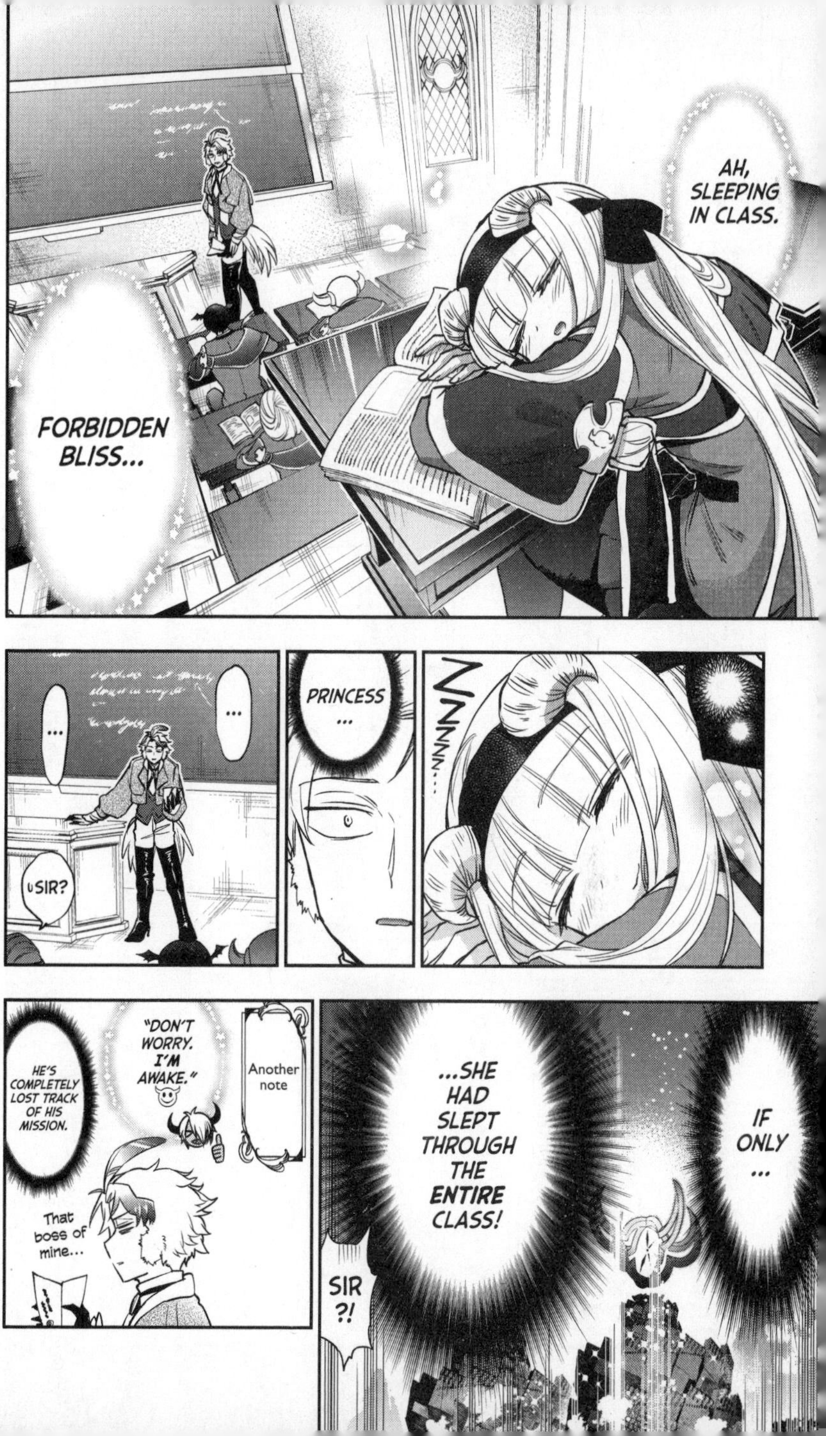
AH, SLEEPING IN CLASS.
FORBIDDEN BLISS...
ZZZZZZ...
PRINCESS ...
...
...
SIR?
IF ONLY ...
...SHE HAD SLEPT THROUGH THE ENTIRE CLASS!
SIR ?!
Another note
"DON'T WORRY. I'M AWAKE."
HE'S COMPLETELY LOST TRACK OF HIS MISSION.
That boss of mine...

218th Night: Dorm Rules

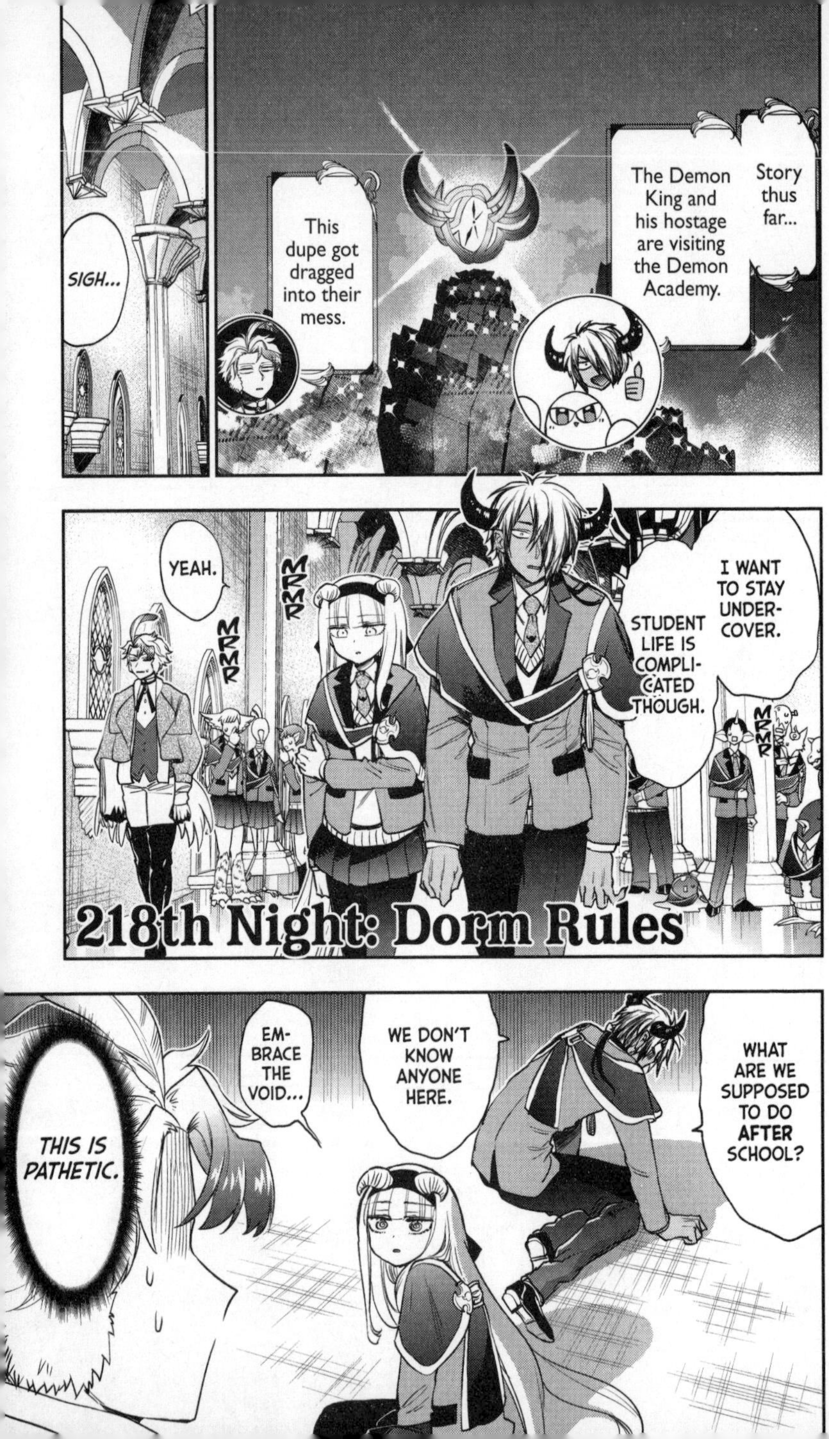
Story thus far...
The Demon King and his hostage are visiting the Demon Academy.
This dupe got dragged into their mess.
SIGH...
I WANT TO STAY UNDERCOVER.
STUDENT LIFE IS COMPLICATED THOUGH.
MRMR
MRMR
MRMR
YEAH.
WHAT ARE WE SUPPOSED TO DO AFTER SCHOOL?
WE DON'T KNOW ANYONE HERE.
EMBRACE THE VOID...
THIS IS PATHETIC.

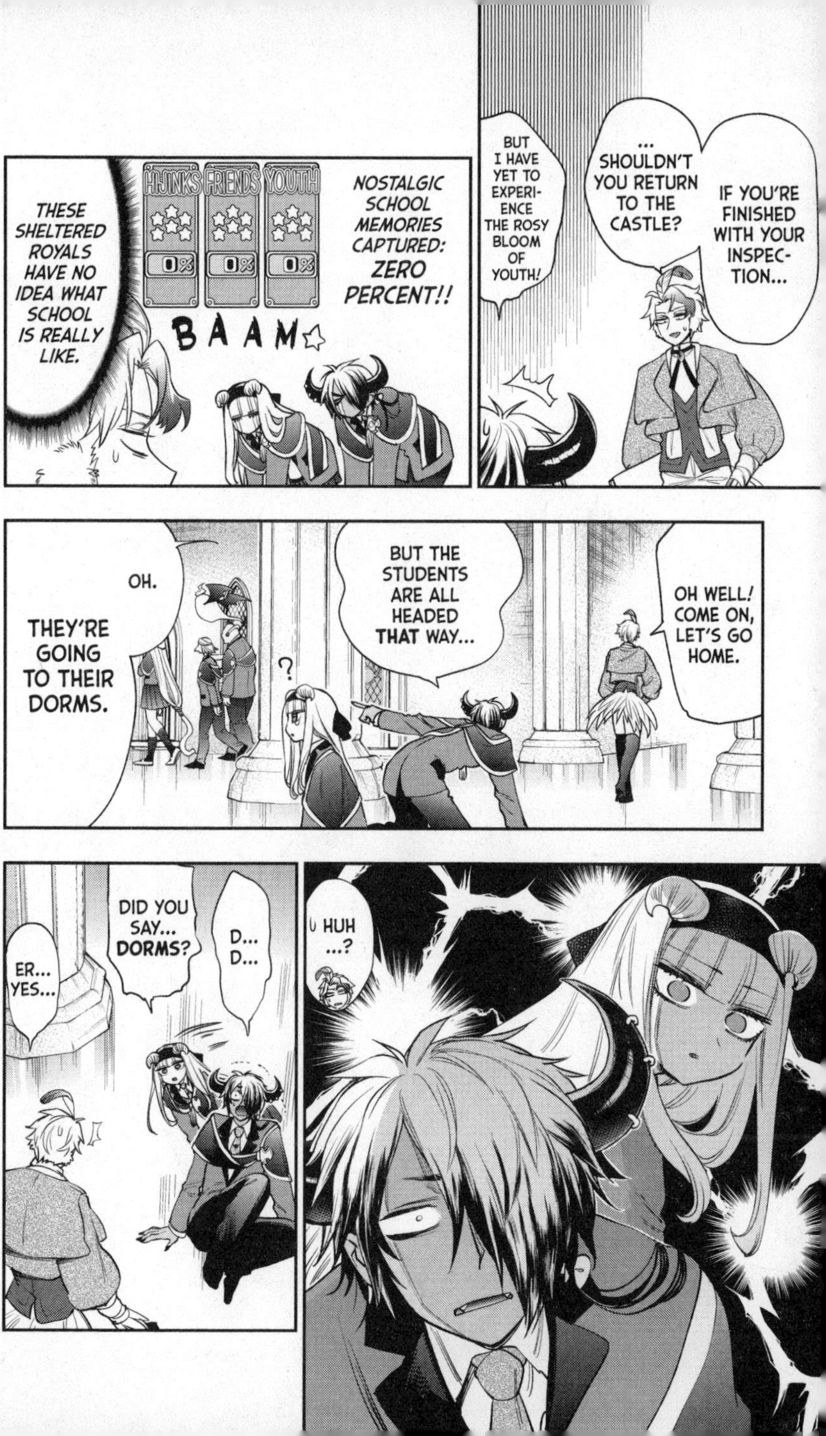
...SHOULDN'T YOU RETURN TO THE CASTLE?
IF YOU'RE FINISHED WITH YOUR INSPECTION...
BUT I HAVE YET TO EXPERIENCE THE ROSY BLOOM OF YOUTH!
NOSTALGIC SCHOOL MEMORIES CAPTURED: ZERO PERCENT!!
HIJINKS 0%
FRIENDS 0%
YOUTH 0%
BAAM
THESE SHELTERED ROYALS HAVE NO IDEA WHAT SCHOOL IS REALLY LIKE.
OH WELL! COME ON, LET'S GO HOME.
BUT THE STUDENTS ARE ALL HEADED THAT WAY...
?
OH.
THEY'RE GOING TO THEIR DORMS.
HUH ...?
D... D...
DID YOU SAY... DORMS?
ER... YES...

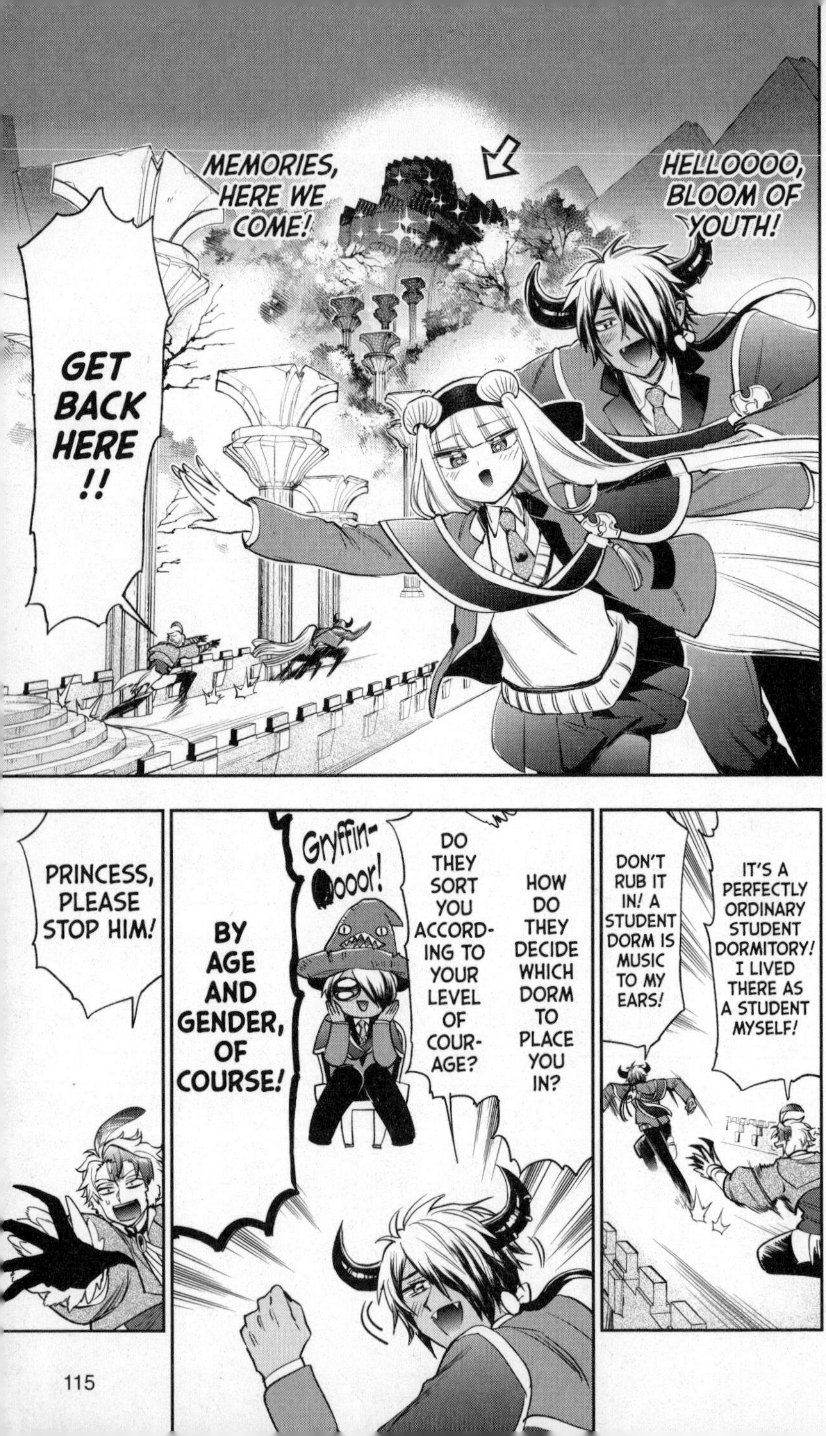
HELLOOOO, BLOOM OF YOUTH!
MEMORIES, HERE WE COME!
GET BACK HERE!!
IT'S A PERFECTLY ORDINARY STUDENT DORMITORY! I LIVED THERE AS A STUDENT MYSELF!
DON'T RUB IT IN! A STUDENT DORM IS MUSIC TO MY EARS!
HOW DO THEY DECIDE WHICH DORM TO PLACE YOU IN?
DO THEY SORT YOU ACCORDING TO YOUR LEVEL OF COURAGE?
Gryffin-Dooor!
BY AGE AND GENDER, OF COURSE!
PRINCESS, PLEASE STOP HIM!

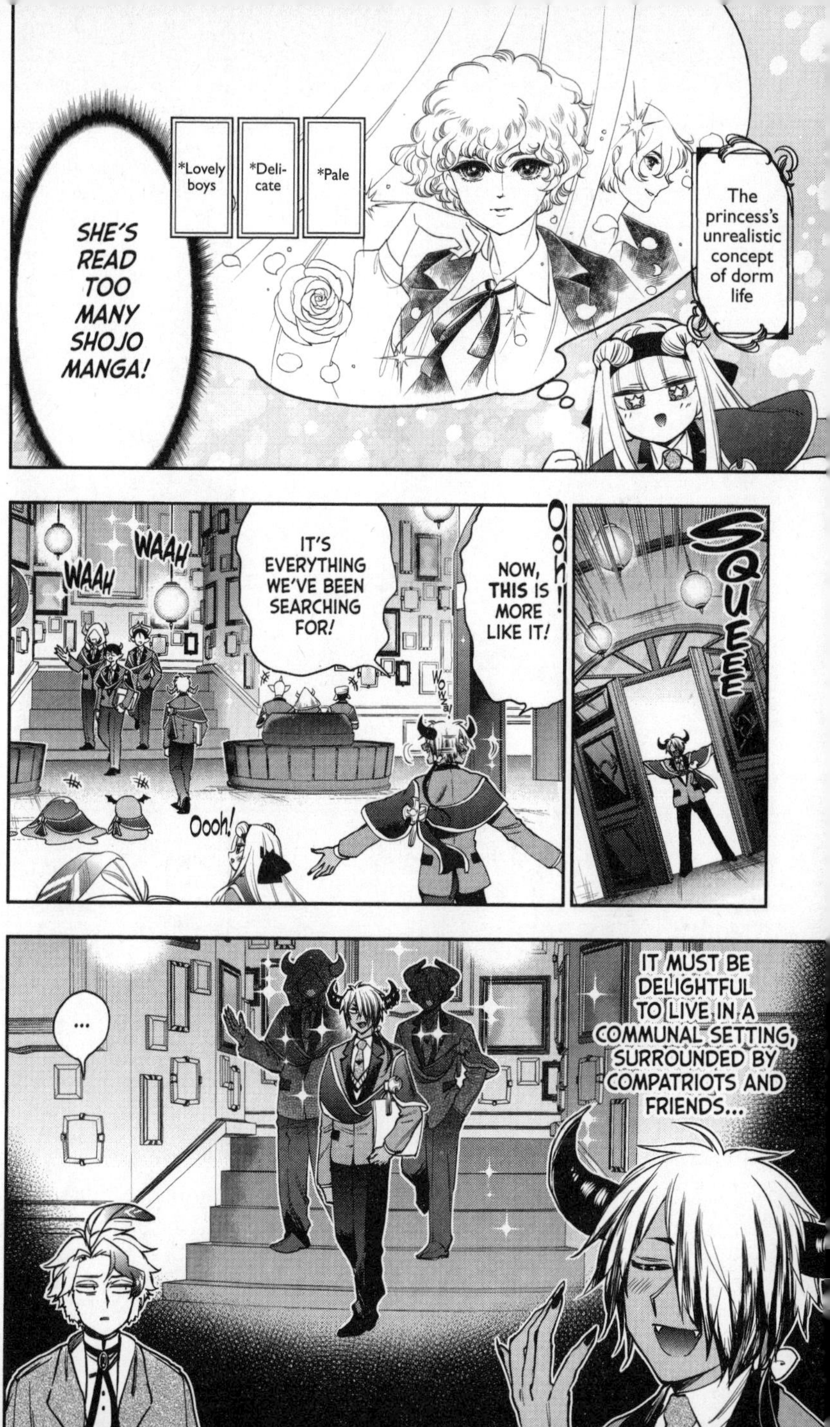
The princess's unrealistic concept of dorm life
*Pale
*Deli-cate
*Lovely boys
SHE'S READ TOO MANY SHOJO MANGA!
SQUEEE
Oooh!
NOW, THIS IS MORE LIKE IT!
IT'S EVERYTHING WE'VE BEEN SEARCHING FOR!
WAAH
WAAH
WOWZA!
Oooh!
IT MUST BE DELIGHTFUL TO LIVE IN A COMMUNAL SETTING, SURROUNDED BY COMPATRIOTS AND FRIENDS...
...

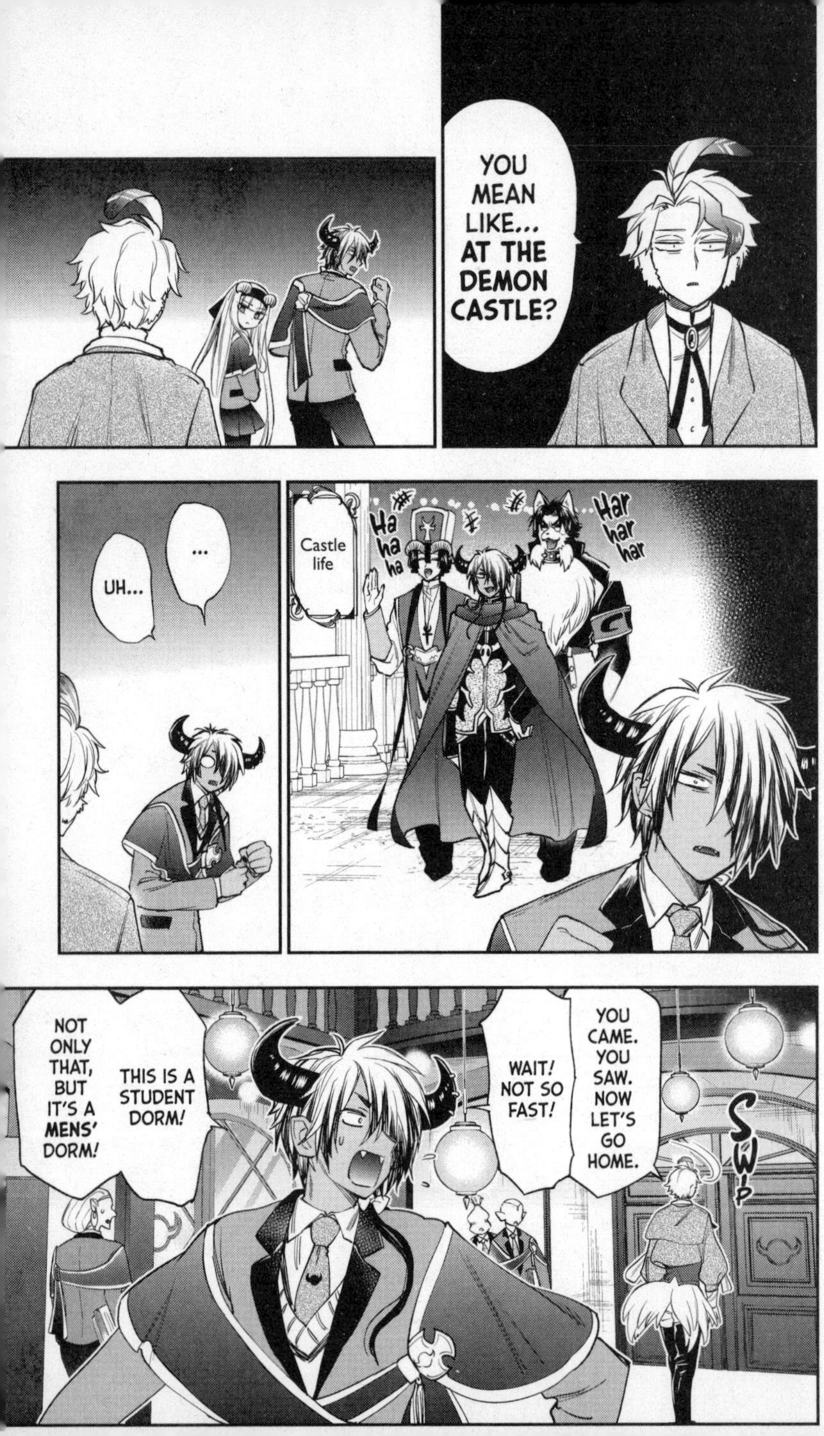
YOU MEAN LIKE... AT THE DEMON CASTLE?
Har har har
Ha ha ha
Castle life
...
UH...
YOU CAME. YOU SAW. NOW LET'S GO HOME.
SWIP
WAIT! NOT SO FAST!
THIS IS A STUDENT DORM!
NOT ONLY THAT, BUT IT'S A MENS' DORM!

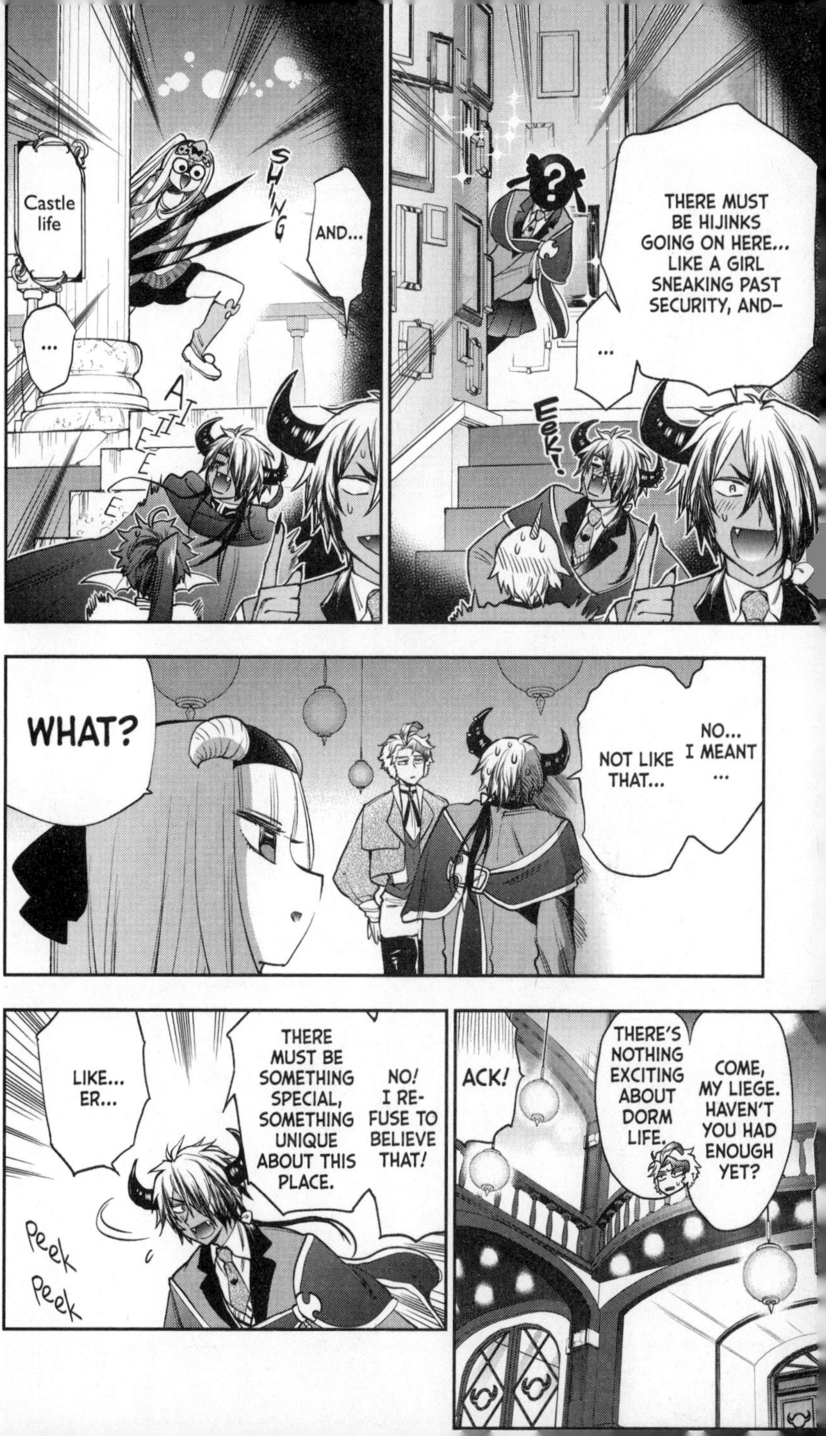
THERE MUST BE HIJINKS GOING ON HERE... LIKE A GIRL SNEAKING PAST SECURITY, AND–
...
EEK!
AND...
SHING
Castle life
...
AIIEEEE
NO... I MEANT ...
NOT LIKE THAT...
WHAT?
COME, MY LIEGE. HAVEN'T YOU HAD ENOUGH YET?
THERE'S NOTHING EXCITING ABOUT DORM LIFE.
ACK!
NO! I RE-FUSE TO BELIEVE THAT!
THERE MUST BE SOMETHING SPECIAL, SOMETHING UNIQUE ABOUT THIS PLACE.
LIKE... ER...
Peek Peek

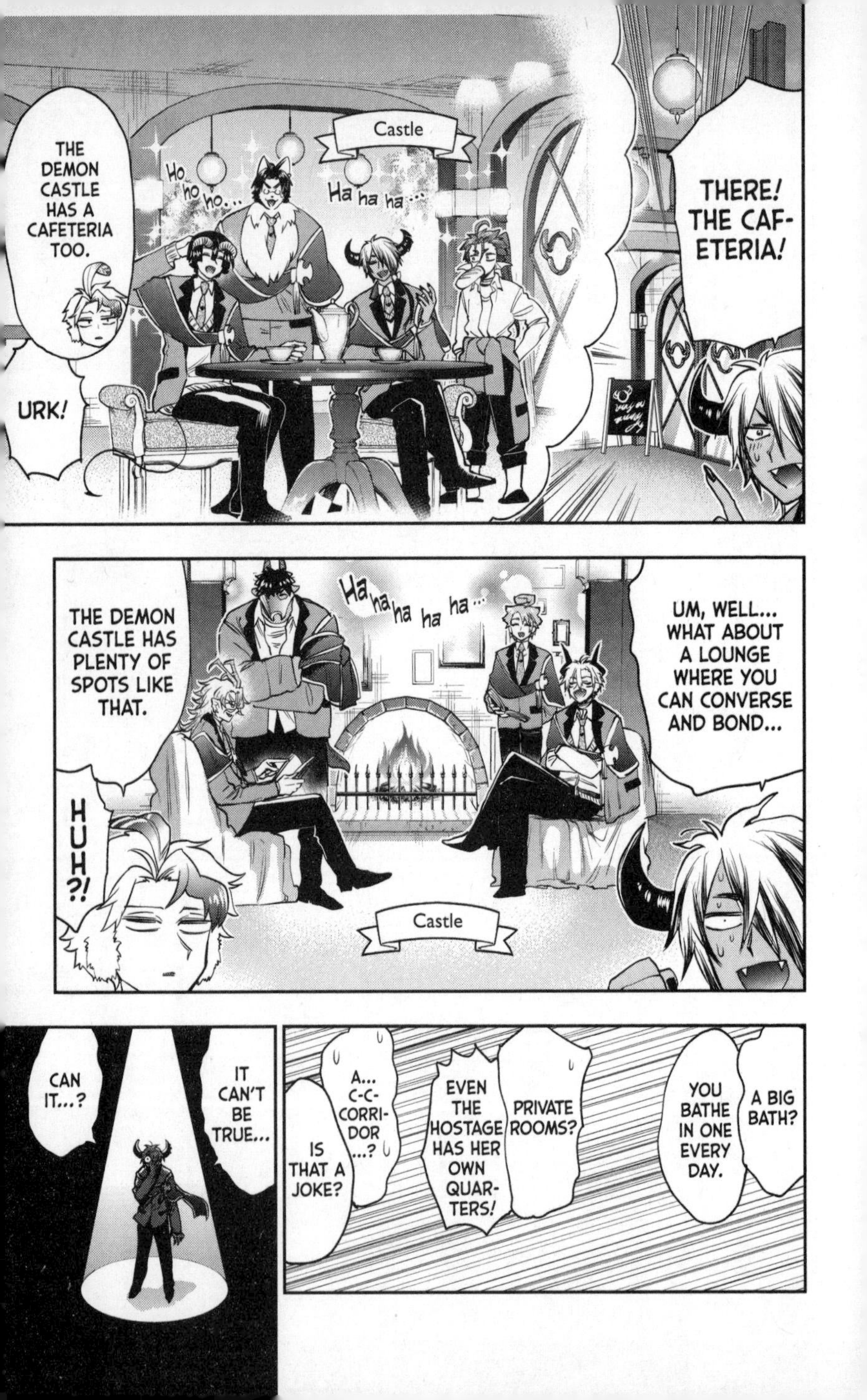
THERE! THE CAFETERIA!
Castle
Ha ha ha...
Ho ho ho...
THE DEMON CASTLE HAS A CAFETERIA TOO.
URK!
UM, WELL... WHAT ABOUT A LOUNGE WHERE YOU CAN CONVERSE AND BOND...
Ha ha ha ha ha...
THE DEMON CASTLE HAS PLENTY OF SPOTS LIKE THAT.
HUH?!
Castle
A BIG BATH?
YOU BATHE IN ONE EVERY DAY.
PRIVATE ROOMS?
EVEN THE HOSTAGE HAS HER OWN QUARTERS!
A... C-C-CORRIDOR...?
IS THAT A JOKE?
IT CAN'T BE TRUE...
CAN IT...?

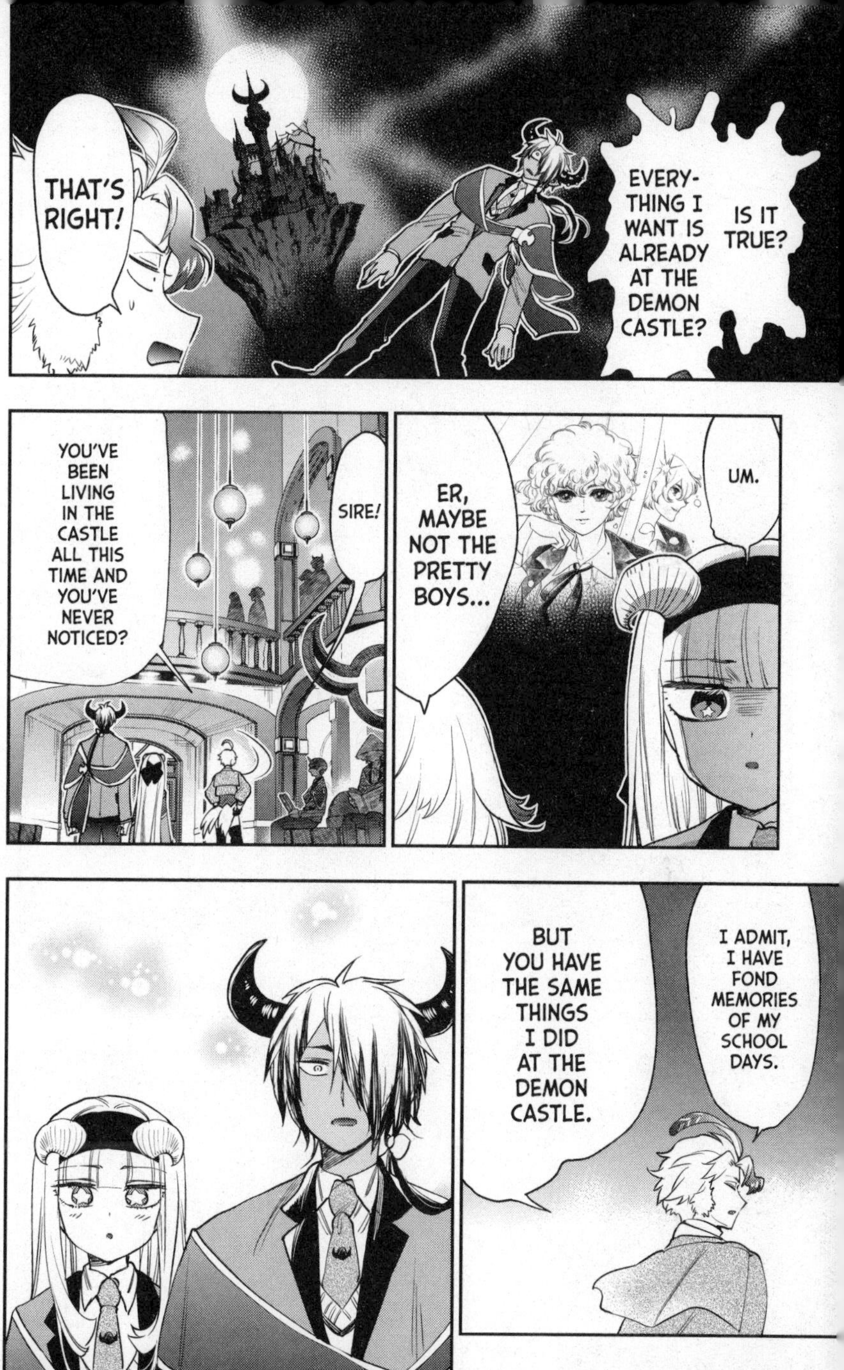
IS IT TRUE?
EVERY-THING I WANT IS ALREADY AT THE DEMON CASTLE?
THAT'S RIGHT!
UM.
ER, MAYBE NOT THE PRETTY BOYS...
SIRE!
YOU'VE BEEN LIVING IN THE CASTLE ALL THIS TIME AND YOU'VE NEVER NOTICED?
I ADMIT, I HAVE FOND MEMORIES OF MY SCHOOL DAYS.
BUT YOU HAVE THE SAME THINGS I DID AT THE DEMON CASTLE.

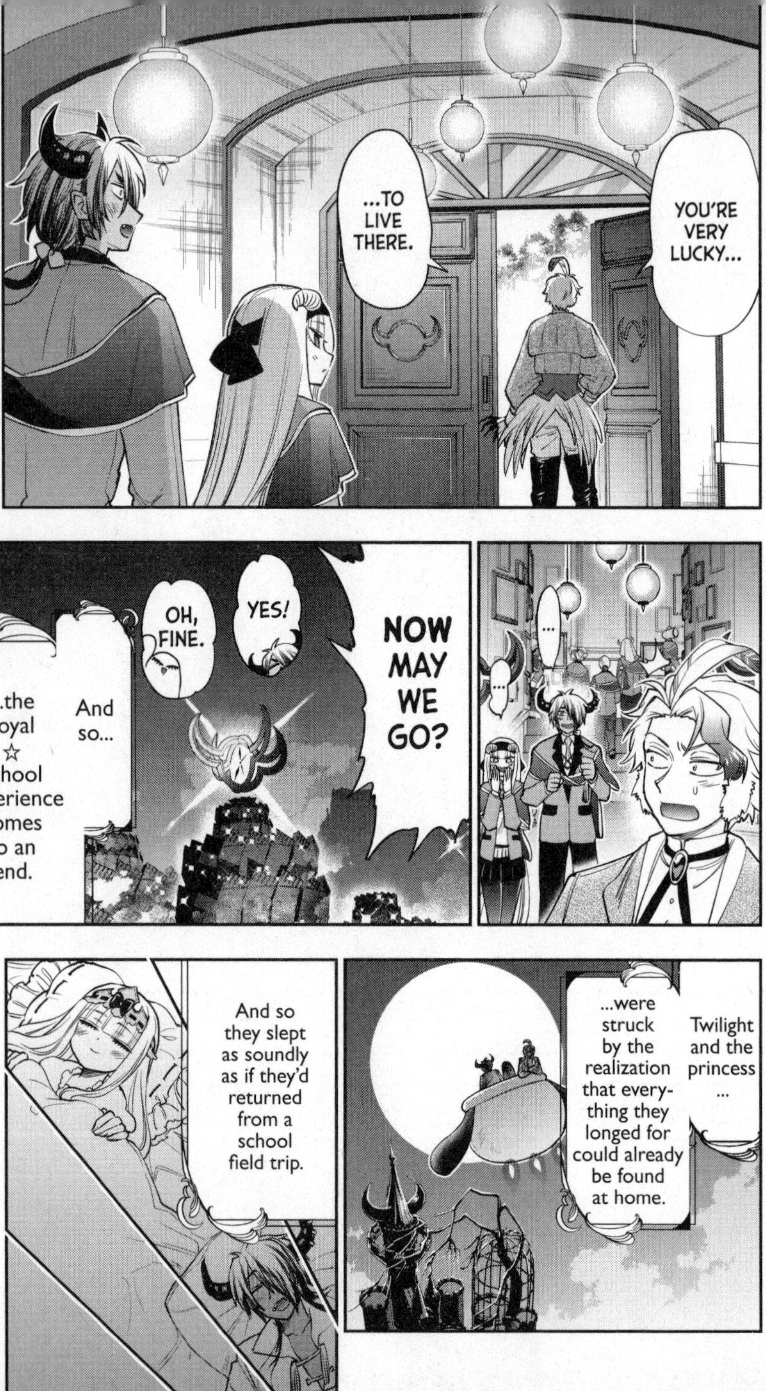
YOU'RE VERY LUCKY...
...TO LIVE THERE.
...
...
NOW MAY WE GO?
YES!
OH, FINE.
And so...
...the royal ☆ school experience comes to an end.
Twilight and the princess ...
...were struck by the realization that every-thing they longed for could already be found at home.
And so they slept as soundly as if they'd returned from a school field trip.

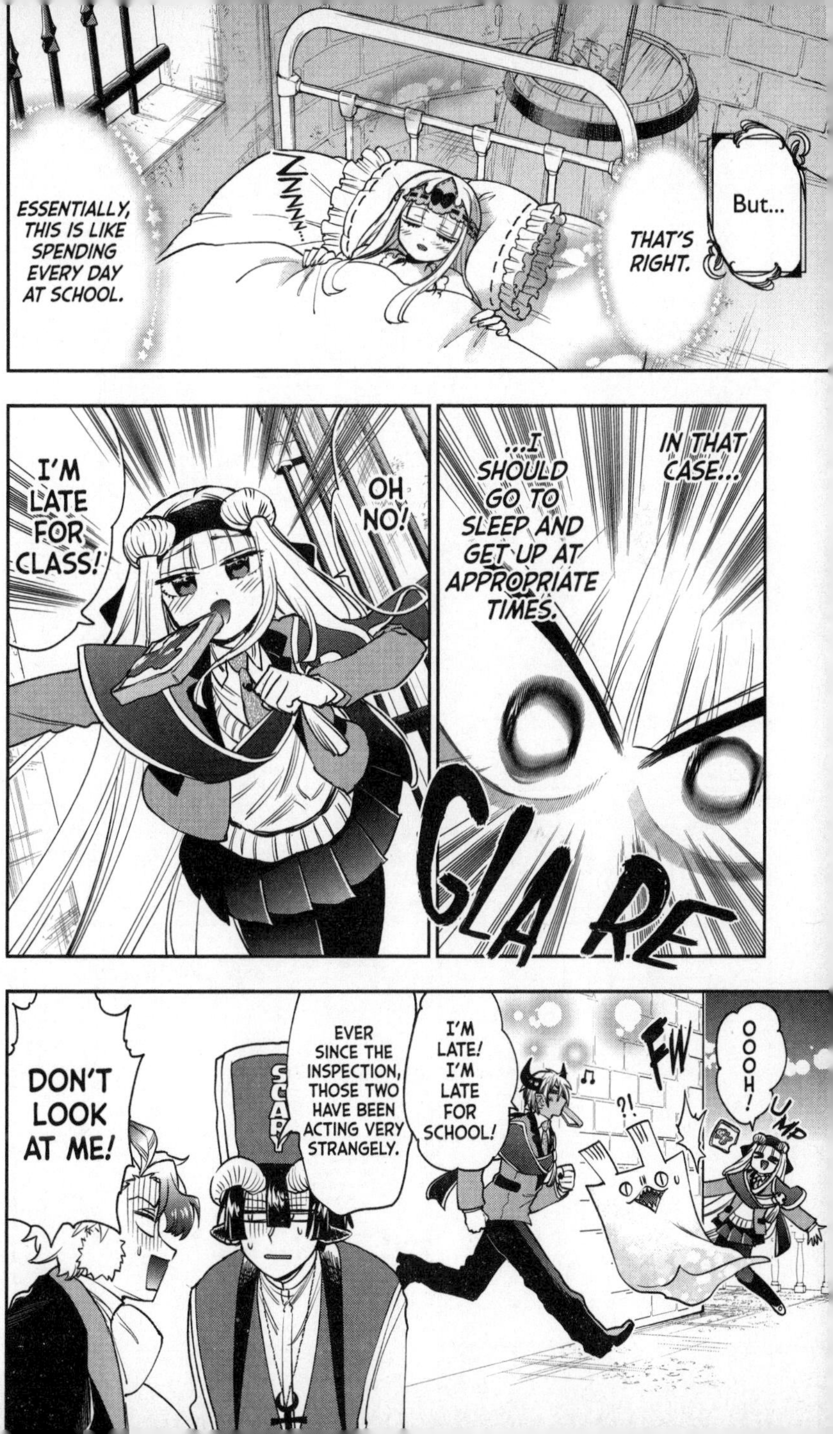
But...
THAT'S RIGHT.
ESSENTIALLY, THIS IS LIKE SPENDING EVERY DAY AT SCHOOL.
IN THAT CASE...
...I SHOULD GO TO SLEEP AND GET UP AT APPROPRIATE TIMES.
GLARE
OH NO!
I'M LATE FOR CLASS!
OOOH!
UMP
FW
?!
I'M LATE! I'M LATE FOR SCHOOL!
EVER SINCE THE INSPECTION, THOSE TWO HAVE BEEN ACTING VERY STRANGELY.
SCARY
DON'T LOOK AT ME!

Demon Castle Question Corner

3

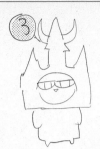

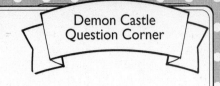

Q Does Poseidon run around like this 24-7?
Doesn't he ever put on a shirt?

A He sometimes dresses up to go out,
but he likes to feel free and easy at home.

Q Why isn't Fire Venom Dragon wearing that triangular headband anymore?
Has his power returned?

A He wore it as a humble badge of defeat, but nobody noticed,
so he gave it up.

Q I want to give the princess
a steaming eye mask!

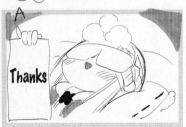

A

Thanks

Q Quilly wore glasses in the past.
Does he wear contacts now?

A Back when he spent a lot of time studying, he wore reading glasses.
But his eyesight isn't too bad,
so he seldom uses them now.

Q The princess failed to turn into an adult in the 59th Night.
If she did, would she look like her mother?

A Pretty much, probably.

Q How does Alazif prey upon the other grimoires?

A Tear and eat! Tear and eat!

Q The Demon King has a unique origin story.
Does he ever wish he had a mother?

A He doesn't have a clear idea what a mother is. Maybe it would be different if the divinity brothers had experienced a normal upbringing and shared it with him.

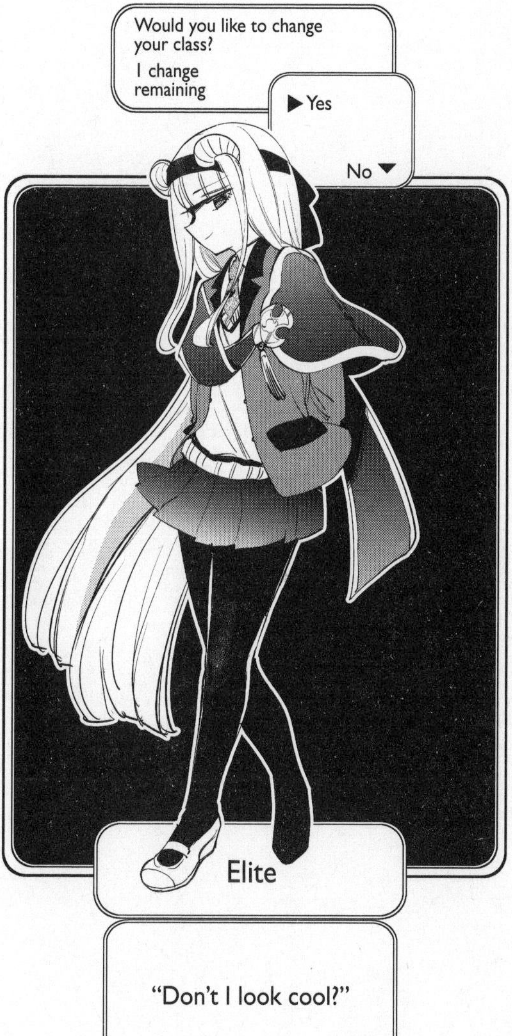
Would you like to change your class?
1 change remaining
▶Yes
No
Elite
"Don't I look cool?"

219th Night: But You Can Still Tune In to *Fly Me to the Moon*

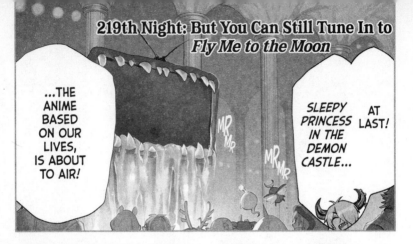

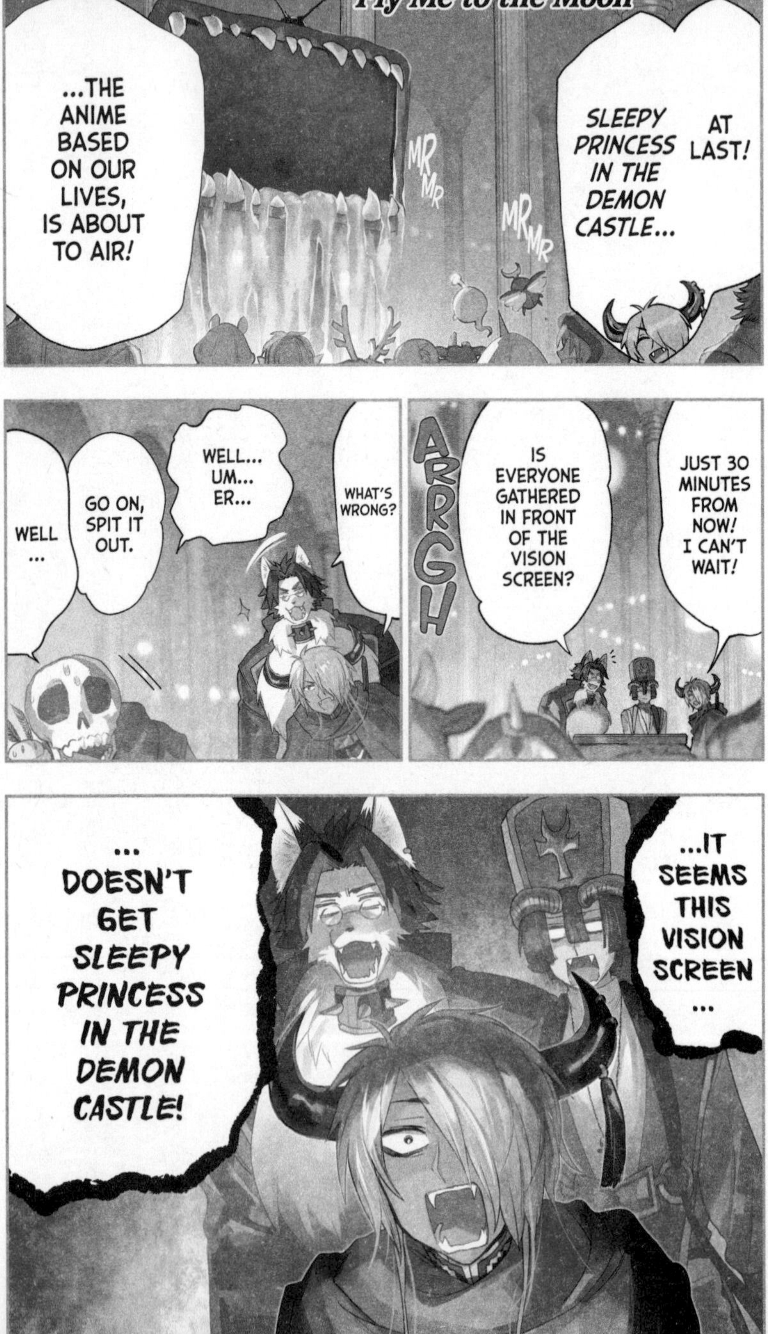
SLEEPY PRINCESS IN THE DEMON CASTLE... AT LAST!
MR MR
MR MR
...THE ANIME BASED ON OUR LIVES, IS ABOUT TO AIR!
JUST 30 MINUTES FROM NOW! I CAN'T WAIT!
IS EVERYONE GATHERED IN FRONT OF THE VISION SCREEN?
ARRGH
WHAT'S WRONG?
WELL... UM... ER...
GO ON, SPIT IT OUT.
WELL ...
...IT SEEMS THIS VISION SCREEN ...
... DOESN'T GET SLEEPY PRINCESS IN THE DEMON CASTLE!

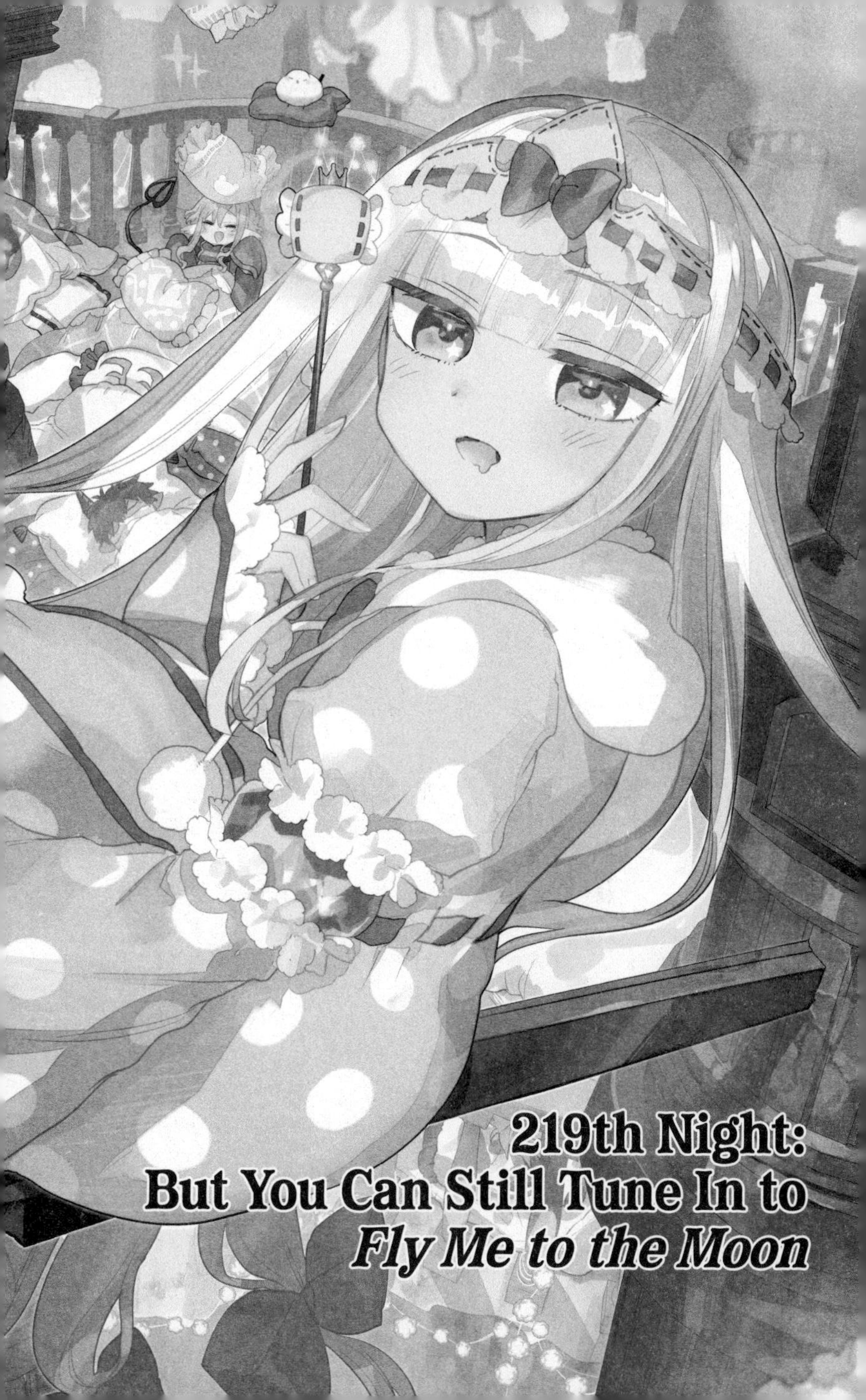
219th Night:
But You Can Still Tune In to
Fly Me to the Moon

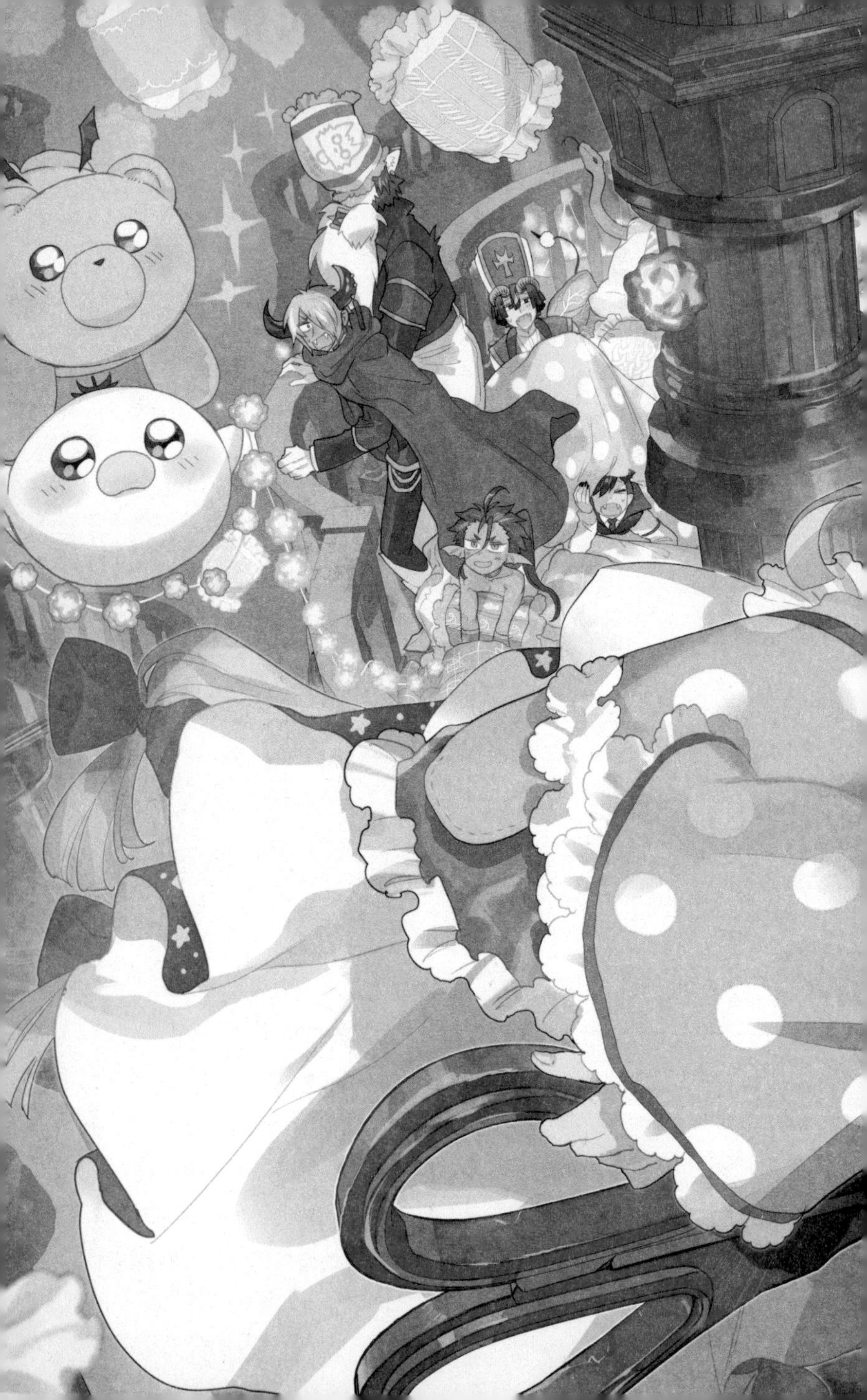

SLEEPY PRINCESS IN THE DEMON CASTLE

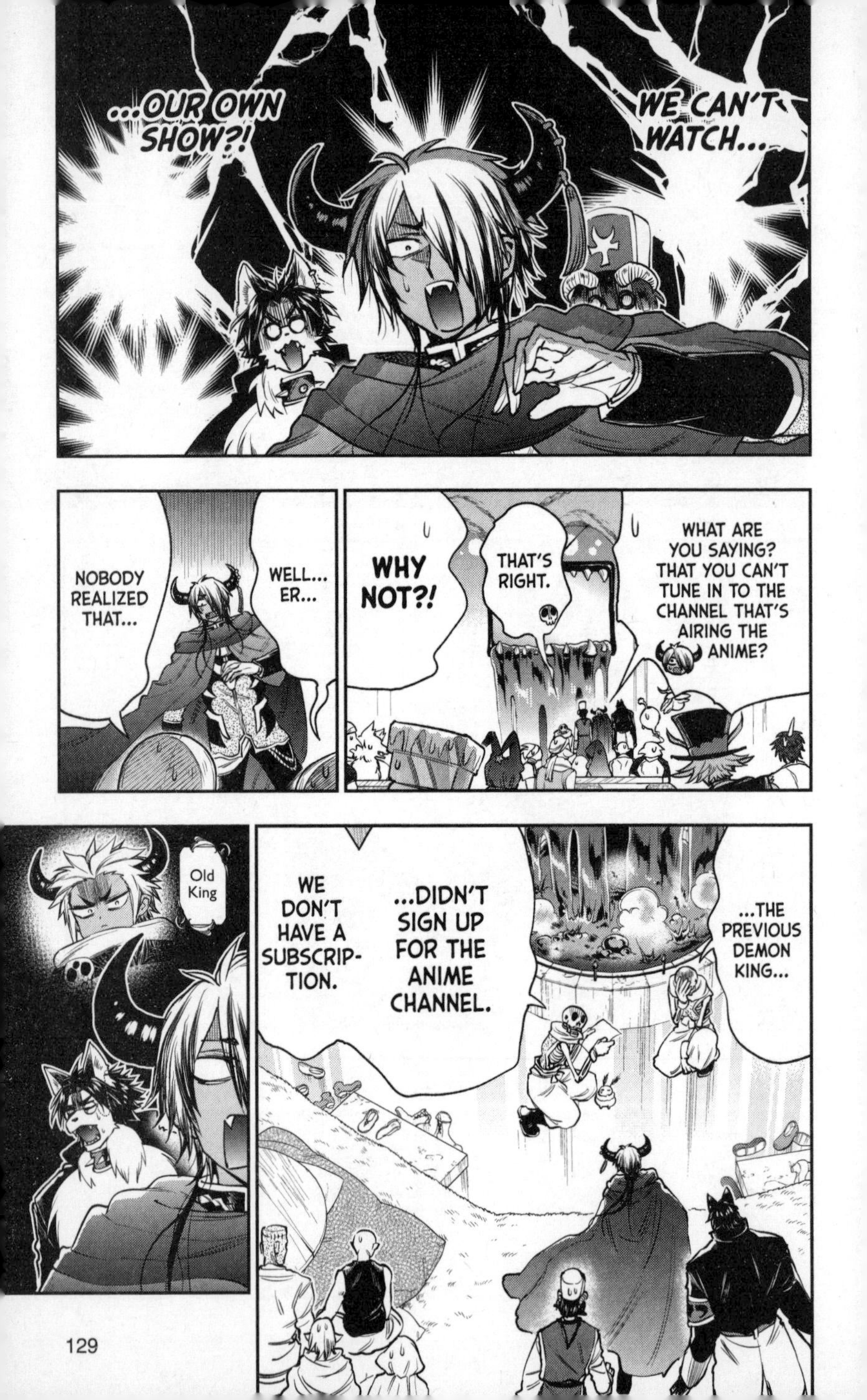
WE CAN'T WATCH...
...OUR OWN SHOW?!
WHAT ARE YOU SAYING? THAT YOU CAN'T TUNE IN TO THE CHANNEL THAT'S AIRING THE ANIME?
THAT'S RIGHT.
WHY NOT?!
WELL... ER...
NOBODY REALIZED THAT...
...THE PREVIOUS DEMON KING...
...DIDN'T SIGN UP FOR THE ANIME CHANNEL.
WE DON'T HAVE A SUBSCRIPTION.
Old King

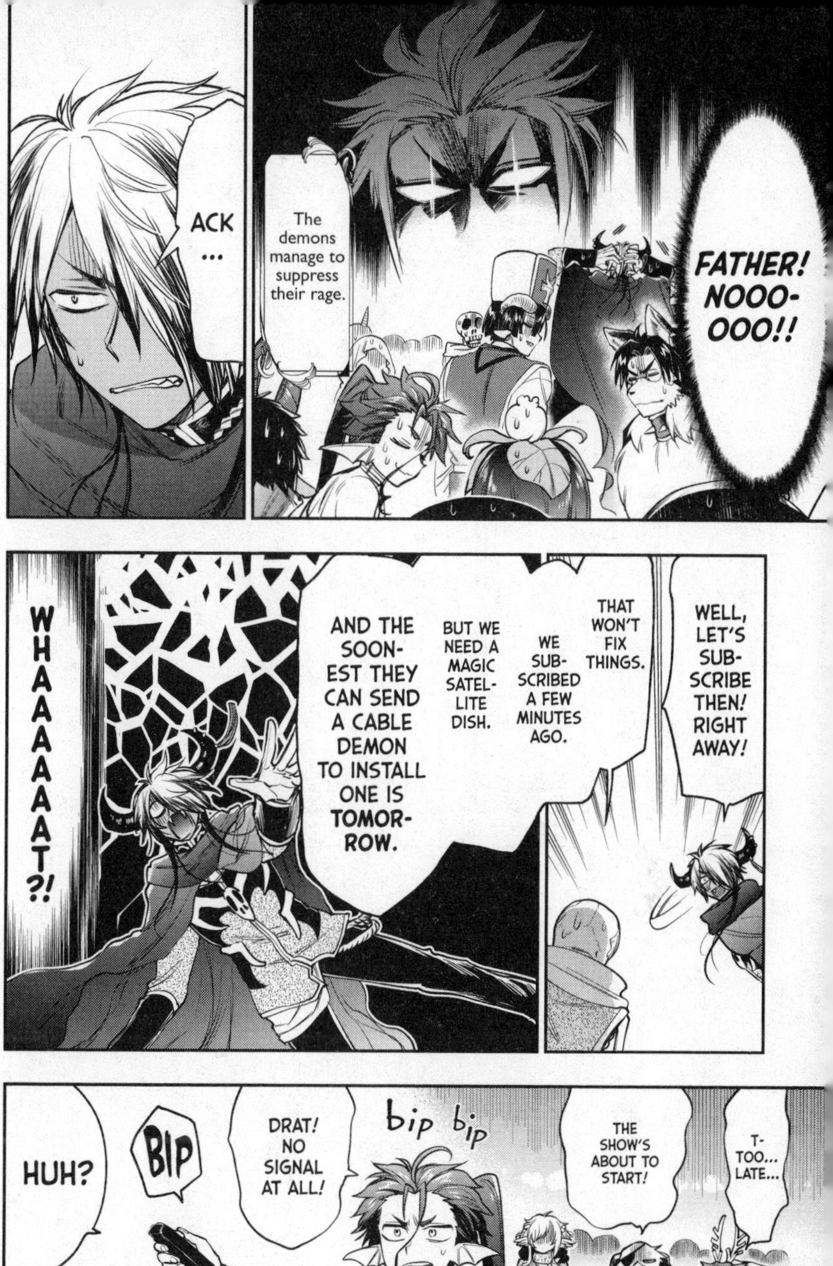
FATHER! NOOO-OOO!!
The demons manage to suppress their rage.
ACK ...
WELL, LET'S SUB-SCRIBE THEN! RIGHT AWAY!
THAT WON'T FIX THINGS.
WE SUB-SCRIBED A FEW MINUTES AGO.
BUT WE NEED A MAGIC SATEL-LITE DISH.
AND THE SOON-EST THEY CAN SEND A CABLE DEMON TO INSTALL ONE IS TOMOR-ROW.
WHAAAAAAAT?!
T-TOO... LATE...
THE SHOW'S ABOUT TO START!
bip bip
DRAT! NO SIGNAL AT ALL!
BIP
HUH?

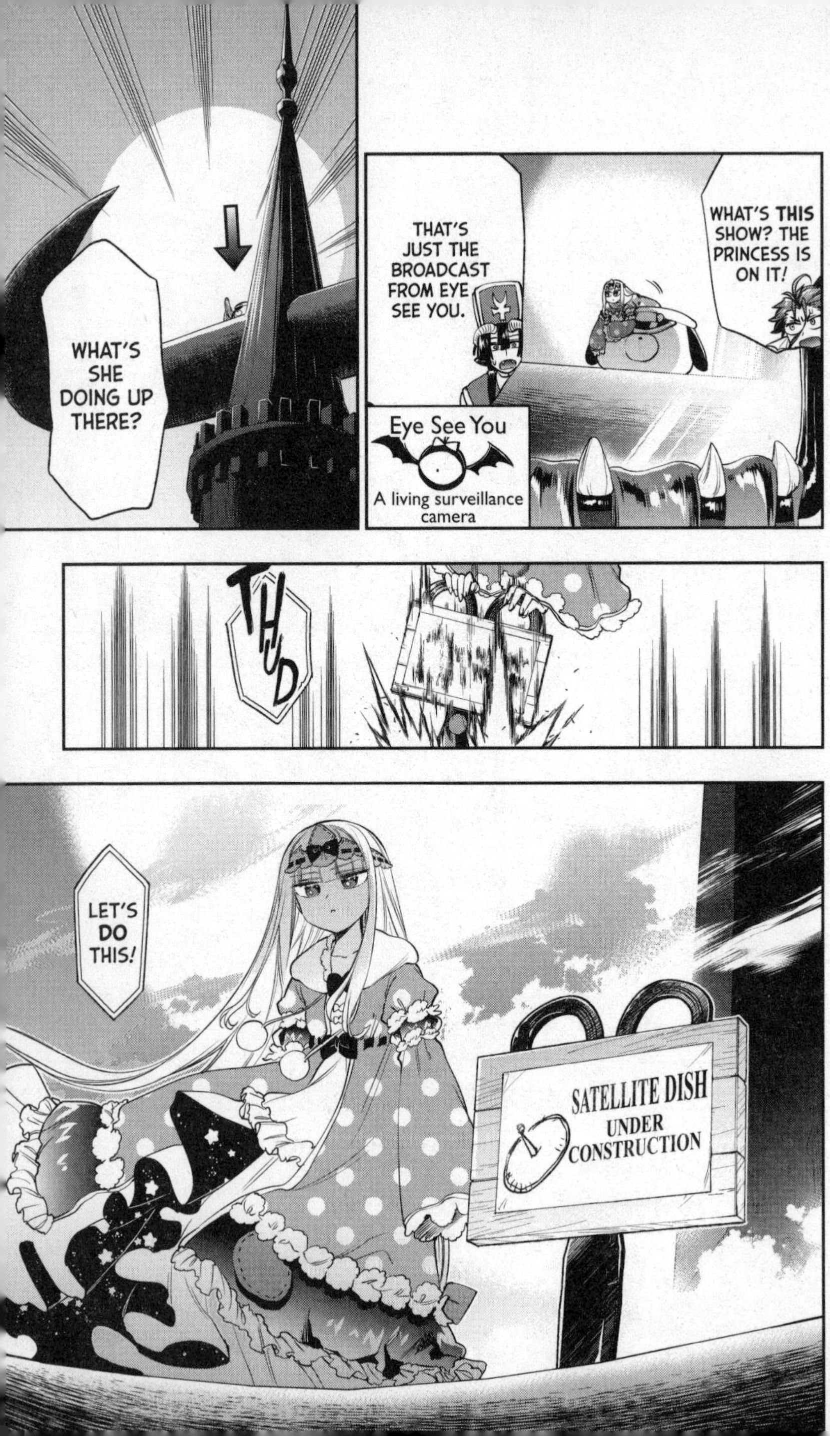
WHAT'S THIS SHOW? THE PRINCESS IS ON IT!
THAT'S JUST THE BROADCAST FROM EYE SEE YOU.
Eye See You
A living surveillance camera
WHAT'S SHE DOING UP THERE?
THUD
LET'S DO THIS!
SATELLITE DISH UNDER CONSTRUCTION

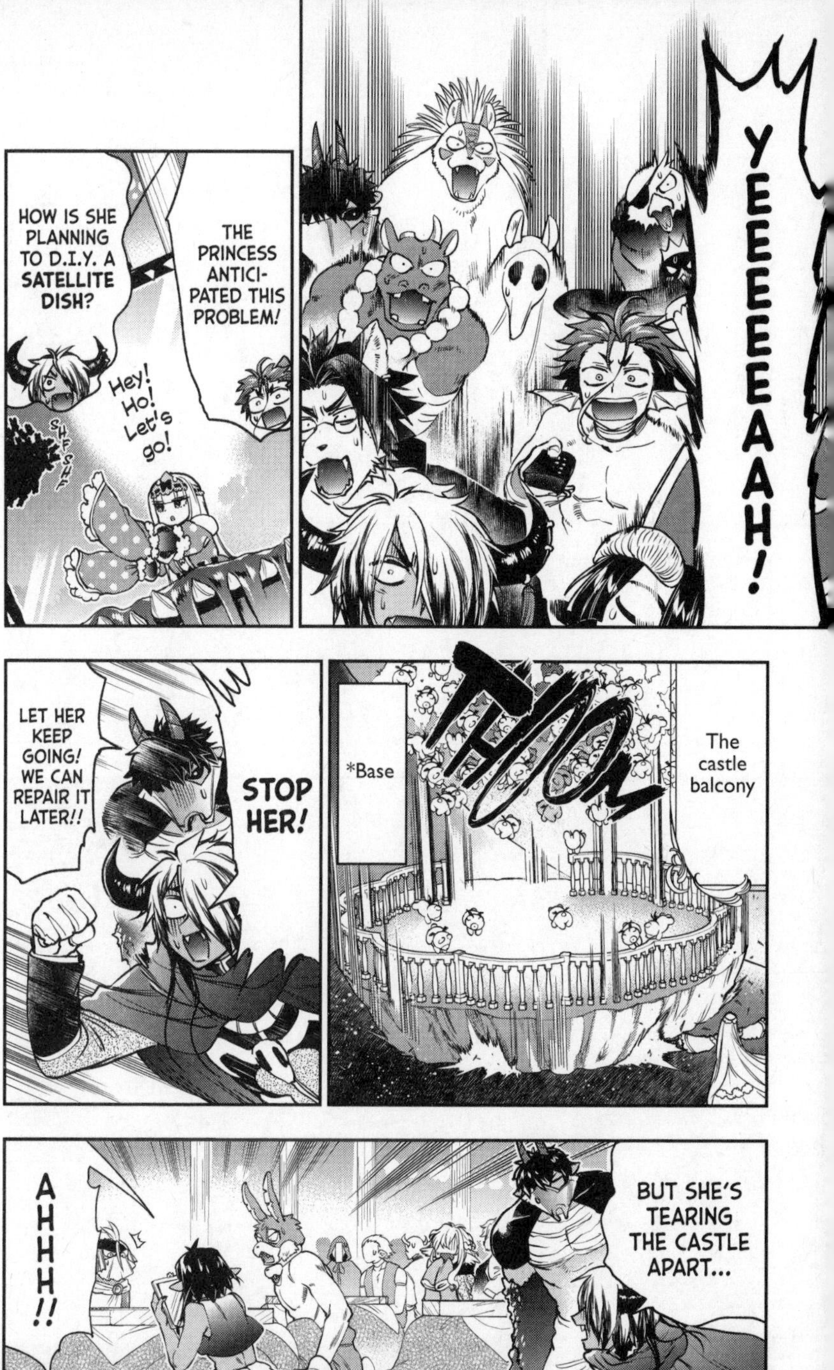
YEEEEEEAAH!
THE PRINCESS ANTICIPATED THIS PROBLEM!
HOW IS SHE PLANNING TO D.I.Y. A SATELLITE DISH?
Hey! Ho! Let's go!
SHF SHF
The castle balcony
*Base
STOP HER!
LET HER KEEP GOING! WE CAN REPAIR IT LATER!!
BUT SHE'S TEARING THE CASTLE APART...
AHHHH!!

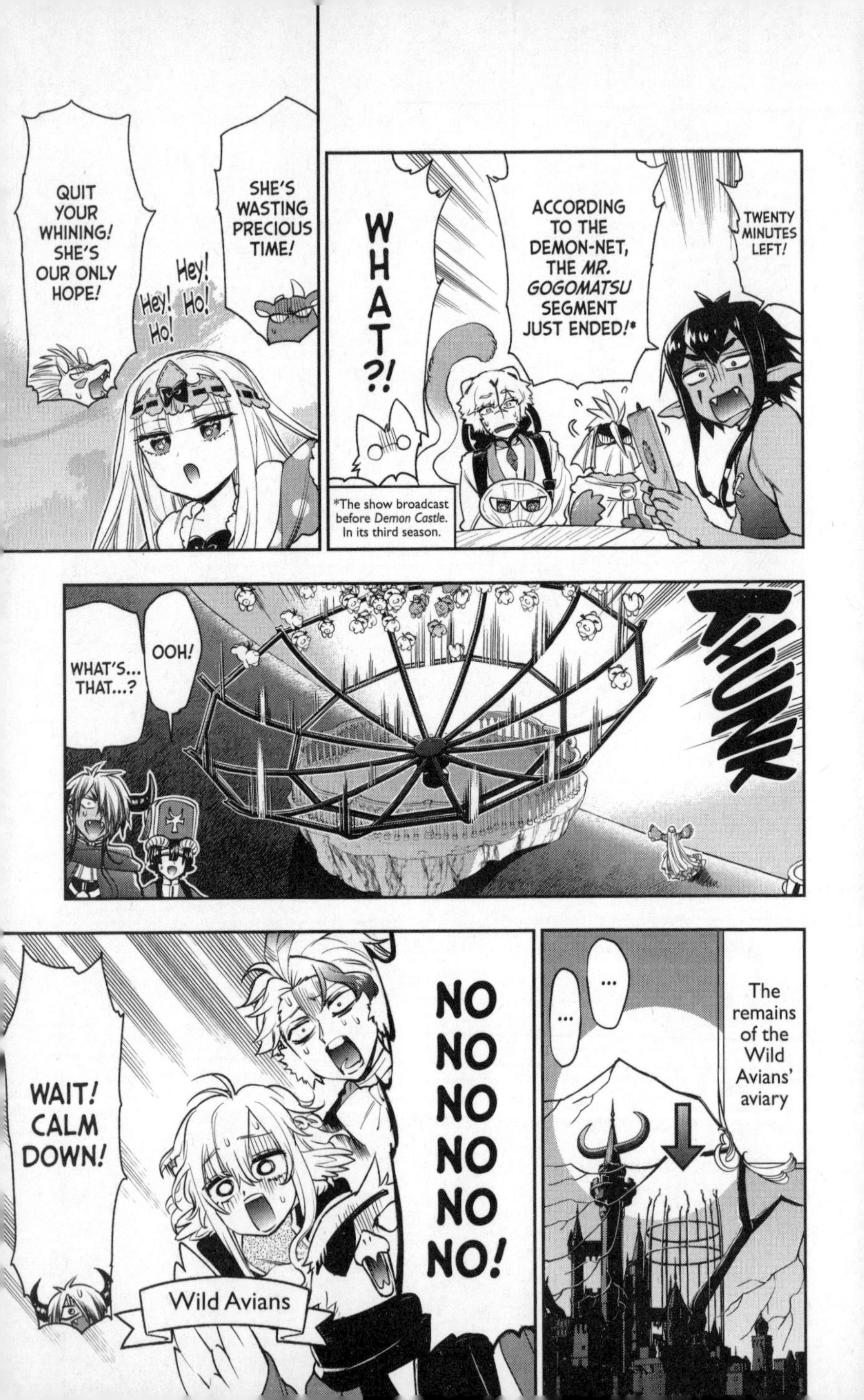
TWENTY MINUTES LEFT!
ACCORDING TO THE DEMON-NET, THE MR. GOGOMATSU SEGMENT JUST ENDED!*
WHAT?!
*The show broadcast before Demon Castle. In its third season.
SHE'S WASTING PRECIOUS TIME!
Hey! Ho!
Hey! Ho!
QUIT YOUR WHINING! SHE'S OUR ONLY HOPE!
THUNK
OOH!
WHAT'S... THAT...?
...
...
The remains of the Wild Avians' aviary
NO NO NO NO NO NO!
WAIT! CALM DOWN!
Wild Avians

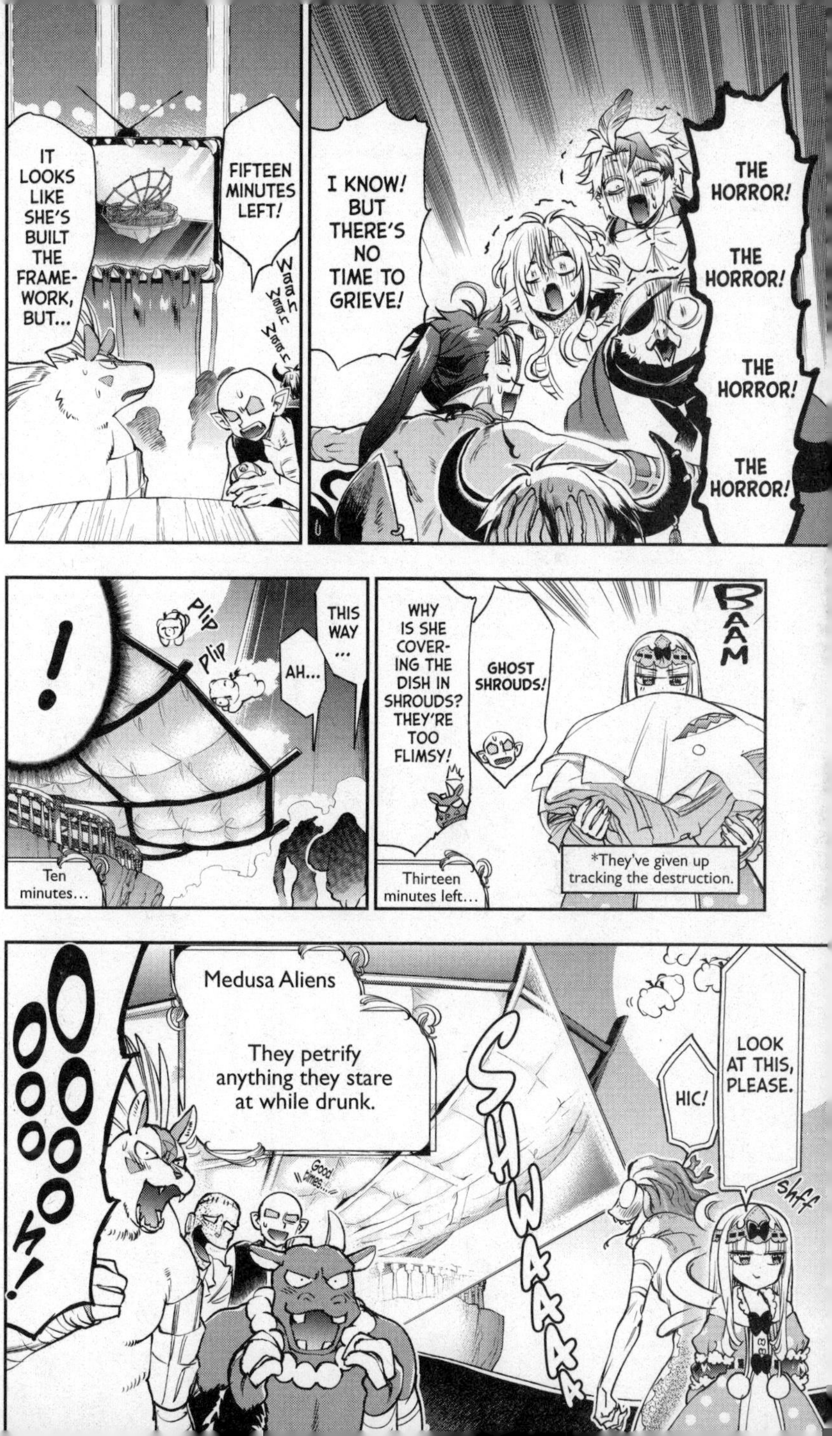
THE HORROR!
THE HORROR!
THE HORROR!
THE HORROR!
I KNOW! BUT THERE'S NO TIME TO GRIEVE!
FIFTEEN MINUTES LEFT!
Waah
Waah
Waah
IT LOOKS LIKE SHE'S BUILT THE FRAMEWORK, BUT...
BAAM
GHOST SHROUDS!
WHY IS SHE COVERING THE DISH IN SHROUDS? THEY'RE TOO FLIMSY!
*They've given up tracking the destruction.
Thirteen minutes left...
THIS WAY...
AH...
plip
plip
!
Ten minutes...
LOOK AT THIS, PLEASE.
HIC!
shff
SHWAAAAA
Medusa Aliens
They petrify anything they stare at while drunk.
Good times...
OOOOOOOOOOOOOk!

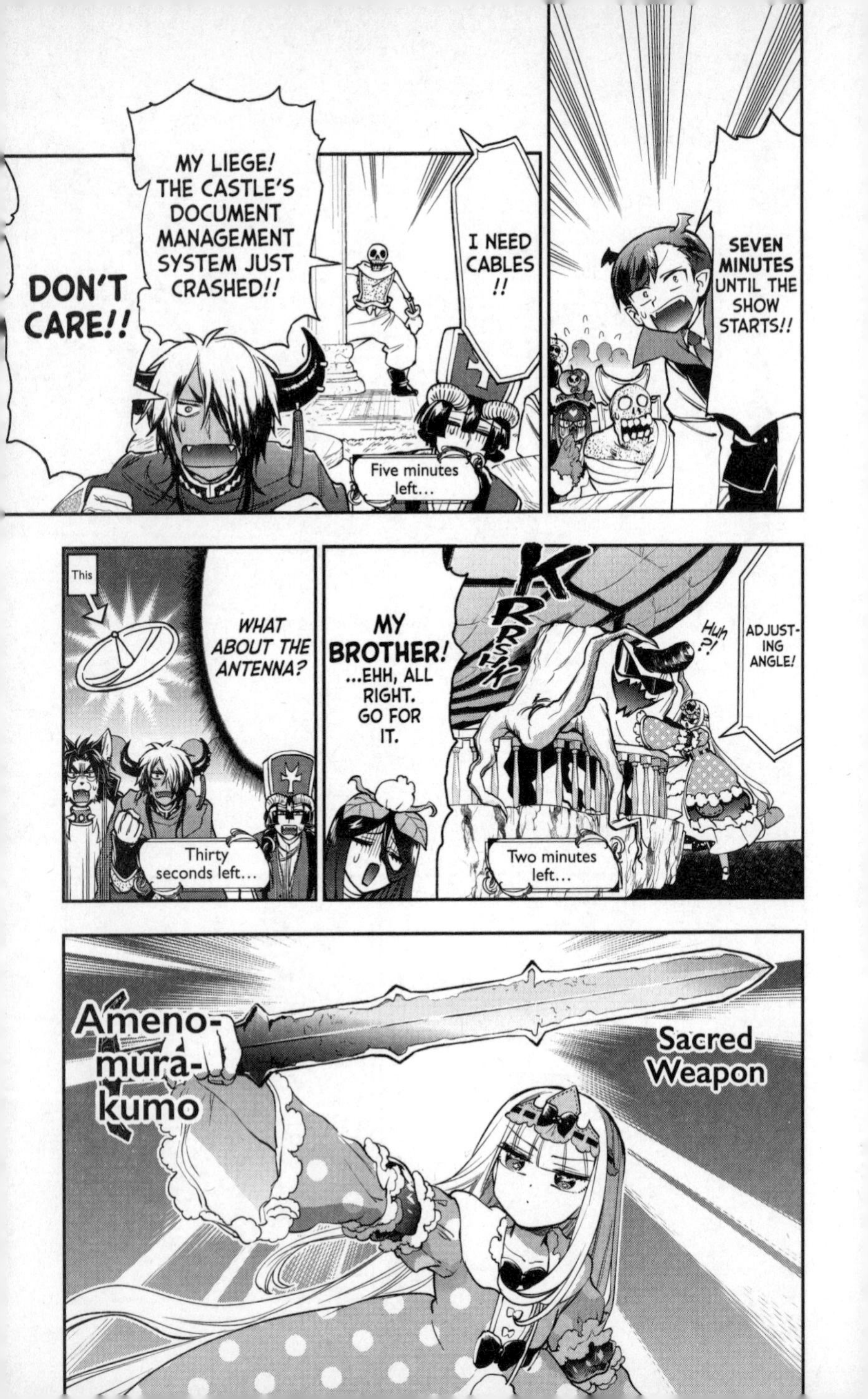
SEVEN MINUTES UNTIL THE SHOW STARTS!!
I NEED CABLES!!
MY LIEGE! THE CASTLE'S DOCUMENT MANAGEMENT SYSTEM JUST CRASHED!!
DON'T CARE!!
Five minutes left...
ADJUSTING ANGLE!
Huh ?!
KRRSHK
MY BROTHER! ...EHH, ALL RIGHT. GO FOR IT.
Two minutes left...
WHAT ABOUT THE ANTENNA?
This
Thirty seconds left...
Sacred Weapon
Ameno-mura-kumo

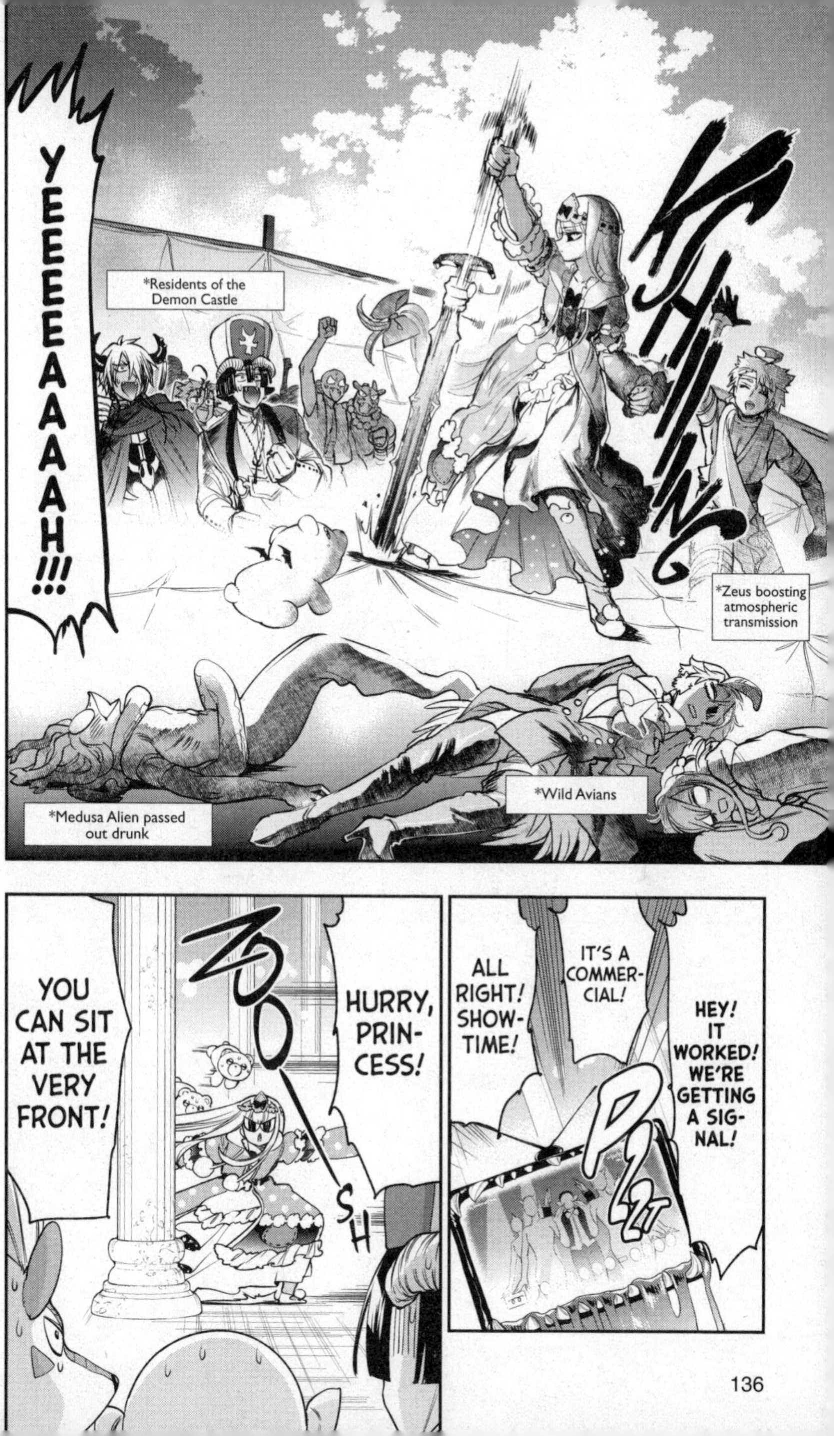

KSHIIING
*Zeus boosting atmospheric transmission
*Residents of the Demon Castle
YEEEEEAAAAAH!!!
*Wild Avians
*Medusa Alien passed out drunk
IT'S A COMMERCIAL!
HEY! IT WORKED! WE'RE GETTING A SIGNAL!
ALL RIGHT! SHOWTIME!
PZZT
HURRY, PRINCESS!
ZOOOSH
YOU CAN SIT AT THE VERY FRONT!

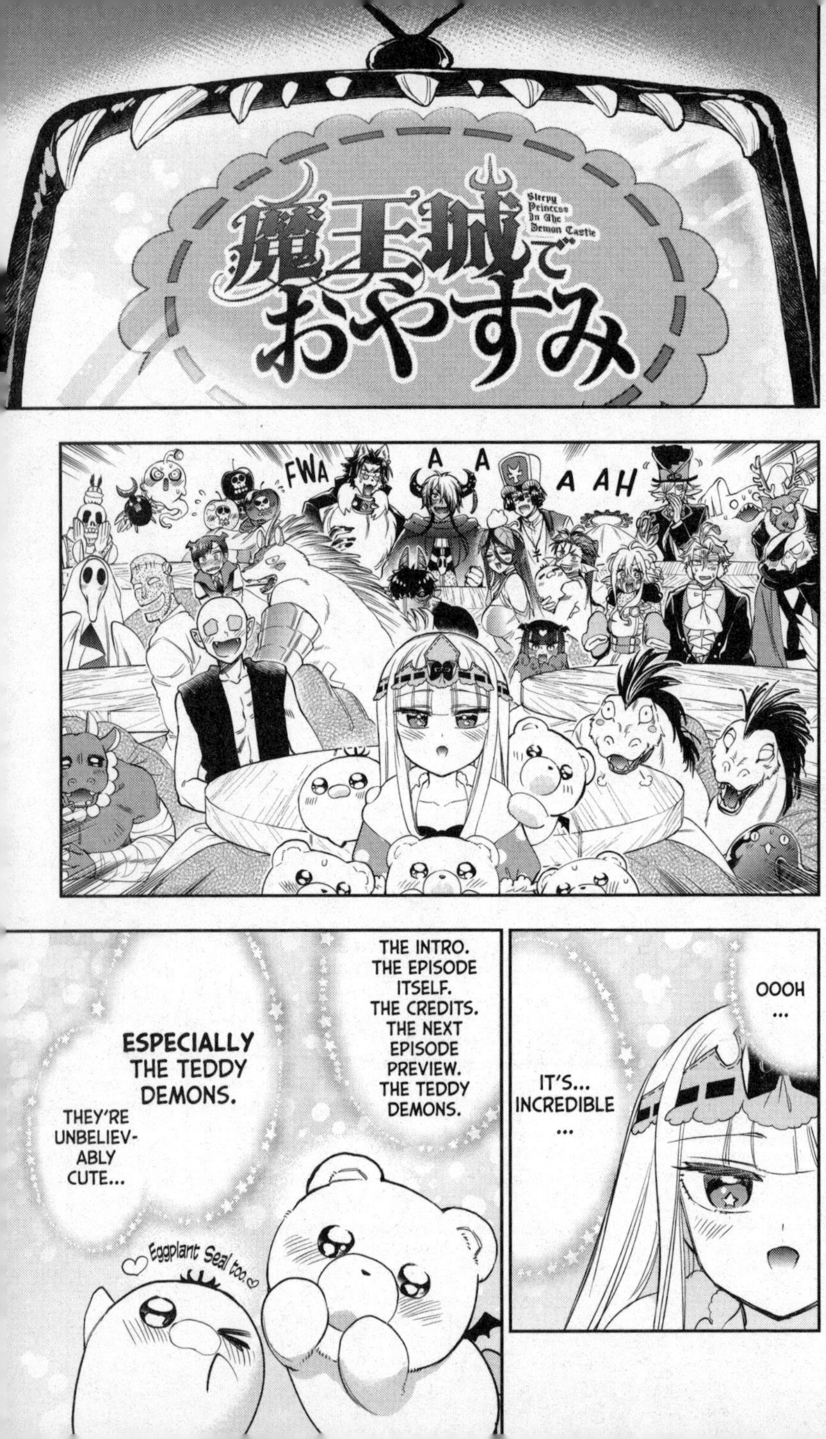
魔王城でおやすみ
Sleepy Princess In The Demon Castle
FWA A A A AH
OOOH ...
IT'S... INCREDIBLE ...
THE INTRO. THE EPISODE ITSELF. THE CREDITS. THE NEXT EPISODE PREVIEW. THE TEDDY DEMONS.
ESPECIALLY THE TEDDY DEMONS.
THEY'RE UNBELIEV-ABLY CUTE...
♡Eggplant Seal too.♡

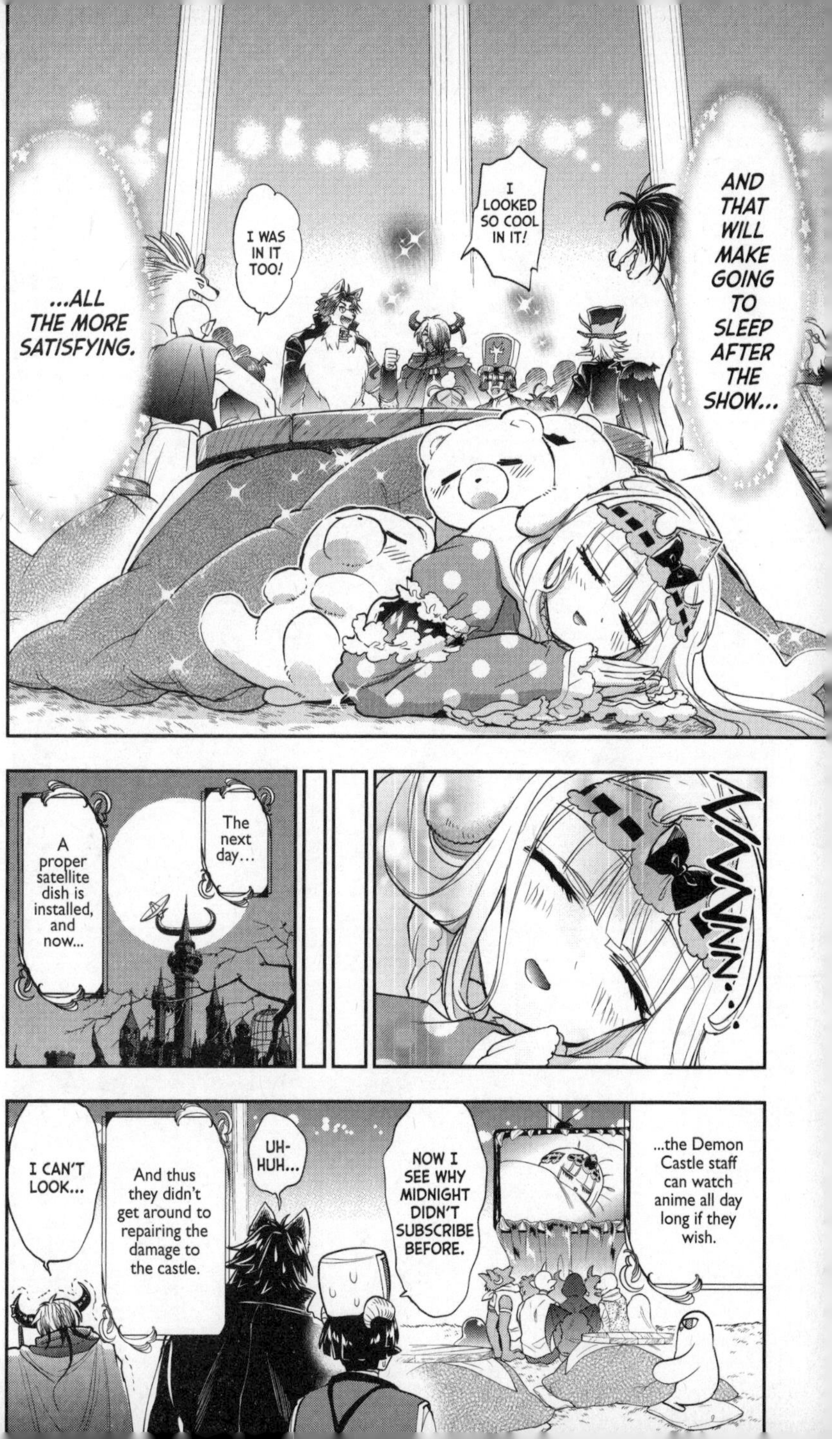
AND THAT WILL MAKE GOING TO SLEEP AFTER THE SHOW...
I LOOKED SO COOL IN IT!
I WAS IN IT TOO!
...ALL THE MORE SATISFYING.
The next day...
A proper satellite dish is installed, and now...
...the Demon Castle staff can watch anime all day long if they wish.
NOW I SEE WHY MIDNIGHT DIDN'T SUBSCRIBE BEFORE.
UH-HUH...
And thus they didn't get around to repairing the damage to the castle.
I CAN'T LOOK...

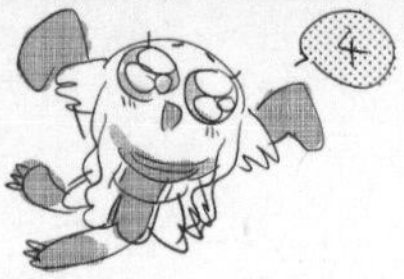

Demon Castle Question Corner

Q What happened to the gangster Teddy Demons after the Princess annihilated the adventurers?

A They're soft and cuddly at heart, so now that some time has passed, I think they've become a friendly biker club. Cute, right?

Q Is the Monster Bird always around Cursed Musician?

A The bird's usually on his head or in his bed. Cursed Musician named it after a musical term, but he won't tell anyone what it is.

Q Is Poseidon the type of guy who always squirts lemon on fried food? If he likes seasonings, which ones?

A He likes to munch on fried chicken with pickled lemon and mayonnaise.

Q Can the gear floating above M.O.T.H.E.R.'s head be removed?

A Yes. It's basically an antenna that connects M.O.T.H.E.R. to a massive library of information. If it malfunctions, it can be replaced.

Q What does the Demon King do to keep his figure?

A Clean living and a healthy lifestyle!

Q I want to know everyone's favorite dessert and what kind of tea they like to drink with it!

A

Princess: King chocolate marshmallow and tea with milk
Demon King: King chocolate marshmallow and demon roasted green tea (hot)
Leonard: Red bean dumplings and demon brown rice tea (hot)
Great Red: Strawberries with condensed milk and demon roasted green tea (not too hot)
Poseidon: Fruit punch and demon barley tea (iced)
Alraune: Liquor-infused cakes and straight iced tea (no sugar)
Fire Venom Dragon: Cheese soufflé topped with demon apricot jam and demon brown rice tea (hot)
Sand Dragon: Almond jelly and Kowloon tea (hot)
M.O.T.H.E.R.: Doughnut (plain) and black coffee (hot)
Hades: Ice cream (rum raisin) and demon roasted green tea (hot)
Zeus: Custard-stuffed pancake and hot or cold water (hardly ever drinks tea)
Harpy: Mille crepe cake and demon green tea latte
Cursed: Chocolate-covered almond bark and black coffee (iced)

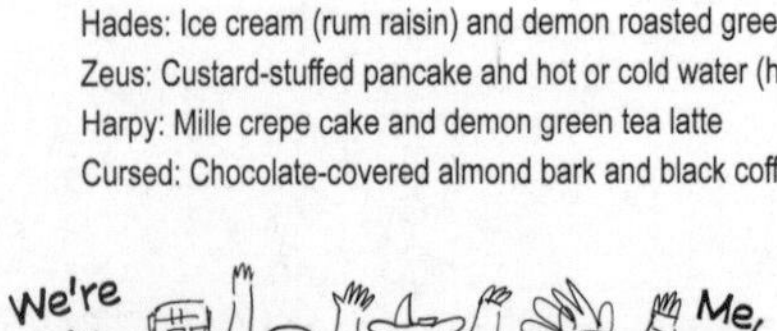
We're big fans!
Me, me!

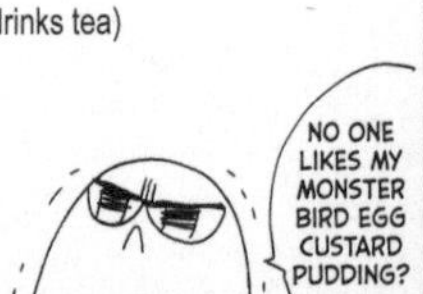
NO ONE LIKES MY MONSTER BIRD EGG CUSTARD PUDDING?

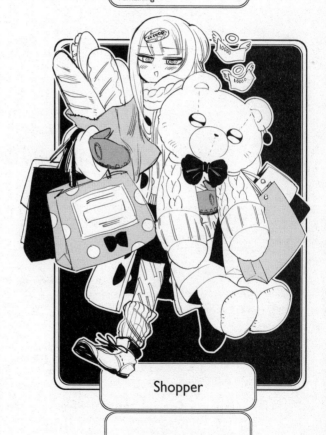

Would you like to change your class?

0 changes remaining

Shopper

"Credit cards are soooo handy!"

220th Night: Fly, Bird Girl, Fly!

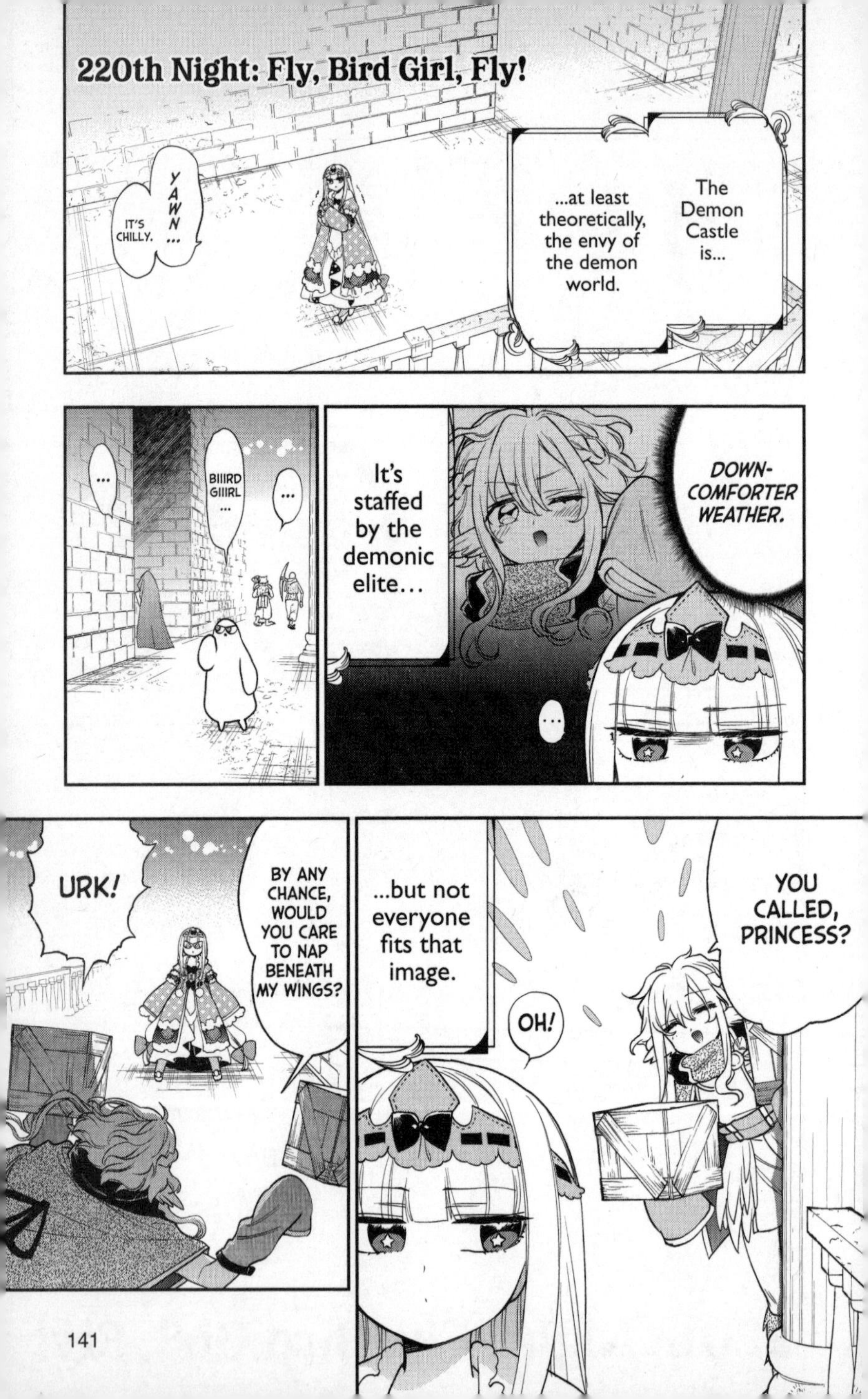
The Demon Castle is...
...at least theoretically, the envy of the demon world.
YAWN...
IT'S CHILLY.
DOWN-COMFORTER WEATHER.
It's staffed by the demonic elite…
…
BIIIRD GIIIRL…
…
…
YOU CALLED, PRINCESS?
OH!
...but not everyone fits that image.
BY ANY CHANCE, WOULD YOU CARE TO NAP BENEATH MY WINGS?
URK!

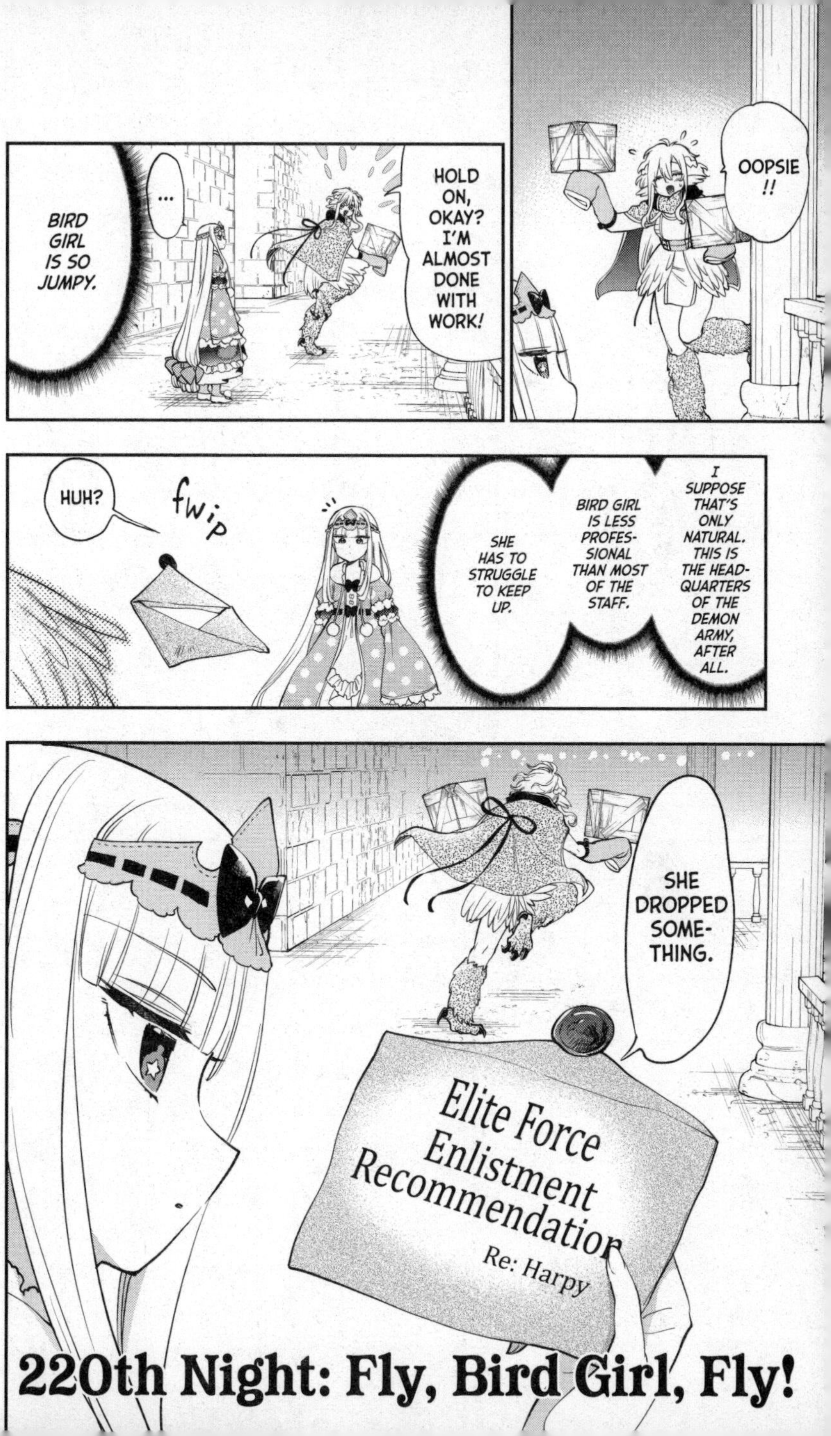
OOPSIE!!
HOLD ON, OKAY? I'M ALMOST DONE WITH WORK!
...
BIRD GIRL IS SO JUMPY.
I SUPPOSE THAT'S ONLY NATURAL. THIS IS THE HEADQUARTERS OF THE DEMON ARMY, AFTER ALL.
BIRD GIRL IS LESS PROFESSIONAL THAN MOST OF THE STAFF.
SHE HAS TO STRUGGLE TO KEEP UP.
fwip
HUH?
SHE DROPPED SOMETHING.
Elite Force Enlistment Recommendation
Re: Harpy

220th Night: Fly, Bird Girl, Fly!

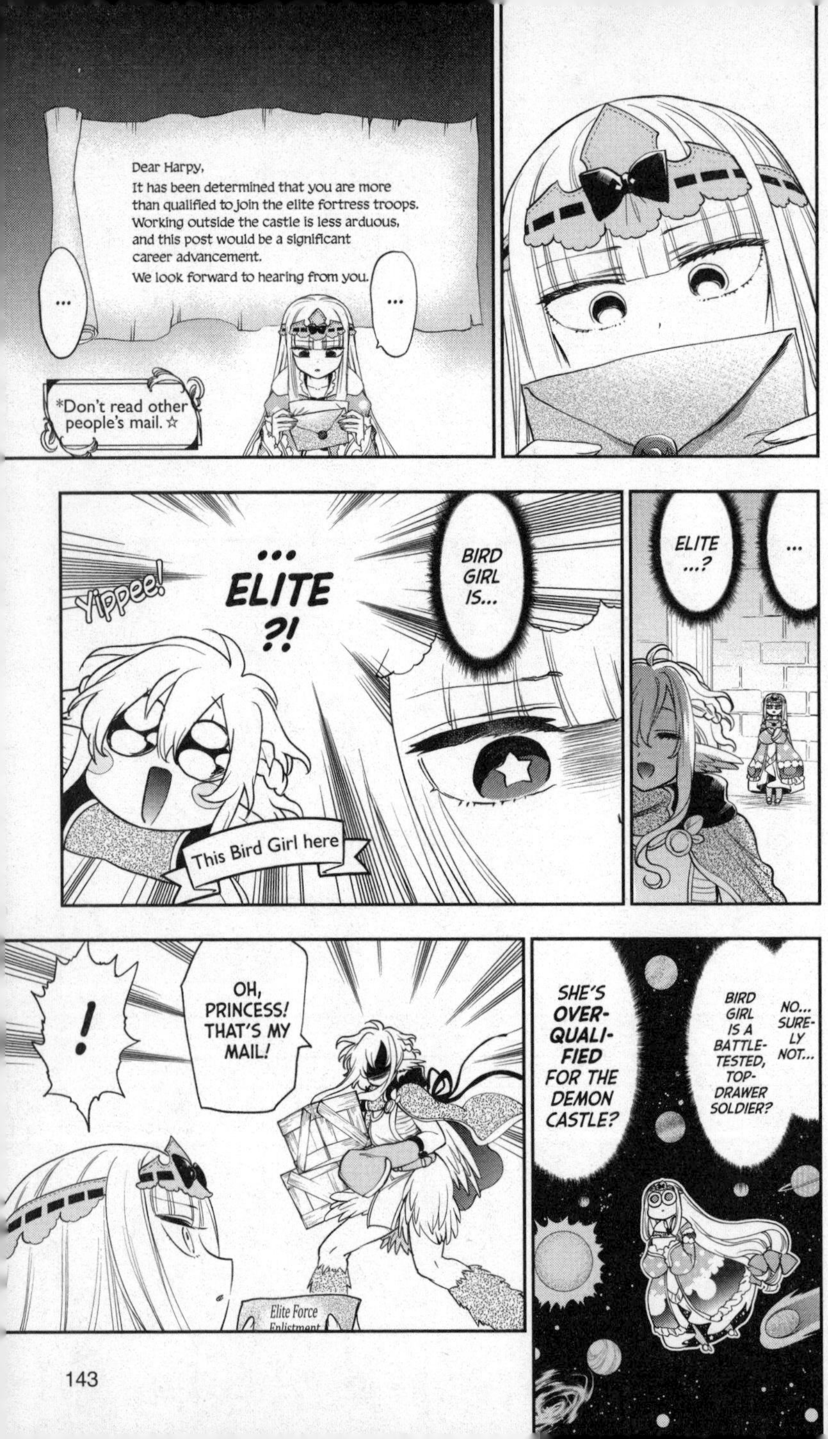
Dear Harpy,
It has been determined that you are more than qualified to join the elite fortress troops. Working outside the castle is less arduous, and this post would be a significant career advancement.
We look forward to hearing from you.
...
...
*Don't read other people's mail. ☆
...
ELITE ...?
BIRD GIRL IS...
...ELITE ?!
Yippee!
This Bird Girl here
NO... SURELY NOT...
BIRD GIRL IS A BATTLE-TESTED, TOP-DRAWER SOLDIER?
SHE'S OVERQUALIFIED FOR THE DEMON CASTLE?
OH, PRINCESS! THAT'S MY MAIL!
!
Elite Force Enlistment

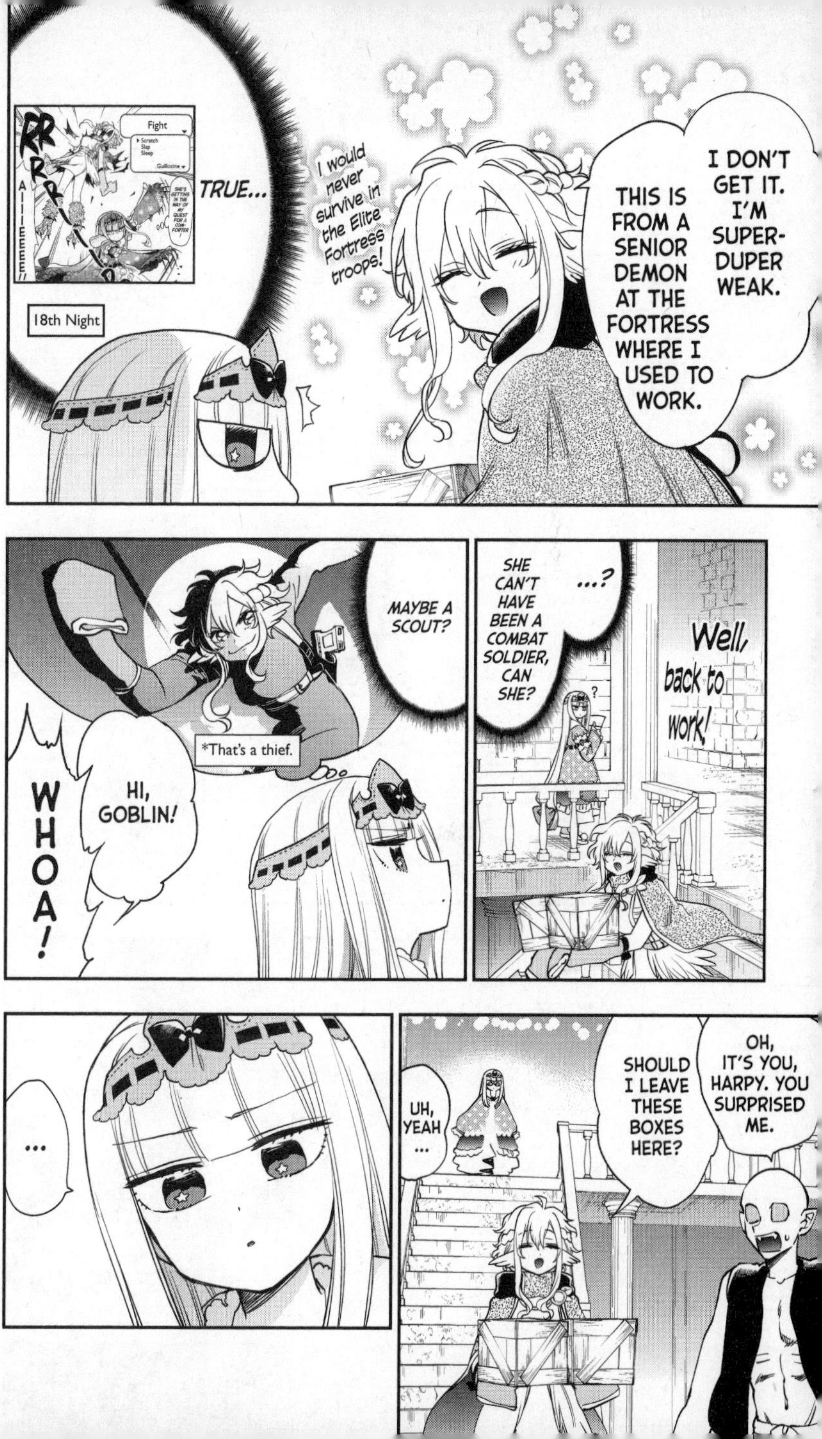
I DON'T GET IT. I'M SUPER-DUPER WEAK.
THIS IS FROM A SENIOR DEMON AT THE FORTRESS WHERE I USED TO WORK.
I would never survive in the Elite Fortress troops!
TRUE...
18th Night
Fight
Scratch
Slap
Sleep
Guillotine
SHE'S GETTING IN THE WAY OF MY QUEST FOR A COMFORTER!
RRRRR
AIIIEEEE!!
Well, back to work!
...?
?
SHE CAN'T HAVE BEEN A COMBAT SOLDIER, CAN SHE?
MAYBE A SCOUT?
*That's a thief.
HI, GOBLIN!
WHOA!
OH, IT'S YOU, HARPY. YOU SURPRISED ME.
SHOULD I LEAVE THESE BOXES HERE?
UH, YEAH ...
...

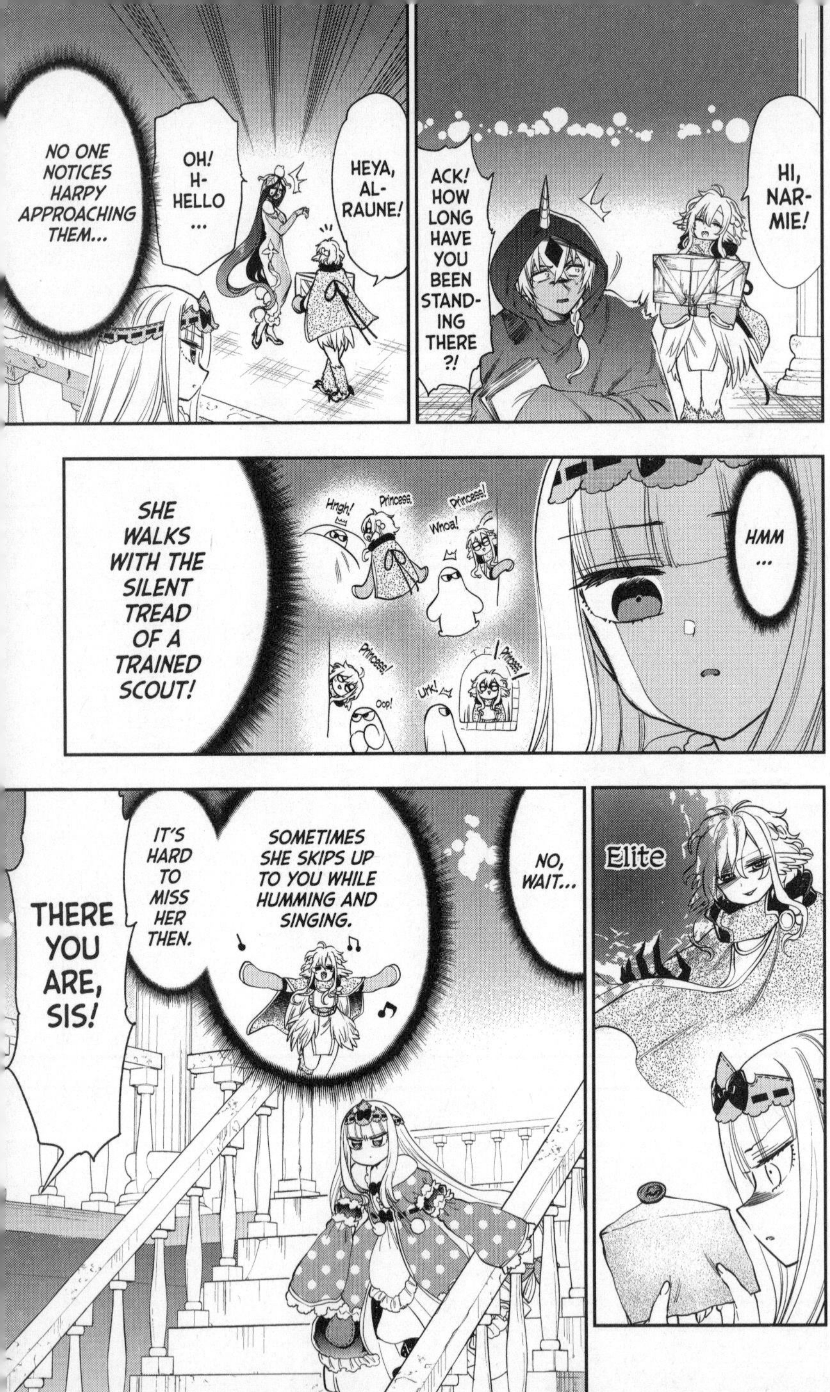
HI, NARMIE!
ACK! HOW LONG HAVE YOU BEEN STANDING THERE?!
HEYA, ALRAUNE!
OH! H-HELLO...
NO ONE NOTICES HARPY APPROACHING THEM...
HMM...
Princess!
Whoa!
Princess,
Hngh!
Princess!
Urk!
Princess!
Oop!
SHE WALKS WITH THE SILENT TREAD OF A TRAINED SCOUT!
Elite
NO, WAIT...
SOMETIMES SHE SKIPS UP TO YOU WHILE HUMMING AND SINGING.
IT'S HARD TO MISS HER THEN.
THERE YOU ARE, SIS!

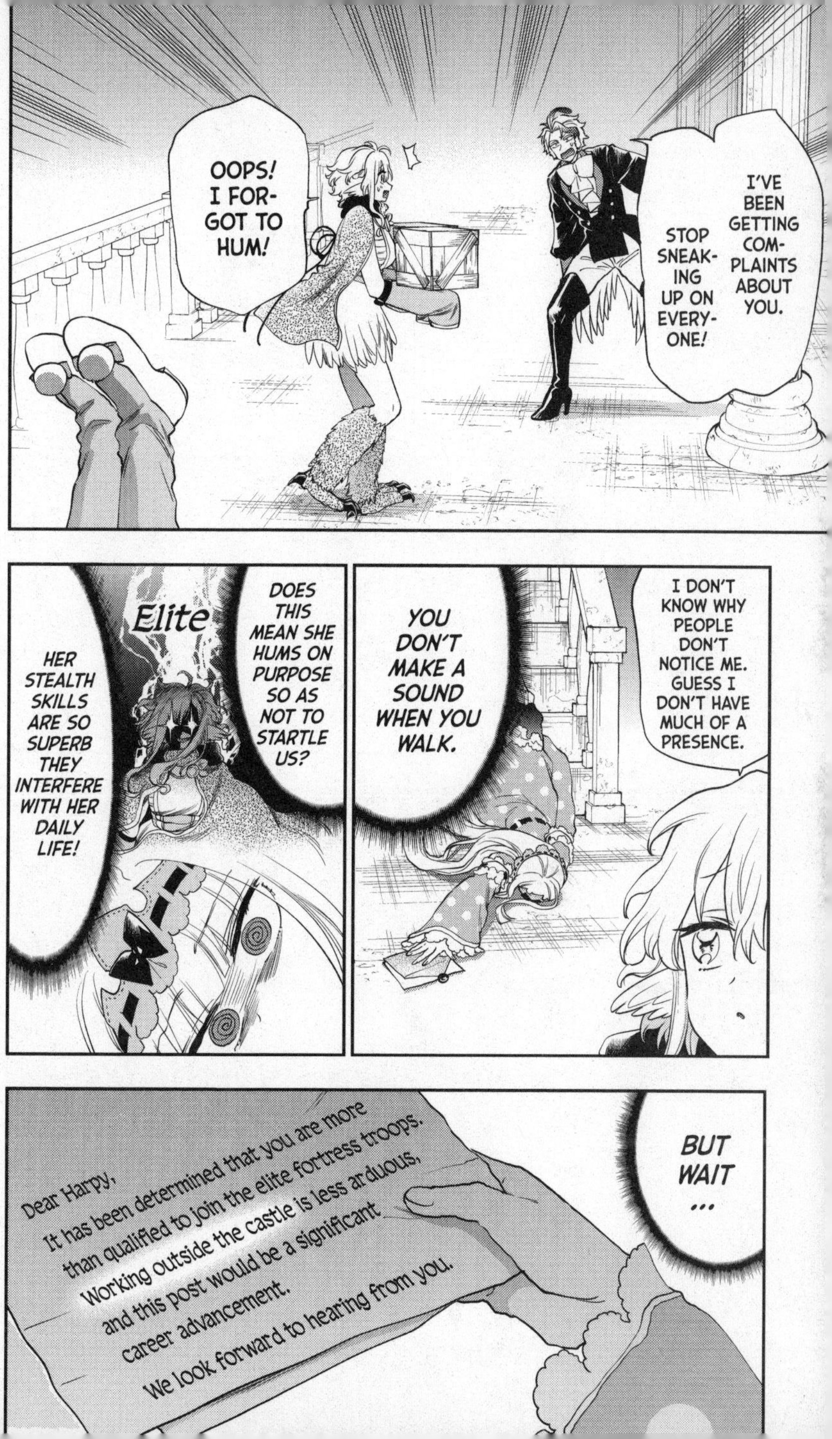
I'VE BEEN GETTING COMPLAINTS ABOUT YOU.
STOP SNEAKING UP ON EVERYONE!
OOPS! I FORGOT TO HUM!
I DON'T KNOW WHY PEOPLE DON'T NOTICE ME. GUESS I DON'T HAVE MUCH OF A PRESENCE.
YOU DON'T MAKE A SOUND WHEN YOU WALK.
DOES THIS MEAN SHE HUMS ON PURPOSE SO AS NOT TO STARTLE US?
Elite
HER STEALTH SKILLS ARE SO SUPERB THEY INTERFERE WITH HER DAILY LIFE!
BUT WAIT...
Dear Harpy,
It has been determined that you are more than qualified to join the elite fortress troops. Working outside the castle is less arduous, and this post would be a significant career advancement.
We look forward to hearing from you.

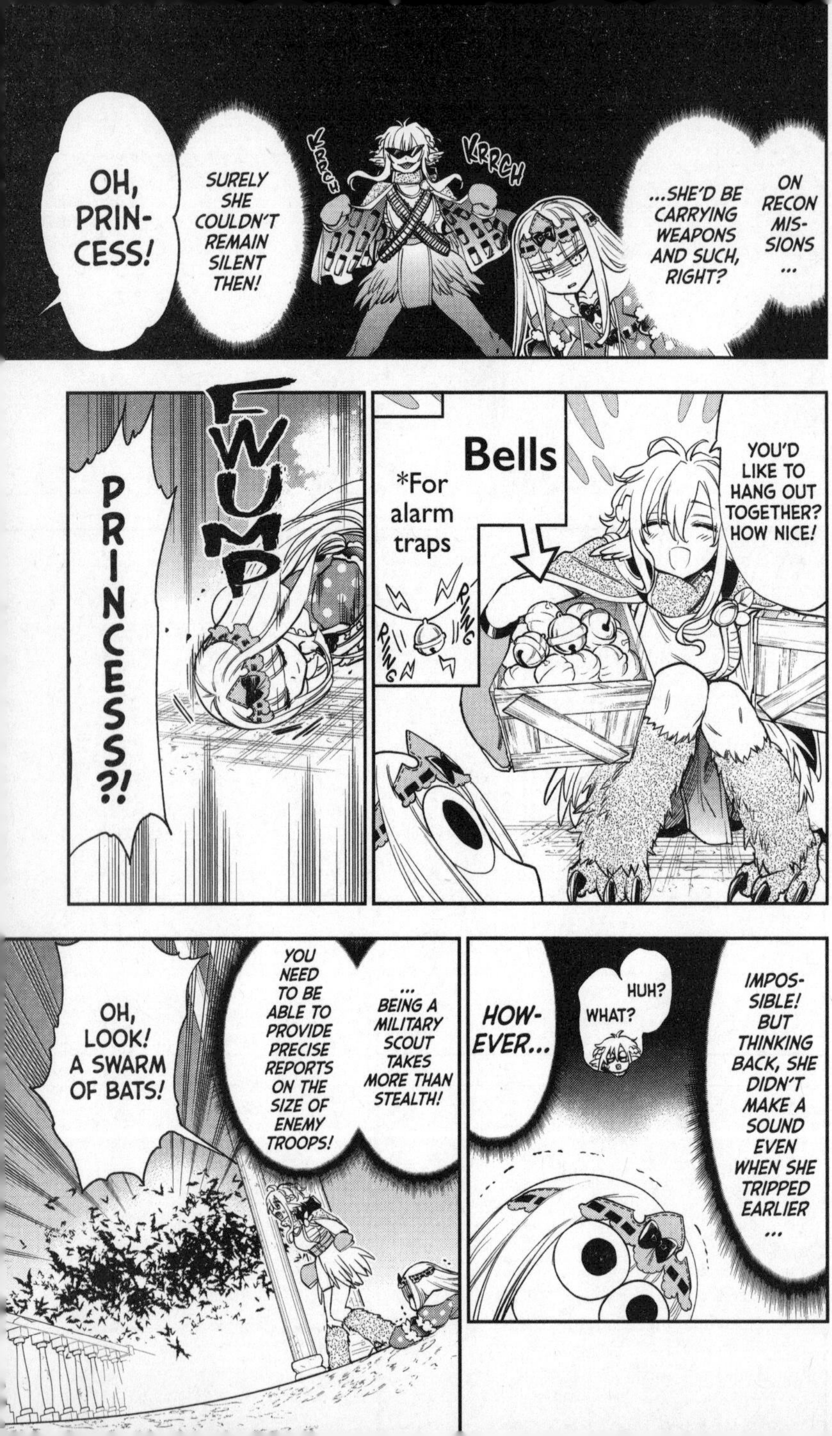
ON RECON MISSIONS...
...SHE'D BE CARRYING WEAPONS AND SUCH, RIGHT?
KRRCH
KRRCH
SURELY SHE COULDN'T REMAIN SILENT THEN!
OH, PRINCESS!
YOU'D LIKE TO HANG OUT TOGETHER? HOW NICE!
Bells
*For alarm traps
RIING
RIING
FWUMP
PRINCESS?!
IMPOSSIBLE! BUT THINKING BACK, SHE DIDN'T MAKE A SOUND EVEN WHEN SHE TRIPPED EARLIER...
HUH? WHAT?
HOWEVER...
...BEING A MILITARY SCOUT TAKES MORE THAN STEALTH!
YOU NEED TO BE ABLE TO PROVIDE PRECISE REPORTS ON THE SIZE OF ENEMY TROOPS!
OH, LOOK! A SWARM OF BATS!

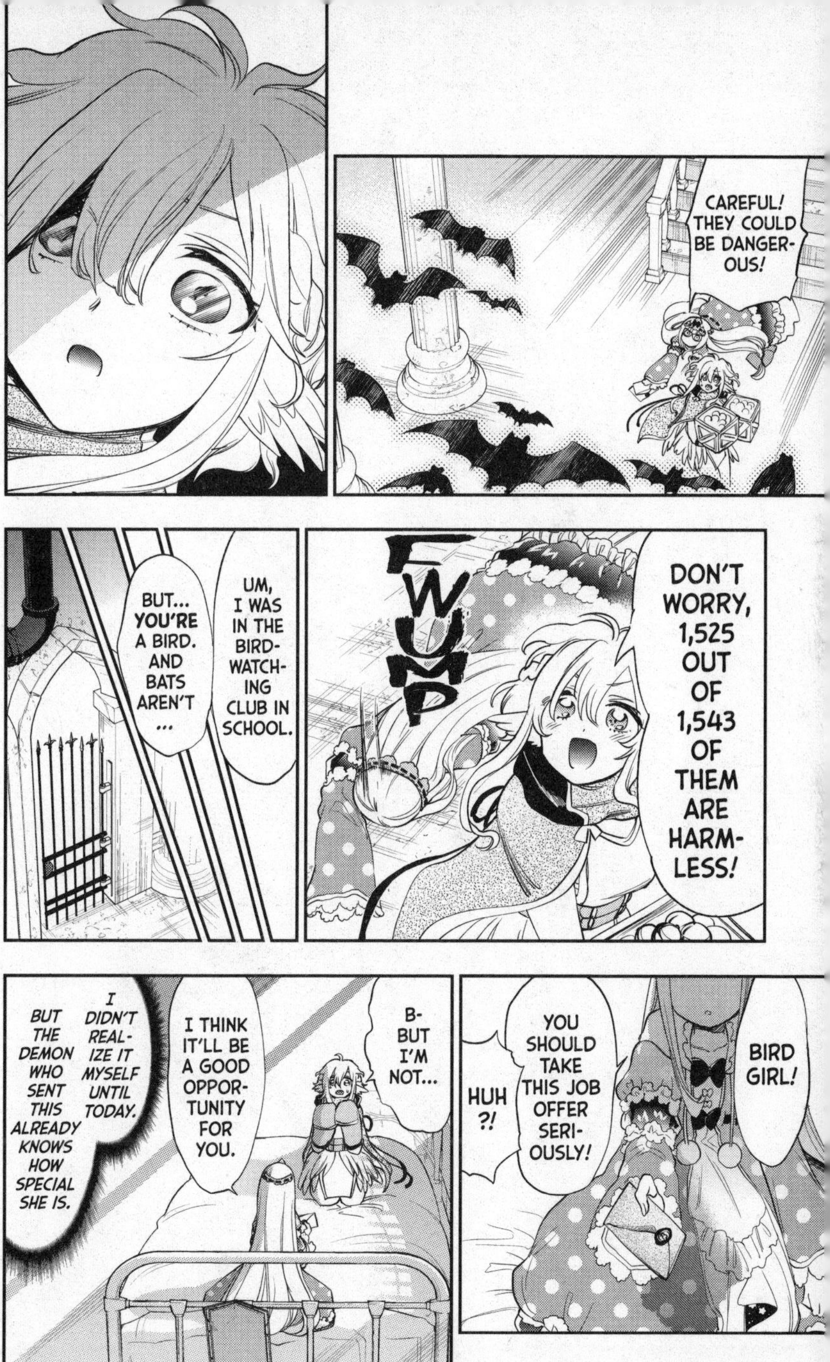
CAREFUL! THEY COULD BE DANGEROUS!
FWUMP
DON'T WORRY, 1,525 OUT OF 1,543 OF THEM ARE HARMLESS!
UM, I WAS IN THE BIRD-WATCHING CLUB IN SCHOOL.
BUT... YOU'RE A BIRD. AND BATS AREN'T ...
BIRD GIRL!
YOU SHOULD TAKE THIS JOB OFFER SERIOUSLY!
HUH?!
B-BUT I'M NOT...
I THINK IT'LL BE A GOOD OPPORTUNITY FOR YOU.
I DIDN'T REALIZE IT MYSELF UNTIL TODAY.
BUT THE DEMON WHO SENT THIS ALREADY KNOWS HOW SPECIAL SHE IS.

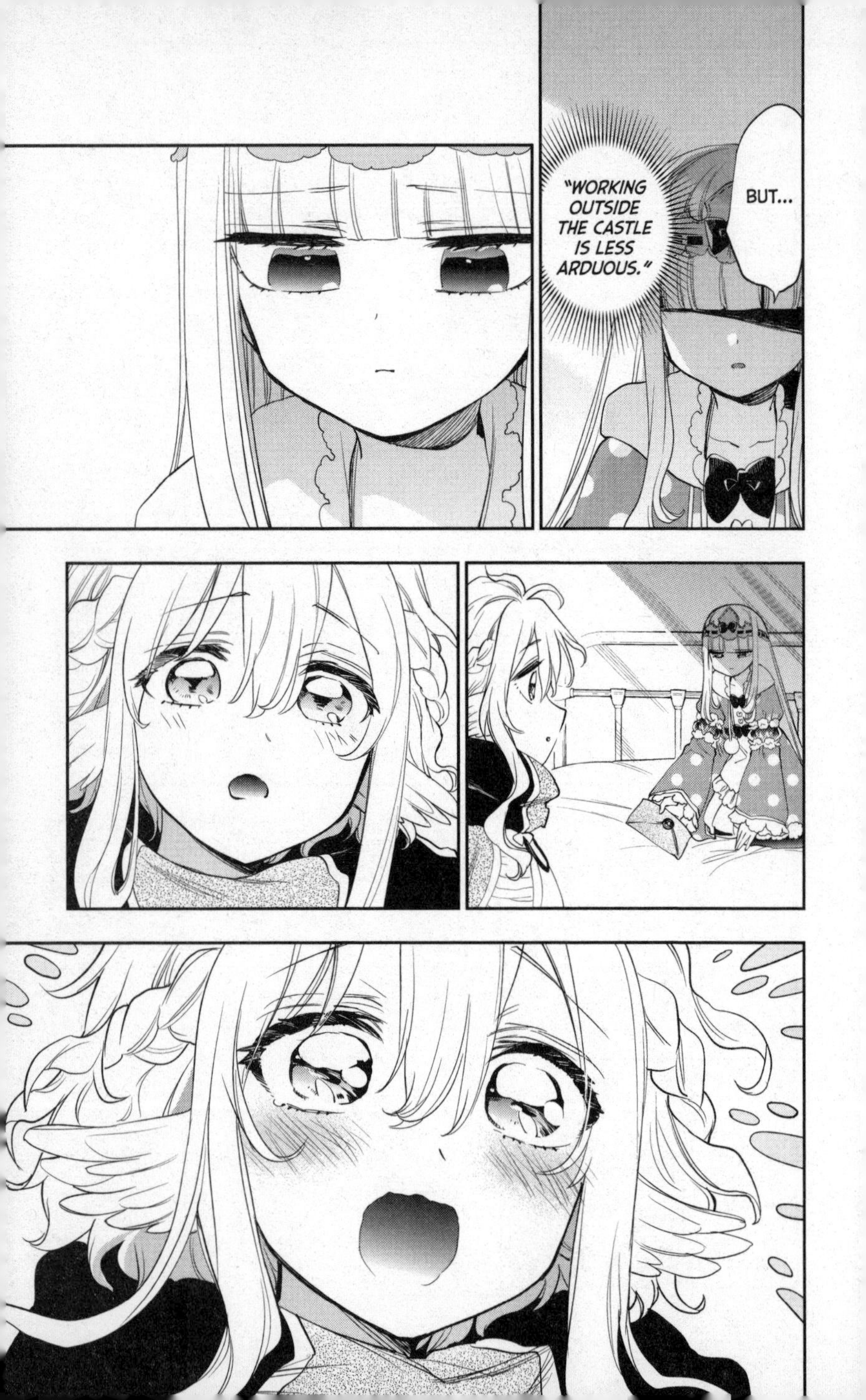
BUT...
"WORKING OUTSIDE THE CASTLE IS LESS ARDUOUS."

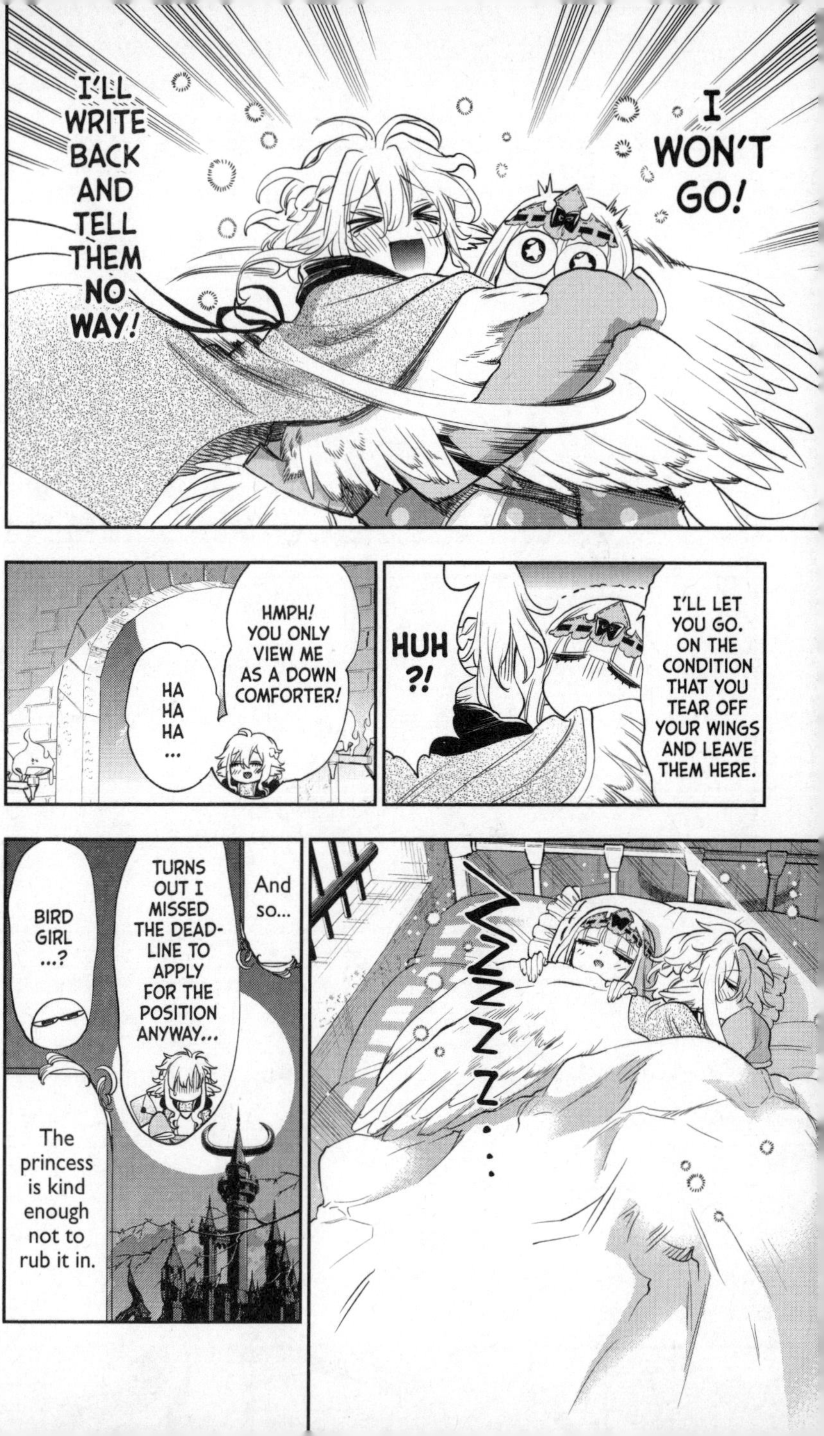
I WON'T GO!
I'LL WRITE BACK AND TELL THEM NO WAY!
I'LL LET YOU GO. ON THE CONDITION THAT YOU TEAR OFF YOUR WINGS AND LEAVE THEM HERE.
HUH ?!
HMPH! YOU ONLY VIEW ME AS A DOWN COMFORTER!
HA HA HA ...
ZZZZZ
And so...
TURNS OUT I MISSED THE DEAD-LINE TO APPLY FOR THE POSITION ANYWAY...
BIRD GIRL ...?
The princess is kind enough not to rub it in.

221st Night: Everything Becomes Princess—the Perfect Potion

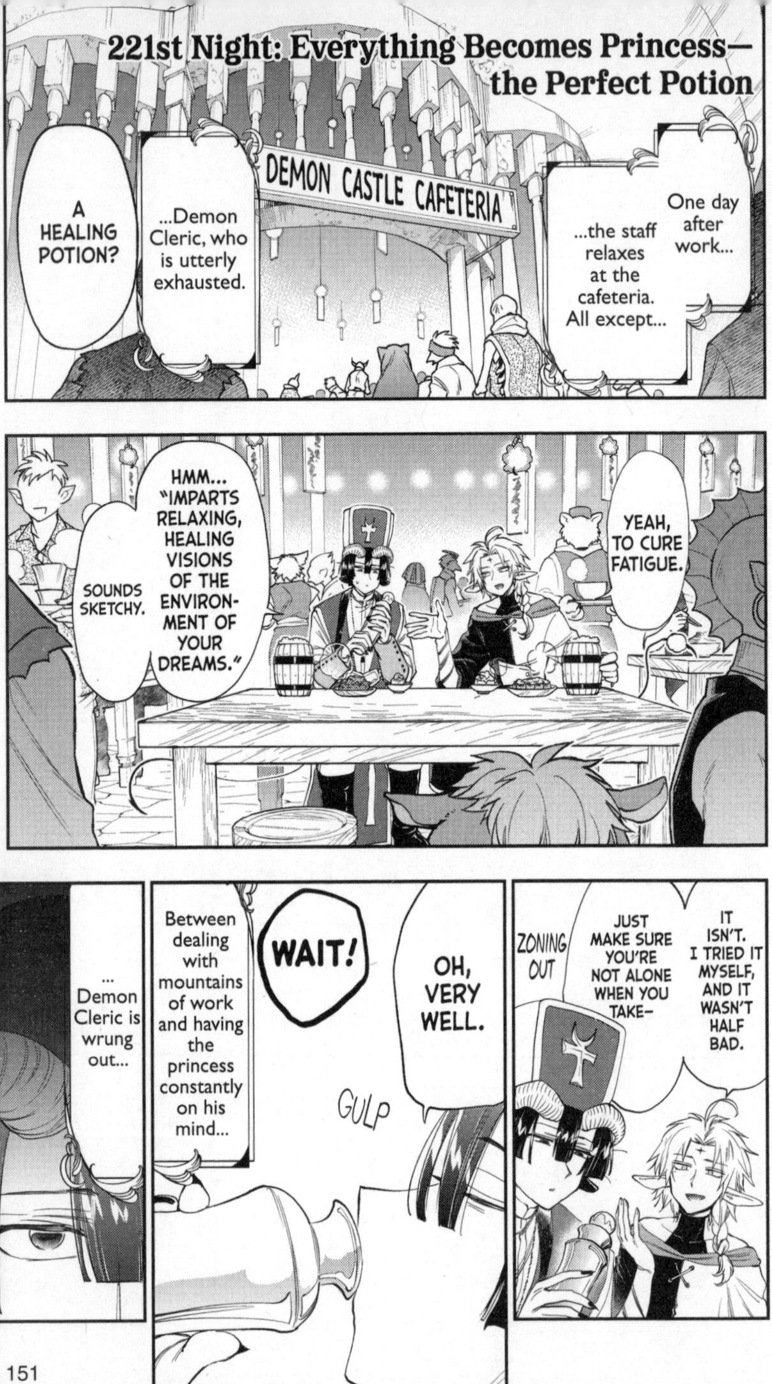

DEMON CASTLE CAFETERIA
One day after work...
...the staff relaxes at the cafeteria. All except...
...Demon Cleric, who is utterly exhausted.
A HEALING POTION?
YEAH, TO CURE FATIGUE.
HMM... "IMPARTS RELAXING, HEALING VISIONS OF THE ENVIRON-MENT OF YOUR DREAMS."
SOUNDS SKETCHY.
IT ISN'T. I TRIED IT MYSELF, AND IT WASN'T HALF BAD.
JUST MAKE SURE YOU'RE NOT ALONE WHEN YOU TAKE–
ZONING OUT
OH, VERY WELL.
WAIT!
Between dealing with mountains of work and having the princess constantly on his mind...
GULP
... Demon Cleric is wrung out...

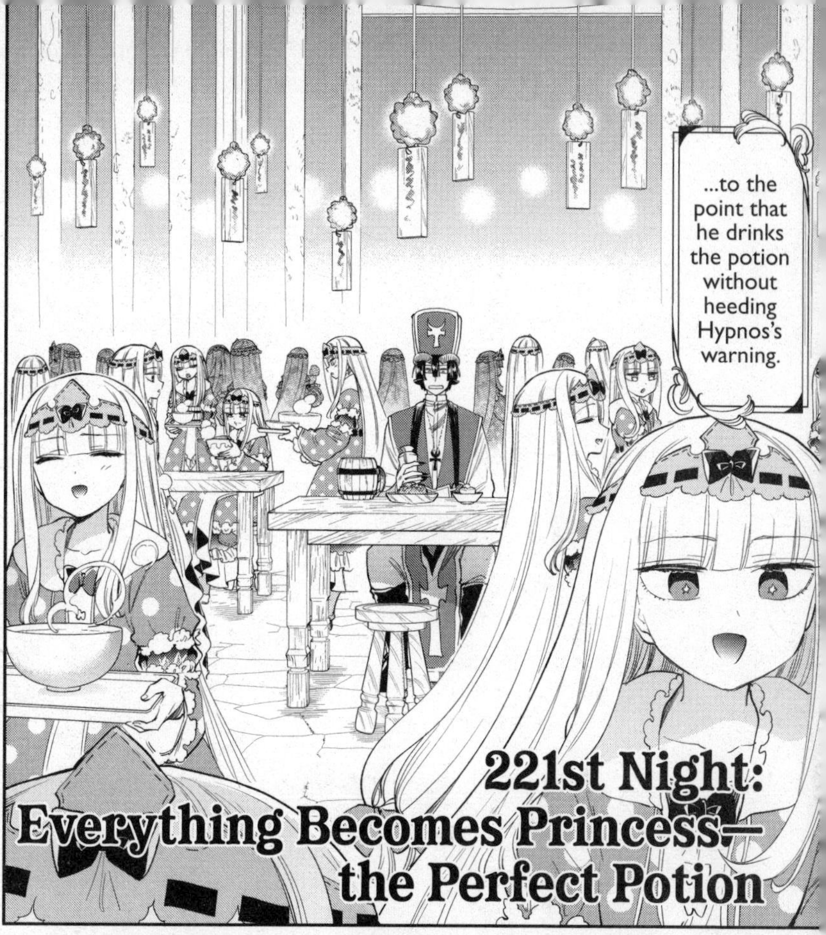
...to the point that he drinks the potion without heeding Hypnos's warning.
221st Night: Everything Becomes Princess—the Perfect Potion
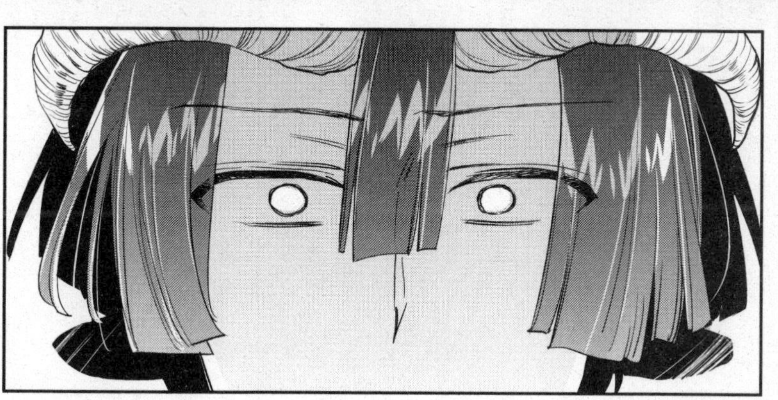

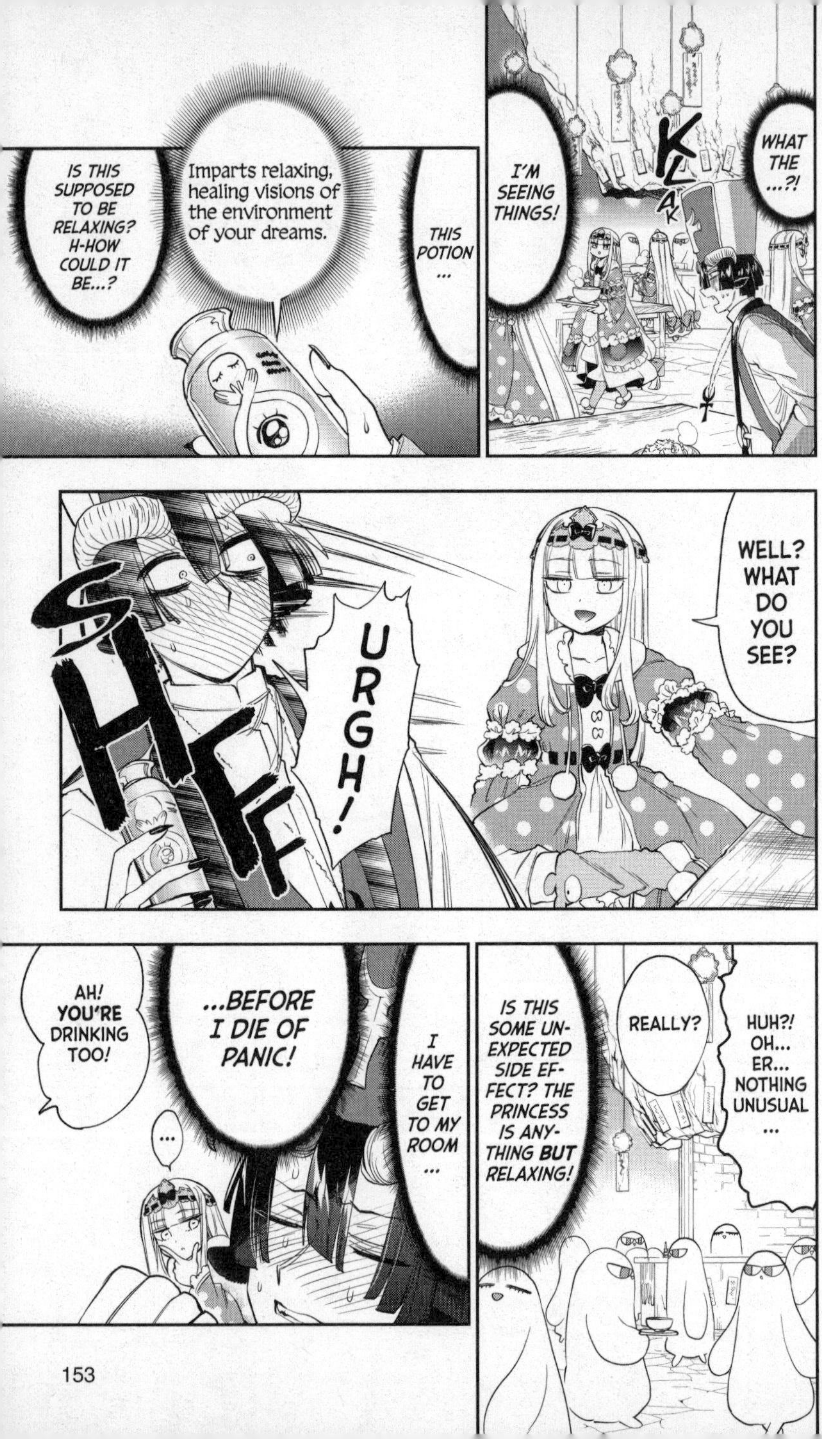
WHAT THE ...?!
KLAK
I'M SEEING THINGS!
THIS POTION ...
Imparts relaxing, healing visions of the environment of your dreams.
IS THIS SUPPOSED TO BE RELAXING? H-HOW COULD IT BE...?
WELL? WHAT DO YOU SEE?
URGH!
SHFF
HUH?! OH... ER... NOTHING UNUSUAL ...
REALLY?
IS THIS SOME UN-EXPECTED SIDE EF-FECT? THE PRINCESS IS ANY-THING **BUT** RELAXING!
I HAVE TO GET TO MY ROOM ...
...BEFORE I DIE OF PANIC!
AH! **YOU'RE** DRINKING TOO!
...

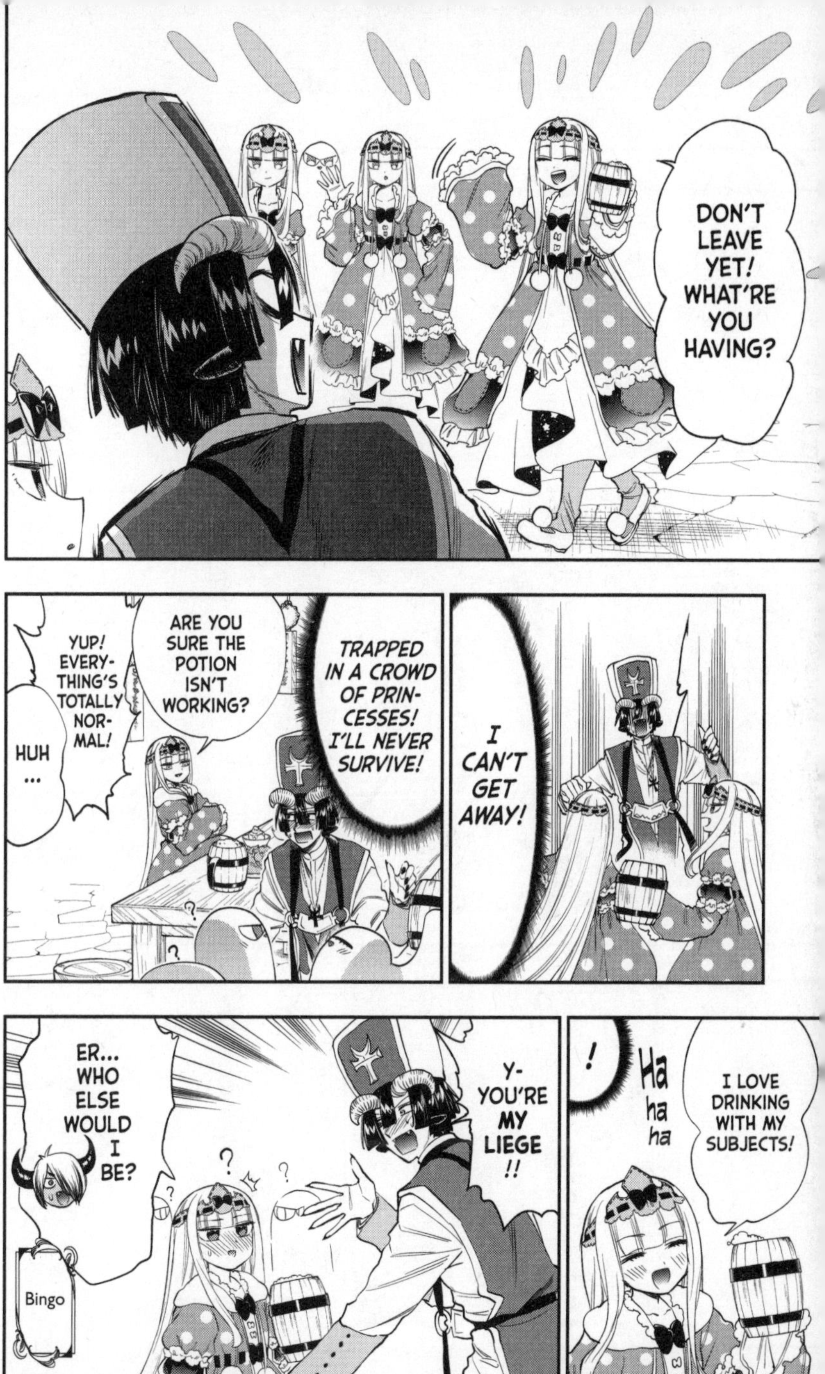
DON'T LEAVE YET! WHAT'RE YOU HAVING?
I CAN'T GET AWAY!
TRAPPED IN A CROWD OF PRIN-CESSES! I'LL NEVER SURVIVE!
ARE YOU SURE THE POTION ISN'T WORKING?
YUP! EVERY-THING'S TOTALLY NOR-MAL!
HUH ...
I LOVE DRINKING WITH MY SUBJECTS!
Ha ha ha
!
Y-YOU'RE MY LIEGE !!
ER... WHO ELSE WOULD I BE?
Bingo

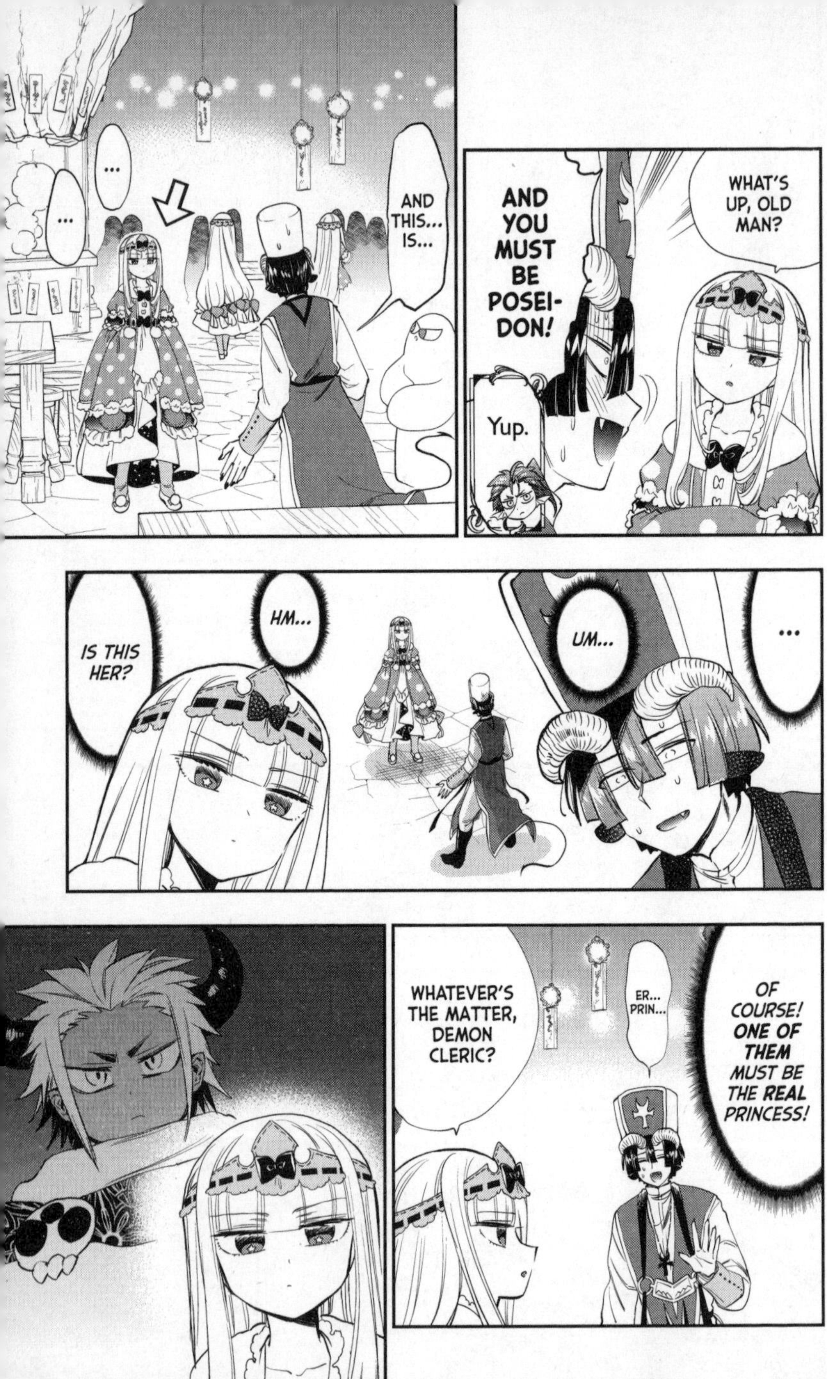
WHAT'S UP, OLD MAN?
AND YOU MUST BE POSEI-DON!
Yup.
AND THIS... IS...
...
...
...
UM...
HM...
IS THIS HER?
OF COURSE! ONE OF THEM MUST BE THE REAL PRINCESS!
ER... PRIN...
WHATEVER'S THE MATTER, DEMON CLERIC?

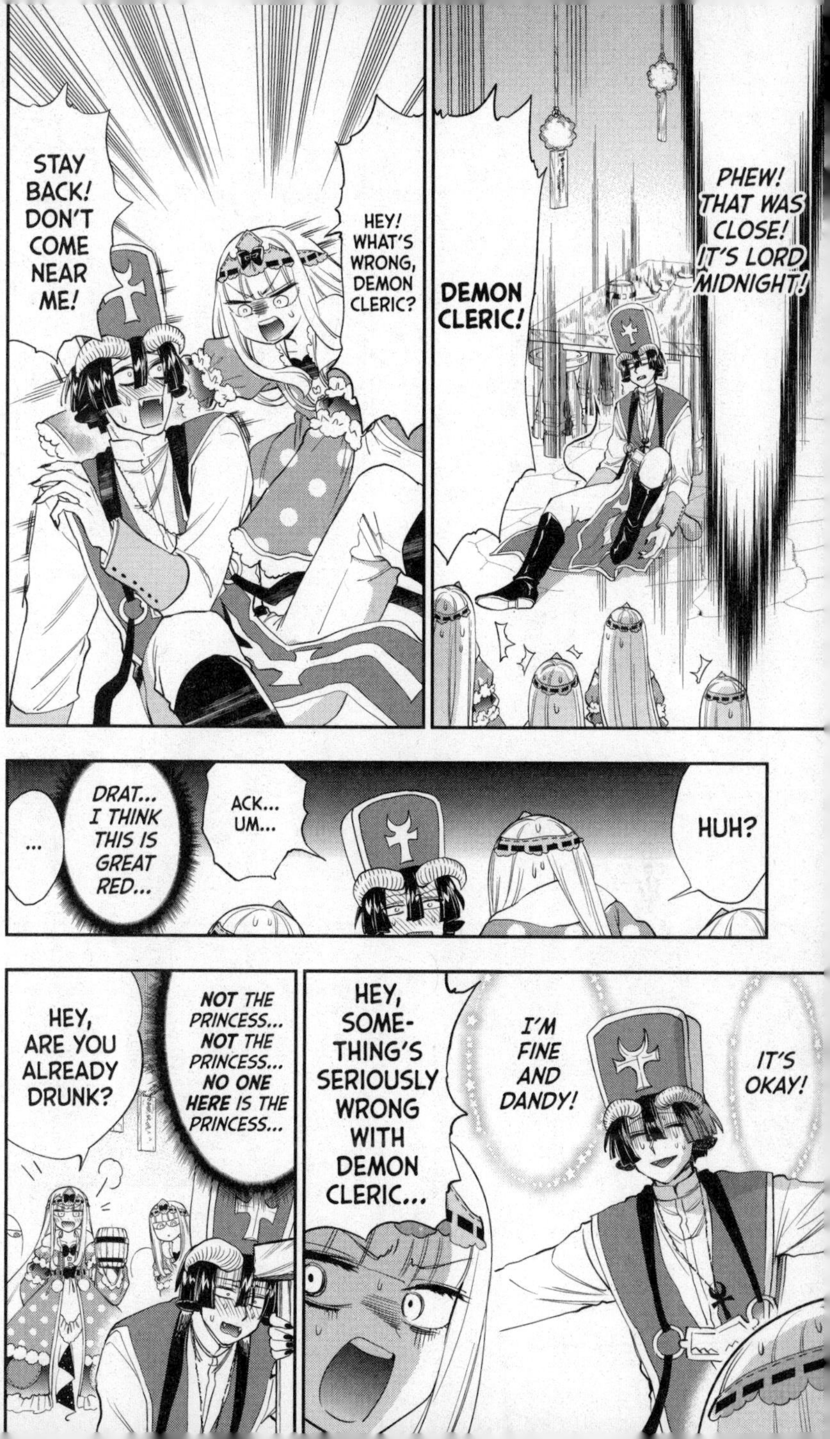
PHEW! THAT WAS CLOSE! IT'S LORD MIDNIGHT!
DEMON CLERIC!
HEY! WHAT'S WRONG, DEMON CLERIC?
STAY BACK! DON'T COME NEAR ME!
HUH?
ACK... UM...
DRAT... I THINK THIS IS GREAT RED...
...
IT'S OKAY!
I'M FINE AND DANDY!
HEY, SOME-THING'S SERIOUSLY WRONG WITH DEMON CLERIC...
NOT THE PRINCESS... NOT THE PRINCESS... NO ONE HERE IS THE PRINCESS...
HEY, ARE YOU ALREADY DRUNK?

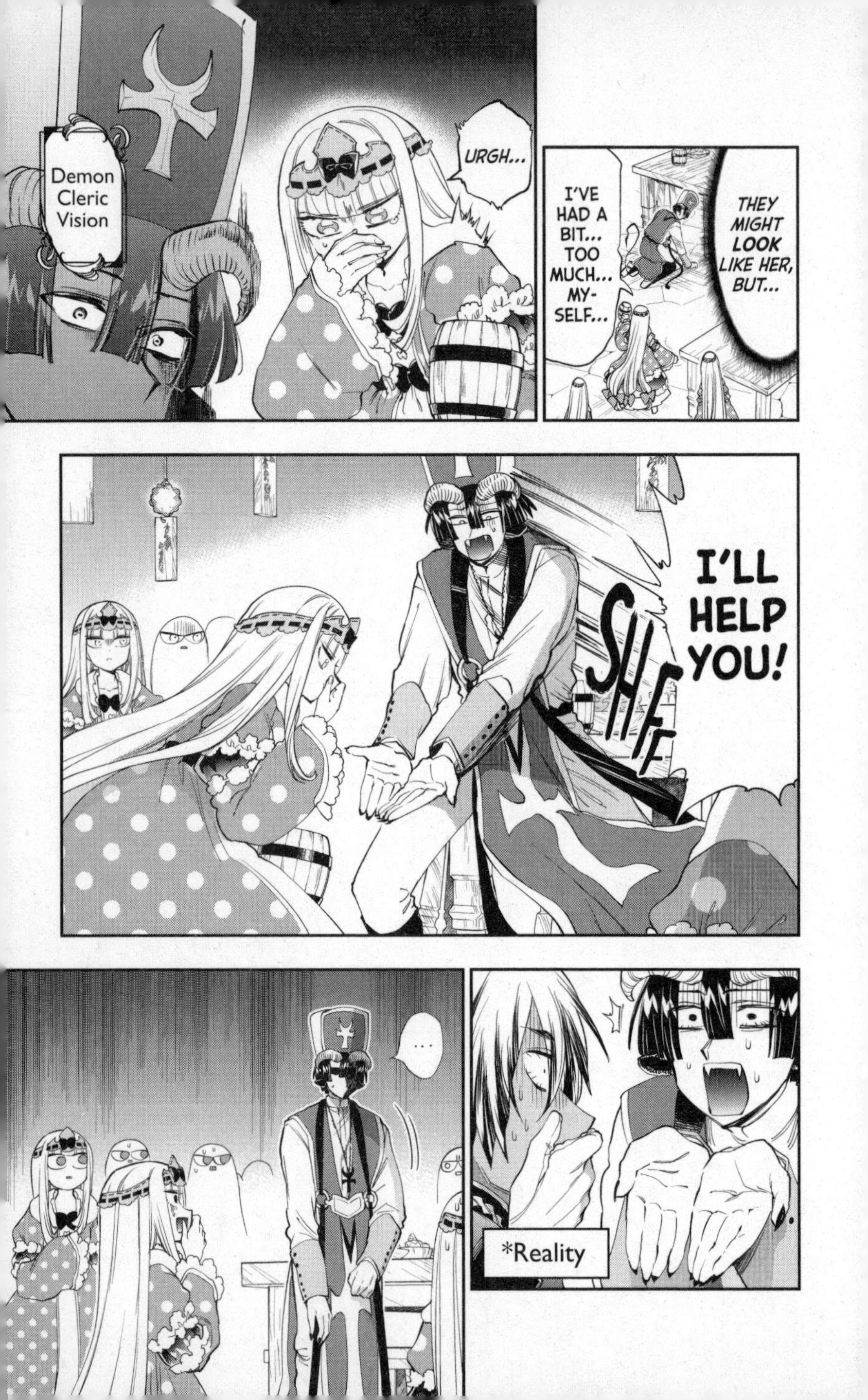
THEY MIGHT LOOK LIKE HER, BUT...
I'VE HAD A BIT... TOO MUCH... MY-SELF...
URGH...
Demon Cleric Vision
I'LL HELP YOU!
SHFF
*Reality
...

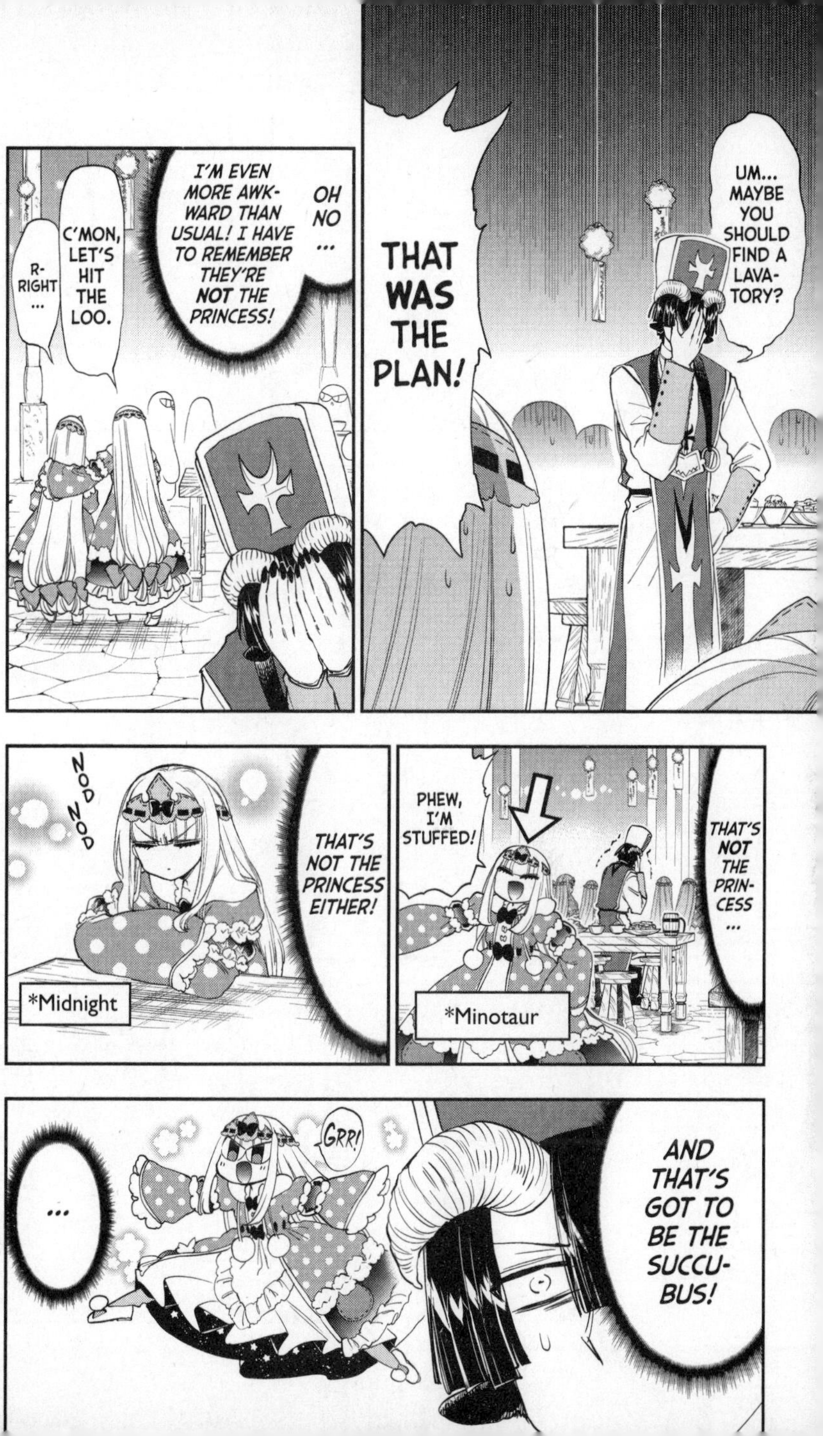
UM... MAYBE YOU SHOULD FIND A LAVATORY?
THAT WAS THE PLAN!
OH NO ...
I'M EVEN MORE AWKWARD THAN USUAL! I HAVE TO REMEMBER THEY'RE NOT THE PRINCESS!
C'MON, LET'S HIT THE LOO.
R-RIGHT ...
THAT'S NOT THE PRINCESS ...
PHEW, I'M STUFFED!
*Minotaur
THAT'S NOT THE PRINCESS EITHER!
NOD NOD
*Midnight
AND THAT'S GOT TO BE THE SUCCUBUS!
GRR!
...

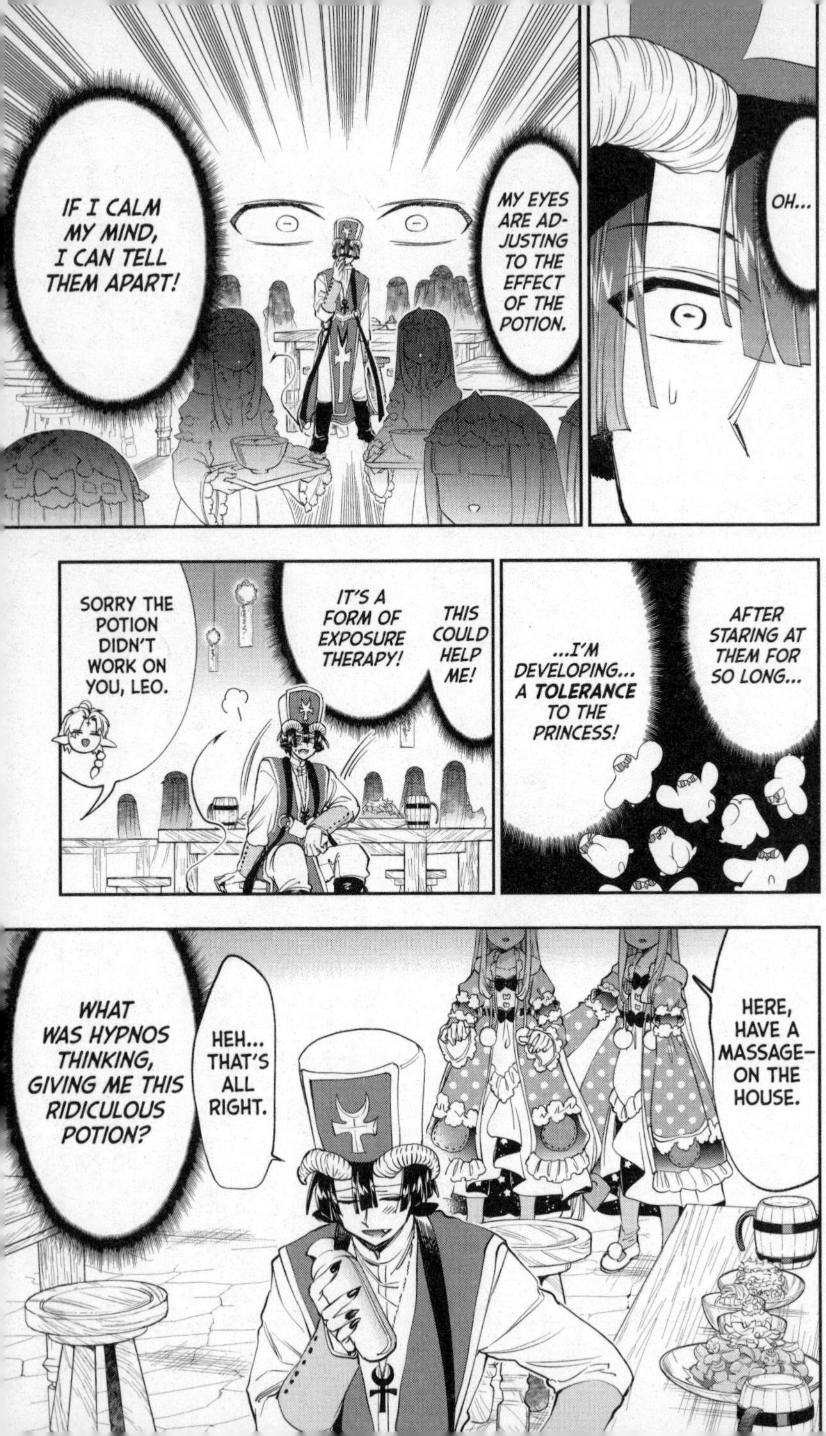
OH...
MY EYES ARE ADJUSTING TO THE EFFECT OF THE POTION.
IF I CALM MY MIND, I CAN TELL THEM APART!
AFTER STARING AT THEM FOR SO LONG...
...I'M DEVELOPING... A **TOLERANCE** TO THE PRINCESS!
THIS COULD HELP ME!
IT'S A FORM OF EXPOSURE THERAPY!
SORRY THE POTION DIDN'T WORK ON YOU, LEO.
HERE, HAVE A MASSAGE— ON THE HOUSE.
HEH... THAT'S ALL RIGHT.
WHAT WAS HYPNOS THINKING, GIVING ME THIS RIDICULOUS POTION?

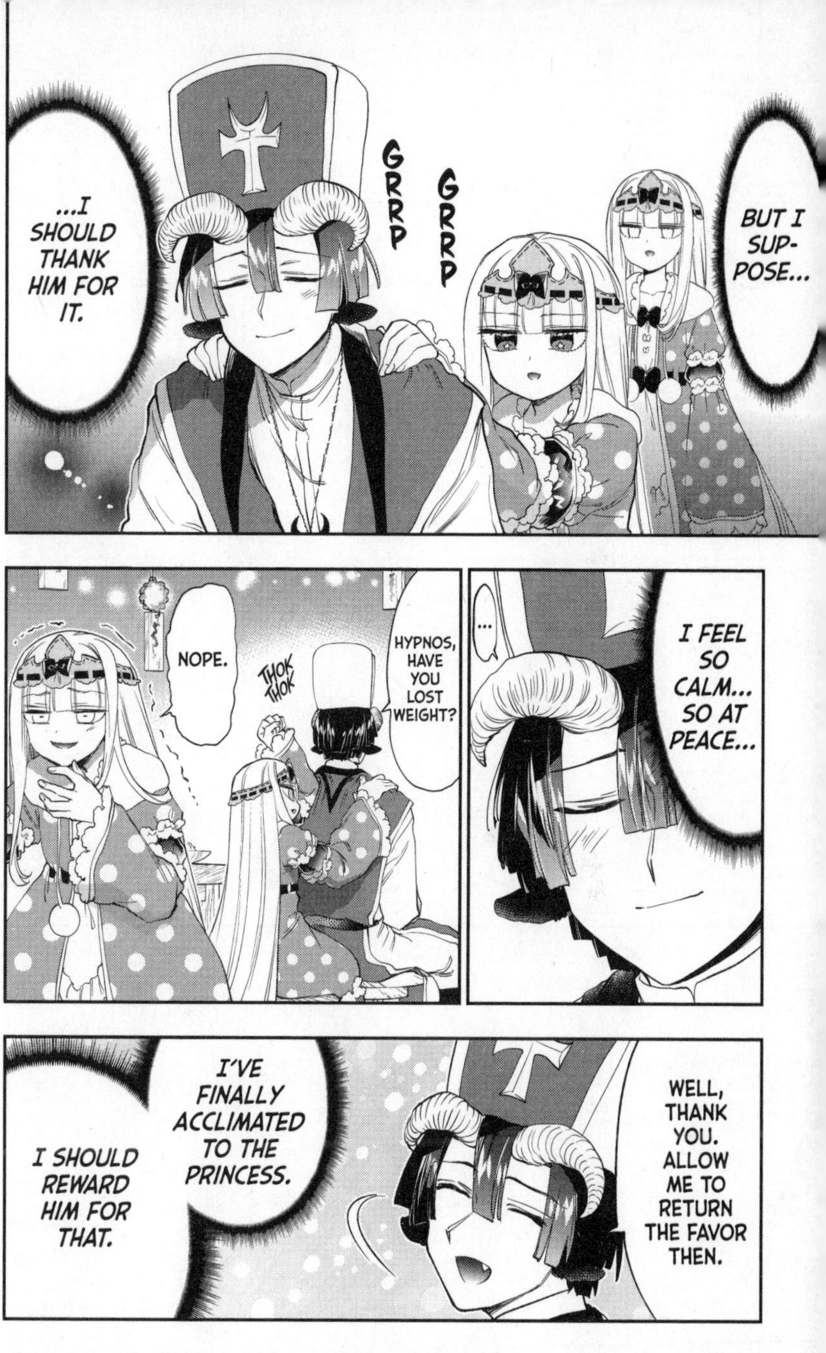
BUT I SUPPOSE...
GRRP
GRRP
...I SHOULD THANK HIM FOR IT.
I FEEL SO CALM... SO AT PEACE...
...
HYPNOS, HAVE YOU LOST WEIGHT?
THOK THOK
NOPE.
WELL, THANK YOU. ALLOW ME TO RETURN THE FAVOR THEN.
I'VE FINALLY ACCLIMATED TO THE PRINCESS.
I SHOULD REWARD HIM FOR THAT.

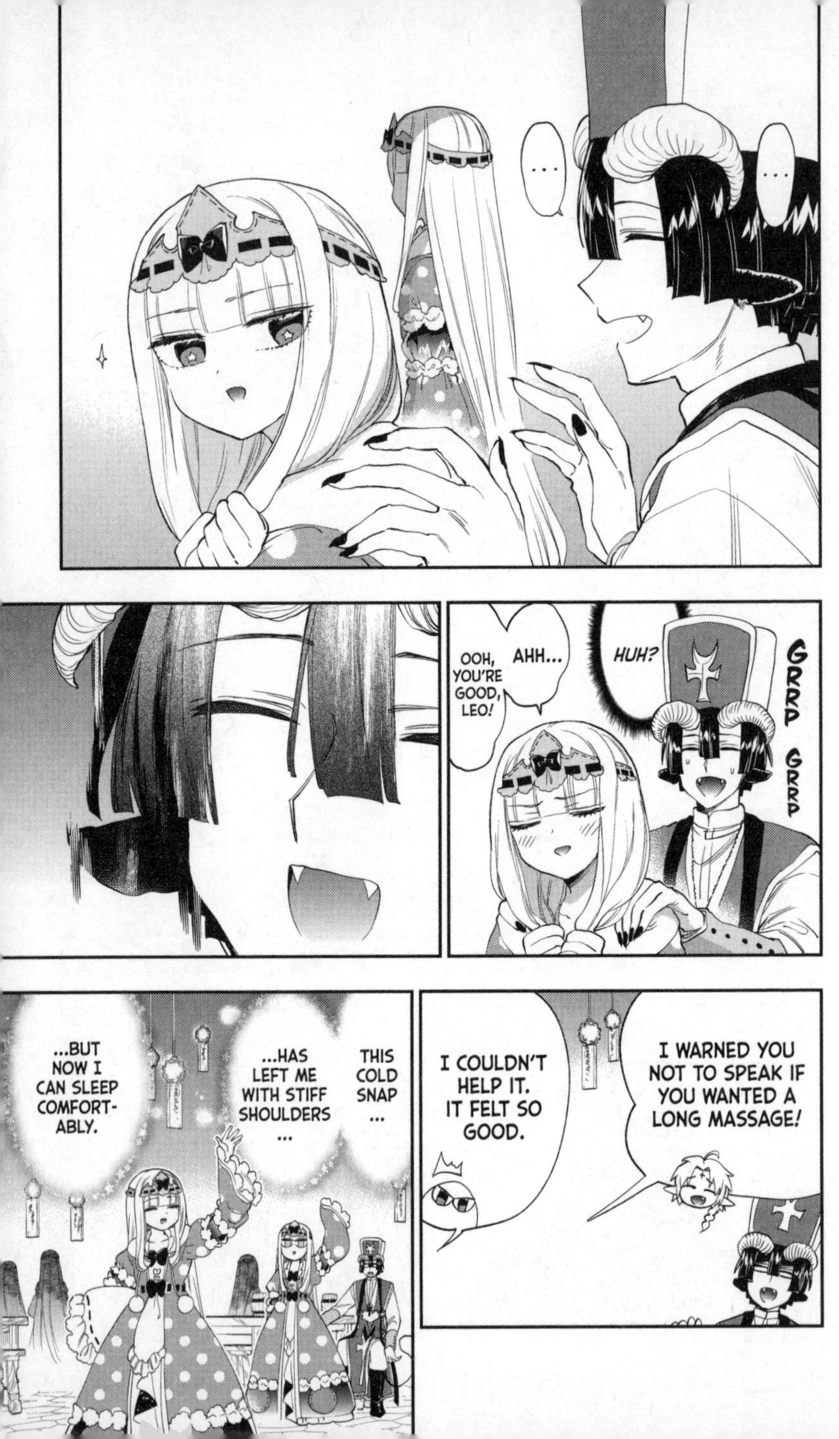
...
...
GRRP GRRP
HUH?
AHH...
OOH, YOU'RE GOOD, LEO!
I WARNED YOU NOT TO SPEAK IF YOU WANTED A LONG MASSAGE!
I COULDN'T HELP IT. IT FELT SO GOOD.
THIS COLD SNAP ...
...HAS LEFT ME WITH STIFF SHOULDERS ...
...BUT NOW I CAN SLEEP COMFORT-ABLY.

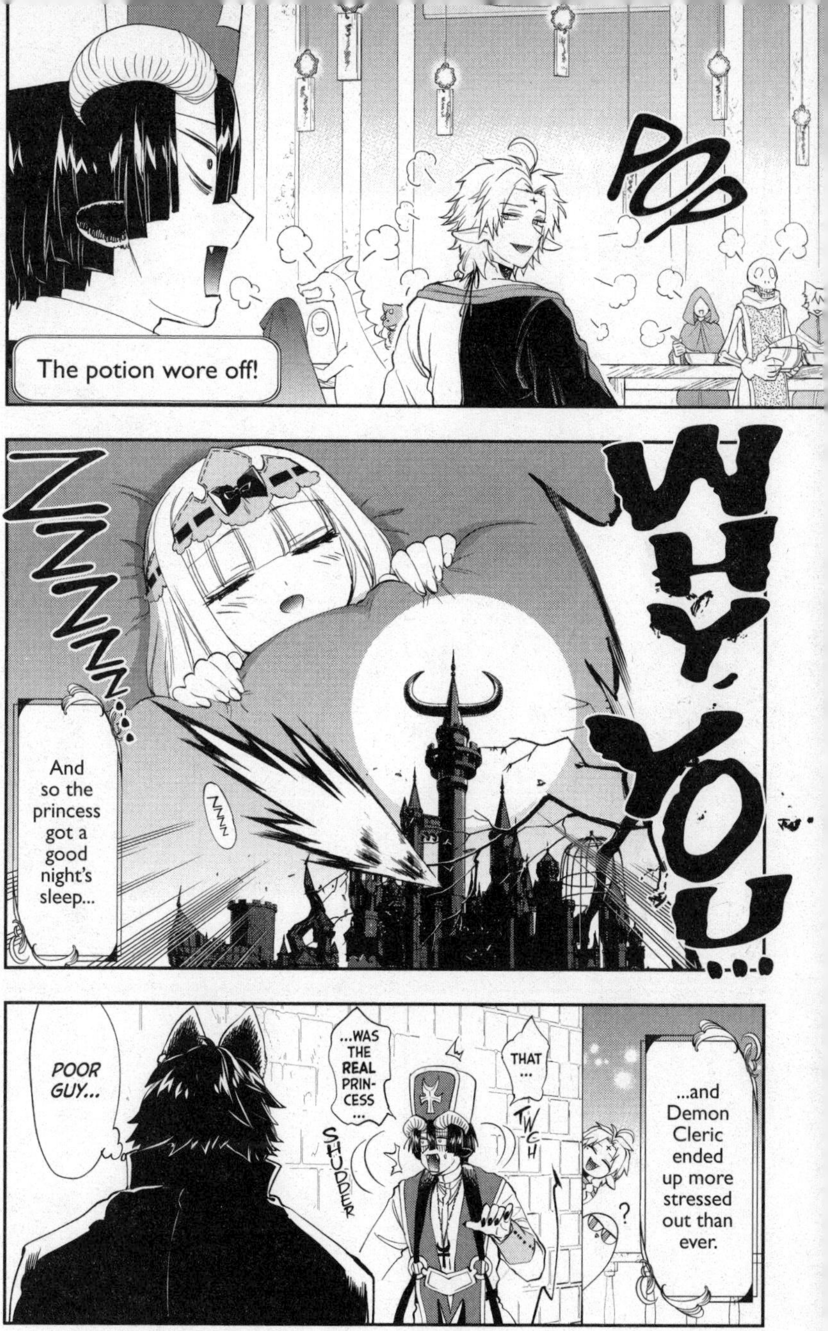
POP
The potion wore off!
WHY, YOU...!
ZZZZZZ...
ZZZZ
And so the princess got a good night's sleep...
...and Demon Cleric ended up more stressed out than ever.
?
THAT...
TWCH
...WAS THE REAL PRINCESS...
SHUDDER
POOR GUY...

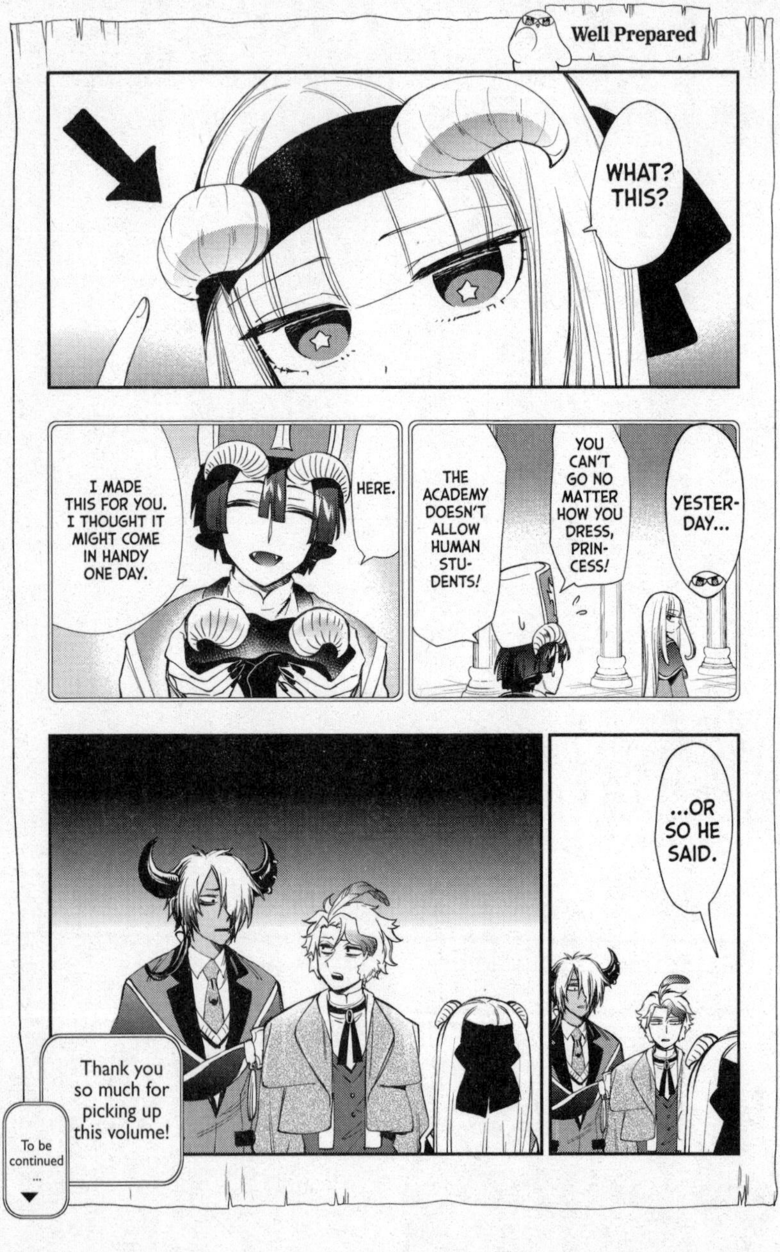
Well Prepared
WHAT? THIS?
YESTER-DAY...
YOU CAN'T GO NO MATTER HOW YOU DRESS, PRIN-CESS!
THE ACADEMY DOESN'T ALLOW HUMAN STU-DENTS!
HERE.
I MADE THIS FOR YOU. I THOUGHT IT MIGHT COME IN HANDY ONE DAY.
...OR SO HE SAID.
Thank you so much for picking up this volume!
To be continued ...

SLEEPY PRINCESS ANIME INTRO

This interview first ran in issue 50 of *Shonen Sunday* magazine.

Q&A with Storyboard Artist Megumi Soeno!

Q: The opening is so unique and fun. When I first saw it, I was astounded!

Soeno: The director, Yamasaki, didn't give me express instructions when she asked me to create the storyboards. I tried to create the vibe of a never-ending carnival or school festival, a place you'd never want to leave.

Q: An endless, dreamlike world? That sounds perfect for *Sleepy Princess in the Demon Castle*!

Soeno: Now that you mention it, you're right! I wanted to create the feeling of a dream.

Q: So many characters appear in the opening. It's a lot to take in.

Soeno: The producer may not want me to tell you this, but (*laugh*) I've been told it's the most fast-paced opening in Doga Kobo history. We used 1,800 cuts. Usually an entire 20-minute anime includes 3,000 to 4,000 cuts. So we basically used enough shots for half an episode in a minute-and-a-half opening sequence.

Q: I was amazed when I saw it for the first time. I thought, whoa, it's so fluid! How is this possible?!

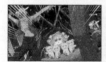 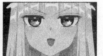

What's your favorite shot?

Q: Is there a specific moment that struck you when you saw the final product?

Soeno: I like the part at the end where the princess is singing really quickly. I believe the right tempo or timing will surprise you and make you laugh no matter how many times you see something. I usually have to watch footage over and over, one or two hundred times, before it's completed. After a while, it feels like I'm looking at nothing but shots with room for improvement.

Q: You can always think of another way to do it, huh?

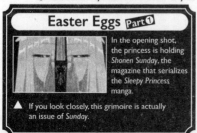

Easter Eggs Part ❶

In the opening shot, the princess is holding *Shonen Sunday*, the magazine that serializes the *Sleepy Princess* manga.

▲ If you look closely, this grimoire is actually an issue of *Sunday*.

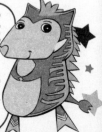

Megumi Soeno PROFILE

A top animator responsible for storyboarding the opening and closing sequences for such series as *Ikebukuro West Gate Park* and *The Seven Deadly Sins: Imperial Wrath of the Gods*.

THE MAKING OF THE

Here's how the irresistible opening sequence was created!

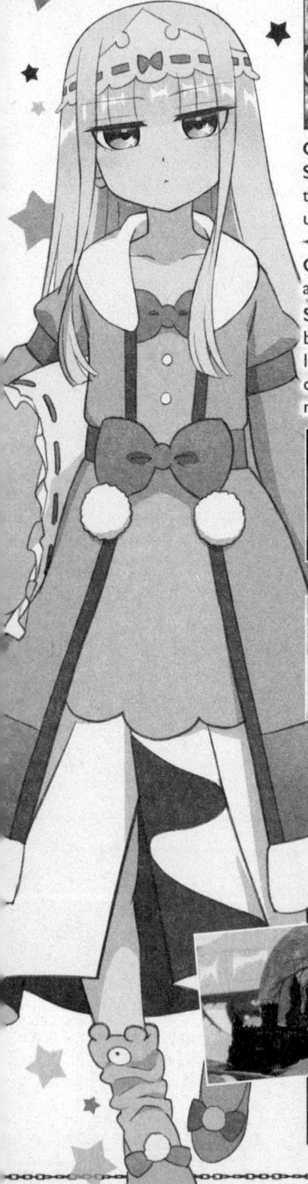

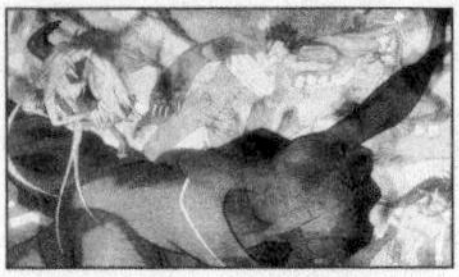

Soeno: Yes. But every now and then, I'll come across a shot that satisfies me and get hooked on watching it over and over. In this intro, I love the bit where the princess chases the demons around until she falls and turns into a tombstone.

Q: Right! It's a very effective moment.

Soeno: I put in a cheesy dramatic shot of the Demon King and the hero to grab the viewer's attention. Then it cuts to the princess, up to her usual mischief. The contrast is a special touch.

Q: I like the shot in the beginning where the princess turns around and a little window opens in the back of her head.

Soeno: When I heard the opening song for the first time, since it's a solo by Inori Minase, I imagined the princess dancing and singing by herself. I could've just gone with that if I wanted to emphasize the princess's cuteness, but I wanted to show her other sides as well. After all, she's not just cute. She can be reckless and dangerous too.

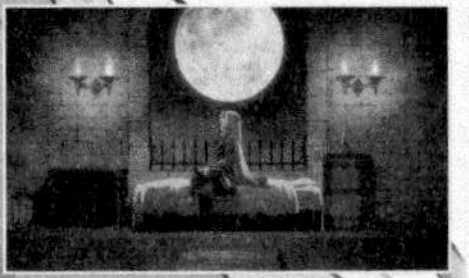

Q: That's right. She's full of surprises.

Soeno: The first half of the intro is supposed to suggest the world of the princess's dreams. Anything can happen in a dream, even a window opening in her head...

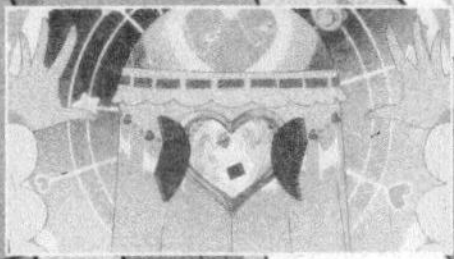

Q: I get it. Anything goes in dreams.

Easter Eggs Part②

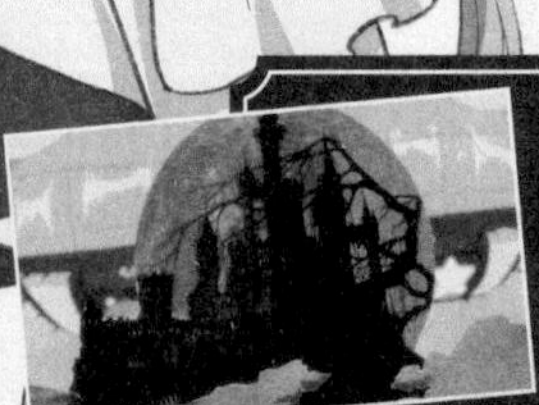

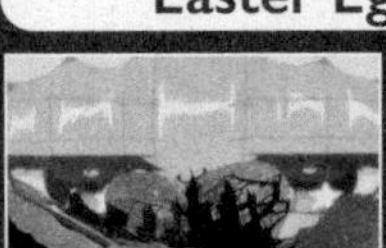

They made a real pop-up book!

▲ The Doga Kobo production department created a physical pop-up book and scanned it for the opening shot.

The Making of the *Sleepy Princess* Anime Intro

A Broadway Musical?!

Soeno: I don't often use this method for an intro sequence, but I included a number of shots designed to look like they were done with a fixed video camera. I wanted to add a touch of Broadway to the festival atmosphere and give the impression that the viewers are watching from theater seats.

Q: Like they're watching a Broadway musical?

Soeno: Yes. When the princess sings about being a damsel in distress, and again when she sings about heading into the dreamworld, I tried to make it look like those moments were filmed with the same camera.

Q: In the beginning the princess is dancing alone, but in the second half she's dancing with the others.

Soeno: In the first half she's trapped in her prison, but in the second half she breaks out and dances with her friends...well, demons.

Q: So the first half and second half were created to contrast with each other. It fits the story perfectly because the princess gradually befriends the demons as the story unfolds.

Princess Syalis is a fun character to draw.

Soeno: The director, Yamasaki, and the producer, Saito, said they'd entrust the opening to me. Trust can be a strong incentive. I'm sure it's the same in any business. You want to live up to others' expectations.

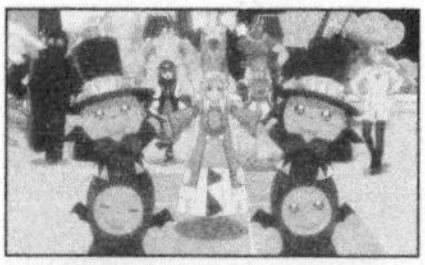

I'm grateful to *Sunday* for letting me work on a character like the princess, who's so much fun to animate.

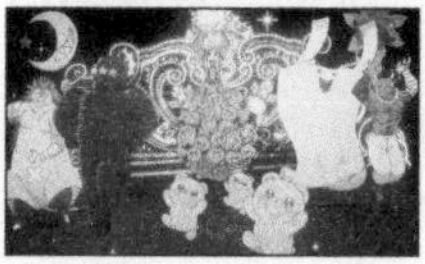

Q: Oh no! We're more than grateful to you, Soeno, for creating something that surpassed our expectations!

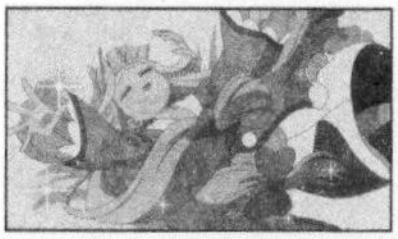

Soeno: It's rare, but fun, to have a character whose movements are more expressive than her facial expressions. It's a lot easier for me to come up with situations to animate if the central character is entertaining.

Q: Talking with you makes me want to watch the intro again! Thanks so much for joining me today.

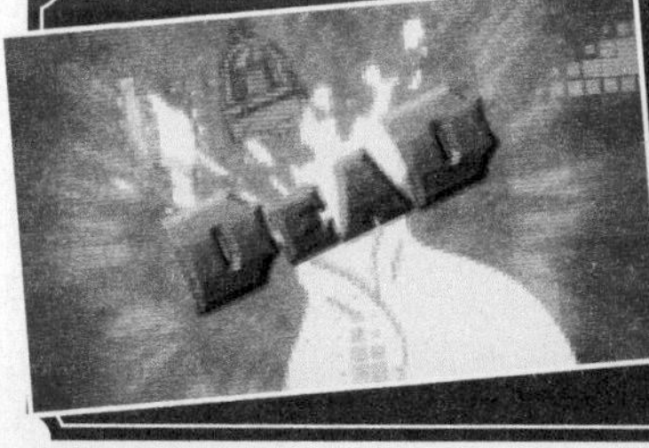
DEAD

Easter Eggs Part③

The pixelated tombstone was designed to look like a video game icon.

◀ There are a lot of gaming references in the manga, so Soeno came up with the idea of including an image that looked like it came from a video game.

Director Mitsue Yamasaki is known for her work on such anime as *Monthly Girls' Nozaki-kun*, *Tada Never Falls in Love*, and *How Heavy Are the Dumbbells You Lift?*

Sleepy Princess Anime Director

Mitsue Yamasaki Q&A

Q: What were your thoughts the first time you saw the storyboards?

I thought they were full of ideas I'd never have come up with! When you're working on a series, there's a tendency to get trapped within the framework of typical anime conventions. Soeno's storyboards were unconventional while perfectly representing the princess's freewheeling charm. Her expressions are really funny and cute too!

Q: What's your favorite part?

I like the shot of the princess spinning around. It's so surreal I had to laugh when I first saw it.

Q: Was there anything you asked Soeno to do when developing the intro?

I told him to keep in mind that the princess gradually becomes friends with the demons. On the other hand, I gave him permission to have the Ghost Shrouds and Slimeys torn to pieces (*laugh*). This is a series with a big cast, so it felt like I had to cut a lot when I gave him the go-ahead...but even after that, there sure are a lot of characters in this intro. And last but not least, I wanted the princess to fall asleep at the end. I wanted to see her sleeping sweetly.

Q: Is there anything you'd like to say to our readers?

If you're already watching, thanks! We've done our best to extract the princess's full cuteness and bring her to life. Please drift off and dream with the anime. And to those who haven't seen it yet, this is an anime about a princess whose obsession is sleeping. It'll make you want to be obsessed with sleeping too! So please check it out!

Director Mitsue Yamasaki, thank you very much!

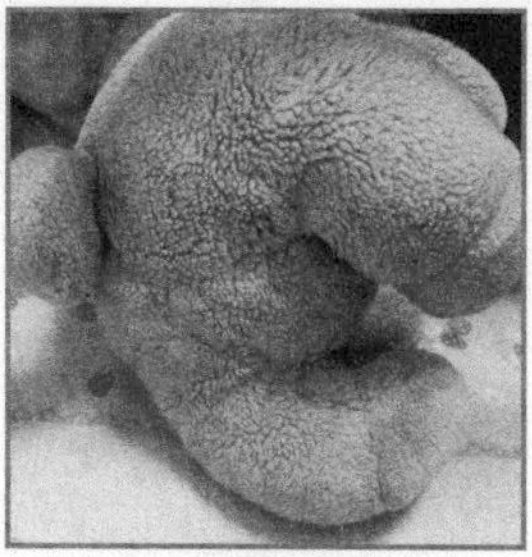

I have so much work to do, Teddy...

– KAGIJI KUMANOMATA

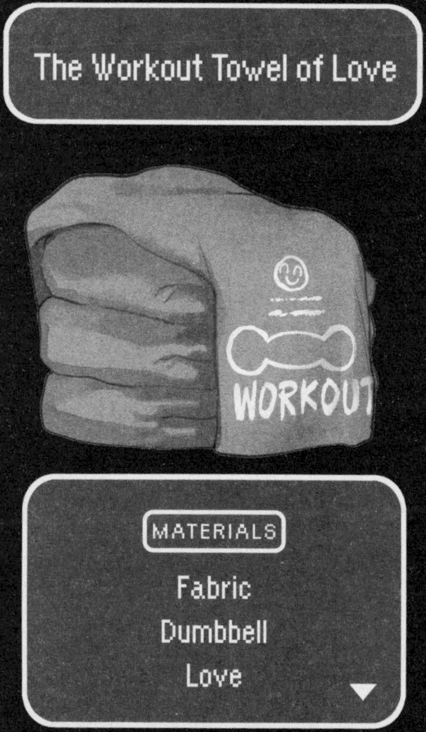
The Workout Towel of Love
WORKOUT
MATERIALS
Fabric
Dumbbell
Love

Those who lurk beneath the cover...

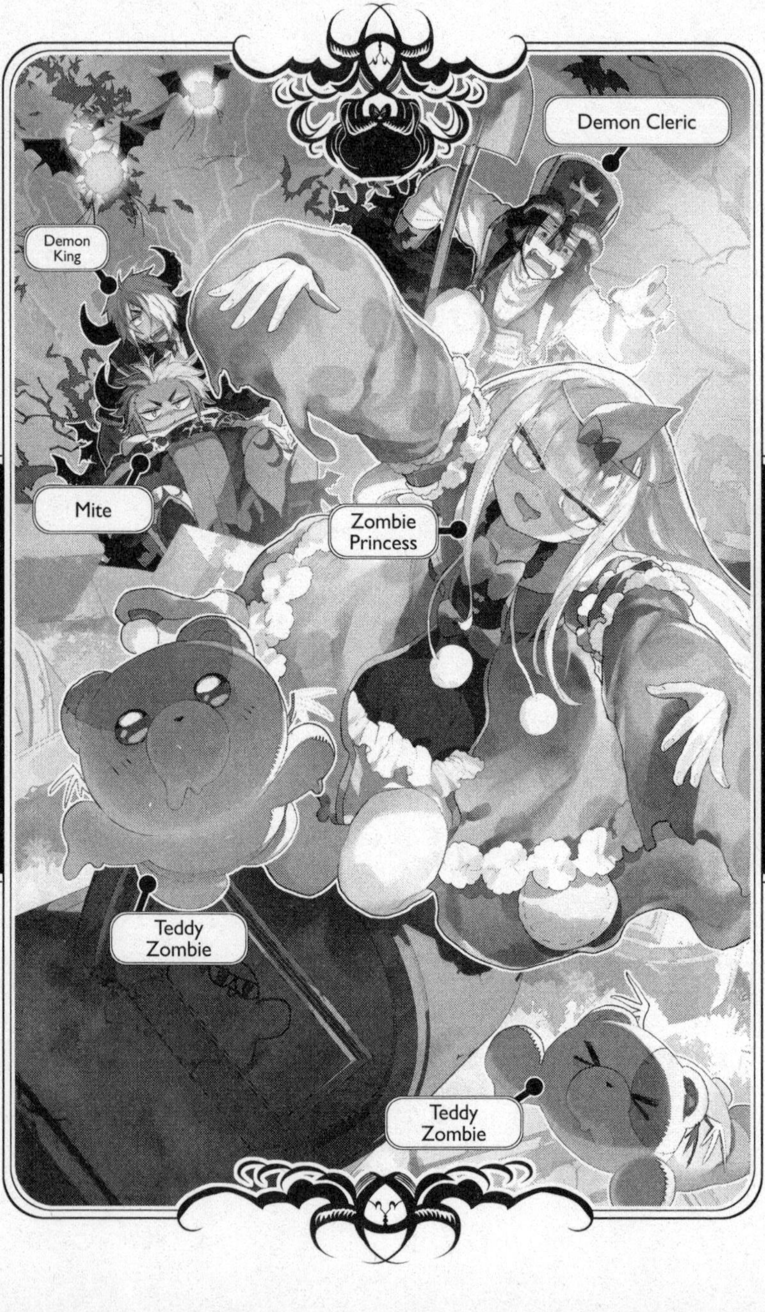
Demon Cleric
Demon King
Zombie Princess
Mite
Teddy Zombie
Teddy Zombie

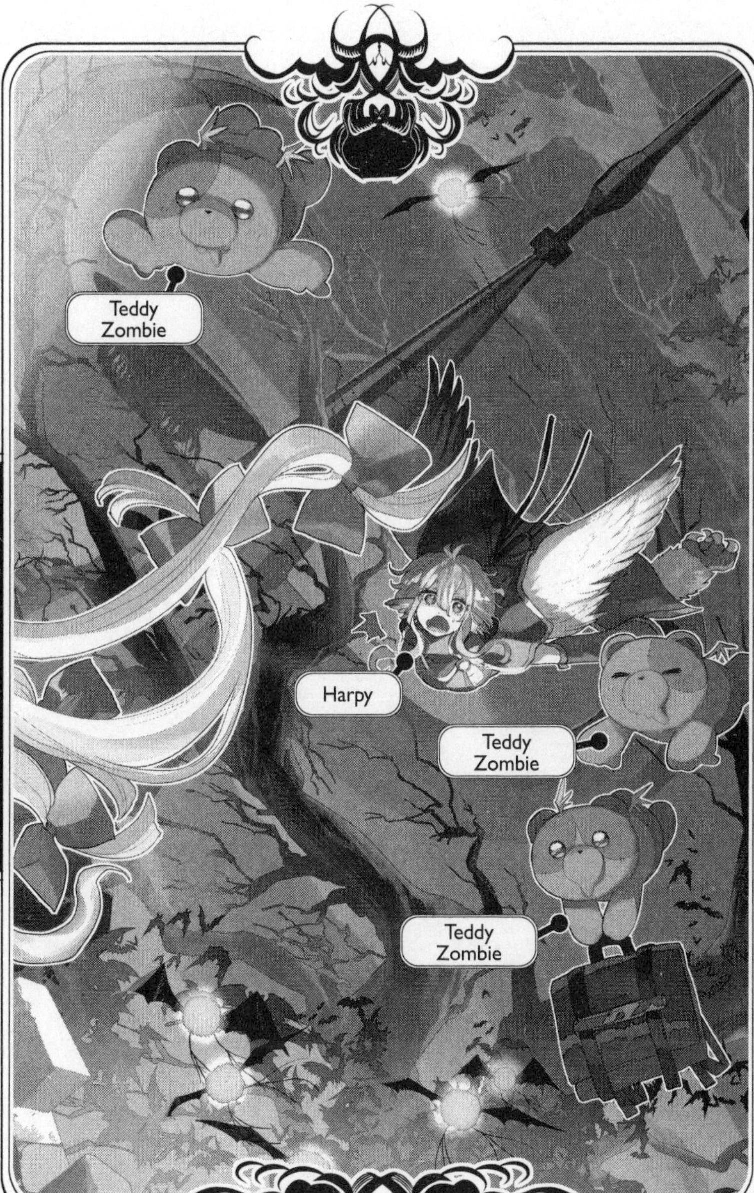
Teddy Zombie
Harpy
Teddy Zombie
Teddy Zombie

SLEEPY PRINCESS IN THE DEMON CASTLE

17

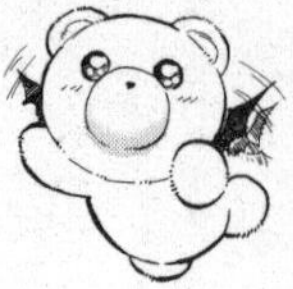

Shonen Sunday Edition

STORY AND ART BY

KAGIJI KUMANOMATA

MAOUJO DE OYASUMI Vol. 17
by Kagiji KUMANOMATA
© 2016 Kagiji KUMANOMATA
All rights reserved.
Original Japanese edition published by SHOGAKUKAN.
English translation rights in the United States of America, Canada,
the United Kingdom, Ireland, Australia and New Zealand arranged
with SHOGAKUKAN.

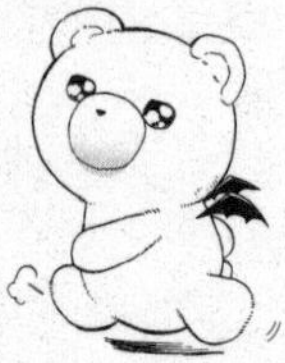

TRANSLATION **TETSUICHIRO MIYAKI**

ENGLISH ADAPTATION **SHAENON K. GARRITY**

TOUCH-UP ART & LETTERING **JAMES GAUBATZ**

COVER & INTERIOR DESIGN **ALICE LEWIS**

EDITOR **ANNETTE ROMAN**

Printed in the U.S.A.

Published by VIZ Media, LLC
P.O. Box 77010
San Francisco, CA 94107

10 9 8 7 6 5 4 3 2 1
First printing, April 2022

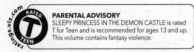

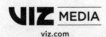

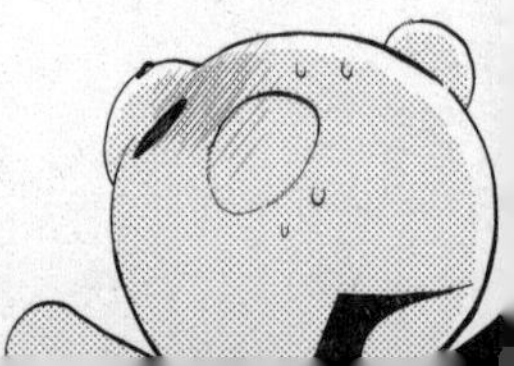

viz.com   shonensunday.com

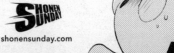

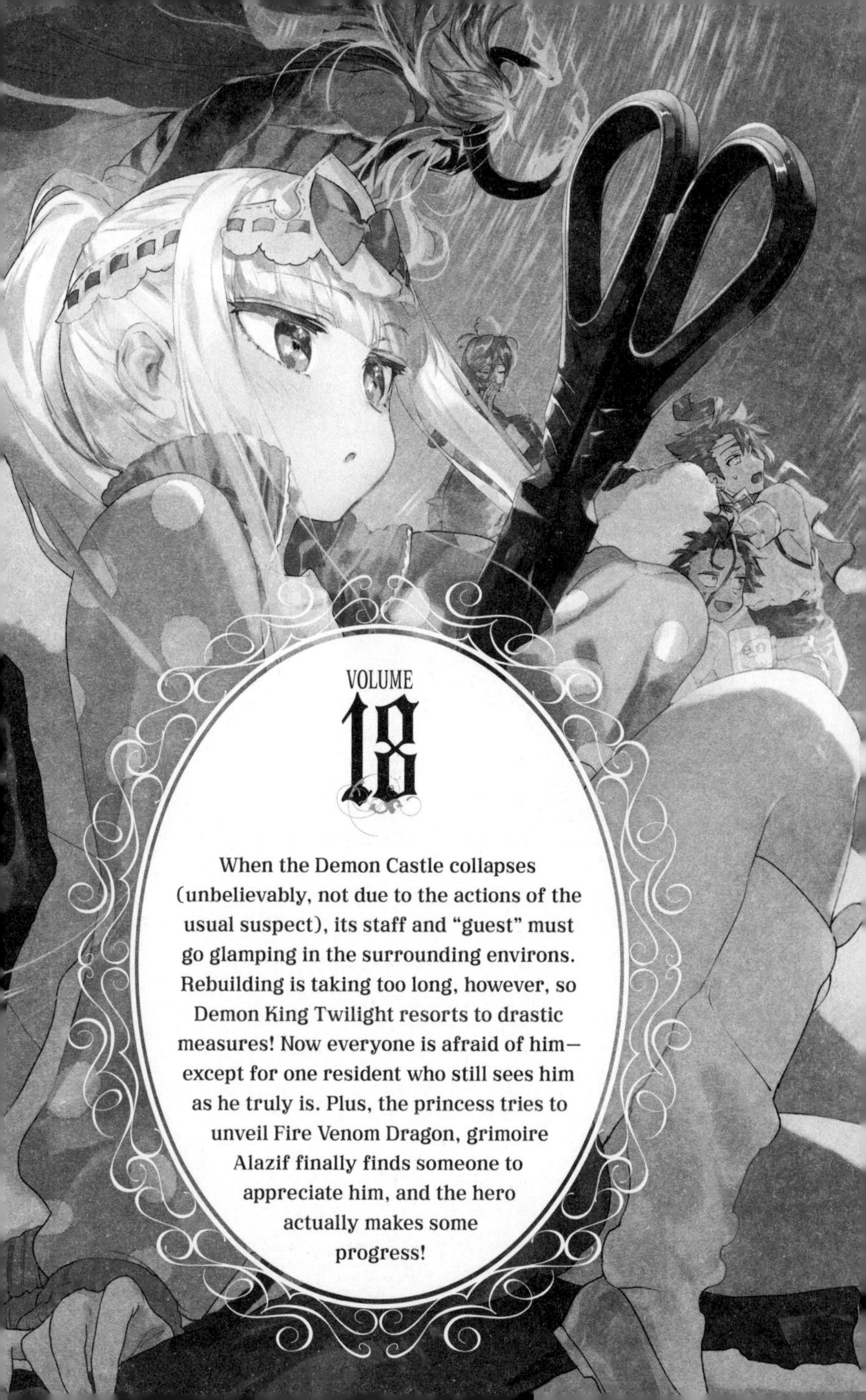

VOLUME

18

When the Demon Castle collapses (unbelievably, not due to the actions of the usual suspect), its staff and "guest" must go glamping in the surrounding environs. Rebuilding is taking too long, however, so Demon King Twilight resorts to drastic measures! Now everyone is afraid of him—except for one resident who still sees him as he truly is. Plus, the princess tries to unveil Fire Venom Dragon, grimoire Alazif finally finds someone to appreciate him, and the hero actually makes some progress!

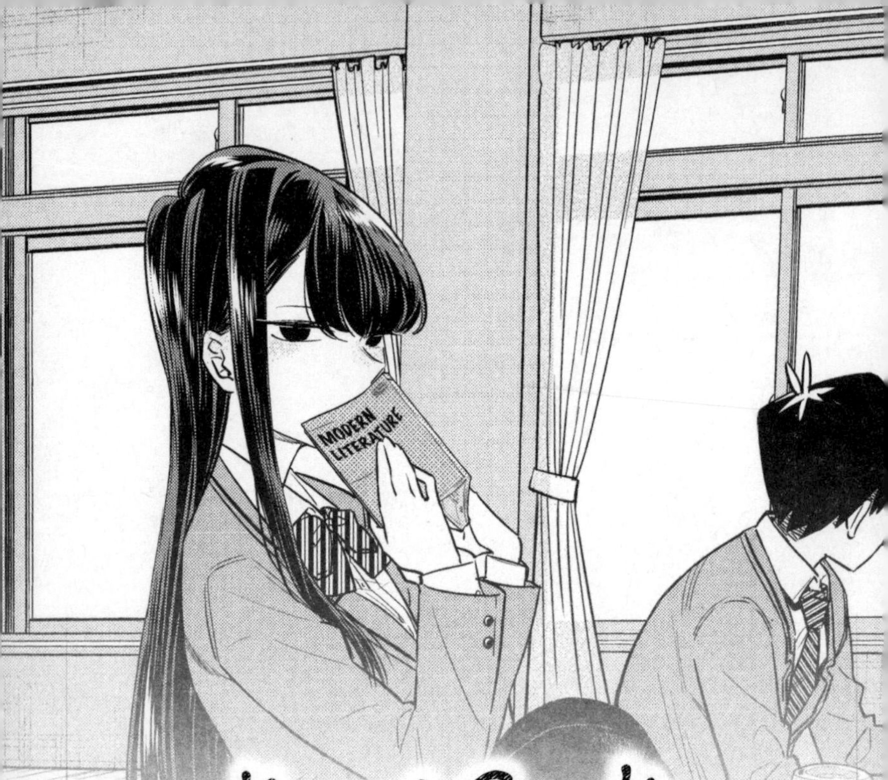
MODERN LITERATURE

Komi Can't Communicate

Story & Art by Tomohito Oda

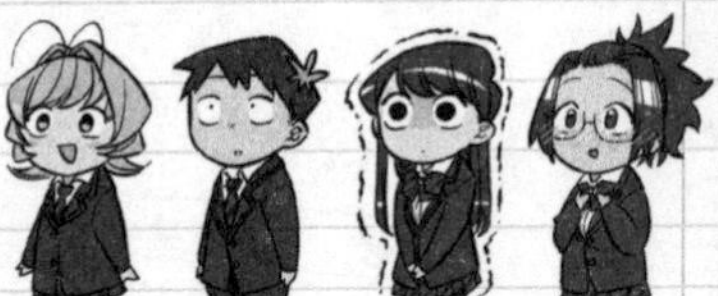

The journey to a hundred friends begins with a single conversation.

Socially anxious high school student Shoko Komi's greatest dream is to make some friends, but everyone at school mistakes her crippling social anxiety for cool reserve. With the whole student body keeping its distance and Komi unable to utter a single word, friendship might be forever beyond her reach.

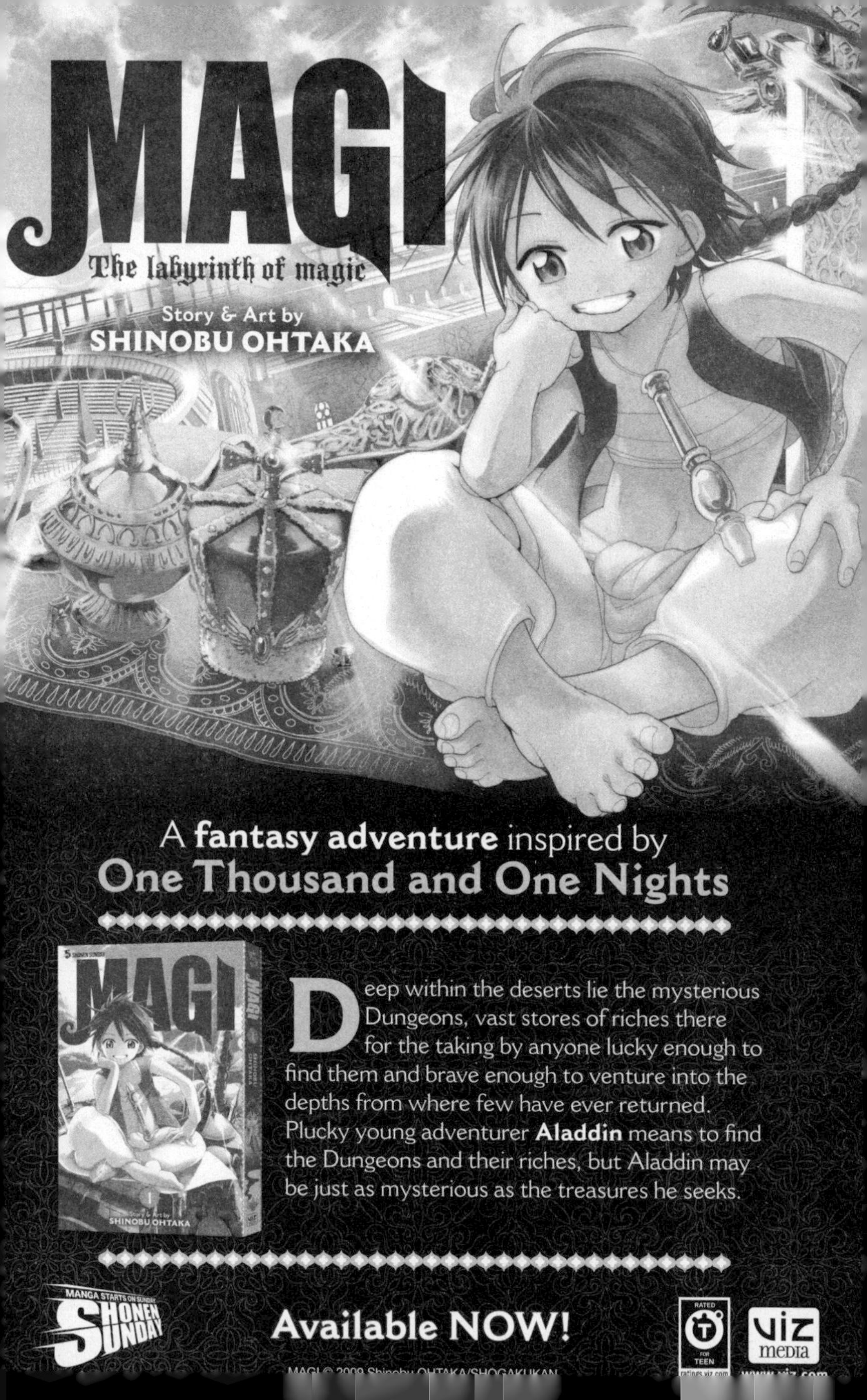
MAGI
The labyrinth of magic
Story & Art by
SHINOBU OHTAKA
A fantasy adventure inspired by
One Thousand and One Nights
MAGI
SHINOBU OHTAKA
Deep within the deserts lie the mysterious Dungeons, vast stores of riches there for the taking by anyone lucky enough to find them and brave enough to venture into the depths from where few have ever returned. Plucky young adventurer Aladdin means to find the Dungeons and their riches, but Aladdin may be just as mysterious as the treasures he seeks.
MANGA STARTS ON SUNDAY
SHONEN SUNDAY
Available NOW!
RATED T FOR TEEN
ratings.viz.com
VIZ MEDIA
www.viz.com
MAGI © 2009 Shinobu OHTAKA/SHOGAKUKAN

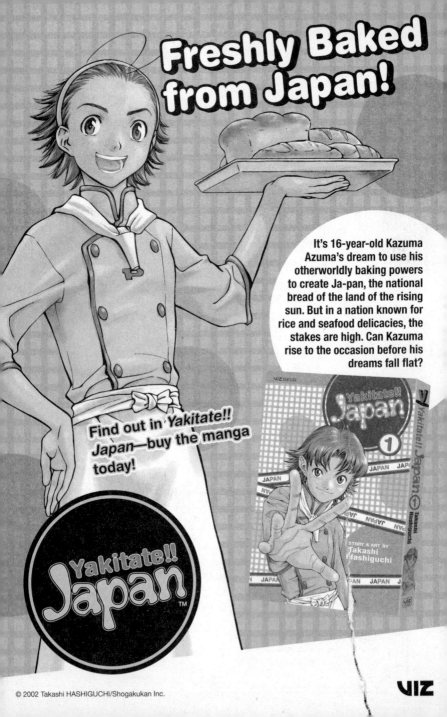

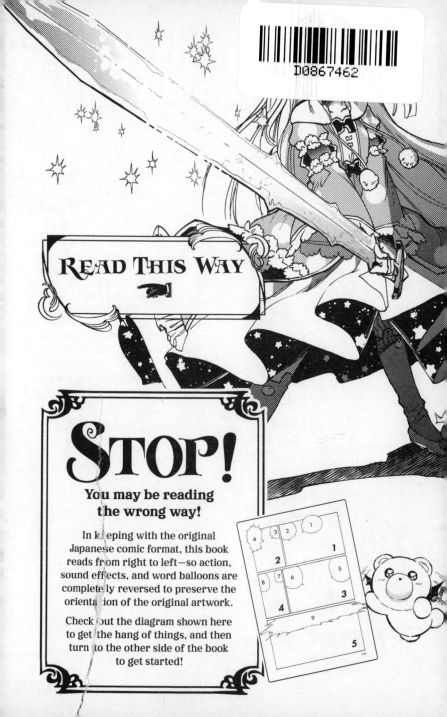

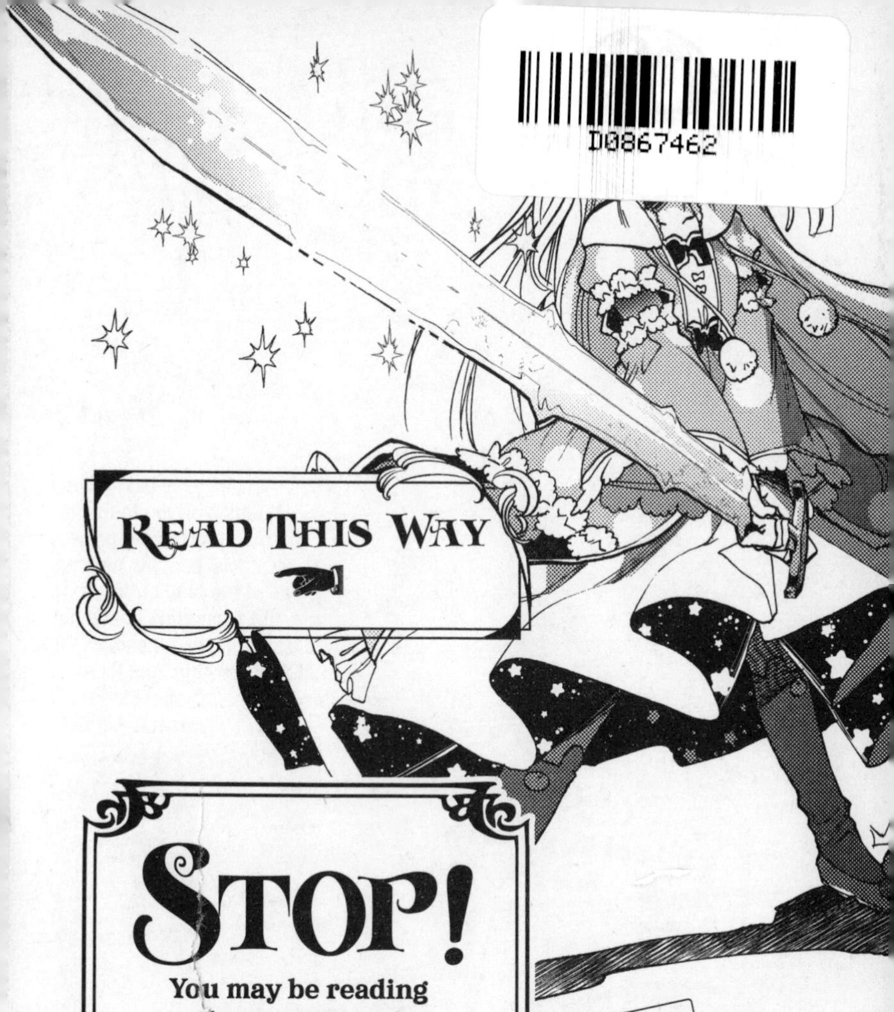
READ THIS WAY

STOP!

You may be reading the wrong way!

In keeping with the original Japanese comic format, this book reads from right to left—so action, sound effects, and word balloons are completely reversed to preserve the orientation of the original artwork.

Check out the diagram shown here to get the hang of things, and then turn to the other side of the book to get started!

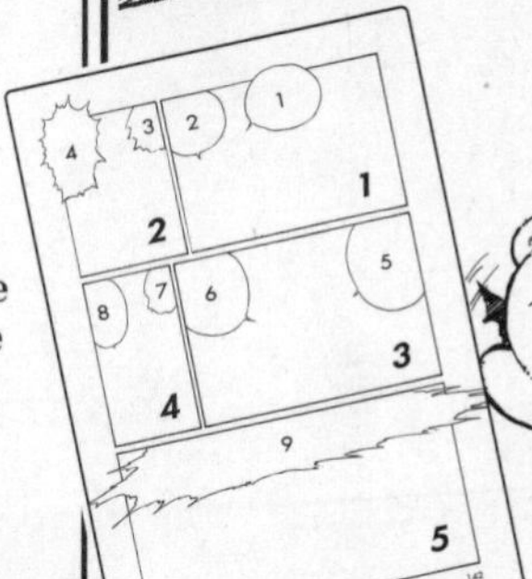
1
2
3
4
5